Annals of the Five Senses

and Other Stories, Sketches and Plays

MacDiarmid 2000:
the Collected Works
from Carcanet

Selected Poetry
edited by Michael Grieve & Alan Riach

Selected Prose
edited by Alan Riach

Scottish Eccentrics
edited by Alan Riach

The Complete Poems, I and *II*
edited by Michael Grieve & W.R. Aitken

Lucky Poet
edited by Alan Riach

Contemporary Scottish Studies
edited by Alan Riach

Albyn: Shorter Books and Monographs
edited by Alan Riach

The Raucle Tongue: Hitherto Uncollected Prose I
edited by Angus Calder, Glen Murray & Alan Riach

The Raucle Tongue: Hitherto Uncollected Prose II
edited by Angus Calder, Glen Murray & Alan Riach

The Raucle Tongue: Hitherto Uncollected Prose III
edited by Angus Calder, Glen Murray & Alan Riach

Hugh MacDiarmid

ANNALS OF THE FIVE SENSES

and Other Stories, Sketches and Plays

Edited by
Roderick Watson and Alan Riach

CARCANET

First published in Great Britain in 1999 by
Carcanet Press Limited
4th Floor, Conavon Court
12–16 Blackfriars Street
Manchester M3 5BQ

A CIP catalogue record for this book
is available from the British Library.

ISBN 1 85754 272 X

The publisher acknowledges financial assistance
from the Arts Council of England

Set in 10/12 pt New Caledonia by XL Publishing Services, Tiverton
Printed and bound in England by SRP Ltd, Exeter

Contents

Contents

General Editor's Preface and Acknowledgements

Of all the books in the MacDiarmid 2000 series, *Annals of the Five Senses and Other Stories, Sketches and Plays* is undoubtedly the most curious.

Here are gathered MacDiarmid's work in prose fiction, semi-autobiographical anecdotes, studies in psychology. Here, too, are collected his divagations and distractions into characterisation, the supernatural, ineffable questions of sexuality and the magical and macabre world of pre-adolescent childhood, which Kenneth Buthlay has associated with the marvels of children's song, where the cow jumps over the moon, just like that. The book ranges from extremes of wearyingly pedantic anatomising of singular mentalities to unsophisticated comicality, from passages appropriate to a psychotic ward's staff-meeting analyses to short tales intended for the readership of the *People's Friend* and the *Scots Magazine*.

The stories fall into four modes. There are the early experimental works of which *Annals of the Five Senses* itself is the fullest flourish. Other sketches of around the same period complement it usefully: the early work drawing on Conan Doyle, H.G. Wells, Stevenson and de Quincey, and the excursions into the volatile mixture of modernism and the Scots vernacular, like the dramatic conversations (more concerned with dialogue than theatre). Then there are the Langholm stories. These probe family and sexuality. Notably, they suggest young Chris Grieve's relations with his brother and their parents, but they also offer a wealth of social and natural detail recollected with love. There are the 'Strange Tales' – ghost stories or weird episodes, like the curious encounter with a character not born of man and woman in 'The Stranger'. Finally, there are the Shetland stories, sometimes mere anecdotes from MacDiarmid's spell in the Shetland archipelago, 1933–42. Each of these groups of stories or studies (and oddities that don't fit any of them) is packed with vivid, memorable impressions.

The teeming mind of the mess-sergeant in World War I Salonika, whose memory is like 'the shooting of frost crystals'; the scrawny, murderous profile of Old Eric of the Shetlands; the eager boyhood thrill of Peter's sledging on Murtholm Hill; Mrs Morgan's Jocasta-syndrome (an antisyzygical answer to the Oedipal cliché) in 'The Never-Yet-Explored'; the puritanical devotion to organised criminality and anti-sociability of Peter MacIntyre, 'A Scottish Saint'; the self-questioning, self-justifying oscillations of the brother who narrates 'Andy' and 'A Sense of Humour': these are unforgettable characteristics and characters.

Equally memorable is the exploration of sexuality in the social mores of the time and the morasses of ignorance and violent jealousies, in the repulsive 'On Being Sold a Pup' and the coldly comic 'Putting the Lid On It'. The depiction of mediocrity and human potential in 'Mrs D' as she stands 'by the pool' contemplating suicide before turning back to a humdrum life of negligible meaning is an intensely affecting miniature, a two-minute bagatelle version of Kate Chopin's great novel *The Awakening*. Even the most outré of the hitherto uncollected items, the ballet scenario 'Barley Break (The Scarecrow)', ends characteristically with the ragged figures of the Lame Girl and the Scarecrow, 'dancing forlornly'. So he reminds us that the chaotic abundance of life just seen depends on and potentially resides in such characters: damned and marginal, but capable of transformation into wild expression, like the 'Auld Wife in High Spirits' in MacDiarmid's poem.

'The dead are as helpless as the living' says the Mother in 'Lechois'. They come and go in many of these stories with alarming ease. There is the ghostly girl in 'A'body's Lassie' returning to haunt the living villagers with recrimination or, more fearfully, with forgetful pleasure; the 'Visitor' who turns up on the doorstep of his later self, and learning that what he might have become is a rather hen-pecked husband, clears off back to the land of spirits. The vulgar squib of debunking superstition in the cloacal bathos of 'Vouchsafed, A Sign' counterpoints the palpable, eerie presence of death in 'Old Miss Beattie' and 'Maria' and the unanswered question (what happened next?) that hovers at the end of 'Some Day'. Yet there are stories full of affection and unsentimental nostalgia, a warmth of recollection for a childhood world of outdoor games with marbles, chestnuts, fishing, berry-picking, adolescent courting in the woods and on the hillsides. MacDiarmid's native place, Langholm, a border mill town at the confluence of three rivers, comes out of this book as lovingly remembered, evoked in complex, sometimes surreal vividness, as in 'The Waterside' where the villagers are characterised by their physical location: 'The High Street folk thocht aboot naething bit themsel's... The folk on the hillside were like the sailor's parrot – they didna say muckle, but they were deevils to think.' But the Waterside folk 'were brainless craturs.

Brains were nae use there. To dae onything ava they'd to use something faur quicker than thocht – something as auld as the water itsel'. And thocht's a dryland thing and a gey recent yin at that.'

This apprehension of animal cunning and fishlike speed is pre- or non-verbal and MacDiarmid gets it in many of the stories of his border boyhood. But there is also adolescent fervour in 'Enemy's Daughter' and adult enquiry in 'The Affair at Hawick'. There are ambiguities that will not allow for easy answers or pious rationalisation. A number of the stories end in ambivalence or without resolution. Is the staunch Scottish isolationist in 'The Frontier' secure in the sense of national identity or is his darkness truly universal? Is the man with the hole in the sock (a dry blend, as if John Cleese or Rowan Atkinson were doing J. Alfred Prufrock) to be ridiculed or pitied? What are we to make, finally, of the five 'Bits' of Miller? Mysteries remain unsolved. In 'The Scab' a leprous patch of barren country begins to expand upon the surface of the earth (like the opening of a J.G. Ballard science fiction novel): general death portends. In 'A Scottish Saint' the conventions of the so-called civilised world encircle and ultimately destroy a last outpost of independence (as if the Scab had morphed into society's most spirit-throttling pieties). The glove discovered by Loch Ness with its inexplicable set of rattling contents remains unexplained, more troubling and scratchingly persistent in the mind than the grosser mystery of its more monstrous neighbour. The legacies of the modern movement, surrealism, the shock of the new, are never wholly absent in these tales of unexpectedness. As MacDiarmid says of Old Eric, the Shetland septuagenarian whose hobby is shooting the cormorants his physique so closely resembles, 'he emerges with his diseased onion of a head in a strange and startling way, like a special creation, incredible as all beginnings are.'

Annals of the Five Senses was MacDiarmid's beginning, first published under the name C.M. Grieve in 1923. In 1917, Grieve suggested that the influences upon him at the time included Turgenev, Henry James, J.M. Synge, Galsworthy, Gorki's *Childhood* and Wells's *Tono-Bungay*. One year later, writing from hospital in France, he says that he has recovered from 'cerebral neuritis' and 'regained' himself through using the 'natural safety-valve' of his writing, 'a sheaf of studies similar in angle of approach to "Cerebral" but dealing with diverse psychological crises and reactions'. He promises to send them out as soon as he has 'purified and concentrated their excellent fury'.

'Excellent fury' characterises *Annals of the Five Senses*. Something of the twisted intensity of Dostoevsky's Underground Man infests their psychopathology. In Chapter IV of Part II of *Notes from Underground*, Dostoevsky's subterranean spaceman dwells on the 'horrendous' and humiliating moments of his life, pacing 'from the table to the stove and back again. "Oh, if you only knew what thoughts and feelings I'm capable of, and how cultured I really am!"'

This furiously defensive desire to assert the complex circuitry of mental singularity activates MacDiarmid's writing here, especially in the fevered pitch and toss of 'Café Scene' and the comic tour-de-force in 'Sartoria' – a cheeky reply to the weighty masculinity of Thomas Carlyle's *Sartor Resartus*. For MacDiarmid, the world of Conrad's *Heart of Darkness* in which 'the women... are out of it – should be out of it' 'completely', was not so distant. The Victorian sense that men should 'help them to stay in that beautiful world of their own, lest ours gets worse' belonged to a world MacDiarmid had lived through and came out of. Vivid curiosity about sexuality is predominant in the depiction of carnal lust in 'The Following Day' or the clever spin on a traditional 'aubade' in 'Spanish Girl' (where morning is, unusually, welcomed for the light it throws on the lover's beauty: 'Sweet is the dawn and fresh / The dawn wind on the bed'), or the exalting act of sex in 'Consummation' or, above all, in the minute attentiveness to familial pressures and sexual jealousies cross-hatching in an individual woman's identity in 'The Never-Yet-Explored'. Here, 'The essence of life lies in the movement by which it is transmitted.' The woman's entry to the modern world of literature signals a new form of human comprehension, and MacDiarmid is fast to reckon her 'many mad desires'.

But if MacDiarmid's concern is pre-eminently with psychological and intellectual states, he complements this extreme singularity with a more encompassing human sympathy. In 'A Limelight from a Solitary Wing' he presents Fred, a hopeful, indeed faithful character, imagining the prospect of 'humanity's bewilderment of thought' as 'a mighty net which somehow holds the whole truth'. This sense of bewilderedness as an essential part of the whole story has come at a price. In 'A Four Years' Harvest' the astonishing description of the symbolic burial of Christ celebrated by the Greek Church seals off the conventional morality of the nineteenth century from modernity. Yet there remains a 'reviving trust in a centre of unity' and 'another tendency equally ingrained in him, the impulse of revolt against "the pale cast of thought"'. If he 'had endured so much either in his own or the rent flesh of others' he is nevertheless always on the way 'to the knowledge of loyalty and faithfulness which kept his vision whole.'

This is neither sentimental nor naïve knowledge but one acquired through 'Wellsian access' – an appetite and aptitude for the whole modern complexity. It comes after a recognition that 'the greatest of all international crimes had been committed in a blind unanimity of enthusiasm with scarcely a voice to protest against it…'. For MacDiarmid, the Great War had degraded Empire into 'a dirty little scheme for taxing the foreigner' and degraded Patriotism into 'sloppy adulation for a little German family and their vast crowd of German relatives and dependents'. The socialist, republican and anti-royalist hope burned fiercely from this forge. And lasted. Over a decade later, in the Shetlands, MacDiarmid was out with the fishermen; one of them later recalled 'sittin aroond da table an facin da table wis dat big boiler, an a front aa boiler dey wir a big roond door, it wis aye red hot. Auld Grieves [as the fishermen knew him] wis sittin looking at yun an he said: "I would just love to see the whole royal family going in there, one by one, feet first".'

In Salonika, the intensest activity counterpointed vast paralysis. As Joyce was defining urban sterility, the bias, thwart and deadlock in *Dubliners* (1914) and *A Portrait of the Artist as a Young Man* (1916), MacDiarmid was approaching an understanding of anti-heroic absurdity, the horrific banality of waste in Salonika: 'a superfluous side-show' – futile, diseased and apathetic, yet right at the foot of Mount Olympus.

So *Annals of the Five Senses* enacts a search for resolution which is achieved and sustaining. The 'attitude' of its author 'could only be described as one of curiosity': 'And now his mind was like a hayrick aflame where, when the wind blows the fire inwards, the portion in flames completely disappears like melting sugar, and the outline is lost to the eye'.

The intensity of heat, the Homeric scale of the context of war, the ferocity and pathos of the effort begun here could not but lead to the work of renewal and revaluation that marked the great career upon which MacDiarmid now had embarked.

Acknowledgements are due to the Institute for Advanced Studies in the Humanities at the University of Edinburgh where I held a Fellowship from February to April, 1995 and December 1996 to February 1997; and to the University of Waikato Research Committee, who have generously supported my work on the 'MacDiarmid 2000' project.

Most grateful thanks are tendered to the staff and the Trustees of the National Library of Scotland, and to the staff of Edinburgh University Library, the Mitchell Library, Glasgow (particularly Hamish Whyte), the University of Delaware Library, the British Library, London (particularly

Richard Price) and the University of Waikato Library, particularly the indispensable services of the reference and interloans department. Especial thanks are also due to John Manson for the contribution of the stories and sketches he discovered in his own researches; these are noted in Appendix 2.

Thanks for personal kindness, support and generosity towards the project are due to Kenneth Buthlay, David Daiches, George Davie, Duncan Glen and Edwin Morgan; G. Ross Roy and Patrick Scott of the University of South Carolina; my parents Captain J.A. Riach and Mrs J.G. Riach; my wife Rae; and my colleagues at the University of Waikato, Marshall Walker and Jan Pilditch. I would also like to make grateful acknowlegement of the trust of the MacDiarmid Estate and Deirdre Grieve, and of the professionalism, commitment and patience of Carcanet Press, especially Michael Schmidt and Robyn Marsack.

In respect for his love of the literature of Scotland, his service to it, and his generosity and support of the MacDiarmid 2000 project, the Editors would like to acknowledge the late W.R. Aitken, eident scholar, fine librarian and bibliographer, Hugh MacDiarmid's good friend. This volume is dedicated to his memory.

ALAN RIACH

Introduction:
'A Strong Solution of Books'

Written by an unknown Scottish sergeant, catering for the RAMC Officers' Mess stationed at the 42nd General Hospital in Salonika in 1917, *Annals of the Five Senses* marks the first signs of a major literary talent, and indeed with hindsight the book can be seen to foreshadow much of what was yet to come from a writer soon to be better known as Hugh MacDiarmid.

Idiosyncratic, exasperating, challenging, cliché-ridden, utterly brilliant and flawed by turns, these 'psychological studies' also stand as a fascinatingly rich document of early modernism, prophetic, too, of a postmodern sense of the decentred and unstable nature of the human subject and the endless intertextuality of literary production.

As he explained in his dedication to John Buchan, Grieve himself did not know what to call these, 'psychological studies, essays, mosaics (call them what you will) which I have (perhaps the best word in the meantime is) "designed"'. The Acknowledgments page refers to 'these perhaps strange fish of mine...discernible almost entirely through a "strong solution of books" – and not only of books but of magazines and newspaper articles and even of speeches.' Indeed, Grieve goes on to list twenty-four sources and allude to many more which 'I unfortunately cannot now trace' and his pages are filled with echoes and borrowings from well-known and obscure writers alike. In this respect *Annals* anticipates by twenty years the methodology of *Lucky Poet*, *In Memoriam James Joyce*, and all the other long world-language poems which marked the last stages of Grieve's extraordinary development as a poet. Here, too, can be seen the prevailing and unifying theme of a vision of endless movement, endless detail, changeless change and yet unity in complexity which was to underlie all his subsequent work.

Largely composed in Salonika in 1917 and completed in the years immediately after the Great War, *Annals of the Five Senses* (originally titled *Cerebral and Other Studies*) had been delivered to T.N. Foulis of Edinburgh by 1920. Foulis had published the first two of Grieve's *Northern Numbers* anthologies in 1920 and 1921, but the firm met with financial difficulties and withdrew their support, although they allowed

Grieve the use of the plates (already set) for *Annals* and he finally published the volume himself in 1923 from his home in Montrose. By that time he had begun to make a significant commitment to poetry, and to Scots poetry in particular.

Alan Bold has noted that 'the transformation of the Grieve of *Annals* to the MacDiarmid of *A Drunk Man* is one of the most exhilarating spectacles of modern poetry. The difference between the writer of English and the master of Scots is startling' (Alan Bold, *MacDiarmid. A Critical Biography*, London, 1988, p.221). This is true, but equally startling is the extent to which the studies in *Annals* (very different to the Scots lyrics) anticipate so much of what the poet's vision was to be, and so much, too, of his writing in the long catalogue poems of the late 1930s and 1940s. Writing in Scots, however, was the last thing on Grieve's mind when he began, and we can learn a lot about these early ambitions from the correspondence with his former schoolmaster and mentor George Ogilvie. The Ogilvie letters in the years between 1911 and 1919 – and especially the years when Grieve served in the RAMC in Macedonia – reveal a young writer's absolute determination to make his mark in literature. They reveal a lot too, of his own excitements and depressions, of the malaria he caught in Salonika in 1916, and they reflect more generally on the heat and the chaos of the forgotten 'eastern front' during the Great War.

Later reflections on the war appeared in 'Casualties' from the *Broughton Magazine* of 1919 (about the Somme), and they also feature in the story 'Nisbet' in which the author's own many conflicting ambitions are divided among three characters 'in post war Glasgow'. 'Nisbet' was actually performed by the Curtain Theatre in Glasgow, with Duncan Macrae in the title role, and the protagonist's name was important to Grieve because he had been prompted to enlist when his close school-friend John Bogue Nisbet was killed in 1915 at the first battle of Loos. Grieve thought of Nisbet as a spiritual familiar – 'part and parcel of the debating society which is my mental life' (letter to George Ogilvie, 20 August 1916, *The Letters of Hugh MacDiarmid*, ed. Alan Bold, London, 1984, p.10).

After yet another bout of malaria in 1918, Grieve was eventually transferred from Macedonia to France and it was there, in a hospital for shell-shocked Indian soldiers in Marseilles, that he completed his work on *Annals* (mostly written in Salonika) and told Ogilvie about his plans for the collection: 'I was certainly in a dreadful condition of mind when I wrote last. No fit of "blues" approaching that in prolonged intensity has ever visited me before – nor have I often lost my depersonalisation so completely. My state amounted to cerebral neuritis almost. However it is over.

I regained myself by using my natural safety-valve and the result which I am busily licking into shape is a sheaf of studies similar in angle of approach to "Cerebral" but dealing with diverse psychological crises and reactions' (to George Ogilvie, 27 December 1918, *Letters*, p.30).

One of the stories written in Marseilles was 'A Four Years' Harvest', a loosely autobiographical account of Grieve's war years in Salonika, and a reminder that the fevered instability of these 'psychological studies' is not so easily separable (like so much in modernism itself) from the despair and the elation, the terror and the boredom, the violence and the absurdity of the times: 'One became unable to size things up: a curious vein of impotence in thought manifested itself. Everybody was either ill or sickening for an illness or convalescent. The pathological element was everywhere abominably intrusive ... the general sensation was of a highly-coloured nightmarish unreality.'

Throughout *Annals*, Grieve's prose style sets out to convey exactly the same sense of 'unreality' in passages of paranoid intensity, reminiscent of Dostoevsky's *Notes from Underground* or the 'estrangement' techniques which the Russian Formalists found in Gogol. For example, in 'Café Scene':

A line between two flagstones on the pavement, suddenly a yawning chasm! A cough behind him which gave him the feeling of being buried under an avalanche! Feet splaying at angles suggestive of the most irreconcilable and meaningless divergences! A tall man instantly precipitous! A woman's waist expanding equatorially! Hands like starfish or stars! Noses like fallen towers! Eddies and undercurrents and cataracts of eyes! Feet under which the ground fluttered like paper! Voices that struck him as if he had been a gong – voices that tortured him as if they had been ferrets and he a rabbit-warren – voices that were charged with astounding and unintelligible prophecies, accusations, threats and pleas.

The 'pathological element' could not be clearer, nor its links to expressionism and the alienated effects of early modernism. Such was the internal geography of *Annals*, and Grieve's lifelong debt to modernism (and indeed the part he played in it) is clearly seen in these 'studies', despite their being largely and sadly forgotten by literary historians of this period. In story after story, the unstable and shifting world of mental sensation and cerebral excitation finds its own eerie echo in the physical realm around it, from coruscating effects of light and weather, to the bustle of the streets, to the proliferation of texts, to the esoteric details (in 'Sartoria') of 'filet crochet-stitch and appliqué':

He could isolate the shy fire of a brooch or arrest a flashing petticoat with a startling instancy and jewel-like completeness where straight down a hill dipped a double row of street lamps displaying a whirligig of figures in the dark space between. A flash of imagination caught an unknown life, discriminating countless shades where the common eye sees but gloom or glare; pursuing countless distinct movements where the common eye sees only whirling perplexity ... He 'lived in the flicker' and darkness was all about. Souls glided in the human river, small green souls, red souls, white souls, pursuing, overtaking, joining, crossing each other, then separating slowly or hastily.

The 'mosaic' technique of *Annals* can be seen in action in this very passage, for the text subsequent to 'he lived in the flicker' is no less than a modification of passages from the opening pages of Conrad's *Heart of Darkness*, when Marlow observes that 'We live in the flicker' of time, and goes on to describe the first Roman voyagers on their journey up the Thames, before breaking off his thoughts, as 'Flames glided in the river, small green flames, red flames, white flames, pursuing, overtaking...'.

Whether such practice is an anticipation of the fragmentary modernist collages of Pound and Eliot, or a pre-figuring of postmodern theories of intertextuality, or just evidence of simple plagiarism, is still under debate. But in so far as Grieve's focus is on cerebration and on how human subjectivity is constructed, it seems entirely appropriate that that subjectivity should be seen as an intricate palimpsest of other texts – 'psychological movements', as Grieve explained in his Acknowledgements, 'reflected through the current reading and cultural conditions of the characters involved'; or even 'an art which [readers] do not understand' as the cheerfully arrogant epigraph on his title page had it.

Each of the six studies in *Annals* explores the inner life of a single character, but all pursue what is in effect, the same sensibility – a sensibility not far removed, in fact, from that of the author himself. Indeed 'Cerebral' and 'Café Scene' could involve the persona of 'A Four Years' Harvest', and what seem to be directly autobiographical allusions are made at several places in that text.

But the true focus of these pieces is on the mental states they describe. Thus the protagonist of 'Cerebral' is a young journalist at work on an article on 'The Scottish Element in Ibsen', and the 'cerebral sense' he experiences is a sensation of endless complexity and endless movement, now harmonious, and now on the edge of 'instability and nameless fear'. Grieve's prose captures this complexity by way of long sentences, moving as if by free association, whose sense is both enacted and also delayed by frequent parenthetical insertions and diversions. Yet this is not a stream-of-consciousness technique, for the protagonist is a curiously detached observer of his own mental processes (Grieves's 'depersonalisation'), even as they spin-out in spontaneous fashion, and the paradox of this condition is enacted yet again by a vocabulary which blends empathetic discourse with a rather abstract vocabulary, for example in 'Cerebral':

> Night and day, city and country, sunshine and gaslight and electric blaze, myriad-faceted existences and his own extraordinarily vivid pictorial sense of his own cranial geography and anatomical activities were all co-visible to him, I say, and perfectly composed, without any conflict or strain. Nor were any of the elements permanent or passive. All of them lived, and each in perfect freedom, modifying or expanding, easing off or intensifying continually. They moved freely, each in its own particular whim, and they moved also with the unity of one impression.

The evocation of exactly this flux was to appear again in Grieve's later work in the poetic symbol of the coils of Cencrastus the 'curly snake', and also in the gloriously Joycean Scots language which he used to celebrate the rivers of his native Langholm in 'Water Music'. (Something of the same spirit can also be seen in the story 'The Waterside' published in 1927, with its delight in 'the dunt and dirl o' the river...shoals o' licht and the crazy castin' o' the cloods and the endless squabble o' the gulls...'.) Before 'Cencrastus' and before 'The Waterside', however, it was 'the cerebral sense' which gave the yet-to-be-born MacDiarmid his first glimpse of the endless plurality of existence which yet moves – both internally and externally – with the 'unity of one impression'. Such were the annals of the senses to be found at work in all six 'psychological studies'. (The phrase 'annals of the five senses' was taken from Gregory Smith's *Scottish Literature: Character and Influence*, 1919 – an influential little book soon to provide another productive concept in 'the Caledonian antisyzygy'.)

The autobiographical links in *Annals* are clearest in 'A Four Years' Harvest', in which a sergeant reflects on an army career very similar to Grieve's own, not to mention a trip home on sick-leave to marry 'Peggy', and some lines quoted from one of Grieve's own letters to George Ogilvie. But, like the journalist in 'Cerebral', he also has a haunting sense of the ideal 'great music' which will achieve a 'logical yet ever new unfolding, the embodiment in the whole composition of richest variety with completest unity...' – once again, the very conditions of what the poet would later call 'the impossible song'.

'Fred' in 'A Limelight from a Solitary Wing' shares his author's own tendency to 'plunge into the full current of the most inconsistent movements ... his aim being to complete every thesis, to see all round every problem, to study a question from all possible sides and angles...' and the conversation of the protagonist of 'Sartoria' – a dandyish connoisseur of women's clothes – was 'a swift, beautiful catalogue of the most delightful and unexpected of interests'. Such lines could just as easily describe 'The Kind of Poetry I Want' and the working method of the autobiographical *Lucky Poet*. 'Mrs Morgan', the female protagonist of 'The Never-Yet-Explored', is haunted by the conventions which impose social and sexual constraints on her inner nature, and that nature is recognised in equally fluid and dynamic terms as an overwhelming vitalism caught up in 'the swirl of blood, the trampling of pulses, the violin play of lightning muscles'. In its attempt to imagine a female psyche in what now seems like a Lawrentian mode, 'The Never-Yet-Explored' is the most ambitious piece in *Annals* and the closest to conventionally imaginative fiction. Here again Grieve chose to use a deliberately intellectual register to describe specifically physical and emotional states – often with rather startling effects, such as 'Her inner soul struggle was acting like a strong developing fluid upon a highly sensitised plate.' Apposite or not, this is the very stuff of early modernism with its distrust of sentiment, and a vocabulary often drawn from the physical sciences. Similar effects can be found in early Virginia Woolf, in Lawrence, Eliot and Wyndham Lewis, all of whom delighted in analytical or alienating analogies:

> Her physical-intellectual being was the sensorium of Nature, but it was also one thing among natural things whose number was legion. It was the mirror in which she viewed the world, but it was also part of the world, the part most necessary for her to know and work upon, and its value to her depended upon her knowledge of its natural distortions and how to test and correct them.

All the characters in *Annals* are caught up in just such a 'sensorium' which is at once part of the natural world and part of the mind itself and hence our only access to the world. In the constant interplay and interconnection between external observation and the inner flow of the mind, the 'cerebral' sense has a lot in common with the contemporary interest in what Henri Bergson came to call *élan vital* by which all living things are bound together in vital impulse and the endless and uncatchable variation of their mental states.

Born of the same fascination, Virginia Woolf's early studies share something of the vision in *Annals*, and revealing comparisons can be made between Grieve's prose and Woolf's *Monday or Tuesday* collection of 1921, with pieces such as 'An Unwritten Novel' and 'The Mark on the Wall'. Writing in 'Modern Fiction' in 1925, Woolf explained her programme in the following terms:

> Let us record the atoms as they fall upon the mind in the order in which they fall, let us trace the pattern, however disconnected and incoherent in appearance, which each sight or incident scores upon the consciousness. Let us not take it for granted that life exists more fully in what is commonly thought big than in what is commonly thought small.

She might have been describing exactly the working principle of the 'cerebral sense' in *Annals* – and also the cultural principle by which MacDiarmid was later to hail the smallest patches of heather on a Scottish hillside as 'multiform' and 'infinite'. In touch with the pulse of modernism from the start, *Annals of the Five Senses* anticipated Woolf's agenda by some five years. In 'Modern Fiction' Woolf went on to praise what she saw as James Joyce's wholly modern concern 'to reveal the flickerings of that innermost flame which flashes its messages through the brain' – a concern which itself stems from the famous 'gem-like flame' of Walter Pater's Conclusion to his 1873 *Studies in the History of the Renaissance*, another key document in the history of modernism. By 1922 Virginia Woolf had published *Jacob's Room*, her first fully impressionist novel in what might be called a Bergsonian mode, but by then Grieve had left creative modernist prose behind, and was concentrating on poetry as the main medium of his imaginative expression. Yet Grieve's early English verse never attained the experimental force of *Annals*, and the next major step in his modernist odyssey was not to be taken until 'Hugh M'Diarmid' discovered Scots in 'The Watergaw' and 'The Blaward and the Skelly' in October 1922. Henceforth, he would cite Joyce, Dostoevsky and Lawrence in the cause of poetry, rather than prose, and although his production of fiction was by no means over, he was never to realise again in a single volume the sustained imaginative and experimental coherence that is *Annals of the Five Senses*. (Actually, Grieve's correspondence contains several tantalising references to novels in progress, and he never considered himself 'only' a poet, but these novels must join the many other projects mentioned in his letters which never saw the light of day. The prospect, however, remains enticing.)

As a working journalist since the age of nineteen, and a poet whose poetry could not support him, Grieve early learned the habits of swift and frequent output. The 1920s mark an extraordinary period of activity during which he produced at least half of the remaining prose pieces in the present collection, as well as writing the Scots lyrics and the poems that were to become *A Drunk Man Looks at the Thistle* and *To Circumjack Cencrastus*, while also acting as editor of, and indeed chief contributor to, *The Scottish Chapbook*, *The Scottish Nation* and *The Northern Review*. During this time he also compiled the three *Northern Numbers* anthologies and contributed material under pen names and his own name to *The New Age* in London. On top of this he was writing literary critical essays for *The Scottish Educational Journal*, sending stories to *The Glasgow Herald* and *The Scots Observer*, and providing over a hundred articles on matters of national and local identity, written by 'Special Correspondent' and 'Mountboy', and distributed to newspapers all over Scotland through the agency of R.E. Muirhead's 'Scottish Secretariat'.

It is against these work-habits, and the constant need to earn a living by the pen that we must see much of the remaining prose fiction in this volume, not least the previously uncollected material traced by Alan Riach and John Manson. (The editors decided that 'fiction' was probably the best description for 'All Night in a British Opium Joint' written for *The People's Journal* in 1912, but fiction or not, the piece stands as a reminder of the vast and ephemeral hinterland of Grieve's journalism which lies behind the stories collected here.) Born of the same economic imperative and among the least successful examples of his fiction, in my opinion, are the more anecdotal pieces, told in the spirit of tales at a gentleman's club, not unlike Edwardian shockers from the pen of Saki – but without his saving elegance. Among these I would number 'The Stranger'; 'The Dean of the Thistle', 'A Sense of Humour'; 'A Scottish Saint' and the unpublished 'In the Gaelic Islands', 'The Lion of Edinburgh' and 'The Loch Ness Mystery'. A similarly anecdotal approach, with a somewhat patronising air, marks 'Enemy's Daughter' and 'Wells'. More original and more ambitious, but relegated to the status of fascinating fragments, are 'Lechois: A Play in One Act' and the sketch for a ballet to be called 'The Scarecrow' or 'Barley Break'.

Although produced for the moment and published in different journals as the need arose, Grieve does seem to have had plans to collect a significant number of his stories into single volumes, as outlined by Alan Riach in Appendix 2. One of these putative collections remains untitled, but the other was to be called, perhaps, 'On Making Beasts of Ourselves: A Scottish Miscellany'.

This latter list draws attention to the fact that many of Grieve's very best stories draw on Scots roots in both language and character, and indeed they are mostly set in his home town of Langholm or the surrounding Border country. These monologues or dialogues in vivid and colloquial Border Scots – twelve of them, from 'Some Day' (1923) to 'Holie for Nags' (1928) – are among the finest things Grieve has done and they show him returning to a simpler colloquial utterance and an unpretentious reassessment of his Langholm roots. The author referred to these pieces, and his hopes to make a separate collection of them, in a letter to Neil Gunn of 28 February 1927: 'I've made a little headway with my own novel (in English) but switched that to one side on a sudden impulse, deciding that my next book would be a collection of short stories in Scots. I've well over half the book written. One of the stories – "The Common Riding" – will appear in the *Glasgow Herald* shortly' (*Letters*, p.215).

He goes on to say that he would like to dedicate the book to Neil Gunn and his wife, and that the title will be 'The Muckle Toon'. The collection was indeed offered to Blackwoods that year, only to be turned down. Grieve went on to re-think the 'muckle toon' project and to reconceive it as the first volume of a massive poetic autobiography (to be called 'Clann Albann') which would collect together the Scots poems on Langholm themes which had appeared in other volumes. This, too, was never realised, although Patrick Crotty's researches have reconstructed what 'The Muckle Toon' would have contained.

Grieve's hopes of pulling together a collection of Scottish stories were revived once again when he was in Whalsay in 1935. (His Shetland sketches in English also come from this period: 'Aince There, Aye There', 'Old Eric's Hobby' and 'Without a Leg to Stand On'.) It seems very likely that the envisaged collection of stories in Scots would have contained much of the earlier work and further pieces such as 'Wound-Pie', 'Vouchsafed: A Sign', 'Sticky-Wullie' and the unpublished 'In the Middle of the Field'. Writing to Fionn Mac Colla in 1935 he described them thus: 'nothing Kailyairdic about them, very varied, simply and straightforwardly written, anecdotal like Maupassant's in kind and without any involved psychologising. They make in fact a very lively collection; I've enjoyed writing them and be confident I've communicated that pleasure' (*Letters*, p.567).

The pleasure is undoubtedly there, as is the delight in estrangement that so characterised the early Scots lyrics, where folk utterance and a certain expressionist eeriness came together to memorable effect. Several of these stories evoke childhood experience and rites of passage in various encounters with death and the uncanny ('Old Miss Beattie', 'A'body's Lassie', 'The Moon Through Glass', 'Maria', and 'The Visitor'); and they all catch something of the extraordinary image-making power that

MacDiarmid found in the Scots language, or indeed in Jamieson's Dictionary. The first line of 'Murtholm Hill', for example, gives us 'The warld's like a bridescake in a shop window the day', and it was exactly this figurative vividness that he had set out to explore in the earlier piece 'Following Rebecca West in Edinburgh'. Self-consciously obscure in its Scots and its determination to bend 'ancient figures of speech to modern requirements', 'Following Rebecca West' invokes the example of James Joyce and illustrates something of the author's own 'Theory of Scots Letters' which was also being published in *The Scottish Chapbook* at this time.

The same interest in marrying avant-garde approaches with folk material can be seen in the mini-drama 'The Purple Patch', an ironic tribute to kailyard religiosity (set in the parish of 'Blawearie', incidentally, ten years before Lewis Grassic Gibbon entered it) which also attempts to generate an experience of literary simultaneity in its reading. It's a special irony that this tale of an alien text (the 'purple passage') accidentally transposed into a minister's sermon, might well describe the working method of the author's own *Annals*.

The uncanny invades other stories in this volume, including three of the most notable unpublished pieces. The dislocating surrealism of 'At Sixes and Sevens' contains passages of complex inner monologue which echo the studies in *Annals* – 'till one's brain is simply a chaos of contending lights, scintillant sensations, like – like a damned chandelier!' And the same style of intense paranoid pedanticism (reminiscent of early Beckett) marks 'The Man with the Hole in His Sock'. Equally discomfiting is 'The Darkie Baby', and indeed that sinister little doll is no less than the tutelary spirit of 'the pathological element' which Grieve had first discovered – living on his nerve ends indeed – in Salonika:

> A glance at it seemed to help me put myself at several removes from merely human feeling. The frisson of the very definitely, yet indefinably abnormal in much of my writing – the attractive awkwardness of many of my rhythms – owed a great deal to the darkie baby. And I am afraid this influence extended to my relations with my wife and child. They became too ordinary, too destitute of any element of surprise, and especially of the sort of ugliness of which I was more and more enamoured.

It's a pity that modern Scottish fiction did not get to hear more from this voice, although its spirit might be said to have been sustained in the neo-Gothic aspects of contemporary writers such as A.L. Kennedy, Janice

Galloway, John Herdman and Elspeth Barker. (Indeed, the highly formal English of 'The Scab' offers a vision of diseased nature and insect horror reminiscent of some of Duncan Thaw's worst visions in *Lanark*.)

The broad humour of 'The Last Great Burns Discovery' and the unforgettably Rabelaisian tour de force which is 'Five Bits of Millar' return us to a more familiar MacDiarmid, to the wonderful energy and grotesquerie which so characterised *A Drunk Man*. But, for me at least, the lasting and most original impressions which remain from Grieve's fiction come from the ground-breaking modernist estrangement of the 'cerebral sense' in *Annals*; from the fluid colloquial ease of the stories in Scots, each with their own hints of the uncanny; and finally from the deranged rationality of the narrative voice in 'At Sixes and Sevens' and that curious and hitherto unpublished manuscript (exactly as if rescued from one of Alasdair Gray's fictions) known here as 'The Darkie Baby'.

RODERICK WATSON

Annals of the Five Senses

The greater part of readers, instead of blaming us for passing trifles, will wonder that on mere trifles so much labour is expended, with such importance of debate and such solemnity of diction. To them I answer with confidence that they are judging of an art which they do not understand; yet cannot much reproach them with their ignorance, nor promise that they should become, in general, by learning criticism, more useful, happier or wiser.

*   *   *

TO

John Buchan

For the encouragement and help he has given to a young and unknown writer (as young as it is possible to be in the Twentieth Century, and almost entirely unknown, at least to himself), I dedicate these poems and these psychological studies, essays, mosaics (call them what you will) which I have (perhaps the best word in the meantime is) 'designed'.

IN ACKNOWLEDGEMENT

The old lady described Shakespeare as being full of quotations. So are my studies: I having deemed it desirable for the most part to show the psychological movements, with which I am mainly concerned, reflected through the current reading and cultural conditions of the characters involved.

As fish are seen through an aquarium so these perhaps strange fish of mine are discernible almost entirely through a strong solution of books and not only of books but of magazines and newspaper articles and even of speeches. What I have done is similar to what is done when a green light on a railway replaces a red light, or vice versa, in a given lamp.

The sources of certain of my quotations I unfortunately cannot now trace. For most of those taken from copyright work I have to thank the various authors and publishers. If inadvertently I have anywhere used copyright material without the necessary permission, I err through no lack of effort to trace my quotations: and hope to have the indulgence of those upon whose rights I may have trespassed.

I have quoted, *inter alia*, from the following: – Elbert Hubbard, S. Cyran, Dr South, R.B. Cunninghame-Graham, Bernard Capes, James Huneker, Shelley, the Bible, James Stephens, O.W. Holmes, G.K. Chesterton, Helen Parry Eden, E.A. MacIntosh, Edward Carpenter, Robert Browning, Saturday Westminster Gazette, Joseph Conrad, John Galsworthy, William Blake, John Masefield, Algernon Swinburne, Francis Thompson, Ian Mackenzie, etc. etc.

To all those to whom I am so indebted – whether authors, editors, or publishers – I make grateful acknowledgement.

                                                                    C.M. Grieve

I Cerebral

> 'At least,' he said, 'we spent with Socrates
> Some memorable days and in our youth
> Were curious, and respectful of the Truth.'

To maintain order, harmony, and excellence in the territory under one's own hat will keep one well-employed.

Prim little gardens ran out of the left side of his head right into and through the discoloured and ink-spotted wall-paper with its long yellow lines and tight little pink roses, and through the wall which was so thin that if the wall-paper had not been put on first it could never have stood at all, and into the next room where his landlady (who was so thin that when she shut one eye she looked just like a needle) sat, at that hour of the evening, knitting the inevitable grey Shetland shawl, with her feet on the shiny fender: and all that quite as a matter of course and without the slightest element of incongruity or confusion, without blurring the yellow bars or the pink buds in the least, or minimising the disfiguring reality of one splash of ink or one stain of damp, without dematerialising the irreducible minimum of wall-power and, above all, without alarming the meagre ungracious spinster (who was so thin that when she shut her eyes she couldn't be seen at all, making him wish, in moments of trial, that she had been born blind), clicking steadily away with her wooden needles, or breaking in on her arid privacy at all!

There everything was, *un chaos decoratif*, on the left side of his head, and all with that cut and coloured clearness which belongs rather to the things of art than to the things of experience: or if the edge of his head and the wall-paper and the tentatively existent wall and the next room with all its ill-conditioned furniture and sordid tidiness, and particularly the Lean Lady herself, were a little duller in hue, impinging a trifle less daintily on his mind than the prim little plots, why so little and such a trifle it was that he was barely sensible of it. (And, indeed, had it been otherwise, he had been greatly put out, for, being young as he was, he still esteemed clarity of vision above all things, having always in his mind the words of S. Cyran when he said: 'The least cloud which is on our mind will spread itself over our papers like an evil breath tarnishing the brightness of a mirror; the slightest indisposition of our spirit is like a worm which will pass into our book and gnaw the hearts of those who read to the end of the world': Or else that sounding passage of his sermon wherein Dr South declares: 'The image of God in man is that universal rectitude of all the faculties of the soul by which they stand apt and disposed to their several offices and operations. And, first, for the noblest faculty, Understanding! It was then sublime, clear, and inspiring, and, as it were, the soul's upper region, lofty and serene, free from all the vapours and disturbances of the inferior affections. . . . Like the sun, it had both light and agility: it knew no rest but in motion; no quiet but in activity. It did arbitrate upon the several reports of the senses and all the varieties of the imagination. . . . In sum, it was vegete, quick and lively; open as the day, untainted as the morning, full of the innocence and sprightliness of youth: it gave the soul bright and full view into all things!' But thus much for the Essay on Human Perfection and the mental well-being of Adam in the Garden of Eden: at all events he was so constrained to keep his mirror bright, and who will gainsay that a sense of the whole is the sign of a sound mind and that there be many who have it sadly to seek these days?)

Nor did the thousand and one other things of which severally and jointly he was just as acutely conscious and just as acutely critical, not even the harvesting of his lively eyes which, looking this way and that, could see the changeful, changeless thoroughfare without, where the trams rode garishly, or the rather more select crescent curving off from it, each with its trees and divers lights and processions of people coming and going, and apricot and lemon shop windows and sphinx houses: nor yet the busy work of his hands under the direction of an insignificant small portion of the lower part of the front of his brain on the typewriter, import the least disharmony or friction, although he realised that if he did not have to go on with that endless typing (Alas! the *Leader* had to have it first thing in the morning – a column article on 'The Scottish Element in Ibsen'), if he could release that little under bit of his brain, freedom from infinitesimal drag would give the whole atmosphere just a perceptible lightening and ease, a roundness and perfection which it all but had.

Night and day, city and country, sunshine and gaslight and electric blaze, myriad-faceted existences and his own extraordinarily vivid pictorial sense of his own cranial geography and anatomical activities were all co-visible to him, I say, and perfectly composed, without any conflict or strain. Nor were any of the elements permanent or passive. All of them lived, and each in perfect freedom, modifying or expanding, easing off or intensifying continually. They moved freely, each in its own particular whim, and they moved also with the unity of one impression. As one thing receded into unreality, the reality of other and ever other things became newly apparent (albeit oddly familiar and repetitive) taking him like trumpets. Colours flashed in and out like trout in clear waters. Surface impressions scuttled everywhere like rabbits with white scuts of discredit and under the ground (the darkness of which, needless to say, had a perfectly penetrable and gracious quality), all manner of strange things led busy but quite undisquieting existences, intricate, yet orderly. But easy comprehension and complete possession were never lost. The transfusing vitality of his interest never failed to discharge to the tiniest detail the demands of that versatility of sensation and speculation. He was athrill with the miracle of sentience, quivering in every filament of his perceptions with an amazing aliveness. All his thoughts were to him (although all the while away down in the unguessable depths of his being, where the egos of his actualities and his appearances debated without end in the forum of the absolute, doubts may have been expressed as to what was becoming in a man of his years), every one of them sweet, careless, fragrant interpretations of the gratitude of being alive – Elysian fields of cogitation where all happy words which had endeavoured in honesty and humility to express for him raptures beyond adumbration, after their patient services of signification, entered into their full felicity – brilliant, joyous, poignant pages of appreciation, as sensitive and magical as the mind of youth ever lent to the wonder of being.

Continually the spirit of poetry broke blossoms about his head. Bits of old song floated everywhere, little sweet verses of adventure, dalliance, inspiration, murmuring of unseen radiances and raptures unimaginable… He made flowered names for his pictorial feelings. To them he dedicated arrows from virgin bows… Constantly a new ego of his nature came in out of the multitudinous darknesses and lit to a flame… It was 'like an Atlas night when the moonbeams fall on domes of house and mosque and light up the green and yellow tiles, making them sparkle like enamels, and long shadows of cypresses cast great bands of darkness on the red sand. Then the croaking of frogs sounds metallic and by degrees resolves itself into a continuous tinkle, soothing and musical. Camels lie ruminating, their monstrous packs on their backs. As one passes they snarl and bubble and give out a faint odour as of a menagerie, mingled with that of tar, with which the Arabs cure their girth and saddle galls. From the Arab huts a high-pitched voice, to the accompaniment of a two-stringed guitar played with a piece of stiff palmetto leaf and the monotonous Arab drum that, if you listen to it long enough, invades the soul, blends so inextricably with the crickets' note and the vast orchestra of insects that praise Allah without intermission, each after his own fashion, that it is difficult to say where the voice ends and the insects' hum begins. Still, in despite of all, the singing Arab, the guitar and the drum, the croaking of the frogs and the shrill pæns of the insects, the night seems calm and silent, for all the voices are attuned so well to the surroundings that the serenity of the whole scene is unimpaired.'

So here!... The conversational exchanges of the Gay Young Woman in the corner shop and Mr Bellairs, Jun., of No. 119, whose bird's-eye bow was inevitably askew and clamorous for her righting, did not prevent him from hearing the Lean Lady behind the wall poke up her sinking fire to a new orange crowning (and the tapping of the grey ashes on the hearthstone made him suddenly most unusually sorry for her!), nor render inaudible the fall of another gooseberry leaf in one of the prim gardens, and that at the same time as he was evolving his old English master's profile from one of the inky stains on the wall-paper, taking a mental note that he must reply that very night to Peggy's letter (the words of which were a starry system in his memory), and changing the paper in his typewriter.

Indeed, and was it not perfectly proper that the clean blues and whites of the Gay Young Woman's chatter, the rosy personality of Bellairs fils with his fatted calves and knicker-bocker check suit, the orange lacing of the stirred flames, and the bright red urgency of not forgetting to reply to Peggy's letter, should float nicely together? But it was a sorry thing, so it was, that he had to change the paper in his Roland every now and again, for what had that to do with the happy art of living?

Was there not an essential and most excellent harmony in all this? He thought of the boy, Jake, blowing the organ for his master. 'The business in hand-blowing was to watch a plummet's rise and fall: you pumped for the fall and slacked for the rise. That was the hard prose of it, but Jake knew a better way. He would imagine himself blowing up a fire with a bellows. When a full organ was needed he had to blow like the devil to keep the plummet down, and then the fire soared under his efforts. Otherwise a gentle purring was easily simulated. At another time he would be filling a bucket at the Well for a succession of thirsty horses and would so nicely time the allowance for each that the bucket was descending again on the very point of its being sucked dry. Or he would be the landlord of the "Bit and Halter" dozing over his parlour fire, nodding, nodding, down in little jerks, and then recovering himself with an indrawn rising sigh. Sometimes when the music was very liquid he would work a beer-engine-one or two good pulls and then the upward flow through the siphon!'

Nor was his happy-headedness perceptibly reduced by his steady subconscious elucidation of the reaction on Ibsen's sensitive nature of the brief white nights, the chilly climate, the rugged Scandinavian scenery, and the influence of the various strains, Danish, German, Norwegian and Scottish (particularly the last), in his blood, giving the gamut of mood – philosophic, poetic, mystic and analytic: nor was he more than most obliquely intent on the motley mob, with anguish in their eyes and features convulsed and tortured into revealing their inmost secrets by their implacable creator, passing slowly by in a vivid and dream-like way – fascinating, inconstant Peer Gynt; Emperor Julian, that magnificent failure; the grotesque Steensgard; the whited sepulchre, Consul Bernick; the doughty Stockman; Gina, the homely-sensible, and Ekdal, the self-illusionist; Rebekka West and Johann Rosmer; Ellida Wangel and the Stranger; Hedda and Lowborg; Hilda and Solness; Asta and Rita Allness; John Gabriel Borkmann, his gloomy brows furrowed; and the entire cohort of subsidiary characters, each one personal and alive – so much so that while he traced the working of the Scottish leaven so strong in the 'Northern Rembrandt', in practice an artist and in his bones a moralist, each one became, shorn of racial stigmata, one of the passers-by in the streets without, and he himself the Ibsen of Edinburgh... Instead he felt matter of fact and easy in this complex, nor was there any element of perturbation or torment in his mutable face. His eyes were happy and active as birds on a summer's morning, and his pipe was drawing evenly. At any minute he knew he might have the Chinese Republic on his head, and he felt quite equal to establishing an encyclopædic interaction with its manifold departments without yielding up the idlest of his present pleasant preoccupations. Or the Russian Duma might meet in the base of his skull and he would take in the whole ensemble, hear every word spoken, weigh up every speaker, discount the particular prejudices of each of his own personalities, educe an aggregate of conviction quite unanimous in its essence and airily at variance in its details – and communicate his impressions to the *Times*!

In a word, anything might happen – and nothing could happen (thus this fleeting mood!) that would surprise or perplex him or find him unequal to the strain. Why, not one of the countless impressions his brain was registering every instant, but immediately it was cleanly stamped, suffered a 'sea-change' into something entirely and most inconsequently different, just as a lightning artist may sketch the portrait of a popular actor, and then with another stoke of his pencil transform it into an excellent impression of a fishing fleet out from Newhaven.

(Perhaps it was because these effects were all so effortless and etherealised that this obscure but poignant sense of being an entirely different person to himself, afflicted him with such a minute sense of unreality. He felt somewhat as Shelley did, when writing his 'Epipsychidion' – fearing that the sentiment inspiring the poem would be associated in the minds of the readers of contemporary literature with the philanderings of the housemaid and the butcher-boy!)

Withal he never for an instant lost possession of the least of his realised personalities, not even of those unborn, for whom he made allowance, even as the Greeks built their altar to the Unknown God. (Yet how could he be sure that he was leaving room enough, making suffcent allowance? How could he be sure what he was to receive from the Unknown – the Unknowable – when he could not be sure, be quite sure, what he was willing to receive from the Known, from, that is to say, even the purest intimations of his Innermost Critic? – But beyond the regulation recognition of complexity modernity demanded, could one not probe too far – these continual allurements to new intricacies of introspection, wherein were they profitable? These were the 'greyflies winding their sultry horns'.) The Cynic, the Poet, the Prig, the Working Journalist, the Mere Human Being, his Father's Son, his Mother's Son, the Social Man, the Beardless Boy, the Seeker, Lazybones, the Innermost Critic, the Impersonal Factor, and an ever-increasing host more of them, all had fair play and carried on their separate activities with the mingled and protean materials of his mental life with the fair effect of social commonwealth in being. His internal economy realised the dreams of the Socialist idealists; the interactions were free and full of enterprise; the tone throughout was healthy; and the Greek Chorus of Recorded-Opinion-Read never failed to moderate timeously. Best of all, perhaps, he was already wary – albeit mindful of Joubert's advice, keeping a corner of his head open and free for the opinions of his friends – not to put his reliance on opinions, least of all on his own opinions, and was becomingly fearful of that 'cursed conceit of being right which kills all noble feeling', whether in himself or others. So that most pervasive of all, perhaps, was the feeling of the skilled operator taking pride in the complicated work of his machine and jealous of its smooth running. Yet at times he could not help wondering, in a subterranean sort of way, whether intelligence itself was not an accident in the creative processes, or really the goal towards which mankind believed itself drifting. Deep down in his nature an elusive thought, for which he had not yet found that symbol needful to transform it into an intellectual reality, disseminated vague distrusts of certitude.

Thus, occasionally, he might have a shadowy sense of the incongruity of convening the Russian Duma under the woolly scalp of an undistinguished Scottish free-lance of two-and-twenty, or a hollow feeling (forthwith exorcised as a mean commercial instinct) that little profit to a fellow in his shoes lay in spending an hour or two as a Chinese Reference Library. He would, with the vaguest sensation of irrevocable poverty (which in the volatile atmosphere of these speculations was like the passing of a light cloud across the face of the sun), acknowledge that he had no standing in the world and that all his way was still to make.

Such prosaic reminders, invading the serenity of his mental life, made him feel in a distant fashion, as he put it, 'like an inside without an outside'. But such aspects thrust themselves upon his consideration with tiny but undeniable insistence – if so far they simply amounted to this – that surrounding all his clear-cut conceptions were diffused colour-effects that still so obliterated design (and indeed they might be palimpsests concealing design upon design) as to leave it indistinguishable from pure colour-regions of delicate palpitant haze from which, perhaps, after seven years, as with Maris's canvases, the faint signs of design might break through the colour screen. Under these luminous washes lay, he imagined, the secret lineaments of destiny – 'dreams of form in days of thought'! Moreover, even when the activities of his perceptions were like the round soft tendernesses of songs, rising and falling, broadening and soaring in high flights, that hung, eddied a moment, and then bore away to more slender and wonderful loftinesses, until their harmonies turned on the very apices of sweetness, dipped steeply, and flashed their joyous returns to the exultations of all his senses, rolling an ecstasy of understanding which gladdened the whole universe of his being, and the sad mortal elements which moved therein, until every nerve was athrill with the goodness and bravery of life, the calm spirit of the Innermost Critic dispassionately disassociated the essence of it all from the modern satisfaction in complexity for complexity's sake, insisting on the impossibility of his having captured more than the most fragmentary strain from the glorious never-ending

> maze of various man
> In coloured music wrought.

So it was that, undaunted, he was always shadowily but effectively repeating in the recesses and byways of his far-going introspection the tremendous words of the Prandial Philosopher: – 'If all that poetry has dreamt, all that insanity has raved, all that maddening narcotics have driven through the brains of men or smothered passions nursed in the fancies of women; if the dreams of the colleges and convents and boarding-schools, if every human feeling that sighs or smiles or curses or shrieks or groans should bring all their innumerable images such as course with every heart beat – the epic which held them all, though its letters filled the Zodiac, would be but a cupful from the infinite ocean of similitudes and analogies that rolls through the world': and was perpetually amused to find that, salutary though the effects of such a reminder were, even that terrific sentence scarcely dimmed for a moment the ebullient gratification of his Prig, who was incessantly chanting, 'I am thinking all these things – I – I!'…

This amusement was, of course, mainly pathological. His sense of actual cerebral disposition was acute and constantly employed. Indeed, one of his favourite recreations was to take a given statement, say Chesterton's declaration that a yawn is a silent yell, and map out the ideographical conditions necessarily obtaining for the production of such a phenomenon. But despite this keen curiosity in regard to the causation of such mental occurrences, although he became stored with unique lore in regard to psychological technique, he sought in vain for any clue towards understanding the selective instincts. Why a man should be set off on a particular line of thought he could account for easily, and the methods in which particular aspects of a case presented themselves to such and such a mind he was able to realise in the most meticulous photographic fashion, but why they should do so was a perpetual mystery upon which he could not secure the faintest light. He could find no centre of motivation and rebelled at times against this spring slavery. He likened himself to a lighted circle, a camp-fire, into which came all manner of waifs and strays from the surrounding imponderable night. Deviously and incessantly, through many a mood that was sheerly pathological, in many an excursion which took him well over the recognised boundaries of sanity, he pursued his investigations. Still, all these mazy meticulated divagations were in his mind only what insect life is in the world as we see it, ubiquitous but infinitesimal. Another obscure ray he knew of which was fused in the broad light of his thought, and with the properties of which a tiny specialist-cell in his brain was constantly experimenting, emanating from his subtle realisation that beyond the individual mind of each man was a collective mind, quite different in its psychology, directed he could not imagine how, or to what ends, employing the symbols of religious systems, world politics and racial instincts. The little specialist was able to use this pretty much as a man uses electricity or radium. The consequence was that he was enabled, indefinably but quite definitely, to trace the thin line of his own mentality through all the incalculable fabric of the thought of humanity. This gave him latitude and longitude on the oceans of speculation.

At times, however, the unnatural aspect of this cerebral sense overcame him and he was seized with sensations akin to the sudden instability and nameless fear which overtake investigators of psychic affairs. This had some horrible effects. The instantaneous realisation of unwholesome abnormality would vitiate all his speculative liveliness. Max Nordau and Lombroso would spring into his mind, and he would suddenly see his brain as a writhing mass of worms. One part would beat like a pulse, growing louder and louder – swell enormously – then burst, deluging his mind in warm blood. He was obsessed – then recovering from the terrible phantasy, nerveless and blanched, he would watch with painful realism the break-up of his mental life. Every one of his separate egos became violently anarchical, creating an unthinkable Babel. Disunity and internecine hostility tore him into shreds. This passing, he would darken into lethargy, thus eventually recovering his poise in sleep, and the memories of such crises were almost indistinguishable from nightmares. Similar at times was the effect of his sense of personal insignificance, of physical inadequacy – of having paralysed his creative faculties by over-reading – of being merely a 'strong solution of books' as 'full of quotations as Shakespeare' – and so forth, and, as will readily be discerned when his youth is remembered, even more pronouncedly was he thus affected by evidences of stupidity prospering and wickedness flourishing like the green bay tree, and by the actual irrelevance of religion, education and art to the facts of life. On the other hand the more clearly participant in his mood the sense of the collective mind, the more comfortable he felt. Everything was then in proportion and perspective, and the humbling and depersonalising effect was soothing and helpful. But bother criticism when everything was really doing its very best so nicely! After all, these contrasting sentiments were only agreeable little differences between one right and another. He remembered a bit of a letter from his Aunt Sarah, concerning a railway journey: 'I must say I always thought it a mistake for the Companies to stop at so *many* stations – people who want to get out at these are so selfish, keeping the other poor passengers packed in the train.' Outside, in front of a red and green chemist's shop, a mongrel was going round and round in pursuit of its tail. He couldn't let any of these small issues dust over any least little bit of his intellectual clearness. In the coloured air he moderated with easy expertness an ethereal see-saw with a subtle pride of obscurity on one end and a glimmering recollection of S. Cyran on the other, and knew that he had solved the problem of perpetual motion. Strange, that within a hundred miles or so inside his brain or on the left of his head, just for a bird's brief flight, there should be thoughts and feelings and experiences 'a whole God's breadth apart' – 'the breadth of death and life'. Then, apropos, apparently of nothing, the Social Man who had travelled a great deal began saying how, when he was among the ostriches on the veld, he had often wondered how it happened that that bird in hiding its head in the sand should make your head so conspicuous. And the Working Journalist said, 'How common these fanciful paradoxes are nowadays, to be sure'. The furthest doubt flashed out again, and he felt almost as if he had dropped an 'h'…. He felt all these vaguer speculations reinforced and running in his blood like wine. *Was* thought then, as we knew it, a disease? he asked for the millionth time.

> Then felt ashamed as they who shout
> When God's own silence is about,
> And turned that he might hide his head
> Because nothing was to be said.

And so, again, naturally he found all the more to say welling up from unplumbed depths in him. The seeker went off again on his mazy endless divagations:

> Oh, vanity of vanities
> And following of wind
> Through the dim avenues and deep
> Abysses of the mind,
> When would his ears be deaf at last,
> When would his eyes be blind?
> Oh, vanity of sorrowing
> And emptiness of mirth
> And wandering fires of thought in clay
> Iniprisoned at his birth,
> When would the wandering fires go out
> And earth return to earth?

In the words of the Irishman 'there was no beginning nor end to it, and it hadn't any bottom'. He must soon tackle seriously this curious question with which he was always playing – why certain sensations and experiences will bear recalling over and over again without becoming exhausted, so that he could return to them after months or years or constantly, and always find entirely new bearings in them which had escaped him on the first occasion. It was most remarkable that this could go on happening time after time, giving extraordinary effects of internal infinitudes, while other sensations and experiences (more vivid and arrestive at the time, perhaps) were exhausted right away and could never be renewed – to all appearances, although, of course, he knew that even the most casual incident or impression could have an underground existence, working away like a mole, unobserved, yet in such a manner as to throw up heaps here and there, and in the most unlikely places. How was it possible that some phrase or concatenation of words, or run of colours, should bear within itself meaning after meaning, horizon after horizon of significance and suggestion? Yet such was undoubtedly the case. Portions of his far-flung reading, certain recollections of landscape or house-furnishing, inflections of voices, smells, sounds, physical and mental sensations, had for him this inexhaustible germinative quality. He returned to them again and again (or they returned to him), and continually he found fresh interpretations lurking beneath the old and familiar facts. Was it like the difference between the actual solid shape of a mountain and the different views obtainable from different sides? Were these mountain-facts of his mental world imaged forth in such a way as to retain this quality of solidity, so that their outlines varied according to the angles at which he approached and reapproached them and the endless variations of his mind? None of these outlines were final, and the ultimate content remained behind and eluded them all…. But this was going far afield – and his article was finished.

II A Moment in Eternity

To George Ogilvie

> The great song ceased
> – Aye, like a wind was gone,
> And our hearts came to rest,
> Singly as leaves do,
> And every leaf a flame.
>
> My shining passions stilled
> Shone in the sudden peace
> Like countless leaves
> Tingling with the quick sap
> Of Immortality.

I was a multitude of leaves
Receiving and reflecting light,
A burning bush
Blazing for ever unconsumed,
Nay, ceaselessly,
Multiplying in leaves and light
And instantly
Burgeoning in buds of brightness,
– Freeing like golden breaths
Upon the cordial air
A thousand new delights,
– Translucent leaves
Green with the goodness of Eternity,
Golden in the Heavenly light,
– The golden breaths
Of my eternal life,
Like happy memories multiplied,
Shining out instantly from me
And shining back for ever into me,
– Breaths given out
But still unlost,
For ever mine
In the infinite air,
The everlasting foliage of my soul
Visible awhile
Like steady and innumerable flames,
Blending into one blaze
Yet each distinct
With shining shadows of difference.

A sudden thought of God's
Came like a wind
Ever and again
Rippling them as waters over stars,
And swiftlier fanning them
And setting them a-dance,
Upflying, fluttering down,
Moving in orderly intricacies
Of colour and of light,
Delaying, hastening,

Blazing and serene,
Shaken and shining in the turning wind,
Lassoing cataracts of light
With rosy boughs,
Or clamouring in echoing unequalled heights,
Rhythmical sprays of many-coloured fire
And spires chimerical
Gleaming in fabulous airs,
And suddenly
Lapsing again
To incandescence and increase.

And again the wind came
Blowing me afar
In fair fantastic fires,
– Ivies and irises invading
The upland garths of ivory;
Queen daisies growing
In the tall red grass
By pools of perfect peace;
And bluebells tossing
In transparent fields;
And silver airs
Lifting the crystal sources in dim hills
And swinging them far out like bells of glass
Pealing pellucidly
And quivering in faery flights of chimes;
Shivers of wings bewildered
In alleys of virgin dream;
Floral dances and revels of radiance
Whirling in stainless sanctuaries;
And eyes of Seraphim,
Shining like sunbeams on eternal ice,
Lifted toward the unexplored
Summits of Paradise.

And the wind ceased.
Light dwelt in me,
Pavilioned there.
I was a crystal trunk,

Columnar in the glades of Paradise,
Bearing the luminous boughs
And foliaged with the flame
Of infinite and gracious growth,
– Meteors for roots,
And my topmost spires
Notes of enchanted light
Blind in the Godhead!
– White stars at noon!

I shone within my thoughts
As God within us shines.

And the wind came,
Multitudinous and light
I whirled in exultations inexpressible
– An unpictureable, clear,
Soaring and glorying,
Swift consciousness,
A cosmos turning like a song of spheres
On apices of praise,
A separate colour,
An essential element and conscious part
Of successive and stupendous dreams
In God's own heart!

And the wind ceased
And like a light I stood,
A flame of glorious and complex resolve,
Within God's heart.

I knew then that a new tree,
A new tree and a strange,
Stood beautifully in Heaven.
I knew that a new light
Stood in God's heart
And a light unlike
The Twice Ten Thousand lights
That stood there,
Shining equally with me,

And giving and receiving increase of light
Like the flame that I was
Perpetually.
And I knew that when the wind rose
This new tree would stand still
Multiplied in light but motionless,
And I knew that when God dreamt
And His creative impulses
Ran through us like a wind
And we flew like clear and coloured
Flames in His dreams,
(Adorations, Gratitudes, and Joys,
Plenary and boon and pure,
Crystal and burning-gold and scarlet
Competing and co-operating flames
Reflecting His desires,
Flashing like epical imaginings
And burning virgin steeps
With ceaseless swift apotheoses)
One light would stand unmoved.

And when on pinnacles of praise
All others whirled
Like a white light deeper in God's heart
This light would shine,
Pondering the imponderable,
Revealing ever clearlier
Patterns of endless revels,
Each gesture freed,
Each shining shadow of difference,
Each subtle phase evolved
In the magnificent and numberless
Revelations of ecstasy
Succeeding and excelling inexhaustibly,
– A white light like a silence
Accentuating the great songs!
– A shining silence wherein God
Might see as in a mirror
The miracles that He must next achieve!

Ah, Light,
That is God's inmost wish,
His knowledge of Himself,
Flame of creative judgment,
God's interrogation of infinity,
Searching the unsearchable,
Silent and steadfast tree
Housing no birds of song,
Void to the wind,
But rooted in God's very self,
Growing ineffably,
Central in Paradise!

When the song ceased
And I stood still,
Breathing new leaves of life
Upon the eternal air,
Each leaf of all my leaves
Shone with a new delight
Murmuring Your name.

O Thou,
Who art the wisdom of the God
Whose ecstasies we are!

III   Café Scene

He wanders lonely as a cloud.

He caught sight of himself in a long narrow mirror– practically a full-length reflection, so vivid that it seemed to thrust upon him almost with vehemence a sense of responsibility for his own identity: as he invariably (almost invariably – there had been times unfortunately – but…), if less intrusively did at this point, just passing the glittering unsteady counter, scintillating and swaying there, into the comparative twilight of the (today somewhat improbably narrow) neck which attached the front shop to the long narrow tea-room behind: and this glance at his external appearance gave him, he perceived with resigned contempt, despite the unnecessary over-emphasis of his physical actuality, an odd irrational sensation of reassurance, a mere animal assumption that with such a composed and natural (whatever that might mean) look upon his face, his state of mind could not really be so terribly seismic and unsafe as he had with a sensation of blanching and blenching (equally irrational – a mere intellectual presumption – mind and matter it seemed must always be playing this little game of over-rating themselves and under-rating each other) felt it to be a moment earlier... all the afternoon, indeed, a peculiar and unsupportable condition when the most casual sounds seemed charged with secret and sinister inflections, most ordinary objects endowed with unthinkable and malign properties, the processes of his brain obscurely altered, the selective methods of his senses subtly different.

Faces that ordinarily his eyes would have passed over without registering any definite impression had come round all sorts of corners, leaping out of crowds in the most inconsequent and inexplicable fashion, and fastened themselves upon his unsteady brain – silly faces that he felt would haunt him for ever, particularly that impossible old policeman... no, that lean girl with the butter-coloured hair was the worst, a masterpiece of indecent cleverness in visual realism! And faces that his eyes had to his relief actually passed over seemed instead to have entered some optical side-door, and long after he had passed their possessors surprised his consciousness in the most outrageous fashion, alarming afterthoughts violently spatchcocked into his very soul.

And it hadn't been faces only. Corners of houses had split into his thoughts like an elbow in the ribs. The glittering motion of a bicycle wheel had communicated a wild dizziness and when deflected to circumvent an omnibus given him an extraordinary feeling of having launched into an insane aberration. All sorts of little everyday things, disproportioned and bedevilled, were picked out by his eyes as if in a spirit of capricious and cruel caricature. That sewing-machine now – a standard make, a world-famous machine, why had it afflicted him with such an agitated and exaggerated sense of its infinite clicking, throbbing capacity to irritate just as if his nerves had been passed endlessly under the needle stitching every little quivering bit of sentience into some fantastic pattern of wanton agony?... The flaming effrontery of a bunch of cheap roses, brutally red! The hot offensive dampness of an afternoon edition! (He had tried to read a perfectly plain little paragraph of news and had not been able to understand a single word of it, any more than if it had been in Chinese or part of the leader, and the shape and size of the paragraph set in a column of similar paragraphs in a quite normal way had affected him as bizarre geometrical experiments which had signally failed!) A line between two flagstones on the pavement, suddenly a yawning chasm! A cough behind him which gave him the feeling of having been buried under an avalanche! Feet splaying at angles suggestive of the most irreconcilable and meaningless divergences! A tall man instantly precipitous! A woman's waist expanding equatorially! Hands like starfish or stars! Noses like fallen towers! Eddies and undercurrents and cataracts of eyes! Feet under which the ground fluttered like paper! Voices that struck him as if he had been a gong – voices that tortured him as if they had been ferrets and he a rabbit-warren – voices that were charged with astounding and unintelligible prophecies, accusations, threats and pleas.

He could not even now, however, help looking at his feet. The mirror cut him off just below the knees with a vicious effect of unnecessary amputation... Of course, his feet were all right down there; shining blackly. What could have happened to them, anyhow, he asked himself bitterly – to move as one? eh? Or to have the boots that encased them go suddenly green or purple? Why the devil must his brain go on tweaking out logical processes to impossible lengths? He was entering (he impressed upon himself firmly and quietly) just the same old room he always entered at tea-time, and, of course, everything was really just as usual (except perhaps that the tea-cups appeared to be twinkling with an unusual rapidity and the little circular tables to be going round at such an intense speed that they deceived the eye, any eye but his, with a seeming immobility! He knew instinctively that if he put a finger on one of them however delicately, there would be a distinct buzz). And he himself, with a sense of shaking his brain vigorously, was just as usual, the same look on his face, the same way of balancing his flesh on his bones, the same slow, quiet gait – this haunting sense of stealthiness was quite unfounded – and in a second or two he would be sitting in his usual chair in the corner yonder, sipping his tea and eating his favourite cakes, nodding to the usual people and having the usual feelings.

Without a doubt! – but an extraordinary sense of intolerable belittlement assailed him between the first little table he had to pass and the second, so congesting and compressing his organs that he felt that he was fighting for breath. It was as if a dwarfing process had set it. He would soon have no more stature than a fly. He found time, with a sense of extraordinary mental agility to reflect that probably his feelings were quite similar to those which must have afflicted those luckless wights in the fairy tales just at the moment when they were being transformed into pigs or pansies.

A titanic figure heaved past him, looming up above his shoulder to his nervous sidelong glance like a thundercloud, a great and oppressive phenomenon, discharging a dark incalculable belligerency directed against the world at large, it seemed, and only incidentally and fortuitously against himself, a doom-dark shape, billowy and lowering, like nightfall and a storm at sea.

He took once more (quaintly conscious of courageousness and even a little amused by his hasty search for symbols and figures of speech sufficiently enormous) a grip of himself, discerning in every mode of his bodily and mental functioning a diathesis of sheer unreason, in which the slightest incident or impression, negligently admitted, might set up unthinkable conditions of terror. Every cell of his body and his brain seemed, separately and conjointly, poised on the very edge of an unknown that was both ludicrous and fatal…

He so impressed himself with the need for intense caution that a second later he found himself staring at the perforated cane bottom of a chair with a powerful fixity as if daring it to declare its hidden nature and do its worst.

He had difficulty in tearing his eyes away from it. There were nineteen little round holes in that atrocious lemon-coloured disk of seating, surrounded by a tight round red cane, and mounted on slim curving legs – three of them!

A preposterous joke imperilled the foundations of his consciousness with its fortuitous folly. 'Three legs – the Manx device – a Hall Caine chair!'

His internal agitation communicated itself to his lips in what was probably but a sardonic and suffering smile, but what (caught in another convenient mirror) appeared to those insufferable and dilating eyes of his, swinging like lanterns, like a wild and dangerous hazard of his facial muscles. There was no knowing where it might stop. It might continue until like the Cheshire Cat he hung on the atmosphere in but a grin. The corners of his lips appeared to be giving way, slitting silently and unresistingly, threatening his ears…

An intense but utterly impersonal interest in this physiognomical phenomenon grew painfully within him – then abruptly and painlessly deserted him. All at once it was as if he had lost his face or had never possessed one… He knew that he had noticed that the Thundercloud (who had passed him darkly and heavily just before that wretched chair had arrested his irresponsible eyes with its irrelevant triped antics) was poised there on his favourite chair in the corner, the old corner yonder – banked up into it blackly, sitting there like Hell itself!

He sat down on the nearest chair – any chair, any table! Nothing mattered now. Destiny was unmistakably upon him and would have its way with him. He must let things take their course. If it had been ordained, set down against his soul and this place and day and hour from the commencement of time, that he must look at things from an unaccustomed angle, see the unfamiliar and unsuspected aspects of all the everyday unfamiliar things that in the sinful arrogance of his individuality he had taken as fixed and fundamental, given and unchanging, it did not matter what sort of angle it was. It was certain to be acute. Geometry be damned! 'Thunder!' He heard his absurd soul telling itself in its pitiful bewilderment, 'Thunder!' Stuff and nonsense! It was only a big man, a very big and stout and brutal-looking man, dark hair, dark moustache, blue-black chin, a swarthy and overweighted face... but only a man! It wasn't a bit of good though. His lost soul kept muttering 'Thunder! Thunder!' as if in amazed and impotent recognition – Thunder about to devour cream cookies in a black and purposive fashion, a tenebrous and terrible tea-taker!

Then the girl came in – a white-faced slip of a thing, emphasising her anaemia with a scarlet blouse without regard to his feelings. No! It was not culpable thoughtlessness on her part. Something in the apologetic bend of her neck suggested that she was pitifully sorry that she was quite incapable of regulating the effect she must incidentally produce, miserably and hopelessly concentrated as she was though no fault of her own on being a pallid, insignificant wraith of a woman, a complex and colourless business. Her whole being seemed to cry out to him and to the world in general, in a white tenuous voice, 'Don't take any notice! I am very sorry, but for reasons which I cannot express, and which in any case you would not understand – not because of any mental deficiency on your part, but because they are essentially unknowledgeable – I must go on, day in and day out, year in and year out, bleaching away. And I must take tea somewhere, that being so, mustn't I now – as a reasonable man, mustn't I?... another Café? What difference would that make? To you, personally, selfishly, yes!... but, generally speaking, considering the effect of my unspeakable ensemble on human eyes as a whole? I'll be perfectly quiet – don't look at me: I shall only go whiter and whiter if you do, you know – or rather you don't know: believe me: my power of blanching is boundless – I'll be perfectly quiet and I won't be long – just a cup of tea and a couple of buns and I shall cease to blight the air about you in this ghastly, unforgivable but imperatively, if incomprehensibly, necessary fashion!'

A sense of dreary goodwill invaded him as he looked at her. It was as if his soul replied, going over and bending earnestly above her bloodless but invincible countenance. 'Sh! Not a word! I know. Don't mind me. Why should I object to your going into a decline just because I happen to be having tea? There's no law compelling young females to carry blood in their faces or, for the matter of that, elsewhere. It's fashionable, of course, but still... ! Quiver away for all you are worth, my dear. You are but a human aspen really. A human aspen faint and frail! Never you mind! Your pallor is almost pleasant, really... Now, what I do object to is an inimical immensity like that...' waving a differentiating finger cornerwards.

The Thundercloud had ordered tea – tea, in a reverberating roar, as if he were pandering brazenly in public to some unmentionable vice. In the aspect of the waitress (a deft and pleasant servant he had always hitherto thought her) hastening to execute the deafening order there was a revolting servility. She shot soullessly along between the tables with a vile velocity. It was almost as if a flash of lightning had emanated from the growing darkness in the corner.

Then he saw an indistinct shape hovering hesitantly – heard the sigh of a spiritless zephyr – and knew that what had really happened had been that the other waitress (who had always hitherto appeared to him sufficiently well embodied) had taken the girl's order. Indeed it must have been so: for in a few moments a small teapot decadently green, a plate of shadowy-looking brown bread and butter and other obscure paraphernalia, dimly coloured and insecurely shaped, of a negligible repast, had forgathered mistily in front of this little white ghost of all the sorrow in the world, whose glimmering hands were apparently making ineffectual passes over and amongst them, an impotent and pitiable ritual, incapable of producing that ancient magic, that friendly and familiar faerie of tinkling metal and shining delf, for which the unhappy girl was in all likelihood desperately striving.

'Bread cast upon dark waters!' he found himself murmuring (could it be audibly?), thinking of the contrast between her tentative fastidious mastication – little bites that were so nearly invisible that they might have been imaginary, tiny sips that involved so little movement of her lips that the cup might most likely have been empty – and the hideous fashion in which ball after ball of bread and bun and draught after draught of tea were lost in some desperate juggling trick, swallowed up and lost in that looming darkness, sitting accumulating in the corner there.

He could not remember having ordered tea himself or having had it brought to him. How much he had already eaten there was no possible telling. As if he had turned a sharp corner and run into himself again, he was horrified to find that he had to all appearances swallowed a great cake whole... He had just caught a glimpse of it being automatically put to his lips by a nonchalant hand: and now it had vanished as if it had never been. Could it have been only an optical illusion? He would know when he got his bill. Madeira cakes, one? Surely not! Hastily seizing his cup he drained it empty in one desperate gulp. Somehow on restoring the cup to the saucer his arm descended with involuntary violence. He had forgotten that the table was rotating at a dizzy rate. Yet, curiously, nothing happened. If he had been subjected to a volley of china splinters, or if the cup had swerved and shot off into space, at least he would have been able to understand it. Was the operation of all natural laws suspended? Beads of sweat started out on his brow. In a moment or two he felt as if he was holding his head under a pouring tap. This was intolerable. He must know one way or another without delay if he was to preserve his sanity. He seized the cup again – a thin cynical light was playing round its fluted body – raised it high above his head, then brought it down with full force – and there it was nesting peacefully in its saucer, intact! Were his thoughts moving so rapidly that he had only imagined he had subjected it to this test – or had the fragile, evil-gleaming vessel actually survived it? How could he really determine? To think the matter carefully out he put his elbow on the table (what did it matter suppose the friction should set fire to his sleeve?) and pillowed his head on his hand, feeling like Atlas during an earthquake.

Just as he was getting the pros and cons of the unspeakable problem carefully and clearly arranged in his mind, however, another matter of precedent urgency presented itself. Leaning forward in this new position he caught a glimpse in another mirror (the place was like that Bar of Bennett's 'all whisky and looking-glasses') of an extraordinary exhibition of necromancy, the effect of a composite reflection bridging the space in some subtle and sinister fashion between the doom-dark figure in the corner and the phantasmal female, and thus secretly) the baneful figure of evil was making deliberate and incomprehensible passes above her witless head, with (of all the instruments of sorcery) a tea-cup, held loosely in an enormous dark and hairy fist, on the middle finger of which gleamed a yellow ring set with a huge and baleful emerald. With his eyes starting out of his head and his brain repeating and repeating helplessly, 'And this, mind you, in a well-known tea-shop, one which I have frequented for years and years… the diabolical ingenuity of it…', he watched these Satanic machinations, the tea-cup swinging above the piteous unprotected head like a Damoclean sword and all behind and around Egyptian darkness.

'The defencelessness of woman!' he said to himself, muttering tensely, and excitedly conscious that he was making up his mind for some inconceivable action of knight-errantry.

He rose as if with a wild leap – almost as if shot out by some catapultic motion of the chair. Why on earth had he done so? He now perceived that what had actuated him had been the fact that the girl and the giant had also arisen, in fact just a second or two before he had, and were now moving out of the tea-room into the front shop. But was the girl there? The broad back of the man, ballooning blackly, blotted out from his view whatever might be in front. He followed breathlessly. Was he really running? He could not be sure. At the pay-desk he almost cannoned into the giant, who was throwing down great clangorous coins upon the vibrant counter. With incredible dexterity he contrived to thrust his head round a pillar of a leg in a cunning effort to discover if the girl was in front, but the giant frustrated his intention with a sudden movement which made him feel he had lost his sight… Blinking, a second later, or how long, he found himself alone, floating it seemed in a sea of suspicion. That was how the cash-girl's face affected him, as if he had been guilty of some monstrous solecism. With a mighty effort he pulled himself together – worlds might go smash but bills must be met – he fumbled in his pockets for coins which eluded him in a manner that, to say the least of it, was excessively ill-timed. Finally his fingers closed on a great round of metal, and he drew it forth, and with an air of mastery which he instantaneously felt had been crassly premature, tossed it on the throbbing counter… With the royal, if fateful clangour of the giant's pieces, which had clashed like mighty shields, still in his cars, it was with a sense of incontinent horror that he heard the inexplicable boom, a very echo, as it were, of the hollowness of life… Years after, he remembered that, stunned in a way as he was, he had yet contrived to reflect on how much the human brain will stand. A second later he knew (though he had no earthly notion of how he had done it) that he had apologised to the cash-girl, tendered true money, noticed a familiar picture endowed with a second meaning which somehow escaped him, and received his change and countless excruciating and simultaneous impressions ranging from a feminine eyebrow twisted into the shape of a question mark to a sense of his boots rooting to the tiles of the floor.

With a sensation of tearing himself up with a soaring motion of his shoulders he flew to the door. Not a soul was in sight! Anything might have happened. Only the worst – an indefinable and unthinkable worst – was thinkable. The street had a mocking emptiness. He seemed to be gazing down a corridor in interstellar space.

A waitress ran up to where he stood poised on the threshold as if on the edge of a fathomless abyss, tendering his hat, which he had forgotten.

He took it dumbly, trying to look at her but finding nothing on which to fasten his eyes; and walked slowly and unsteadily away, carrying his hat in a petrified hand.

IV   The Fool

He said that he was God.
    'We are well met,' I cried
'I've always hoped I should
    Meet God before I died.'

I slew him then and cast
    His corpse into a pool,
– But how I wish he had
    Indeed been God, the fool!

V   A Four Years' Harvest

I

O Memory, Lord of broken and broadcast
Fragments of life, like scattered cyclades
Set in the dark illimitable seas
Of Time...

The crisis was over once again – once again. He lit his pipe which had gone out. The struck match gleamed cheerfully and the atmosphere seemed to throb as he sucked at the stem. The window was open.* Vast and awful shapes of cloud with clear-cut edges were cleaving their way across the sky, spreading like enormous fans. All the light that had flooded the heavens seemed to be concentrating before the menacing advances into such random patches as were yet uninvaded, so that an interstice in the ragged purple here, an irregular belt just above the horizon there, had a peculiar ghastliness as of some human disease. The world was full of the

Red darkness of the hearts of roses,
Blue brilliant from dead starless skies,
And gold that lies behind the eyes,
The unknown unnameable sightless white
That is the essential flame of night,
Lustreless purple, hooded green,
The myriad hues that lie between
Darkness and darkness...

* Sections Lahore Indian General Hospital, Sergeants' Mess, Marseilles.

With what an abruptness storms sprang from the blue at this season here! All at once a change had made itself felt. The sunshine seemed less brilliant, the shadows less solidly, less sharply etched. Very slight, very uncertain! It required close scrutiny for assurance that it was not fancied, – a change in his blood! The sky might have been ransacked to discover the smallest shred of cloud: but never so faint a gauze had been drawn over the face of the sun, faintly bedimming without obscuring it. At the same time the air which had been hot all day, hot but buoyant, stimulant, seemed to become thick, sluggish, suffocating – to yield up its vital principle and fall a dead weight on the earth. And this effect was accompanied by a sudden silence.

Not a bird twittered! Not a leaf rustled! The world held its breath. And his thought that went on babbling, babbling, was a very part of the silence, accentuating and underscoring it. Still no rack of cloud was anywhere discernible...

Then suddenly the higher grounds were lapped in obscurity. The cloud spread, and sank, cancelling the sun, shrouding Cap Janet to its waist, curling in smoky wreaths among the houses of Les Abbatoirs and La Calade aloft yonder; turning the sea from sapphire to steel; filling the entire valley with a strange mixture of darkness and pallid light.

Overhead it hung like a vast canopy of leaden-hued cotton-wool: westward it had a fringe of fiery crimson beyond which a strip of clear sky on the horizon diffused a chill metallic yellow like tarnished brass... His window looked to the East: but still he knew that it had been so. He had felt the fronts of his teeth disproportionately black... Then there was a violent gust of wind, cold, scattering everything before it, dust, dried leaves, the fallen petals snow-like of fruit-tree blossoms; making the trees writhe and labour like wrestlers in grips with invisible opponents; making the short grass and his hair shudder; corrugating his brow and the surface of the bay.

> And the dark fell. There grew
> Himward a sound of shaken boughs
> And ceased above his intricate house.

The lightning tore through the dark cloud canopy in long blinding zigzags. The wind moaned, howled, hooted, and the chamber in which he sat was full of the chill and the smell of it.

So the storm had begun, and still the lightning played torturingly across the swart swelling bosom, and a muttering of thunder came as from a throbbing heart within it. It looked quite solid and he thought, 'If it reaches that electric light down there struggling so fiercely it will surely fall and then....'

A flock of night-birds passed, flying low and swift. He could hear their quills beating the air and they cried to one another. The black geometry of the system of breakwaters in the bay was a congeries of moulds holding the dulling lead of the seas. Farther out a dark mist hid the Château D'If and the islands. Just outside the window – an outstretched hand could touch them – the stripped boughs of a poplar were swelling and rippling like negroid muscles. A mass of green-black shrubbery hid the base of Cap Janet but a sudden irradiation of yellow in the thick leaves told of a tramcar rounding the hidden corner. He rose and moved to the window. Yellow lights gleamed in the stormy chiaroscuro – a smoking shell – of the Abbatoirs quarter up the hill. A wrinkled bit of the steep water-worn ascent was discernible in the thin light of a couple of lamps. Just below him the tents were ghostly shapes like fallen and faded moons. From behind the yellow squares of the little windows of the Indian Y.M.C.A. hut at the bottom of the hospital grounds, inexpressibly remote as it seemed, came the crying of strings, a screeching lugubrious and fierce in its alien transport, as if it were mocking his sad and earnest conviction of irrelevant inevitability, the crowning torment and inward pride of his dexterous and irrepressible intellectuality. Bhim Dyal, probably, the mad little Gurkha, strummed with vertiginous speed, with fury, and the distracted clamour of his voice wrestling madly with the ringing madness of the strings ended in a supreme shriek. A low and applauding murmur flowed to his ears – the austere acclamations of connoisseurs. He depicted to himself their shapes, squatting thickly round the music-makers, their fierce gesticulations, their ear-rings, bound heads, the incomprehensible expressions on their brown grimacing faces, whitening with sudden teeth.

In the tension of his imagination he beheld them as plainly as anything seen with the eyes of the body, and with his sharpened hearing catching every word with preternatural distinctness, felt as if, with the ring of Gyges on his finger, he actually squatted in their midst. Nor was he able to disengage his attention, it seemed – his ears were apparently held by this barbaric cacophony (which, proceeding doubtless all the while, he had not previously heard) as by some ancient mariner's eye of glittering insane sound... The gay truculence of the hollow knocking, the metallic jingle, the shrill trolling, went on crescendo to a burst of babbling voices, a mad speed of tinkling, a thundering shout... The sudden silence pulsated with the ponderous strokes of his heart.

Then there came a sound of men laughing ('honest English laughter!'

– he had a ridiculous imitative sensation in his own throat, as if some physiological memory had been sympathetically excited) in the Rest Camp across the way. He sat down again some way back from the window, feeling more than ever cut off and desolate. In the darkness of his mind (as if something of the darkness and wildness of the night had struck in upon him) swirled the fallen leaves of his thoughts.

II

He had a fancy that many of them (and by 'them' he meant that section of the 'interpreting class', as John Buchan termed it, who had been actually in the Army and overseas during the greater part of the war) when finally restored to their 'old ways of doing' would look back upon those years of war pretty much as a man looks back across the gulf which a sudden serious illness cuts into the familiar landscape of his life. 'Though we speak with the tongues of men and of angels we shall not be listened to unless we prepare for ourselves a hearing.' It was difficult enough to listen to himself as it was. He was conscious of the bewildering hopelessness of trying to sort out his impressions and come to any considered conclusion. Looking in upon himself, working away feverishly in that teeming brain of his at any section of this multitudinous task, he realised with unerring instinct that he was capable at best of being even to himself in his final attitude, whatever that might be, only glittering but ill-poised, sincere but unconvincing.

Malloch and he were agreed that the real literature of the war could not possibly be written for a few years – possibly for a good few years – if ever. They had not come to that momentous conclusion without wrestling mightily with themselves. But it was ineludible – he following himself with an air of indignant mystery, Malloch glaring whitely through his spectacles.

He recollected with a painful embittered reluctance the chorus in the *Bacchæ*: –

> Knowledge, we are not foes!
> I seek thee diligently
> But the world with a great wind blows
> Shining, and not from thee;
> Blowing to beautiful things
> On amid dark and light,
> Till life, through the trammellings
> Of Laws that are not the Right,

Breaks clean and pure and sings
Glorying to God on the height!

He found it impossible to express, even with any minimum of intelligibility, his consuming sense of the utter and impermissible estrangement of practically all that had been spoken or written – thought was perhaps another matter! – about the war from the facts as he had seen them in Macedonia, in Italy, and in France, – or to indicate the cause of the desperate and agonising impotence that seized him whenever he was constrained (as he was so continually, so inexorably) to consider the ways and means by which his experiences might ever become even in the remotest degree – no, not acceptable – but merely expressible. So great was the conspiracy of misunderstanding that even general knowledge (to soldiers) on various aspects of the subject was as incapable of proof, or citation (to non-soldiers), as the theory of a new dimension.

A few months ago various correspondents had taken a young English writer (Alec Waugh) severely to task for an article on 'How the Soldier saw the War'. The reception accorded to that article, and the impression which he knew it had created in the minds of friends of his own who had read it and who by all pre-war standards were accounted intelligent and high-spirited men – made him shudder to think of the morass of useless misunderstanding into which he would plunge if he ever managed to put upon paper any record of how he saw the war.

Not yet, if ever, could he realise the desire a friend had expressed when he wrote, apropos of certain wildly unrelated manuscripts he had sent him from Salonika: 'There may be a method in your madness an old fogey like me cannot be expected to detect. I am ever in danger of underrating the strength of tide in these new times, and of forgetting that your inconsequent excursions may subtly represent the many and diverse channels it is cutting out for itself in minds like yours. Still, to continue the figure, I don't want your "bore" to run to sea in a delta, but in a broad and navigable waterway wherein we may anchor one day to our great delight.'

Not yet, if ever!

III

A bit of another soldier's letter occurred to him as, at a loss, peering out into the storm and the night he reflected that, in Conrad's figure, the few gas-lamps on the up-way to the Abbatoirs, showing up a bit of brickwork here and there, a fragment of tree-trunk, a flight of stone steps, an angle of a house, appeared in the blackness like penny dips in a range of cellars.

'It will be of little use, I suppose, asking you to spare a moment from making the millennium out of recast German guns to consider the woes of a soldier. But spare it if you can. I wish to forget that it is Christmas Day and to call it only the 25th of December of any old year. So I want a book or two. You who are so happy at home now you have won the war don't know how we feel out here. I feel about as victorious as yesterday's *Daily Mail* in a horsepond. Compared with me the man who never smiled again would have brought the house down at Hengler's. I am not going to explain to one of the heroes why that is so – but send a book or two quick. No blessed novels. No Dickens. Don't be funny either and send me Bairnsfather or things of the giddy kind. But I should like some old voyages if you know how to lay hands on them. I don't mean Stevenson or anything this side of 1870. Something without a comment in it, like Bates, only further back. In your exhilaration do bear me in mind and act at once; for now the silence has settled on us survivors, we are inclined to be rather thoughtful while still out here....'

Old travels!

> I too have prayed to feel desire no more,
> To find in little things a small content,
> No longer from the green and friendly shore
> To swim a waif in the huge element.
> My spirit darkens, my heart beats fitfully:
> A power descends upon my soul and shakes
> The calm of tranquilising song and breaks
> The doom-dark wave of passion over me,
> And every tumult in my being wakes;
> A power not friendly to me but divine
> Troubles the current of my trembling line.

Not for him the other side of 1870 – or of 1914 – whatever might betide!....There was always this reviving trust in a centre of unity, a reassembling of his faculties for action in the faith that some inner purpose would be developed and confirmed. He believed recurrently that his own thought was part of the consciousness which sustained the world, and he expected to find a rational quality in its final outlines as well as in human history. He started anew from himself around an anthropomorphic universe, and went in search of a larger self which was the reflection and confirmation of his own (thus temporarily chastened)...an impulse this deeper than all philosophy... but, just because it lay so deep, it conflicted with another tendency equally ingrained in him, the impulse of revolt against 'the pale cast of thought', the feeling that if he could only escape from his mind's anticipations he should find himself face to face with things as they really were... Could he never do justice both to himself and to what was independent of him?....Anyhow he was continually hauled back in a most humiliating way from wherever his thoughts had carried him to what was simply given – his poverty, his comparative ignorance, his follies and inequalities – torn away from contemplation of this over self which was dazzling, and from the thought which magnified its preconceptions.

His thoughts were like a flock of grebe... He remembered an article he had written about nine months ago: Why has so little War-poetry been produced in Salonika? The leisure for thought is greater than on the Western Front, but then war-poetry soars like a bird with shining wings out of a dark and tangled thicket of tumult and despair. Is it that the close perils and constant high excitations of Flanders intensify feeling to poetic pitch while on the contrary the comparative stagnation and monotony and gruesome dull routine of disease and misadventurous death, unaccompanied by the flame of guns and the glitter of steel, blunt the perceptions? The truth cannot be here, because in point of fact, although the difficulties and dangers of the two campaigns are entirely different in character the same great elemental factors are through each working constantly in the minds of sensitive participants – the sacrifice of youth, the long, hard separations of lovers, the rush of death, the insupportability of the apparent triumph of the powers of darkness, the deep thoughts in the sentinel night, the sharpened memories of home constantly coming with an unspeakable newness, that strictly professional feeling, difficult to define, peculiar to the imaginative callings whose primary appeal lay in the suggestion of helpless opening to incalculable revelation, in the suggestion of restless adventure, a sense of waiting upon an event secret from their knowledge, longer than the measure of their experience, an aspect as from a strange world, not only infinitely remote but superior with a greater destiny, 'chimerical with gathered lives'.

And their further exile should surely have produced nostalgic poetry of even a more spear-like poignancy and slender gleaming desire than the wonderful poems of home-thought with which soldiers on the Western Front had imperishably enriched their literature. Think, too, of the wonderful associations of Salonika, with 'high Olympus' across the blue and silver waters of the gulf. The slightest tendency to poetical expression could surely not lie fallow there.

It would be an easy enough matter for a deft historian in the days to be, when the official documents were available and the censorship no longer applied, to detail accurately the complicated course of the campaign, but a pen no less subtle, a sense of colour and psychology no less delicate and infallible than that of a Pierre Loti, a Theophile Gautier or a Lafcadio Hearn would be needed in the writer who was to reproduce for posterity the atmosphere of the Salonika front.

For the soldier the rush of impressions had been tremendous, beyond the possibility of assimilation. The course of events had been so rapid and so tortuous withal that it had been well-nigh impossible to follow it, although paradoxically it had often been their complaint that 'nothing ever happens out here' – their common excuse for meagre and unsatisfactory letters home, and true enough in its own way too – and equally strangely the impression had obtained at home that but for the prevalence of certain diseases life in Salonika would have been little short of a picnic. Salonika during these times had been perhaps the most cosmopolitan city the world had ever seen. What Boyd Cable or 'Sapper' had done for the Western Front only very much more dexterous penmen could have accomplished for Salonika. It would have taxed the pen of a Henry James to do justice to its intricate contrasts, its amazing juxtapositions, its colourful complexity – a Henry James with a richer spiritual sense! 'Ole Bill' was unknown. A Beardsley and not a Bairnsfather was demanded. A bloodless Revolution and one of the world's greatest conflagrations had been dates in their diaries. They had grown familiar with life and death in every shape and form, praying one instant for additional skull space to cope with the onrush of novel and exciting impressions, and the next confessing to an abject sterility of mind incapable of maintaining a passably decent correspondence, whilst at home 'man in the street opinions' swung between finding them an insoluble enigma, the victims of another 'error of judgement' or holiday makers.

On all sides the mind was baffled by paradox – the incredible malignancy of a city which outwardly was so wondrously fair, with its white minarets set in cypress bowers gleaming in some magical Eastern sunrise ('Geometry, lines and planes, smooth edges, the ordered horror of perspectives….In this country there are pavements bright and sleek as water. The walls are precipices to which giants have nailed a perpetual cataract of marble.') The incalculable treachery of weather which in one day could produce cases of heat-stroke and frostbite; the incomprehensibility of a campaign which bustled so tremendously and variedly at the base and was apparently lost in impenetrable mists up the line; the impossibility of determining whether they were a superfluous side-show, or, as the Bosche boasted, 'the cheapest internment camp they had'; the co-existent sensation of living on a volcano edge and of being bored to death on a front comparatively uneventful to others; and so on. After a few months out there a famous scientist had declared every man became slightly 'puggled', some malignant endemic influence destroying a tiny cerebral membrane – and he believed the statement to be true. One became unable to size things up: a curious vein of impotence in thought manifested itself. Everybody was either ill, sickening for an illness or convalescent. The pathological element was everywhere abominably intrusive. Mails ran so irregularly: censorship was so strict, and news either so limited or so belated and always so untrustworthy that a curious sensation of being marooned in a Kathleen Mavourneen manner was produced. The absence of accurate information created an unstable atmosphere in which credulity and cynicism acted as cyclone and anti-cyclone. The total effect created by the accumulation of all these obscure and unusual factors on the psychology of the troops, varying with each individual soldier, was scarcely describable, but the general sensation was of a highly-coloured nightmarish unreality.

The feat of transforming a raw recruit into an effective soldier was a very elementary exercise compared with that of adapting one's mind to the polychromatic chaos there – and the average British mind, lacking chameleon-power, confessed to a feeling of bewilderment and stultification full of unseizable qualities and with a general mental effect as different from any it had received before as a Japanese painting was from the accustomed oleograph at home. Infrequent and independable links of correspondence scarcely held their hearts to their old moorings against tides of inverted incredulity. One's former life haunted one almost like an undemonstrable belief in a fourth dimension. There was no obvious connection between past and present. Now seemed hopelessly at variance with then...

There had been that Frenchman's Diary in Hospital: 'The atmosphere all afternoon has been heavy with thunder and my nerves have vibrated the more in accord with the electricity charging the air, the peals of thunder synchronising with the pulsations of my blood under the bandages. I see the sky as one great grey blotting-pad against which the branches of the trees appear like gashes of ink. About 8 o'clock the storm which has burdened our blood all day breaks at last. We have never seen the like in Salonika. The garden rattles with the shrapnel of the heavy drops. The branches are weighed down. The long leaves are streaming. Electric wires that their weight and the wind bring into contact fuse suddenly. And the formidable claps of thunder roll in the violet mountains which make the northern horizon, just as in the bay, where our boats dance like walnut shells, mauve glimmers or flashes of lightning swiftly illumine the shadows. After the storm there is an appeasement unknown till then. Oppressed lungs breathe freely. The wet earth exhales a heavy and healthy smell. The sky has regained its infinite limpidity and in the calm night I dream and I can at last write....' 'When one mounts the curve of a hillock and looks towards the sea, there is in the air, clear and pure after yesterday's rains, a brilliancy of light which fills the eyes. On the night lies the city and its white minarets like an army of house-tops which goes to assault the old red walls with which the Turks fortified the summit of the hill. In front lies the gulf, its curving blue speckled with the straggling uneven shadows of our ships, and the sun is setting between Olympus, and the city among pale reds and old gold. As the night grows cooler, in the calm garden where I dream my dreams, behind the spikes of a cactus I feel for an hour as if this is my own little kingdom....' 'Through the open door I can see through the garden almost at the height of my eyes clusters of flowers laid out in squares, a quadrangle shaded by the stout branches and heavy blossoms of an acacia, the foliage of which fills the rest of the field of my vision. At its roots at the bottom of the garden behind a thin hedge a low railing separates us from the street where the commotions of life continue despite our repose – an uninterrupted procession of passers-by, tramway cars, automobiles. And it is a strange contrast, this ceaseless feverish cacophony of the boulevard of Queen Olga and the four hundred foot square little garden where a blackbird, preoccupied and grave, walks by itself!....Between the branches the sky has a great intensity. One by one the stars come out. In the chequered twilight, and where rays of light run, gentle white figures flit, and, suffering in the great sweetness of the falling night, I understand in a sense, impossible in happier, heedless days, the goodness of Woman.'

And he thought how he had thought of Peggy three thousand miles and more away –

I have found in my lady many beautiful things:
The dawn-glad song of the bird and its light quick flutter of wings
And passionate joy in living a life that sings.

And of how, invalided home, he had married her... and the verse that came to his mind (his eyes bright as the eyes of a lizard, his lips shut very tightly, a colourless face with a curious fullness at the corners of the tucked-in mouth, folded about the stem of his pipe, which isolated the expression) –

You are truth and the world is illusion: faith, it is doubt,
It wraps its disaster in darkness and you shine out,
And the liquor that drugs to endurance is not for your drought.
Pass on to the waste and the fells! I stay and forget
Your breasts and your hair and your laughter like suns that are set,
Despise me, forgive me, but leave me. I love you yet.

Then he remembered some friends he had made out there... Their mothers had been sisters. The two cousins had the same dark flame in their oriental eyes. Their classic beauty was remarkable even in that great cosmopolitan centre where every race had taken root and soldiers mingled drawn from every quarter of the globe. Madame L – , the junior of the two, very spare, very tall, very haughty... like an Athenian or Corinthian lady of the old Greek type. A coyness which covered the face with the hands, prettily displaying the forearms, modernised her. Musical as a Polish girl she was full of vivacity. Intellectually she was engrossed in problems of psychology presented in the world around her and in literature dealing with the like. Madame J – , very mature, with great dark eyes under her languid lashes, and with heavy earrings which contrived to give a Levantine note to her slightly maternal appearance. Time had not dimmed the splendour of her tresses. The lines of her figure betrayed generations-long dalliance on the silken cushions of the divans where dreams are wrapt in the blue smoke of scented cigarettes. Her daughter was on the contrary the quintessence of both types; the dull colouring under the brown curls; the forehead just such as Phideas gave in his ivory statue to Pallas; the arcs of the eyebrows so impeccable that they seemed to have been traced with the pencil of a Japanese artist, the deep brown eyes veiled by a discreet lowering; eyebrows which cannot be seen otherwhere than in Smyrna; a deeply intelligent look already singularly sceptical, readily lit with malice, the mouth of a child but with lips almost too thin in their narrow scarlet oval, a long fragile neck, a figure *svelte* and supple, even a little willowy, expressive of a femininity that knew only too well what it was about; and that elegance in the lines of the limbs and the feet which Asiatic Greeks alone of all the peoples of the Levant possessed. She was nevertheless very Frenchified, in her ready laughter, in her rapid intuitions... She was sixteen years of age.

Characteristically thoughts of women led to thoughts religious. He found himself re-experiencing his impressions of the 'Epitaphios', the symbolic burial of Christ as it was celebrated by the Greek Church on Good Friday. 'Someone great and famous, you would have said, was carried to burial in Salonika on Friday last. The dust, soft and warm about your feet, the sky dark and very high above you, you went, pushed by some major emotion, towards Saint Sofia. And there were whispers and words from the obscure houses about you which you divined to be almost emptied; on the balconies the feet of a few women only moved; the words of a few women flickered out and died in the hush of the deserted earthen street; and faces of women appeared to you like white shadows against the grills that closed them in. The words, the shadows, the hollow clacking of their shoes above, all pointed to some festal expectation for which they waited. And you passed on. In front of you there grew up out of the encompassing dark a haze of gold, a warm stream of light: it invaded the air and made of the night a thing shining and decorated. It was diffused, you saw soon, and scattered up by point after point of processional flame, each point yellow as honey and illuminated like sunlit amber. They twined and defiled before you, confounding your perspective, across the narrow street end; and, as you approached them, you heard populous movement and the wail of metal. At once you knew that men were mourning with some tragic mourning. The ululation of the brass, the stamping of the muttering muffled drums, the crying of the people drew around you as it were and pressed upon you their own grief. Certainly someone great and famous, you felt, was being borne to burial at this unfamiliar hour with this pomp and keening. You hardly wondered any longer who it was: you had become so akin to those mourners that, whoever it might be, you would follow them to his grave. With them you would salute the unreturning Dead... At last the hurrying numbers swept you aside and on, their tapers smoked hot against your face, their shoulders and their bodies pushed and pressed you. It was a tide that set round one thing and that thing came near... High above it white arches of flowers looped, pale as artificial things are pale, without weight or fragrance. The brass walled. Thin cracked voices of intoning complaining priests pierced the murmuring air. The crowd stopped and shuffled and moved on; and through that flaming river of men it came, the sad and sacred thing. Gold-crowned, gold-coped, with Jewels in his crown and tiny coloured pictures shining from it, with the golden serpent-headed sceptre swinging to and fro in his hand as he paced, the high priest led it. Swarthy and grave, their hair loosened like women's, the down of their uncut beards about their oval faces, with high black biretta and the long sweep of black robes, walked its sacerdotal escort. The white-flowered arches still stooped and looped above it as they came; small boys, imposing above their size in crimson hieratic garments that trailed to their feet, passed with it, peering and childish and indifferent, black crosses upon their round tall hats of straw. And as it was carried past them, the sacred imaged pall that was the Bier, men and women bent and kissed its edges... Who was it that they carried thus to a brief and partly happy burial? Someone great and famous, someone honourable and renowned, someone, too, not utterly mortal! You would have known whose Bier it was a few hours earlier. The lamenting dirges had chanted His praises and our sorrows and His great sorrows also. Level and measured and wailing the cries had mounted up under the blue and golden arches of St Sofia.

"Thou who didst set the measures of the earth, thou inhabitest today in a narrow tomb.

"For thee the holy Mother tearful dirges wept and wailed, most motherly; how shall I mourn thee, O my son?

"With a sword I am pierced most terribly and my bowels are torn asunder, looking upon Thy death unjust and murderous.

"O Light of my eyes, my most sweet, sweet Son, how art Thou hidden now in the tomb?"

'And then as the keening passed in alternation to and fro, the high priest, stiff with gold, came down from his throne and bowed before the holy Bier and took in his hand a silver phial.

"Coming very early in the morning, the women bearing myrrh sprinkled the tomb....Coming very early in the morning the women bearing myrrh sprinkled the tomb...."

'Three times he cried it, passing round the Bier. And he, too, these many ages after, made that Bier fragrant with sprinkling. So it was that in Salonika they carried to burial on Friday last Someone very great, it seems, and very famous....'

On Friday last! It would never be further away again for him. He thought of his wife's only brother, her 'big brother', gay and gallant in his green-black kilt with his soft dark hair curling out below his cocked glengarry and his blue eyes shining down over his red cheeks, who had been best-man at his wedding a few short months ago, and yet, a little later, within a few days of his landing in France, within a few weeks of his nineteenth birthday, had been blown to fragments, scattered on the shining indifferent air... and a great wave of darkness soared out of his heart and toppled at a dizzy height and broke and roared down again....

> He died too late for hope, too soon for faith.
> So we, who have seen the end and had no scathe
> Shall die. But they who fell with hearts aglow,
> Whose hopes went with them to their burial,

Are happier. They are dead and do not know
What fools rejoice, what thieves hold carnival.

This unendurable conclusion was forced in upon him in a thousand
shapes: –

> The faith by which we stand,
> The laws we made and guard,
> Our honour, lives, and land
> Are given as reward
> To murder done by night,
> To treason taught by day,
> To folly, sloth and spite
> And we are cast away.

It was one of those ideas which when he tried to put it away developed
that remarkable power of internal resistance by which a dog makes himself
practically immovable by anything short of a kick... This habit of pursuing
general matters in a peculiar manner between jest and earnest was
becoming confirmed... He was like an ant-heap stirred: thoughts and
memories ran about in all directions at the same moment. He relit his pipe,
the flame of the match making scarlet the hollow of his hand. 'Lord have
mercy on the young, for grief is very hard until a cry becomes a prayer.'
'Let that day be darkness. As for that night let darkness seize upon it: let
it not be passed into the days of the year, let it not come into the number
of the months...let the stain of the twilight thereof be dark... because it
shut not the doors of my mother's womb: nor hid sorrow from my eyes.' It
was too dark, now, to see the difference in tone between the earth and the
sky: between outside and inside – save where broken lights of the city
gleamed like the flashing of a shield and where in the irregular illumination
of La Calade causeways flagged with irregular slabs of stone ran beside the
low-browed houses and disappeared round acute and unexpected corners,
and he caught glimpses of doors open within doors, of strange nooks and
little courtyards, deep eaves darkening sinister windows... Did he sit alone
here in this upper room of a deserted world with 'his unlit lamp and ungirt
loin?....' 'I stick fast in the mire where no ground is....' Then, below, at
the foot of the drive, human shapes, appearing mysteriously as if springing
from the dark ground, skimmed the edge of the uncertain light thrown
down by the lamps. The sight restored him to actuality – to the facts of the
hospital...

Let us go to the most feverish patients!
They have strange exhalations.
In the middle of them I cross a battlefield with my mother.
Let us go to the weakest.
They have strange perspirations.

They were pruning trees round the prison,
They were bringing medicines one afternoon in June,
And meals of patients were being spread at all the horizons....

Then –

There are stags in a town that is besieged
And a menagerie among the lilies;
There is tropical vegetation in a coal-pit!
A flock of sheep is crossing an iron bridge!
And the lambs of the meadow are coming madly into the room.

There is a conflagration in the sun
And I cross a forest of wounded men....

He pulled himself together again... His memory was like the shooting of frost crystals on a window-pane: never was there a crystal which was not attached by traceable lines to the main body, yet no one could prophesy whether each fine filament might strike out on its undivided adventure. What he sought would come slowly and in its own way. When the great music came it would not be such and such a bit of tone-colour, nor this or that sonority, but the soaring or tender curve of the themes, their logical yet ever new unfolding, the embodiment in the whole composition of richest variety with completest unity....

He did not fancy that he was subject to fits of delirium but by a sudden and alarming aberration he became aware of a troupe of trained dogs dancing on their hind legs....

Here is a jewelled token Homer brings
And there a ruby phrase of Wilde glows red:
In the far corner ghosts of seabirds' wings
Which Conrad garnered as a slim craft sped:
A bright keen diamond word which Johnson said;
Sweet perfumed tapestries from old Montaigne.
There glimmers Dumas' heavy signet ring,
The thought that flamed through Henley's hours of dread.
There is a store of little scraps of things

Hid in the dim cobwebbed nooks within my head:
A dusty pile of half-rememberings,
The doubloons and the silks of books I've read.

Veritably a spring-cleaning! In all this embarrassment of recollection,
sensation and desire he resembled the man having all Eden and sighing
for a pippin!....He thought of Barrie getting that grip on the heart which
is the prerogative of genius with an apparently hopeless apparatus of
charwomen and winkles... And he thought of him whose weary invariable
comment had been: 'It is all just bloody nonsense.' (A devastating
recollection which reminded him obliquely of the Johnsonian sentence
which Andrew Lang claimed to have evolved from his inner consciousness
by making his mind a blank and letting his pen write what it would:
'Observing the down-grade tendency of the sympneumatic currents, the
Primate remarked that he could no longer regard Kafoozleum as an aid to
hortatory eloquence.')

IV

He sat with the blood swinging in the hollows of his feet, steeping his
thoughts in profounder views of the subject, conscious that, though the
room was as black as a cave in Himmon, even if the light were switched
on, he would still sit in a state of mental gutta serena, totally deprived of
light, yet with no obscuration visible from without to any incomer... As it
was, however, the obscurity of the air and the obscurity in his mind closed
together in a black fraternisation....How to unroll the panorama of shifting
tastes and backgrounds, varying theories and shattered waves of
enthusiasms!... They were not fictional jumping jacks of absurd and utterly
false heroism and cheerfulness. Let any reader feel with them the
deadening weight of the pack, the grind of the shoulder-straps, the
exasperation of the obstacles in a trench – all those seemingly trivial
miseries which had piled up into an unpayable debt of hatred against war-
makers. A sensitive man who had suffered was a man, whether he had
endured the monotonous epic suffering of an infantry private or the
continual spectacle of pain in a Casualty Clearing Station, who returned
not altogether sane. He had endured so much either in his own or the rent
flesh of others that he brought back to civilisation an ardour of revolt, a
sharp bitterness, made up partly of hatred and partly of pity. He saw with
eyes different from other men's – clearer or more blurred, anyhow not the
same. His state of mind was grievous. He suffered not only for himself but

for others. Old ideas, old standards were inevitably judged with an acrid bitterness which sought to destroy and to cast into oblivion the oldest and most respected of human institutions – anything, if war be made impossible. He came back with an *idée fixe* – never again must men be made to suffer as in these years of war... Book after book was coming out now on this theme, each in its own way, according to the temperament of the author, formulating an indictment of modern society....It was curious that the very people who were most anxious to stifle this harsh real war-literature were those who were most ecstatic early in the war at the thought of the masterpieces which would be produced by contact with reality...but 'by instruction a man can learn to handle the normal and expected, but only inspiration will enable him to handle the abnormal and unexpected, and especially the most unexpected and abnormal of all things – his fellow-man – aye, and even more so himself!' – 'Bold is the donkey driver, O Khedive, and bold is the Khedive who dares to say what he will believe and what disbelieve, not knowing in any wise the mind of Allah, not knowing in any wise his own heart and what it shall some day suffer!'....And after all what is the noise of one hard Buddhist student, desirous of admission to a monastery, struggling with the elementary problem?....A cloak of darkness covered everything netherward while aloft the stormy sky looked down with a strange and disfigured face.

> The world is charged with the grandeur of God,
> It will flame out, like shining from shook foil.

* * *

> Thou mastering me
> God! giver of breath and bread;
> World's strand, sway of the sea;
> Lord of living and dead;
> Thou has bound bones and veins in me, fastened me flesh,
> And after it almost unmade, what with dread,
> Thy doing: and dost thou touch me afresh?
> Over again I feel thy finger and find thee.
>
> I did say yes
> O, at lightning and lashed rod;
> Thou heardest me truer than tongue confess
> Thy terror, O Christ, O God!
> Thou knowest the walls, altar, and hour and night:
> The swoon of a heart that the sweep and the hurl of thee trod
> Hard down with a horror of height!

The water flows to the sea and the little stones find their places.

> Christ plays in ten thousand places
> Lovely in limbs and lovely in eyes not His.

… Time peered at him through his domino of days. With a sense of telescopically extending his mood he visualised the hearts of men during the crises of history. Times of great human calamity had always thrown men back on first principles: challenging both the optimisms and the pessimisms developed during periods of comfort and security, compelling men to reconsider their working creed of life in the light of terror and tears.

'The destruction of the Roman peace by the barbarian produced the "Re civitate Dei" in which Augustine definitely abandoned the one "City" built by men for serenity and enjoyment, to lodge his hope and all the hope of humanity in that "City of God", which was building like the Republic of Plato, somewhere "beyond the fixed stars". The earthquake of Lisbon produced many attempts to reconcile the popular buoyant Deism with an event so purposeless and brutal; and one immortal work of genius which rendered that buoyant belief incomprehensible for evermore. He thought of the effects of the Age of Anguish on the great writers who saw "reality" suddenly substituted for realism – Renan "renouncing both Judea and Israel", and thenceforth "doing nothing, thinking nothing," only clinging to hope; Taine in the face of "dying men, flowing blood, burning cities", with heart dead "feeling as if living in a mad-house", "in a continuous state of dumb anguish and despair", with all his scientific and positive system of human progress turned into dust and ashes; Flaubert dislodged by these nightmare visions from his boasted security in detached and dispassionate art, "haunted by the one idea of the powerlessness of literature", and convinced that it was impossible to rise again after such a blow…

'Once more "dying men, flowing blood, burning cities" had challenged both the affirmations of progress and social amelioration in the region of practical affairs: and the ultimate assertion beyond them of any intelligent or moral order of the universe. To some indeed the very call to action from thought which had lost itself in blind alleys and wandering mazes came as a relief and an inspiration. These had found in the call to arms a tonic and inspiration not given in the stagnant civilisation of a world grown "too old". They entered the combat with rejoicing, and had gone down into the darkness singing.'

> Lost adventurers, watching ever
> Over the toss of the tricksy foam

> Many a joyous port and city
> Never the harbour lights of home.

But in him the spirit of exultation had been rapidly overwhelmed by the spirit of questioning and disturbance. He had seen his dreams of human betterment vanish like the spider's web, his ideals of improvement for the hard lot of the masses of mankind torn to pieces or indefinitely postponed to some remote future beyond the space of his allotted days. He had been forced to wonder insupportably if any purpose could be discerned beyond the blind forces of human madness, hate and passion, making and unmaking without pity and without end. (All this with a sensation of twisting his head this way and that, desperately striving to get huge sections of life into focus!)

He descried on many sides an exhilaration in the spirit of the world's youth as they looked out on the universe now, on the edge of peace: and it afflicted him like a recurring decimal – with a sense of inexorable emptiness. But there it was. The very troubles of the time, the strained mental toll to make a league of nations, the insistent claim of workers to know all about the finance of commerce, to share more and more the profits, the perils and the management of industry, the hungry yearning for a better life, a roomier house, a 'place in the sun', a chance to develop and display: all these (with a sickening sense of ancient illusion as if the confidence trick had been successfully worked on him), seemed to be bracing young men again: giving colour, interest and adventure to living. A new world was being born and in its time-honoured fashion youth knew that it and it alone could tackle the obstetrical propositions. Great things would happen in England but he would have no part in them. A quotation from Wordworth's letter to Matthew seemed to adapt itself to the expression of the purposes of his spirit: 'I know that the multitude walk in darkness. I would put into each man's hand a lantern to guide him and not have him to set out on his journey depending for illumination on abortive flashes of lightning or the coruscations of transitory meteors.'

And as he sat framed highly in the besetting storm he seemed to win some of the light of the lightning and much of the emptiness of the thunder, exclaiming with Valére Gille,

> We have thought until
> The world is but the shadow of our dreams…
> The mind has ravaged space and we are ill
> With what we know: yet knowledge only seems
> Upon life's verge a net of cheating gleams.

'O Euphranor! he who looks into the bottom of things and resolves them into their first principles is not easily amused with words.'

> Whichever way I turn I find
> The path is old unto me still.

'The locust years! How these three words ran like lizards in and out of the thoughts and memories that flocked to battle with the vicious phrase. His judgment found it hopeless to repudiate it utterly, but he hurled retorts at it, beautiful things remembered, wonderful things still desired... Every day is a king in disguise... But the years are locusts... The locusts cannot touch the soul. No, but they can undermine the spirit... The spirit feeds upon life and grows the stronger by fearless contact with it... The truth is the other way. Life itself is the great vampire and feeds upon all things...a bitter endless duologue between pessimism and optimism... Life had assuredly played the vampire to every instinct in his breast...how his cynicism, distorting him beneath his mask of recklessness, his secret impatience with superficial things, his hidden intolerance of others, increasing to an asperity that he could only counter by the most anomalous fierce futilities of *camaraderie*, had grown!... and yet how quickly he revived from each consuming crisis, these gala-banquets of the Great Vampire, life...

'Locust years beyond denial: but though the locust might devastate, it devastates merely the surface and that only for a season. Green hopes are eaten – but Earth, the treasure-house of green things, cannot be eaten more than the sun: the earth remains even as the heart remains, an ever-springing garden. Again and again he fought the stinging phrase with weapons of reminiscence. The years have been compact with other things than blood and tears. One might be passing rich in the possession of trivialities. These locust years had been full of life: the episodes in these years of trial were based upon such as upon little gritty worthless pebbles. Yet even these trivialities had made a rough basis for hard-earned repose, and one sufficient perhaps for a continuity of effort. All sorts of scraps of comedy cemented together these inconsequent finite trifles, comedy of juxtaposition, of the incidents of miscellaneous campaigning, of the incidents of personal experiencing... All manner of grace hovered somewhere at hand, often too far out of reach for intimate delight but never too far for fleeting consolations. War pitiless, hideous, Godless, changed its face. Its crabbed pages became slowly legible. Philistine it remained, all-consuming like life it still proved yet as all-enduring and all-compensating as life. Everything was lost in it but everything was to be found in it.

'The reading of the great book of Armageddon became for a little while, at least to one of the soldiers, a thing which made good the waste of the locust years. The wine of things, the zest for existence, shone behind those odd scraps of thought, these sudden glimpses into the motives of humanity in the mass. Justice and order, intrigue and egotism fought a great fight continually, and their grotesque instructive battle news travelled through any channel. Even in this wide Philistia were citadels – small enough but yet citadels – of art and faith which the pushing impulses of materialism could not disturb. Colour and form were there… The music of various man remained ever divine and more than a solace, a great fount of exhilaration, a motive power, beautiful, inexhaustible, a thing that existed apart from the pink and white and red and gold concert rooms of the chancellories of empires and kingdoms, from schools of technique and commentary and criticism… He visualised how, even now, the Goddess of Victory was strutting about the boulevards of Paris in a Megan toque.

'The story of the odd labour of these four wild years raced by him like a panorama. Such a gallimaufry as it was of all that was frivolous, absurd, luminous, suggestive, depressing, exasperating and farcical! Such a mosaic of hot haste and fatigue, overheated brains and mobs, over-produced nothingnesses, shams and jumbles! And through it all peered the faces of men and women, each one eager for acclamation and for gain. Moreover, to each of these things hung others, the odd fruitage and gleanings of this odd life, insane confidences, strange privileges, glimpses into bottomless horror, terror, emptiness, visions of sacrifice and heroism and endless glory and goodness. "With a royal sense of this world and how it passes away, with a catch at the heart of what is to come! And still the sense is royal: it is the majesty of art. We feel that we are greater than we know. So on the surge of our emotion as on the surge of Prospero's island is blown a spray, a mist. Actually it dwells in our eyes, bedimming them: and as involuntarily we would brush it away there rides in it a rainbow: and its colours are wisdom and charity, with forgiveness, tender truth for all men and women growing older, and perennial trust in young love."'

> Earth, sea and sky are not as once they were
> To us: there is no aspect of all things,
> No pulse of heart or brain, no whisperings
> Of truth's grave music to the inward ear
> Unaltered or unglorified: the mere
> Being of life, intense as song-swept strings
> Is like a breathless sense of soaring wings

Loosed in the spirit's boundless atmosphere!
We are not as we were! Our feet have ranged
The summits of imperishable hours:
Life is a lordlier hope: and we, estranged
In secret and at heart from all control
Walk in the wide new futures of the soul
Charged as with incommensurable powers!

V

A sky so wide that it could hold all sorts of weather at once.

He passed out again into the crowded world of his experiences, full of movement as a river, his eyes occupying every function of sense, touching his memories, traversing them from head to foot, inquiring darkly and passionately concerning their bodies, looking through them, ravishing them, draining them, and leaving no physical or mental part untouched... tongues of air ferreting out the secrets of life!

From far, from eve and morning
And yon twelve-winded sky
The stuff of life to knit me,
Blew hither: here am I.

In a bird's-eye view, as Milton's Satan first saw Paradise, he caught glimpses, like a jigging of flames, of the keeper of a village shop explaining that his kippers are 'mountainy herrin's and great pets... I catch them in the garden at the back of the house... Last winter when the snow was on the ground they'd come into the kitchen and sit for hours on their tails round the fire warming themselves and them as tame as cats,' or how, returning trom a wake, 'just as I was passin' this very place out steps a tall, respectably-dressed ghost about forty-six years of age'; of a man of middle age, with a pointed beard, a jolly-looking man, a forceful face and a lovable one, roguish a bit, with that old Gallic spirit that makes fun in public of the things that Englishmen laugh over in private, yet benevolent – the face of a man who begins life as a delightful companion and ends it as a delightful grandfather; of peaceful countries, tinged with the early Spring, trees and fields, belfries and far-off hamlets, all under a sky sad-coloured and beautiful as that sky which dwells for ever over the 'Avenue near Middleharnis'; of Sorley's 'we were fighting not a bully but a bigot'... of Chapin hating the gregariousness and publicity of Army life with a deadly hatred interspersed by daily longing for his home, his wife and his little child... of Tom Kettle dropping pearls....They have nailed their leader to the mast.' 'Mr Healy is a brilliant calamity'... of the Grenfell brothers, of Anthony Wilding, of Donald Hankey, of Frederick Keeling... of all the snapped stalks of incomparable youth; of one walking resolutely onwards into 'the great red light': of the anxious face of a poor little sucking pig; of the troubled surface of a river wherein the stars, reflected and distorted, shone like broken spear-heads; of a long straight improbable village, with its bridge, its ancient stone cross, its irregular pink and white houses, as improbable as a street in *opéra bouffe*, with a thin cloud of dust rising, a thin screen of white dust, which, in the sun, looked like a fume of silver; of planes of light and darkness outspread; of a great-grandmother surviving on the verge of her hundredth year to mumble chestnuts over the fire of a Kentish farm, and the great-granddaughter of a Spanish dancer who married in the early thirties of the previous century a rather ordinary British soldier, inheriting her wild, passionate nature inextricably intermingled with British reserve, just as the dancing mouse will sometimes reappear amid the brood of a common domestic rodent; of a void of blind-eyed water; of the shooting of a pitiful rotund little mayor strutting gamely to the end; of a woman dying very quietly at last on the floor of a cart, and her husband's unspoken annoyance with her just before her death because she did not as usual respond to his sympathy; of the chaotic formula, pyrrhic = trochee = pæon = choriamb, *i.e.*, $2 = 3 = 4 = 5 = 6$, the effect of which until scientifically measured remained the sphere of possible personal illusion; of the engaging spectacle of a home-loving working man whose only ambition was to rise by steady work, to be elected to the Glee Club and the Social Club, perchance even to the Town Council, and probably with dreams at dizzy moments of becoming mayor of his native town and dying at last amidst universal regrets for our 'highly-respected fellow-townsman'; of graceful and proportionate figures-of-eight heads going off into random facial angles; of the rays of male vision which seem, as Hardy says, to have a tickling effect upon virgins' faces; of cats going into various arched shapes and fiendish convolutions; of lights flapping as if reflected from phosphorescent wings crossing the air; of a rising fire brightening a room with the brazen glare of shining majolica; of the most hen-like waiter in France; of a distinguished novelist producing a new volume written like many of its predecessors round the boot and shoe industry in Northamptonshire; of how the other day when he had been in the city a particular little group of two became individualised out of the side-walk crowd like a particular wavelet which gleams from the lap-lapping of a river with an instantaneous personality of its own; little houses on the grey hillsides of Eskdalemuir; the cluck of hens about the doors on a hot summer's morn; the crying of plovers in the windy Aprils; the smell of peat smoke; of how the 'Charge of the Light Brigade' had been written round a phrase in a newspaper account and of how the 'Solitary Reaper' owed its two most famous lines to a phrase from a guide-book; of how a lugworm sang with its grey and muddy mouth;...war memories crowding in upon his mind in their images of misery and horror and brutality, 'word upon awful word' with a truth that denied and a courage that terrified, and then, when his endurance was at breaking-point, lo! how he came upon lovely things, a land of wine and music, the touch of fur, the kiss of sea-borne winds, the peace of sleep, the scent of roses in the dawn...by these paths returning to the knowledge of loyalty and faithfulness which kept his vision whole.

> To the Heavenly Power I cry,
> Foiled by these dreams of immortality,
> 'Let be as Thou wilt,
> And the foundations in Thy dark mind built;
> Even infinity
> Be but imagination's dream of Thee;
> And let thought still, still
> Vainly its waves on night's cliff break and spill.

> 'But Heavenly Power,' I'd cry
> Knowing how, near or far, He still is nigh,
> 'When this burning flesh
> Is burnt away to a little driven ash
> What thing soever shall rise
> From that cold ash unseen to unseen skies,
> Grant that so much of me
> Shall rise as may remember Thy World and Thee.'

So on and on: he recalled a girl with the unnecessarily pungent name of Sapphira; a man whose nose was so thin that it would go through a cambric needle, shoulders so hard and sharp that they would cut tobacco, his head dark and bushy like the top of a hill and with fingers which could be likened to nothing; another who was clean gold, heaven about the sun, a silver vessel having wine in it; a wide general sensation that seemed like

> A tossing and lifting of bodies lost and drowned
> In the huge indifferent swell, in the waters' wandering sound,

then, instantly a verse –

> Often have I seen in fields the little birds
> Go in between a bullock's legs to eat,
> And what gives me most joy is when I see,
> Snow on my doorstep printed by their feet;

the fact that every Cathedral choir in England contains at least one former member of the choir of Leeds Parish Church – unpromising machinery getting home to his heart as swiftly and unerringly as Mozart, so that he was brought trembling before the eternal verities by means of a gay libertine, a comic lackey, or a stone statue tramping in to supper; or by four charwomen, a fussy curate and a massive kiltie with hairy legs taking tea and winkles and talking in a nice derangement of epitaphs culled from the Sunday Papers, crude and vulgar, but belonging to the world of poetry and not to the world of fact.

Then isolated items from his omnivorous recent reading came upon him like a cloud of insects... the sickness of acquisitive society – the present need of an aristocracy (making his brain a hall of mirrors in which he caught countless reflections of every theme in as many shapes and sizes) – searching expositions of theories of industry and life, one holding that industry is and must be conducted for private gain, another that it must be subordinated to social purpose, another stressing the need for a recognition of race values and even of family values in human progress, holding that the equality which exists between men by virtue of their possessing each an immortal soul involved an even distribution of justice and protection of law without distinction of persons but did not involve the admission of any claim to equality of action or the denial of varied status, since race values, both of the gens and of blood, invariably entered into and established differences in character, in intelligence and in capacity which could not be permanently changed, save with the slowness of metamorphosic rock, by education, environment and heredity (taking up thus, as he felt too, one after another great subjects occupying the minds of thinking people, as they are ludicrously called, and thinking intelligently round them, a practice all too common, and, for capable minds, fatally easy) – the reflections of an accomplished thinker who believed that man is immortal in that the brain communicates to the ether vibrations which influence other brains through an indefinite period of time – a consideration of Plato, Socrates, Bacon, Spinoza and Nietzsche with the view of showing that the social problem has been the basic concern of the greater philosophers, that the social problem must be approached through philosophy, and that philosophy must be revitalised by being approached through the social problem – a discussion of the extensibility of co-intuition – perambulations occasionally Bacchic and a company lurid but criticisms never blatant or vulgar, resting always on refined appreciations, and a trip to that fabulous inn 'The Chequers' at never mind where, a fairy hostelry (not without a hundred miles of London), where the landlord played Mozart's Sonatas and the police sergeant in the bar read Boswell and preferred Gluck to Debussy – off betimes on a spring morning to Amersham or to Boxhill – dreaming of the time when Limehouse would once more be free and easy, Soho flowing with Chianti and real macaroni, and khaki faded from the Strand (seeking vainly that English, to be found in *Gulliver's Travels* or in Bunyan, which is a kind of rare and dynamic language, as straight as a ray of light, the result of passionate morality that happened to be gifted with the complete control of full expression)...

In a huge Wellsian access, he thought how the greatest of all international crimes had been committed in a blind unanimity of enthusiasm with scarcely a voice to protest against it... of movements, causes, obsessions, defects and animosities; the degradation of the Empire into a dirty little scheme for taxing the foreigner; the degradation of Patriotism into sloppy adulation for a little German family and their vast crowd of German relatives and dependants; the invincible ignorance of governing Bourbons who learn nothing and forget nothing; the fatuous refusal of the Universities to give the future governing classes the faintest idea of what they would have to govern; the enormous self-satisfaction of the Public Schools at their wholesale manufacture of young men 'with the outlook of clean, serious bricklayers' labourers, densely ignorant and intensely opinionated'; the evil influence of the hordes of rich idle women kept at vast cost in great expensive houses, using the labour of innumerable people, terrorising the poor, consuming (like sacrifices) huge pyramids of sheep, cattle, birds, and bottles of wine and in return devastating the land with animosities and bitter class hatreds; humanity, under the surface of the portraits which pursue and persecute, through the medium of the pictorial papers, incessantly – the vivid scum of politicians, intellectuals, artisticals and detrimentals – heart-broken with millionfold bereavement; of miners and factory hands in the North of England who did not care about increasing their wages or living in bigger houses or wearing finer clothes, but discussed Greek history with men like Zimmern, Greek poetry with men like Gilbert Murray, Greek philosophy with men like Hadow: and so of a great diversity of thinkers, from the materialist out for revolution to the old 'Stunt-Maker' flinging his hat in the air with three cheers for

Nature, and the student sitting up the night through at his books and going straight from them to the shop...

> So he stood and eyed me hard,
> An earnest and a grave regard,
> 'What, lad, dropping with your lot?
> I, too, would be where I am not,
> I, too, survey the endless line
> Of men whose thoughts are not as mine.'

And still he thought of ordinary sorts of working men at home developing into good soldiers and snipers of peculiar genius, with private and tragic and utterly ridiculous reasons behind their passion for killing Germans, moving to berserker and heroic ends; of pale people craving trash to divert their minds from the horror of great darkness, rent by thunder of guns and the lightning's devouring flame, which, for an eternity, had brooded over them and robbed them of all joy in life; of intolerable writers seizing the chances and the casualties of the battle-field as a means of disentangling the impossible knots tied in the destinies of their under-created puppets...

Most extensively he recalled a woman writer whose professed aim was to record the spiritual tendencies of the hour and to stimulate thought about them. She had perhaps what would be quite generally deemed to be a great deal of ability, but sometimes she had a glib fluency which gave an impression of superficiality and rushed her through dubious statements on to preposterous epic paths. 'Intellectual chaos and moral despair is the spiritual portion of the best men and women of today.' 'The doctrine of verbal inspiration with its inevitable implications is revived for the moment in practice if not in theory. The God of Battles whom we salute today is Jehovah, the Tribal God... ' The second part of her book discussed the modern tendency to discredit reason in comparison with instinct (the frequent quotation of *élan vital* supplying the shibboleth), the return to the primitive in art and in the science of humanity; the new developments of psychology; the growing insistence on personality as the moving force of history, the 'herd instinct' only to be combated by personality and dangerously fostered she thought both by the Church and the school. 'For the moment in my judgment passion unrestrained and instinct all unmoralised do seem in unexpected measure to rule our life. Reason and religion are submerged beneath the flood....'

There was so much to be read that there was hardly time to think. How could he digest the marvellous, the epoch-making truths which every day put before him! And the still more marvellous lies! The war-time lies, the press bureau lies, the eye-witness lies, the lies of accusation and the lies of defence; thousands of liars, nations of liars, conscience-impelled liars, and liars for the love of art! The truth as an abstraction had disappeared. They might in the dim future again approximate it. They would never reach it. 'The Germans mutilate the Belgians', 'the Belgian civilians ambush the Germans', 'the English use Dum-Dum bullets', 'the Germans mount machine-guns in Red Cross ambulances', 'Germany caused the war', 'England craftily planned Germany's destruction', 'Russia attacked Austria', 'Austria planned the destruction of Serbia', 'France planned to attack Germany through Belgium'. There was no end. There never would be any end.

He had feverishly devoured every book, magazine, pamphlet, newspaper, Government paper and statistical report dealing with the war on which he could lay a hand. He had read bushels of briefs, barrels of explanation, pounds of technical data. He had dreamt of the German fighting machine, of the French seventy-five mm. guns, of the Belgian dog-drawn cannon, of the Hungarian cavalry, of the sotnias of Cossacks, of forts, trenches, aeroplanes, submarines, tanks, lyddite and melinite shells, of forty-two centimetre howitzers, of batteries and charges until his brain refused to absorb any more, and then he had joined the Army and been in the thick of it ever since.

He had read the White Papers of England and Germany, the Grey Papers of Belgium, and the Orange Papers of Russia. He had waded through Mr Bernard Shaw's harangues, Mr Arnold Bennett's reply and Shaw's rebuttal. He had listened to Mr Hilaire Belloc world without end. He had seen it through with Mr Britling. Mr Rider Haggard's articles had excited his ghastly amusement, and Mr Harold Begbie's his nerve-shattering detestation. Dr Demberg and Count von Bernstoff had not been lost on him. And he had read and reread *Germany and the Next War*, and those splendid books, Professor Cramb's *Germany and England*, and *The New Map of Europe* by Professor Gibbons. Dr Armgaard Karl Graves had not been overlooked, nor had the countless letters to the press, which had added to the weirdness and mysteries of life. And he had heard Mr Lloyd George passionately aver at Bwfydle that this war, like the next war, is a war to end war. And now he had commenced to dream of writing extensively about it himself which was weirdest and most mysterious of all.

* * *

And now his mind was like a hayrick aflame where, when the wind blows the fire inwards, the portion in flames completely disappears like melting sugar, and the outline is lost to the eye.

VI

Here the truceless armies yet
Trample rolled in blood and sweat.
They kill and kill and never die
And I think that each is I.

Under a Homeric cloud of thought, feeling himself now in the penumbra of infinite tragedy, he retravelled the battlefields of the Western Front... stood again in the Belgian line looking across to the steeples of Dixmude, his ears suffocated with the booming of the big guns, the rattle of the mitrailleuses and the ping of the rifles. There was no rest day or night. The roar of artillery was continuous on all sides. He was encircled by guns. They were everywhere.

How would he describe the battle-field of the Somme? A broad road leading through an open country, rising and falling in conformity with the configuration of the ground. A long stretch of that road covered with traffic of all kinds: huge guns being dragged along by heavy traction-engines; great motor wagons in an interminable line, carrying food, ammunition, clothing: men marching towards the front, either fresh from their training or from rest camps...making once more towards the hell of the trenches; others returning from the battle-ground covered with a caking of mud and yet fretted with an odd cheeriness despite the strain through which they had passed and the bitter cold that bit to the bone: long strings of horses...

On either side of the road were camps for men, camps for horses, parks for reserve vehicles and artillery dumps. Energy, and activity unceasing. The monotony of going through such traffic hour after hour, day after day, year after year. Overhead aeroplanes went to and fro in a very sky that was becoming crowded and peaceless.

A little farther on, entrenchments, barbed wire, shell-holes, hulls of houses. The traffic thinned, wagons were stopped here. Horses switched off the road there. Then that part of the road, and the lifted ground where over it goes where the first heavy fighting in the Somme Battle took place.

This was the very heart of the trench-crossed, shell-pitted, mine-caverned battle area. As far as the eye could see on each side of the road there was nothing but desolation. All had been cultivated ground, studded with villages, farmhouses, villas, and here and there a château. Pleasant woods had risen up in parts... Today a few stumps showed where the woods had been, a few heaps of bricks remained of the villages. Even the piles of bricks were few and far between: in most cases the last vestiges of habitations and of the materials whereof they had been composed had been utterly obliterated.

Away to the right and to the left lay the British and the German lines... They were close together until the days of the first offensive. In broad daylight the pins flashed in different directions and the shells droned as they sped to their objectives. A whole district stretching for miles in every direction with zigzagging trenches, wire entanglements, shell-holes, dug-outs, little crosses marked with the names of men who perished... These cemeteries and crosses met one everywhere... They lay quiet, these soldiers. The busy traffic on the road passed them by. The inquisitive visitor went from trench to trench, from dugout to dugout, read the inscriptions, gathered curios and passed on. They had gone for ever and would come again no more.

These villages that were dust and a brick or two might have been more nobly planned, their buildings larger and newer, their streets broader and better kept... He could not forget the coming and going of generations who had lived their quiet, however varied, lives, had experienced their joys and sorrows, their hopes and their fears, beneath the humble roofs that had been cast upon the indifferent air.

The same desolation had been spread from Riga to the Black Sea. In the Caucasus, in Mesopotamia, on the Austro-Italian frontier, in Macedonia, the same picture of incomputable woe! – an interminable series of swaying campaigns.

And he thought of the 'one-thousandth performance of the comic war-play, *Carryin' On*, which brings the humours of carnage so amusingly across the footlights', of the 'interest in European affairs diverted to cocaine', of the 'mass meeting of Bishops to agree upon what Bishops ought to say about the teaching of Christ and the war when they are so ill-advised as to say anything', of the Archbishop of Canterbury's Grave Warning 'against taking the New Testament too literally in war-time', of the pungent pictures showing the 'Christianity Shortage: Scene in Yesterday's Queue at Westminster Abbey' and 'Escape of an Awkward Fact from the Press Censor's Office', and of Lord Northcliffe directing the removal of Mr Lloyd George's statue from Printing House Square with two press-photographers in attendance....Dryden had spoken somewhere of a connoisseur of news wearing 'three nations in his face.'... A memory kept 'liddening' through his brain of Seinkiewic's titanic historical trilogy running serially for eight long years through the Warsaw *Slovo* – of its translation into English in about twenty volumes and of how, in spite of the comparative obscurity of its setting, it had achieved quite a reasonable success – in America. 'Impatience, the mother of stupidity, praises brevity, and then men want to comprehend the Mind of God in which the universe is included. Oh, human stupidity! do you not perceive, though you have been with yourself all your life, that you are not yet aware of the thing you possess most of – that is, your folly?'…How he abhorred the man who lacked the sense of filigree! (His mental playing was now very soft. He was dreaming over something similar to one of those bizarre fantasies of Schumann which reflect the setting of his sun in a red haze of madness.)… He could not see any internal centre from which sprang anything that he thought or did… His attitude could only be described as one of curiosity. Material might be found in a dream forest of Africa, or a new red-brick house among stubble fields, in the hot-houses of Kew or cave-dwellings of Auvergne or in sheer enchantment or faery. Within these extremes lay the golden mean of interest he should take. How should he discipline his sympathies? How order the jungle of his sensibilities that his spirit might dwell there profitably? Herrick wrote of Julia's silks, Milton of the activities of Satan, Chardin in a kind of stagnant ecstasy painted a clear black-green bottle and an onion, Goya a bullfight, and Degas a ballet-dancer adjusting her shoes as if in eternal life… Perhaps it would be better if he dedicated himself to evolving a fantasia in the shape of a cabbage or a poem in the form of a dog.

> Reason has moons but moons not hers
> Are mirrored in her sea:
> Confounding her astronomers
> But ah! delighting me!

*　*　*

Then strong and swift and instinct with perfect purification there flowed back upon him the full tide of a stirring lay sermon which a Socialist comrade had delivered once during the war when he had been home on leave.

Hazlitt had told how he walked twelve miles to hear Coleridge preach in a Unitarian pulpit, 'a romance in those degenerate days.'… As Coleridge gave out his text, 'And He went up into the mountain to pray *Himself alone*', his voice 'rose like a stream of rich distilled perfumes', and when he came to the last two words, which he pronounced loudly, deeply and distinctly, it had seemed to him, who was then young, 'as if the sounds had echoed from the bottom of the human heart, and as if that prayer might have floated in solemn silence through the universe'.

So this friend had begun with the words from the Song of Solomon, 'Set a seal upon thine heart, as a seal upon thine arm, for *Love is as strong as death*' – and a similar spell had been straightway cast upon the congregation. Save when two women with grief on their features broke down and left the church, nobody stirred.

'The essence of death,' he said, 'is that it separates. There is probably no one who has not resisted the separation… Even when we believe in the all-watching care of a loving God we cannot bring our minds quickly to believe that all is ordered for the best when Death uninvited enters the home, and like the Angel of the Passover, leaves weeping and lamentation where there has been love and laughter.

'The lives that have been laid down in Flanders or in Gallipoli, on sea or on land, have not merely been laid down once and for all. Without this faith how could the mind remain unhinged? The strength of death must be great if it can, having separated man from man, keep him away from God.

'In our own hospitals, at the bedsides of our friends, Love is at this moment refusing to believe in it, even though we know that the sufferer cannot live. In actual fact Love has its victories over death. Love is the incentive of everything that is good.

'It is what inspires men to search out the deep things of Nature, to uncover her secrets; it is what prompts our men of science to analyse the properties of matter; it is what leads our doctors to study the human frame; it is what leads our savants to study the history of men and things, to reveal to us the laws which regulate the great movements in thought; it is what leads our poets to seek the beauty of life and sing to us of its wonders, 'Glorying to God on the height'; it is what impels our saints and men of religion to find the relation of the soul to God; it is what compels a man to search his own soul, for it is only when a man is really in love that he sees the defects in himself and his position, sees them with a preternatural and startling vividness – if he is a man.

'Love laughs at Death! It is the great merit of our faith that nothing can intervene between Christ and us that cannot be overcome.'

And he saw in the dark lineaments of the man he was to become some such resemblance as Stephen Graham saw in a portrait of Robert Louis

Stevenson to a painting of Christ in a Russian Monastery – a Christ, albeit
a little cynical and with a cigarette in his mouth!

> The babble wren and nightingale
> Sang in the Abyssinian vale
> That season of the year.
> Yet, true enough, I heard them plain,
> I heard them both again, again,
> As sweet and sharp and clear,
> As if the Abyssinian tree
> Had thrust a bough across the sea,
> Had thrust a bough across the sea
> With music for my ear.

Like a clear sky after a tempestuous night of wind and rain the thin
rhythm stole into his numbed and blinded brain, admirably sustaining the
leap and bound of his imagination, and swinging gently under the strain
like a supple branch that bears the weight of a bird.

So his moods came and went, shining as Excalibur, beautiful as the spear
of St George. They were like grasses in the winds, one rubbing the heads
heavily, one raking them piercingly, and another brushing them like a soft
broom: and he heard the voice of his overself, deep within him, with the
'unwinded clearness and unnatural sequence' that informed the controlled
and muffled notes of Farmer Oak's flute 'boding an incommunicable
thing.'

VI   The Following Day

Scene – *A remote Shooting Lodge beset with antlers of the wild red deer.*

> 'My house is crowned with horns
> – Transpiercing horns of deer!
> As were His brows with thorns.
> Between two thieves He hung
> Upon His Cross,
> As here 'twixt earth and sky
> Hang I.
> A song a soldier sung

Jocundly in the dark
As now my heedless heart
– Oh, hark!
Defiant of its loss,
Jocundly in the dark,
My heart that crucified me here!

     'I nailed Him high
     'Twixt earth and sky
     And Heaven shut
     Its flaming eye
     But
     Be nights as Hell
     I know full well
     My way to you, oblivious slut,
     Who all my roaring blood shall glut!
     Shall glut,
     Who all my roaring blood shall glut!

     'And when they loose Him from the tree
     At break of day
     I shall not care and shall not see
     – At break of day.
     My snoring head between your breasts
     Will snugly lie,
     Will snugly lie,
     My snoring head between your breasts
     Will snugly lie.'

Every tine when morning came
Caught and held a flying flame,
But between her breasts he lay
Lost to day,
And between her spent breasts fell
Spent, to Hell!

'And I who have been crucified
Go light-foot in the morning-tide
– But hark!
The jocund notes like birds of prey
Go dark
Between me and the clarity of day!'

VII   Sartoria

> Oh I have thought how Una wore
> The linen cloth below her chin,
> And if the poet, Rudel, bore
> A scrip with all his songs therein;
> I know the shoes on Bice's feet
> When Dante met her in the street,
> And I could tell how Florence made
> Lorenzo's marriage festival,
> And how young Friar Lappi played
> In cloth unfriarlike withal!
> And in a thought I stretched my hand
> To touch the dress of Heloïse…
> Yet of this diverse company
> Of people dead or fabulous
> What one of them could come to me
> Had he the power and speak me thus:
> 'Chosen and placed of all of these
> I am that one you understand'?
> Since maybe who beholds the dress
> Searches for no deep loveliness.
> And yet – and yet, there is no mind
> That, being found, is wholly kind,
> And better finger silk and lace
> Than look too fully on one face.

'Pluskow was found hanging from a saddle-strap secured by a nail in his rooms. He had been strangled. Feet, knees, hands and elbows were secured with straps behind his back, and a remarkable feature of the case was that the dead man wore long women's corsets and white gloves to the elbow.' A peculiar trick of emphasis focused my interest on this last fantastic detail with an intensity which disturbed me. He added a comment dealing with representations made several years before by a distinguished and lean-brained journalist* which had resulted in an order to Potsdam officers that white parade breeches were not to be worn on Sundays. And a second later, apropos of something else (he was always like that; it was

* Maximilan Harden, 1899.

practically impossible to get *en route* with him; his mental processes were extraordinarily difficult to follow, and when followed landed you in such a glimmering atmosphere of netted irrelevancy as made you doubt, not exactly your sanity, but the sanity of sanity itself) he set the whole matter in a most intense and surprising light by explaining that in the Convent of the Jesuits at Lisbon there was a picture 'representing Adam in Paradise dressed in blue breeches with silver buckles and Eve with a striped petticoat. And why not? Why not?'

That was the man's method. He overflowed with sudden appreciations. New founts of the most unlikely delight were constantly breaking in his ingenuous and unaccountable mind. A quietly-dressed, unobtrusive little fellow, with the softest and brightest eyes I ever saw in a masculine head, his life seemed to be a perpetual toast to 'The Ladies – God bless them!' inimitably proposed, something between Conrad and George Moore, with a wealth of whimsicality, an unerring if unusual taste, a refreshing volubility, an enchanted and enchanting air. As he spoke I would think of Rupert Brooke's *Great Lover* – his conversation was just like that, a swift, beautiful catalogue of the most delightful and unexpected of interests. He seemed to stick a verbal flower on everything he saw. A scrap of information retailed by him in his quick, quiet voice, flavoured with infinite reminiscence, glittered like a precious stone in a quaint and surprising setting. How his company made of a crowd a thing composed, designed, vibrant, calling to me and making a call in my heart! Pale sunlight suddenly gleamed down upon tall chimneys and a sprawling metropolitan mass shrunk away into an obscure significance while life spun on a single pointed toe, a hat broke into song, or grey houses were neatly bound together with a bow of orange ribbon.

He could isolate the shy fire of a brooch or arrest a flashing petticoat with a startling instancy and jewel-like completeness where straight down a hill dipped a double row of street lamps displaying a whirligig of figures in the dark space between. A flash of imagination caught an unknown life, discriminating countless shades where the common eye sees but gloom or glare; pursuing countless distinct movements where the common eye sees only a whirling perplexity; with just time to speculate, to appreciate, to commemorate in the instantaneous gratitude of a perfect phrase – and his eyes moved on. He 'lived in the flicker' and darkness was all about. Souls glided in the human river, small green souls, red souls, white souls, pursuing, overtaking, joining, crossing each other, then separating slowly or hastily. So he seemed to see life. His eager interest seemed to pass lightly and brightly along the heads, throwing up faces here and there (and always a face worth throwing up), swaying the bodies, running along like a ripple on water, like a breath of wind on a field. I see it now – the multitudinous surge, a pair of eyes here now and there now shining out suddenly like stars through loaded boughs and vanishing again, mutable and amazing faces glowing for an instant between darkness and darkness! When he spoke he always made me think of that passage in Conrad's *Youth*: 'I watched the procession of headlights gliding high, and of green lights gliding low in the night, when suddenly a red gleam flashed at me, vanished, came into view again, and remained!' Remained! As if I could ever forget the way in which as if conducting some subtle ministration in the service of beauty he would murmur, 'Soft tones of pink, rose, geranium, champagne, beige, lime, purple, helio, nigger, havana, ivory and black,' or the manner in which he said 'The present price of gloves reminds me of the advice given to a debutante by an elderly lady who had been through the circle of Society functions and had grown grey and wise. "My dear," she said to her young friend before her first ball, "you are too old now to scale garden walls and old enough to know never to waste white gloves on a younger son".'

It might have been written of him that 'he had the Old Dog's eyes in his head. They watched the door she (Beauty) passed through; they listened for her as dogs' eyes do. When she hung on her lover (Time) timidly and went forth, he followed without an idea of envy or anything save the secret raptures the sight of her gave him, which are the Old Dog's own. His sensations cannot be heroic but they have a fulness and a wagging delight as good in their way.' He was a witty, feminine, indecorous lover of mobility, grace, beauty and genius, whose song of thanksgiving was always 'a song of flourishes; one of those beflowered arias in which the notes flicker and leap like young flames'. To be pointedly rational was a greater difficulty to him than a fine delirium. His farrago was wonderful and winning. He loved things 'extreme and scattering bright'. It was difficult to distinguish the true edifice of his mood for its pinnacles, cupolas, turrets, infloriations and flying buttresses.

I remember discussing with him once the subject of modern stage production. Actor-managers were for ever complaining that Shakespeare did not pay. 'Let them take a leaf out of Mrs Kean's book,' he cried, 'and substitute a lounge suit and spats for the buskin and doublet and they will have bumper audiences and a queue at the booking office. After all, the play's the thing: the rest is only leather and prunella. How Orlando, a dashing young fellow with varnished hair dressed in a nicely cut sports coat and flannel bags would fetch the Matinée girl! And think of Rosalind in a pale blue charmeuse cut on the bias, flesh-coloured stockings and a têtede-negre straw hat trimmed with muslin and poppies. Juliet in a night-dress of aeroplane linen would sit on the balcony knitting a jumper while she waited for her Romeo, who would come in evening dress with a shirt by Messrs Dick & Dinkey's... Juliet in a nightdress of aeroplane linen!' How the repetition and the pause conveyed an almost uncontrollable excitement to me while he held me with ecstatic eyes!

'Nor,' he continued after a little, 'would Malvolio's lines suffer if that gentleman were brought up to date and dressed in a neat Irish tweed with spats and a monocle. Hamlet, of course, would wear morning dress and top hat, while Henry V at Harfleur could hardly be better dressed than in khaki with red tabs. Othello gives the *lingerie* firms plenty of scope in the bedroom scene. Desdemona would be in silk pyjamas with a dainty little mob-cap, while Othello, to show his savage origin, would adhere to the obsolete and barbarous nightshirt. The bed – an artistic four-poster draped with futuristic cretonne – would be supplied by the Alpha Workshops, price lists at the box-office... '

All this going down Princes Street one sunny afternoon! As I saw the fashion in which his eye fastened on to a sale poster the fine frenzy of the caption, 'Furs! Furs! Furs!' seemed to half suffocate my soul. By the time we had reached Shandwick Place he was busy elaborating another characteristic theme.

'In these days,' he said, 'fastenings had become what our grandmothers would have called precarious. The multitude of hooks and eyes which once maintained dresses was unknown, and even the pressed button had declined in popularity. Garments were hung on the shoulders and crossed at the waist or just confined under a belt, and there was little lacing or hooking or buttoning anywhere. Even the corset was but the shadow of its former self. For evening it was no longer just the neck that was *décolleté*, or even the shoulders, but the entire back, and as low as possible in front. Anatomical studies abounded. "Where is the back of the dress?" I asked foolishly in one shop. "That, my dear sir, is provided by the lady," was the reply. "But surely it isn't quite – well... " "Perhaps not, but it is going to be very fashionable." "But with a dress that begins and ends – er – there, how can a woman wear anything underneath?" "Very simple. She will leave it off. Corsets will not be worn with the new evening gowns. The new *lingerie* is specially designed not to interfere with the back view...." I went out a great deal that winter. I have my memories. There was, for example, a frock of white silk jersey cloth made with a little bodice and tiny short sleeves. The skirt from a front view appeared to be composed of three wavy flounces of the material, whilst around the waist there was a loosely knotted

belt. But from the back just a plain white foundation was to be seen, the
flounces were absent, and, in fact, the jersey cloth altogether had ceased
to appear, having stopped short at each side, bodice included – bodice
included! The effect was odd and gave a peculiar impossible look to the
frock, unparalleled in my experience!'

He stopped short and looked blankly into my eyes, so conveying his
sense of an altogether irrational effect in a most thrilling fashion.

'This season,' he resumed, in a subdued fashion, as if he had just evaded
a crisis, 'caprice and novelties there are many but no drastic change of
silhouette. No!' reflectively, 'no drastic change of silhouette. I have in my
mind's eye a toilet designed for a lady who is noted for her taste in dress.
The frock is of Nattier blue taffetas – after seasons of noiseless silks you
will agree that it will be enchanting to hear the soft rustle again! – simple
in style, with a *lingerie* collar and cuffs, and a *gilet*, the only note of colour
a girdle of orange silk in *filet* crochet-stitch and appliqué with corn-flowers
and leaves. Over this will be worn a cape of blue taffetas with a fence collar
and trimmings, bands on the front and the bottom of the cape of crocheted
orange silk. The silk repeated, of course, in the georgette crêpe lining!…'

We walked for a few yards in silence. Then he bought the latest edition
from a running newsboy. The first item to catch his eye was a notice
respecting a forthcoming furniture sale. 'Listen!' he cried (I cannot hope
to reproduce the colourful gusto of his voice), 'the wonderful world!…"Old
blue and white Spode supper service of a hundred pieces. Antique bow-
front chest drawers; set of eight Chippendale chairs, two with elbows; Buhl
show cabinet; three-light candelabra; trophy of armour".' Trophy of
armour! What brave and clangorous scenes his inimitable inflections
invoked… 'Crystal!' He passed on to another advertisement, and there was
contagious rapture in his zestful reading. 'White coutil corsets – very low
bust with whole silk elastic tops, deep-fitting over hips, and finished with
lacing eyelets at foot of bust… Black corsets with dainty pink silk spot,
finished at top with black silk embroidery threaded with ribbon. Four
suspenders! Truly a mystic number! And a pink silk spot"!'

'Listen to this!' he cried again, and I had never seen him so vivified, so
carried away before. '"Two demure blondes took the beach by storm when
they suddenly appeared among the gay throngs garbed in black from head
to foot. They had crêpe veils flowing from their tight-fitting bathing caps
pinned back in regulation mourning style, the veils falling to the waist-line
in the back. The only touch of colour was the narrow white edging round
the bottom of the front of the cap. The bathing attire included dainty
pumps buttoned across the ankle. The widows did not go near the water

but contented themselves with promenading on the beach".'

He stood and looked at me. He had communicated to me a new sense of the mystery and magic of life. The excited air seemed to hold up to my notice the wonderful stitchery on what Swinburne called 'The lifted hem of the garment of Love'. I understood what Francis Thompson meant when he wrote

> The rustle of a robe hath been to me
> The very rattle of love's musketry.

And suddenly I divined how the Saviour had known that someone had touched the hem of His robe. 'For she said if I may touch but His clothes I shall be made whole.' And again I remembered, 'Friend, how camest thou in hither not having a wedding garment?' And again how 'His clothing became white and like the flashing lightning, whiter (said Mark with just the quality of emphasis in his utterance my friend would have used had he been there) than any fuller could bleach it.'...

I left him at the Haymarket standing in the centre of the pavement murmuring over and over again, 'Nainsook Directoire knickers trimmed with Swiss insertion.'

My brain fluttered and filled and my thoughts wound in and out like slender ribbons of honey-coloured silk.

> You never see life's common things or know
> Their strange unfathomable loveliness,
> Till with reluctant tread you too must go
> Down the strange darkened road of silentness.
>
> Your happy room, old books and sunny flowers,
> Jewels that shine through silent floods of hair,
> And glittering cobwebs diamonded with showers,
> Moonlight that slowly climbs to the darkened stair.

And, like moonlight so climbing, may be my readers share in this angle of vision and vesture.

VIII   Spanish Girl*

Is then Aldebaran the star of hell
Lifting alone upon eternal night
One rose of light?
Ah! Fateful lamp
The blood of all mankind is oil for thee at last.
Upon the orgies of oblivion you cast
Your purple glooms.
My lost life quivers redly in your flame!

O Light that callest me by name,
Whom judgment's hoofs could not outstamp,
What deathless spell
Put you upon me still that I
In whose soul shrivelled all the sky
Should loose me from the detriments of dooms,
Shatter the shackles
Of incomputable debacles
And step incompetently free?

Can one light in a midnight single
One shadow from the rest,
One shadow when all shadows intermingle
– One passionate behest
Sever from night what day casts out,
Refuse to death what life repudiates?
O rose that will not let me rest
Espying me in the chaotic rout
What ghostly life now recreates
In shadow shape the man I was, and sets
Me with crepuscular passions quivering?
– Hell's parody of love in silhouette
Upon the stage of dissolution set! –
Can emptiness arise and sing?
Lethe my mouth of ashes wets
And puts a sung song in my heart.
My hollow loins acknowledge whom thou art.

* A recollection of Salonika.

My dusty veins are filled
With the red light that streams from thee.
I rise and come as thou hast willed,
O Light that makest me!
Nay, not Aldebaran but the rose you wear
Red in your cloudy hair!

Am I a disembodied memory
Embracing thee?
Your great breasts rise
In my imaginary hands.
I lie in endless impotence
Vague on your surging life,
Like lights in chaos are your eyes.
Me bodiless
Your arms constrain in ineffectual bands.
Dully I hear
What far distress,
What immemorial strife?

...Burn clearlier, Life, and penetrate
This partially-resurrected sense,
Half corpse, half ghost.
In this confusion dark and dense
But sounds are heard and meanings lost.

...Loosen the rose and put it to my ear!

Surely this urgent throbbing I have heard before
Knowing the whence and wherefore?

Burn more intense.
Clasp me as in a vice.

...Ah no –
I am a void
Impossibly employed.
Vaguely I know and do not know.
So doth the sea
Receive infinity

Upon its whirling breasts.
I hear a multitudinous roar
And see within your eyes the flashing crests
Of tides that reach no shore.

... O weltering womanhood
On whose dispurposed mood
Flotsam
I am!

...O scarlet light of lust
Frenzying the disjunct dust!

... O thou who bearest me
Upon thy wildered courses timelessly
Hither and thither
And in the end no whither
When will the tyrannous rose wither
And let us lapse together
Vacant in space?

...O Whirlpool of Oblivion
Whereon my derelict life is spun
Cease your vain race
And let me like a shadow fall
To depths for ever held in nescience' thrall!

* * *

Morning
And quick winds scattering spice!
You let a ray of sunlight in.
Stand by the lattice – Sin
Bodied in living ivory
With dawn and darkness equal on your head
And one red rose
Flaming triumphantly
That down a white cheek throws
Impossible memories of the Night!
... Hark, the birds sing!
Throw wide the window to the light.

It shall not fall on flowers anywhere
Fair as your breasts are fair
Pulsing and glowing there.
It shall not hold
In momentary gold
Aught younger, aught more old.
The deft beams seek
With gestures sleek
Each nervous beauty in your conscious flesh.
… Sweet is the dawn and fresh
The dawn wind on the bed.

Why should I weary of my fate
Where sunlight is insatiate?
It is good to lie here
In endless mornings pale and clear
And see the roses trembling on the sill
And your breasts quivering still!
O thou whose unremitting lust
Constrains my dust!
And as the day declines
The red rose shines
Unspent,
Omnipotent!

IX The Never-Yet-Explored

Here in the flesh, with the flesh, behind,
Swift in the blood and throbbing on the bone,
Beauty herself, the universal mind,
Eternal April, wandering alone,
The God, the Holy Ghost, the Atoning Lord,
Here in the flesh, the never-yet-explored.
– Masefield

All creation gave another smell beyond
what words can utter.
– George Fox

She was like Galsworthy's lime-tree, coldly fair, formal in her green-beflowered garb – which yet shakes, when the wind enters her heart, with the passion one sees when bees are swarming, a fierce humming swirl of movement, as though she had suddenly gone mad with life and love – tumults soon dying away; leaving her once more perfumed, gracious, delicately alluring.

Are you, did not Galsworthy ask (with that terrible accent of his), the essential tree when you are cool and sweet, vaguely seductive as now, or when you are being whirled in the arms of the wind and seem so furiously alive? When shall I see your very spirit?....And as he fought in his dream towards his vision of the Lady of the Lime-Tree, separated from him by a gulf of nothingness which was soft and cool to the touch of his face and hands, one of her ears lit up by a great buttercup, her eyes velvety and dark and dewy there, her body lovely though nearly hidden by creamy flowers growing stiffly round her as might asphodels, 'on her lips came the sweetest and strangest of all smiles'. Seeing her smile thus he struggled desperately against the cold smooth nothingness, and while he struggled he saw her quiver and writhe as though she, too, wanted to come to him. Her breast heaved, her eyes grew deeper, darker, they filled with glistening moisture and seemed to entreat him... Straining with a furious strength he never thought to have had against that colourless impalpable barrier, he crept forward inch by inch, and as he came nearer and nearer to her he saw her eyes liven and begin to glow sweet and warm as the sun through heather honey; shivers ran through her limbs; a lock of her hair drifted towards him.

A lime-blossom loosened by the bees and wind had drifted across his lips, its scent was in his nostrils. There was nothing before him but the fields and the moor and close by the lime-tree. He looked at her. She seemed to him faraway, coldly fair, formal in her green-beflowered garb, but for all that he knew in his dream he had seen and touched her soul... And in her dream? There was nothing before her but the red and yellow expanse of the carpet, the familiar furniture gleaming or misty in the strong sunlight beating in through the windows, and herself, this Mrs Morgan, far away, coldly fair, formal in her pale silks... She looked at herself.

She tried to define her nature. 'Colourable and plastic, fashioned by the words, the looks, the acts and even by the silences and abstentions surrounding one's childhood; tinged in a complete scheme of delicate shades and crude colours by the inherited traditions, beliefs or prejudices – unaccountable, despotic, persuasive, and, often, in its texture, romantic,' – 'a mobilised and moving equilibrium! Much once central is now lapsed, submerged, instinctive, or even reflex, and much once latent and budding is now potent and in the focus of consciousness for our multiplex, compounded, or recompounded personality.'...

She left it there and took, as it were, as the terms of reference for the particular inquiry she was now about to conduct, certain quotations from her recent reading which timeously recurred to her. The first of these was Richard Middleton's dexterous observation that 'nearly all the real sorrows of youth are due to this dumbness of the emotions. We teach children to convey facts by means of words, but we do not teach them how to make their feelings intelligible.' The second was Pearsall Smith's statement that 'the older kind of names for human passions and feelings, we may call "objective". That is to say, they are observed from outside and named by their effects and moral consequences... Most people must have felt at one time or another the incongruity of ugly names like greed or malice for feelings delightful at the moment, and a nonhuman observer from another planet might be puzzled to find that the passions and propensities that were called by the least attractive names were the ones that mankind most persistently indulged.' Introspection, she thus realised, was often, quite rightly, condemned as an unhealthy tendency, for it was very common and very disastrous to study feelings in order to increase their pleasantness. As a consequence language had become quite apathetic, generalised until it was without meaning. It was necessary that she should (sitting up a little and drawing her legs in) not sink into a warm bath of self-contemplation but make the coldest effort to regard her own organism as merely one among others. Her physical-intellectual being was the sensorium of Nature, but it was also one thing among natural things whose number was legion. It was the mirror in which she viewed the world, but it was also part of the world, the part most necessary for her to know and work upon, and its value to her depended upon her knowledge of its natural distortions and how to test and correct them. Next she 'staked down' as it were, with an odd sensation of sudden successfulness, a quotation the source of which she could not remember, 'Immaturity, degeneracy, disharmony, aberration are conditions of consciousness in which no communion with reality can take place', and her mind seemed to tremble with an imminent efflorescence of spirit, an opening-up of faculty, the breaking forth of new life upon high levels of joy, and she was full of the strange and insatiable craving for reality, 'the diadem of beauty'.

This brought her swiftly to her next point. 'The essence of life lies in the movement by which it is transmitted.' And she felt that she had satisfactorily completed a most delicate and difficult task when she discovered ready for this end in her mind these lines from the strange drama 'In the Name of Time': –

> If there be judgment it shall be required
> Of women what delight their golden hair
> Has yielded – have they put its wealth to use
> Or suffered it to lie by unenjoyed?

And now she saw as from a wooded height the land of fulfilment but not the road thereto.

She knew that she was in a most subtle and successful fashion alienating the affections of her youngest son Frank from his *fiancée* Jessie Butler – adopting methods against which Jessie was too young to defend herself, and against which, constitutionally, Frank had no defence – for reasons which were so indistinguishably woven into the texture of her incomprehensible life as scarcely to admit of being most fugitively recognised by herself in her keenest moments of self-analysis; reasons which expressed themselves definitely, effectively, and yet indefinably, without her volition and often against her will, in the arguments of her eyes and the subtlest persuasions of her contours and colours. That was all – and yet it was proving enough. No! It was subtler even than that – a matter of involuntary tremors and unaccountable viewless vibrations; of co-intuitioning nerves; of incessant arterial heliographing in codes of infinitesimal pulsations indecipherable by any of the separate senses; of obscure and unseizable interactions of personality; wine-like and wind-like; going by unknowledgeable personal channels… by flames passing from sensation to sensation.

In the recesses of her own consciousness Mrs Morgan admitted that she did not care. She was never, when she was in a genuine introspective mood (whatever she might be when her consciousness was limited and hampered by the presence of her husband or others, or when the functioning of her mind was altered by the pressure of any of the various normal external preoccupations incidental to wifehood and housekeeping) a victim to that uneasy pain of conscience 'which seizes both the head and the parenchyma of the heart and thence the epigrastic and hypograstic regions beneath'.

It was an instance of a specific aboulia. 'Specific aboulias in real life,' she knew, 'invariably prove when analysed to be due to our unconscious repulsion against the act that cannot be performed' (*i.e.* her acquiescence in this proposed match). 'In other words, whenever a person cannot bring herself to do something that every conscious consideration tells her she should do, it is always because for some reason she does not want to do it.

This reason she will seldom own to herself and is in the great majority of cases only most dimly if at all aware of.'...It was even with a tonic and penetrating thrill that she recognised the extensive abnormality of her awareness... In other moods she went through the customary conscious processes that so involve and conceal the core of an aboulia. Time and again on such occasions (generally when her husband or other members of her family, all unsuspecting and safely external, were present) she worked herself up, pointing out to herself her obvious duty, with the cruellest self-reproaches, lashing herself to agonies of remorse and once more falling away to calm and by no means unpleasurable recognition of the impotence of her conscious self to control even in her own case the hidden effective factors of human intercourse guiding and enticing all life irresistibly and incessantly to unimaginable ends.

She frankly admitted that she could put into words no conceivable objection to their union. She knew of no bar or impediment. On the contrary, she was perfectly satisfied that Jessie was in all likelihood a more suitable mate than any other Frank was likely to choose or have chosen for him; that she would beyond doubt make him a true and faithful wife, that she possessed graces of mind and person which in conjunction with Frank's would almost infallibly conduce to what the world (and themselves) would recognise as a happy and successful marriage – quite as happy and successful as her own had been, which was, as matters went in the world at the time,* no inconsiderable happiness and no small success from any normal point of view.

She recognised it as typical of her character that in realising that she was thus working, involuntarily but no longer unconsciously, against what in all likelihood were her son's best chances of human happiness (not to take Jessie into consideration) she was not so much concerned with the direction in which her influences were operating, or with the probable consequences, as with the unphraseable puzzles of the causation of that tendency, with the mysteries of her own motivation. If means only existed or could be devised not so much for expressing in words, but for thinking exactly about, such matters, how much nearer she would get to herself; vast regions of perceptions and correspondences eluded the imaging powers of her surface consciousness. What a small part of the whole real experience could the tiresome cerebral pantomime of voice and vision contrive to represent! She sought after clear instances of audition, distinct 'interior words', whereby she might translate her intense intuitions into

* The beginning of the twentieth century – a terrible period.

forms with which her surface mind might deal. She was actuated by motives conforming to a rhythm too great for her to grasp, so that manifestations of it appeared erratic and unprepared.

She rubbed the tip of her nose between the ball of her thumb and the knuckle of her forefinger. For a moment she was startled as it occurred to her to ask what had prompted her to do so. She had stumbled on a clue. Instantly, however, she realised that it was a clue which she could not follow up, and it was with impatience that she permitted her thoughts to seize upon it, knowing that they would require to come back, in a little while, nonplussed, to this point of departure....Undoubtedly, so far, it seemed that the solution must lie in the direction of rendering intelligible her obscure olfactory intimations rather than those of any other sense. Was the nose the key to many of the closest mysteries of human motivation – the nose, that strange winged instrument of an incalculable sentience, which, as it were, contributed to the mental atmosphere potent and pervasive elements appreciable only – and even then unintelligibly – in the crudest terms of their most obvious effects? How could she read the riddle of this sphinx squatting between her eyes? It was not any abnormal fineness of smell she possessed, but far-reaching intuitions that were somehow obscurely bound up with her olfactory sense, appreciable even by herself, and that only in a most rudimentary and fugitive fashion in their relation to nasal sensations, not to be disengaged by the subtlest efforts of her intelligence from the general complex of any normal psychological and physiological situation and yet most potently determinant of action bound up most intimately and effectively with the innermost secrets of her personality – in themselves, in fact, almost solely determining her 'disposition'. She felt that if she could only 'clear her nose' she would come instantly to self-knowledge. Her thoughts turned back again, as she had foreseen, slinking like dogs with nasal catarrh:

> My thoughts are fixed in contemplation
> Why this huge earth, this monstrous animal
> That eats her children, should not have ears and eyes.

She recognised from the outset that to endeavour to arrive at any systematised conclusion as to the reasons for her attitude was bound to prove futile, reminding herself that we cannot concede even to the brute data of sense that fixity and security which a comfortable realism demands. Only by noting an infinitesimal and fugitive detail here, the flitting shadow of a sensation there, by patiently recalling the tiniest nuances of difference in the effect upon herself at different times of different perceptions –

shining shadows of difference – by making as it were here and there points in the shifting landscape of that part of her recent emotional history relevant to the matter in mind, and so endeavouring to triangulate that district of her soul whence these influences emanated, could she hope to arrive at even the most fragmentary conclusions.

She cunningly discerned, however, that to imagine that this district or these purposes were central to her nature was probably fallacious. And to understand that her husband (that strange man, with his lumbaginous licence of movement, at once ponderous and erratic), her children, her friends, her enemies, each of all her acquaintances, had in relation to her more or less definite, and widely differing, conceptions of what her nature was – none of which, of course, in any way approximated to the indeterminable reality any more than her own conception before she adopted her present agnostic position had done – made her problem multitudinously difficult.

Her realisation definitely that the whole 'amazing reality of her concealed nature', for no reason that could be discerned by her conscious self, was set dead against this marriage had come one afternoon when she had been going out with Jessie's mother for a saunter down the river-side. When she arrived, Mrs Butler was in the act of dressing. Her face shone rosily. She tried hard to recall in their initial vividness every sensation she had experienced in the presence of that phenomenon. She failed to discover by ransacking her memory that she had received the slightest unhealthy (unhealthy, not disagreeable – unhealthy for some incomprehensible but very urgent reason was the quality of which she was in search, and not unhealthy in any virtual way but merely in antipathy with the secret standards of her own functioning!) impression.

Patiently her visual imagination recreated the big red face, the smile, the little twinkling eyes, half-birdlike, half-piggish, each separate crow's-foot in itself and in respect of the contribution it gave to the expression as a whole, the under-swell of the chin, the disposition of the throat, the way of the hair – over the ears particularly, and in the effect of the fashion in which it was pulled up from the nape... Mrs Butler had been in petticoat and camisole. The petticoat was negative – a cancelling stripe – that was to say, it did not affect her as if it had been one of her own (it would be to overrate her perceptions, however, to say that its effect upon her was exclusively Mrs Butlerian), but it aroused no speculations of any kind, and the legs beneath it were apparently quite irrelevant. There had been something, however, about the bust – unconnected with the quality of the linen into which it was somewhat negligently stuffed, with the details of the lacework or the ribbons or the way in which they were crossed and tied. Nor could she definitely attribute it to the remotest sense of geometrical impropriety in the fashion of the bunching and gathering.

It was a matter of a line, some indescribable faint flaw in moulding, an almost invisible 'indisposition' of flesh just over the right breast, an elusive indetermination of form. She endeavoured with a conscious impossibilism to reproduce on paper, to achieve with the stub of a pencil the faintest approximation which would in any way make this feeling of hers more definite. The effort was hopeless. Then, suddenly, with a swift, soft movement she crossed the room displaying as she walked that lengthening of the joints as when a desert mare canters along the sand. Her fingers glided swiftly down the buttons of her gown. In a second she had freed herself from its ensheathing. Garment after garment fell until she stood almost naked – naked but for a single filmy garment, slipping slightly off her shoulders. Then she turned to the mirror. The light deepened the hollows of her delicate temples and the double furrow between her clever irregular eyebrows. Her eyes held the shady look of long-suppressed desire. Her ears threw red stubs down the shadowy orange of her neck. Her glittering earrings were reflected like flecks of moonlight in the clear golden skin at the angles of her cheeks. Her face was more characteristic than beautiful, belonging as it were to 'an upper plateau' with a 'savage poignancy in serenity' stamped upon it, intrepid, individual. Nine men would pass it: the tenth sell his immortal soul for it – if he had one....She had never met one of these tenth men... The paleness of some strong feeling tinged her face. A slight trembling ran through her frame. Her inner soul struggle was acting like a strong developing fluid upon a highly sensitised plate. Passion, self-contempt, cruelty, ruthless curiosity, humour, impotence chased one another like shadows across her cheeks. Naked flesh, her own or another's, always affected her thus. Her bare wrist, slender and nervous, had something of the look of a leopard's claw or the leg of a gazelle... She pressed her palms slowly down under her thighs. A purple vibration waved across her face. Then with a sudden gesture she ripped off her remaining garment and stood squarely in all her throbbing nakedness.

She was conscious now that her thought was pursuing a passionate method that was ubiquitous, that was inadmissible, a method ancillary to a conception not as (impotently recognised in an atmosphere of competing flashes of insight!) one could claim to function, but as, for two pins, one fine afternoon, it might become pathologically patent that one did, insomuch as the carnalities inherent even in the best could no longer be subordinated. 'She looked out of herself,' westwards in the flesh as it were, 'into the world of men and there she saw a sight which filled her with unspeakable distress. The world seemed simply to give the lie to this great truth of which her whole being was so full. The effect upon her was in consequence, as a matter of necessity, as confusing as if it denied that she was in existence herself.' If she looked into a mirror and did not see her face she would have the same sort of feeling which actually came upon her as she looked upon closely woven humanity in which such a small moiety of the incommensurable sentience of which she was so throbbingly conscious was utilised – a panorama of insensate maceration. She felt capable of producing a wholesale labefaction of life by simply daring to be herself. Civilisation made life 'a sad science of renunciation', – condemned her to a fractional existence, her permitted courses an inconsequent commentary on the margin of her uncomprehended soul, ending in the intolerable anti-climax of her animal death!

She had never felt before to any similar extent the cruelty of Nature's law, exciting sensations which could not be gratified and desires which could not be justified – never realised so clearly that Nature had no respect for the conventions of society about sexual commerce. 'Blessed,' said Hawthorne, 'are all simple emotions, be they bright or dark; it is only the mixture of them that is infernal.'

She rigged up in the forefront of her mind hasty skeletons, characterless as Pope's women, of civilised conceptions – hollow colourless forms in postures of paralysis corresponding to nothing ever entertained in a human heart – grotesque puppets – and her mind quivering anew with a simultaneous recognition of the wild unphraseability and utter ordinariness of her sensations and desires, destroyed them again 'with a crash of broken commandments'. 'Women' – she remembered Meredith's dictum – 'who dare not be spontaneous! This is their fate only in degree less inhuman than that of the Hellenic and Trojan princesses offered up to the gods.'

Who was this mighty and magnificent and terrible female creature, with lightning in her flesh and thunder in her hair, – with hooded imponderable eyes and bosoms like fog-bound mountains; allied with the ultimate precipitous splendours of life; a votarist of incalculable powers and majesties rather felt than conceived; a lonely, passionate and hungering spirit in a marvellous and intolerable form, set apart for tragedy to come?... She was carried headlong by the rushing rhetoric of her longings.

> Impériales fantaisies
> Amours des somptuosités,
> Voluptueuses frénésies,
> Rêves d'impossibilités.

She thought of her pitiful measures of accomplishment, the preponderance of her forced renunciations, her impotent hungers of heart, outwith the swirl of blood, the trampling of pulses, the violin play of lightning muscles – bound in upon her silent bones, sealed into anæmic courses, marooned in barren continences!

The reduction of the intricacy and wonder of womanhood into a 'rag and a bone and a hank of hair' was not more inhuman than would be her present dwindling back from this amazing stature of her spirit into a commonplace size in suburban wives.

By what secret mechanism did she and all other human beings so dwarf and confine themselves, and why? It made her think of the author who wrote that 'he followed a small maid into an even smaller room.' Because civilisation exalted morality at the expense of life its conventions seemed abortive and unconscionable and its effect unnecessarily withering. Such institutions as these portrayed a clear outline of the appalling commonplaceness which scenes of involution assume when they become a conscious environment – and yet to how fine a degree a woman might develop her sensibilities and her balance in a monotony of needless inhibition!

This Mrs Morgan that she was – would become again as instantaneously and effortlessly (slipping on a *peignoir* and having had 'one of her headaches') if her husband or one of her children should come in just now – was so aptly and economically contrived, to all appearances spontaneous and free in the consciousness that conceived her; moving with a specified grace, displaying a recognised variety of discreet and appropriate gesture. So tense and subtilised was this accepted fiction of herself, that she had her being within it without any sense of imprisonment. Thought of it did not affect her as if this Mrs Morgan was any mere automaton, any stuffed shape staring glassily out of irremediable posture... nor even as a separate personality assumed at her convenience for certain purposes... but as a fairy, the face of which was but a screen, vividly visible on which the suitable selection of her emotions was cast like the lights and colours of a film. With a curious sense of pride she recognised the artistry of that life she was able to contrive under such unconscionable limitations, conjuring up the effects she made as sharply painted as recollections of a dream: and saw herself doing so – leading that usual life of hers, being so perfectly, dexterously and daintily what people thought her (people who could not think) – and her husband and the rest of the company like flittering ephemerides of the spirit under the profound and radiant gaze of her real self.

The artistic temperament. Did not most artists at the end of their careers become discontented with the form in which they had worked? They had succeeded through obedience to that form, but it seemed to them that a rare success lay uncaptured outside these limits. They were tempted by what seemed lawless in life itself: by what was certainly various and elastic in life. They were impatient with the slowness of results, with their rigidity, inside these inexorable limits. The technique which they had perfected seemed too perfect: something cried out in chains and they would set that voice, that Ariel, free... But could she?

She stood square to the mirror and drew herself up to her full height, hollowing her back a little, like a gymnast on the horizontal bar, and, looking at herself, she realised with a sudden fear how her new knowledge imperilled her in her relations with her husband and her sons, remembering what Angela of Foligno said... 'because of this change in my body therefore I was not always able to conceal my state from my companion or from the other persons with whom I consorted, because at times my countenance was all resplendent and rosy and my eyes shone like candles'.

Closely she scrutinised her breasts. In the shifting of a contour, in the motion of a shadow on the skin, she sought for the slightest clue to this elusive recollection of – was it a movement? – an effect. All in vain! Beyond a vague tantalising sense (as when something is 'on the very tip of one's tongue' yet stays unspeakable) of knowing that somewhere along the line of this strange and subtle speculation lay the truth, she achieved nothing. Before leaving the mirror she closely examined her nose, breathing – 'nostrils of investigation' as if in some incomprehensible fashion, the effect for which she was seeking – that fugitive sensation of shape – would be reproduced in a quivering motion of the wings. but no!

Turning again with a sense of having been arrested suddenly in the wild course of an inexplicable aberration and becoming, as with eyes like those of a dreamer suddenly awakening from a vivid adventure to confront familiar things (a good instance of a common and somewhat indescribable sensation analogous to by-psychic duality – the fortuitous phenomenon by which spirits are often uncertain as to whom they really represent), related again to the actual facts of her existence – vulning herself, as heralds say of the pelican, in her piety – like a Greek chorus the furniture awkwardly obtruding its crude significances stood round her passionate soul in travail. Oh, the grotesque, stupid, pitiful interpositions of pictures, chairs, ornaments, needlework! Her household gods had acquired all the repulsive and puerile crudity of heathen idols – the whole room was stuck

like an incongruous gargoyle on the tower of her mood... And through the
window in the oblique light 'mere circlings of force there, of iron negation,
of universal death and merciless indifference!' with, nearer, a light shallow,
an outer reach, a swaying edge of the deep metropolis (like a windless tide
invading an unknowledgeable shore, remotely and with infinite gentleness,
lapping the abysmal dark foundations of the soaring house, alone of all
things alive with its dark and durable secrecy, in which she so inconceivably
lived), making an electric ravel, full of inconsequent glitter, and with little
black unsteadinesses of people, like masses of flies on the broad blond
pavements between which the streets were hung like long fine nets,
quivering with a close-working subtlety of movement, holding a congested
haul of cabs and cars and vehicles of all kinds and colours, endlessly
miscellaneous but merged and dwarfed and suppressed into the tiniest
courses, almost indistinguishable... all so small, swarming infinitesmally
away down there, sown through the thready complicated radiance...
seeming little more than swarms of midges hung in endless fine nets of
flashing and failing light in a nethersky; drifting through strands of light
and heat... now, with a sense of panic, steepening about her as if the lines
of her vision were miraculous dry paths between precipitous seas and all
these but exposed sections of the infinite fisheries of fate... now quiet, and
decided and remote, rather beautiful, and yet seeming to have some
strange, cold power over her... and again all so mild, so very old, so faint
and floral, with a far-off life of its own that came stealing in upon her, very
faint, swelling, sinking, festive, mournful,... lustrous, mild and illusionless.
This thin glitter and fume, this white and fawn presentment below, the
shaken kaleidoscope of a metropolitan fragment, did not exist really...it
rested upon solid darkness, one with the mighty irresistible darkness, upon
which she was hoisted into this bright room and existence of hers...like a
gleam of coloured oil upon dark water...like a fair faint dream in an
Egyptian night (her ears appraised the marvellous *fioritura* of the view, a
graduation of small light sounds) but what was it? – nothing! Just nothing!
'It is amongst such communities as these that happiness will find her last
refuge on earth, since it is among them that a perfect insight into the
conditions of existence will be longest postponed.' Very strange and
immaterial were these glitterings of a toy civilisation away down there in
the fair blind fabulating streets, a pale calm through which the generations
flew like shadows, and the windows high as her own over the way were
blue as crystals full of sorcery, shining with a fascinating fatality. In a
sudden dizziness as she looked they seemed to rock a secret and their panes
seemed luminous, transparent, as if the secret were burning visible in

them. Was it true of her, as of Coleridge, that the further she ascended from animated nature the greater in her became the intensity of the feeling of life?... Could she dismiss her problems merely by going downstairs?

She crossed the room and threw herself down on a sheepskin rug in front of the fire... turning her thoughts now into another channel, recalling the way, or rather the ways, she had been affected by seeing Jessie's father walking in front of her up the street. He was a tall man, spare, with a slight stoop, a stiff fashion of the arms and legs. It seemed impossible that in that precise and mean *ensemble* she could find anything so stupendously objectionable as to mobilise her every instinct to avert this marriage, despite the fact that it was so pre-eminently a satisfactory proposition from every social, material, sentimental and ordinary point of view. Yet such was the case. And she could not discover wherein her objection actually resided, or how it had been stimulated by a back view of Mr Butler. It was, of course, pathological or psychological – practically, here at all events, synonymous terms. It was the invisible and indefinable power that controlled her life. Vaguely she felt that the purposes to which these instincts were directed had practically nothing to do with herself as an individual, or with Frank or Jessie – that they were phylogenetic, intimately implicated with the whole reproductive mechanism of humanity, that in something similar if not identical lay what beneath all the *camouflage* of love, interest, ideals, beauty and so forth, occasioned the suicidal attraction of this man or that man to this woman or that woman... Every crease of his trousers, the whole geometrical arrangement of his frame, the clicking black boots, the bony hands, the shape and angle of his head, and the way in which his ears were fastened to the sides of it, the curves of his bowler, came back to her, but nowhere could she isolate the slightest suggestive detail.

She evoked Jessie herself, with her sherry-brown eyes and flat back, visualising her with an indescribable completeness and accuracy, subjecting her to a thorough pre-mortem, going over her from head to heel, every line, every tint, every habit of her body and mind – unavailingly. She only got near it when the concentration of her mind reached such a pitch that this visualised Jessie seemed to become part of herself, sharing the same vital functions. Then she had the most obscure sensation of something that did not harmonise, that escaped from this imaginary unification, of an unplaceable flaw – of a tiniest discord, as it were, immediately swallowed up and lost in the orchestrated sentience of which she was conscious, of a something unamenable to this twining of their entities. Somewhere the wind of passion failed to keep the sails full and the foam at the bow. Jessie was a pitiful bow for the brave bending of sex...a glittering toy where she should have been a golden torment.

Thoroughly she worked this demoniac strain of sensuality which she had found in herself... criticising every movement, detecting every little inadequacy in her, every tiny congenital inability to respond to the uttermost, to give all and to give enough. Frank would probably be only very remotely if at all conscious of a disappointed muscle here and of there a vainly clamouring pulse, but... ! She thought she saw Jessie looking up at him with her mildly bulging eyes shaken and with a batlike bewildered flicker in their depths. Were these to be given to him in lieu of his birthright – 'eyes terrible as an army with banners'?

These speculations were full of that notion of being captured by the incredible which is of the very essence of dreams. How to understand, then, what made the truth of her mood, its meaning, its violent and invisible essence? It was impossible. No processes of thought could convey that sense of blood running blindly through a net of glimmering surmises; of thought that was but as a mesh of cheating gleams on the verge of the incalculable floods of life.

She who had thought herself bankrupt (and whom civilisation insisted upon treating as if she were) discovered in herself a secret hoard of evolutionary momentum. Wave followed wave from the sea of her soul. She was taken by new billows of largesse. After a period of stability and rest her unstable tendency to variation had broken out with tremendous force, with an abrupt access of vitality, rolling up she knew not whence, breaking old barriers, overflowing the limits of old conceptions, changing her rhythm of receptivity, the quality of her attention to life. She was entinctured and fertilised by a new upwelling of her submerged life. She was on the verge of saltatory developments. The Cloud of Unknowing had passed over. This realisation came like the winds of March. Experiencing it she participated in the deathless magic of eternal springs, full of emotional efflorescence, with an enhanced vitality, a wonderful sense of power and joyful apprehension, as towards worlds before ignored or unknown, flooding her consciousness. Her life was raised to a higher degree of tension than ever before, and therefore to a higher perception of reality.

How like Frank was to what his father had been when she married him. How curiously the same body had been transmitted from father to son and how tragic was the likeness when these two bodies of the same flesh were made to contain so different a spirit. At a little distance it could hardly be told which was the old and which the young, so exact a copy was the son of the father. Close, Frank made her forget the years almost, made the relationship between them impossible, so exactly did he reduplicate not only what his father had looked like but what she had thought he really was when she married him, and renew the sensations and desires within her which she had had then and had long ago had to suppress so cruelly. How much happier she would have been if his father had had her son's nature – how much more she could have had from life – how much more she could have given. If she had married Frank instead of his father surely she would not have remained a mere adumbration of her destined meaning, a magnificent provision of organs intended for functions which had never developed. She thought of Frank – the bright burnish of his crisply curling chestnut hair, the back of his splendidly moulded neck, full and round and strong, bronzed to the collar line, white as milk below, the first two or three articulations of his spine softly rounded, so deeply embedded in muscular tissues as to be scarcely discernible,... of 'his clean blueness of eye and whiteness of tooth and puissancy of neck and wrist ripe brown with stored sunshine.'

Oh, merry love, strong, ravishing, burning, zestful, stalwart, unquenched!... She saw herself again with parted lips and panting rounded breasts and a dancing devil in each glowing eye and a throbbing darting tongue and quick biting teeth, giving muscle for muscle and vein for vein, while the wild music in her heart rose, now slow, now fast, now deliriously wild, seductive and intoxicating... She could feel the answering shiver that quivered up to her.

'Is it beyond thee,' her spirit seemed to challenge Jessie's, 'to be glad with the gladness of this rhythm, to be tossed and lost and broken in the whirl of this fearful joy? All things rush on, they stop not, they look not behind, no power can hold them back, they rush on, keeping steps with this restless rapid music, seasons come dancing and pass away... colours, tunes and perfumes pour in endless cascades in the abounding joy that scatters and gives up and dies every moment.'

It was getting dark. The furniture shone in the fitful firelight dull and livid as old armour.

> Her white breasts gleamed;
> Her neck seemed conscious of its loveliness;
> Her lips, tired of tame kisses, parted with
> The expectancy of proud assault; she was
> As one who lives for a last carnival
> Of love in which she may be stabbed and torn

By large excess of passion....
    Her heart now leaps with life
And now lies sleeping like a coiled snake.
But in tonight's cold moon she burns and glows.
Her heart is housing many a mad desire....

X   Consummation

Ablaze yet unconsumed I lay in thee
And instantly flame blended into flame,
As in a rising wind the light fires came.
Curve after curve climbed shining into me
I felt light flowing from your hands and feet,
I lay in incandescence 'twixt your thighs,
And saw the radiance mounting in your eyes
And heard your soaring heart's delirious beat.

Ablaze yet unconsumed I lie in thee.
Once lit such fires blaze to the end of time
To keener, clearer flaming still set free.
The spirit like a wind moves to and fro
Until in crystal heat, O Love Sublime,
One with eternity our bodies glow!

XI   A Limelight from a Solitary Wing*

Said Jesus, on whom be Peace, 'the world is a bridge : Build no house on it.'

---

* 'A spiritual snapshot', in his own phrase, taken in the spring of 1910 by the Secretary of the St Ninian's Church Literary and Debating Society (the meetings of which Fred had attended regularly throughout the winter, taking the liveliest part in the debates and giving a couple of papers himself), who, in a covering letter, is careful to explain that this is merely the impression Fred communicated to him of his religious position at that time. 'It must be remembered that I had only a single point of contact with this extraordinary personality,' he adds, 'and that I had at that time no knowledge whatever of his other and quite irreconcilable

Just when we are safest, there's a sunset touch,
A fancy from a flower-bell, someone's death,
A chorus-ending from Euripides –
And that's enough for fifty hopes and fears.
As old and new at once as Nature's self
To wrap and knock and enter in the soul,
Take hands again and dance there, a fantastic ring,
Round the ancient idol on his base again,
The grand Perhaps!

And the indefatigable self-analyst in time gets to know and anticipate all these variations and permutations, weary of the whirl of the pool, sick to death of the ever-changing changelessness, knowing just how the circles run, just how the lights and shadows of his moods will play upon them. It is not healthy to live for ever in a mental cinema, least of all when you have, with slight differences in the screenings and accompaniments, seen all the films before, and over-familiarity with the technique of production has bred contempt... But because of the faith that lay away deep down in it this mind realised even in the darkest of the distracted hours it spent in the great mazes of futility and jungles of false conceptions that 'I cannot see the good of it' was one of the worst of reasons for ceasing its struggles. Much of the best work is work done of which one cannot see the good at the time of the doing.

He breathed Stevenson's prayer perhaps: 'Help us with the grace of courage that we be none of us cast down when we sit lamenting among the ruins of our happiness or our integrity: touch us with fire from the altar that we may be up and doing to rebuild our city.' Thus worked in him one of the unrecognised powers of faith; its repellent power; the power by which (this both of course for good and evil, but, at all events, in these regions of uncertainty for good and all!) it rejects new ideas which conflict with its own root certainties. And after all it is a fact of human nature, as William James has put it, that men live and die by the help of a sort of faith that goes without a single dogma or definition – the bare assurance that

activities. I did not know that he was known in other circles as a philosophic anarchist; nor that he was the author of the powerful Neo-Catholic articles which created such a sensation in the autumn of 1909 and won so many converts for Rome. Nor had I the slightest of suspicion of his dipsomaniacal tendencies nor of his countervailing eroticism. Even now, however, with all the material at my disposal, I am satisfied that I have accurately depicted here the attitude in which without the slightest trace of hypocrisy he was then approaching spiritual realities.'

this natural order is not ultimate, but a mere sign or vision, the external staging of a many-storied universe, in which spiritual forces have the last word and are eternal. Only, of course in matters of this kind, the critical and creative mind cannot afford to be behind the scenes, but must have a good view from the front. From the first religions are not the product of logical reflection and experiment, but of sentiment and aspiration, coming into being as pure intuition and afterwards invading the provinces of reason and assimilating the thought of centuries in their own sympathies. He was now quite certain that the imagination had some way of dealing with the truth, which the reason had not, and that commandments delivered when the body is still and the reason silent are the most binding that the souls of men can ever know. So far so good! But this left for his journalistic mind the more difficult problem of communicability. Truth, without the progressive belief of mankind in it, seemed vague and helpless. Of what little avail are the profoundest thoughts if they contain no germ of comfort! The difficulties of the world were not to be solved by one young fellow's subconscious perceptions. And the notion of human progress was derived from just such demands of the spirit. It is all very well to say that the pleasure is in the chase – that 'to travel hopefully is a better thing than to arrive', and that the true success is labour – but surely all the activities of man, all his efforts and all his enterprises, presuppose a hope in him of attaining an end. Once kill this hope and his movements become senseless, spasmodic and convulsive, like those of someone falling from a height. Many times a day at this period he suffered from vertigo on the brink of such abysses. These were the times known to all active minds, when one feels oneself above any and all human books, when music, art, reading all fail as resources to alleviate or interest, and one becomes possessed of an irresistible desire to go forth and find some pain keener than one's own, to meet people more unhappy than oneself (and he knew that there were millions such). Never did he too greatly exaggerate his own trial; he was always indeed cynically conscious of his youthful immaturity, but he only knew that his heart ached night and day, and that the only solace possible would seem to be to find other hearts which ached night and day with more reason than his. And because of these impulses he felt a goodness in this subtly and slowly developing religion of his, nourishing thus a sentiment of the infinite value of existence, of the necessity of continual contact with living men and women, allied, as he felt it to be, with the best in him against the worst, and holding for ever before him the necessity of becoming a new man, making him understand that pain is a deliverer, increasing his respect for the consciences of others. And it was his steady if largely subterranean development along these lines that reassured him most. He was not one of those who would scream with the rabble, feel the pleasure of a gush for the moment and then sink back again to commonplace levels (however much to superficial observers his labouring spirit might seem to be irretrievably overwhelmed in chaos). He was continually recognising new duties above those whose observance had already commended itself to him, seeing, as it were, beyond the circle of conventional obligations, the dim forms of new claimants on his heart and service, moral innovations, enlargements of human life, horizon after horizon... how many such had still to arise?... And in such 'Utopian' dreams he saw arising new kingdoms of the spirit set far above the aspirations of the politicians, beyond all the projects of social betterment, a republic of souls in which, above mere right and sordid utility, above beauty, devotion, holiness, heroism and enthusiasm, the Infinite would have a worship and an abiding city. But he realised the while that it would be essential to eliminate all such suffering and iniquity as is preventible and germane in defective social arrangements, before it would be possible to return to spiritual goods. What he looked for, worked for, prayed for in these beliefs was a nation where class should be bound to class by the fullest participation in the treasure of the one life; where the members of each group of workers should find in their work the development of their characters and the consecration of their powers, where each citizen would know and be strengthened by the knowledge that he laboured not for himself only, not for his family, nor for his country, but for eternal good. So long as there was fear between man and man, so long as there were looks askance, there could be no communion. The new city must be a city of friends and lovers. – And thus in all the surge of new claims, in the encroachments of a thousand interests, in leisure that diminished until it was a marvel to his friends that he could cram so much activity into twenty-four hours, he was sustained by the belief that whatever multiplies the bonds between man and man makes him happier and better. Friendship being essentially hygienic his soul was never more sanitary. The brotherhood of men as an actual fact, soul to soul intimacy, very blood relationship, he deemed fundamentally essential to the real and endless advance of humanity, and when his fastidious and recusant intellect rebelled, he chastised it by recalling dicta such as Bacon's: 'In my course I have known, and according to my measure, have co-operated with great men, and I have never yet seen any plan which has not been mended by the observations of those who were much inferior in understanding to the person who took the lead in the business', or,

Were there no oxen feeding in the stall
    The crib were clean,
But without oxen harvest would be small,
    Housekeeping lean,
Wherefore we may not be too prim and nice,
    There is no good that doth not cost a price.

Thus would he stand with his eyes widened at the mysteries around him, remembering that, in spite of all his book-lore, what he knew was but a trifle and that the smallest detail of the world was infinitely greater than his own immortal mind, and recognising, too, in that prodigiousness of the universe a safeguarding excellence, since it must hold infinite resources and he might allow it some credit without accusing himself of improvidence. Since the fish were still spawning in the waters and a million mothers were smiling at their babies and the publishers' catalogues were increasing in number and growing in size and interest, he found fresh courage to be a mere man and to commit the rest to the numberer of the stars.

He fell back on the old, old feeling that something of everything is wanted to make a world – that it takes all sorts and conditions of men and women – that every human being born has his or her ultimate franchise – and that if every opinion is equally insignificant in itself humanity's bewilderment of thought is a mighty net which somehow holds the whole truth.

Live and let live. Think and let think. So his tendency was always to the whole, to the totality, to the general balance of things. Indeed it was his chiefest difficulty (and an ever-increasing one that made him fear at times cancellation to nonentity) to exclude, to condemn, to say No. Here, probably, was the secret of the way in which he used to plunge into the full current of the most inconsistent movements, seeking – always in vain, until he was utterly exhausted, not having failed, however, to enrich every one of them – to find ground upon which he might stand foursquare.

He was always fighting for the absent, eager for forlorn hopes, a champion of the defeated cause, for those portions of truth which seemed to him neglected: his aim being to complete every thesis, to see all round every problem, to study a question from all possible sides and angles… And thus his dreams were edged with the redeeming inconsistency, the saving dubiety, and he held with Browning the great central liberal feeling, a belief in certain destiny for the human spirit beyond and perhaps even independent of, our sincerest convictions, and could not see

What purpose serves the soul or world it tries
Conclusions with, unless the fruit of victories
Stay one and all stored up and guaranteed its own
For ever by some mode whereby shall be made known
The gain of every life.

* * *

And if I may be permitted just a word in the light of what I now know (and
that incompletely) with regard to his subsequent career, it shall be simply
this, that to my mind the storms of circumstance which have buffeted him
so terribly are laden with this message: 'And so shall our commission be
accomplished which from God we had – to plague His heart until we had
unfolded the capacities of His Spirit.'

XII   A Last Song

The heavens are lying like wreaths
Of dead flowers breaking to dust
Round the broken column of Time.

Like a fitful wind and a cold
That rustles the withered stars
And the wisps of space is my song,

Like a fitful wind and a cold
That whistles awhile and fails
Round the broken column of Time.

Published Stories and Sketches

The Black Monkey

Jim (as I christened him for the twin-sake of convention and convenience, as the Shamus which was constantly on the tip of my tongue would have made rather a bizarre cognomen for a monkey, and one apt to stimulate awkward questions) went into violent convulsions about midnight last night, 'rehumanized' as I expected for about a second and 'mummified'. Certain well-intentioned friends, who have all along expostulated with me, and pointed out how utterly absurd it was for a harassed and not over-wealthy GP (general practitioner) to reserve an entire suite of rooms and a special nurse for a 'dirty little chimpanzee' entered their last futile protest against the oak shell and brass fittings. Oliver thought an empty orange-box, painted black if my conscience insisted, would be quite good enough. Dick Bennet suggested that I was just pulling the india-rubber a bit too far: it might be all very fine in the case of a rich old maid and her pet poodle – but a needy medico and a filthy ape! Dick's common-sensical shoulders gave one of those shrugs which suggest that one might do worse than visit a brain specialist. Fred Henderson thought cash might easily be wasted to better advantage: I gave him what he wanted. It may be the last time. Unless I can get away from my thoughts – unless I can blot out from my memory last night, and that more terrible night of Jim's birth, I shall go mad. To cut away the black embroideries my imagination is for ever weaving about the ghastly facts, and set the tragedy down plainly and concisely here may bring me some relief: it will certainly explain to my friends many things which previously they could only account for to each other by mysterious and by no means complimentary brow tappings.

* * *

Shamus Doyle and I lodged, studied, and were at college together. Doyle was ever a brilliant student, with a perfect genius for psychology. 'Our budding Lombroso,' the class wit christened him. To those who were expecting a bright and shining climax to his brilliant course, his slacking in his fourth year was a bitter disappointment. That the magnet which drew him from his studies was Love but made the case worse to our sour scientific minds; and it went against the grain somehow to see a chap neglecting what was obviously his destined life-work, to set his tie, or discuss shades in gloves with obsequious shop-men. Then one day when I came in he was waiting for me, radiant, with a bulky blue letter in his hand. With no hypocritical grief, he announced the death of his Uncle Silas, a little matter of £800 a year, and what that meant to an impoverished 'medical'.

'When's the wedding to be, then?' I asked, *à la* Sherlock Holmes.

'The what?' he cried in scarlet dissimulation.

'The banns are in your face,' I returned. 'Congratulations!'

We shook hands heartily, and he came away with a cataract of the usual sentimental froth. They were to be married in three months.

I felt a tiny professional disappointment, despite the whole-hearted joy I had in my friend's happiness, for now I knew the most brilliant promise of the year would never bear fruit, and in a good husband the world would lose a great pioneer psychologist.

Alas, alas, for the vanity of human thoughts! No wedding bells rang in three months' time. The shock nearly killed Shamus. Then his heart was consumed with a terrible wrath, and curses flamed in his eyes – with never a tear. My generous big-hearted chum had become as a pillar of bitter iron. He cursed whoever was responsible for Death – his fiancée had been run down by a motor 'bus – and vowed he would never rest again until he had torn the secret of life from the relentless gods. Then he went from my ken for thirty years. Occasionally I heard how he worked like one obsessed, away in some inaccessible corner of the West Highlands, resting neither night nor day in his fierce search after the Elixir of Life – that chimera of science. Wonderful rumours were afloat, to which, however, I paid little heed. It was whispered that he had indeed succeeded in his quest. That he himself – although now on the shady side of sixty – had the elastic step of twenty-one; in spite of the most strenuous study not one grey hair; in spite of night and day work, the minimum of sleep and exercise, the tan of perfect health. He saw no one except his one man-servant, who cooked his scanty meals, went his messages, carried his letters, and sometimes assisted him in the more mechanical part of his experiments.

Then his voice came out of the thirty years' silence, in the shape of a picture post card, saying that he would arrive by the 8.30 train, and hoping that I would be able to put him up for a day or so, or perhaps longer.

I was astounded at my old chum's appearance. Except for an enormous raven appendage to his chin he looked pretty much as when I had last seen him. We shook hands and were silent for a few minutes. We stood in the very room in which he had received the fatal telegram – the breath of Death which burst the bright bubble of his hopes.

'You remember my last words?' he began abruptly. 'I have abolished Death – at least I think so. That is why I am here. I will have you leaping again – a boy at seventy; a boy at a million, Alister.'

'Glad to hear it,' I replied. 'It will be a comfort to get the pokers of age out of my legs and arms.'

'Yes! And I'll make your grey hair as red as it used to be' – he laughed, then sobering suddenly – 'thirty years ago!'

After supper, he detailed his intentions to me. He wanted me, with five or six eminent surgeons and savants, to take four months' furlough and journey North with him. 'And,' said he, 'you'll see this black beard of mine drop out and my chin become as soft as it was before my first scrape. Hitherto I've experimented solely on animals. Now I want a human subject, and propose to risk myself first, of course. You remember Gyp?'

I remembered Gyp – a shaggy little Scotch terrier he had had in the old student days.

'You do not mean to tell me that Gyp is still in the land of the living?' I gasped.

'Indeed, I do,' he answered. 'As much alive as ever he was; no older than when you last saw him, and likely to live as long as the earth's round.'

In the course of the next few days we called on Sir William Barks, the eminent morphologist; Dr Johnston Cairns, the electricity man; Frederic North, the brilliant bacteriologist; Peter Scott, the hypnotist; and Albert Napier, the popular novelist. The reporters had made the most of their crumbs, and a tremendous excitement had been aroused all over Britain. Not one of the five busy men but jumped at the offer – under bonds of secrecy, of course. We journeyed North together.

Doyle explained to us what he desired of us, showing us two little octagonal tabloids – one whitish in colour, the other a magenta red. He would go to bed and swallow the white tabloid. Almost immediately he would pass into a state of trance, indistinguishable from death. In that state he would lie for three months, at the end of which time we were to administer the second tabloid in a little milk.

Having completed his arrangements and prepared a special bed in the centre of a large and exceptionally well-ventilated room, where the temperature was kept at a certain pretty high fixed level, he lay down and swallowed the first tabloid. In three seconds he was to all appearances a corpse, save perhaps for a pink flush about his brow and cheeks, which, however, soon faded. In a week the mirror gave but the faintest shadow of breathing, and he had assumed a more waxen hue. Soon the most delicate tests failed to register any breathing whatever, and yet there was none of the decay of death – and putrefaction is the only sure sign of death.

After six weeks we pricked his arm with a needle, blood flowed, showing that he was certainly not dead. As the time for administering the second tabloid drew nearer and nearer, we all became infected with a nervous excitement. At last the three months were up, and we were all grouped round the bed – six of us, of whom I alone am left.

Sir William Barks prised the colourless lips gently open and administered the red tabloid, half dissolved in a drop of milk. Watching narrowly, we discerned a faint swallowing movement. The glass soon began to show breathing. The waxen hue left the cheeks and was replaced by a greenish yellow colour, which passed into pink. The breathing had become almost normal when the pink tinge suddenly deepened into brown, and then into a dark mahogany.

Surely something was far wrong. We were all terribly unstrung. The colour turned still darker; the skin began to gather and pucker; the black hair crackled into bristles; the ears knotted and wrinkled; the hands withered – and a living monkey was on the bed.

* * *

We all swooned except Sir William Barks. Old Dr Cairns went suddenly out of his mind, passed into strong convulsions and died in ten minutes.

Last night was the horrible curtain to the tragedy. I had noticed all day that Jim was not as well as usual, and I was expecting I knew not what – a chill presentiment of something alien. Nurse rang the bell for me about a quarter to twelve. Jim was taking fits. I hurried nurse out of the room and double-locked the door behind her. Jim was writhing in terrible agony, but I did not try to alleviate the pain. Soon, however, he quietened, and seemed to fall asleep. The puckering left his skin, the mahogany changed to brown, the brown to a dirty white, and Shamus Doyle lay breathing on the bed. He opened his eyes, a joy seemed to quiver through them – then the whole frame seemed to shrink and shrivel. The bones knocked together, and the skin fell parched and hard about them. The eyes had withered to mere black kernels, and for all the world the object on the bed resembled an old Egyptian mummy, discoloured, brittle, and dusty.

All Night in a British Opium 'Joint'

HEAVENLY HALLUCINATIONS DON'T COME OFF FOR DRUG HAS A
SOUL-DESTROYING EFFLUVIUM

I number among the many unpresentable acquaintances which it pays a
modern journalist to possess a man of mixed nationality, who has
considerably more things up his sleeve than Scotland Yard suspects. His
vast and peculiar intimacy with the mysterious underworlds of most of our
great cities is the sort of thing one seldom meets outside detective stories.
To him I apply when duty or inclination take me 'below the crust' and he
it was who acted as my 'guide, philosopher, and friend' while I was raking
the slums of Liverpool in search of 'copy'.

'If you really want to "hit the flute" (have an opium orgie),' said Corp,
as he is not called, 'get a move on.'

There are precious few vices with which the amiable Corp is unfamiliar.
His lips are stained and blistered with countless cigarettes. His forearms
are punctured all over with hypodermic needles. In one or other of his
pockets he always carries a little flat bottle of white tabloids of morphia.
All the curious drugs and illicit decoctions of heathendom have at some
time or other in his career titillated that imperturbable palate.

The flickering flame of the lamps in Park Lane, Liverpool, gave to the
muddy street the semblance of a sluggish river. In the neighbouring square
there flitted, silent and impassive, men of the East whose complexions
subtly harmonised with the prevalent gloom. Clustered round the narrow
doorways of places pretending to be shops, groups of dusky aliens, all more
or less in Western garb, stood smoking their inevitable cigarettes, and
listening while the man in his shirt sleeves – the boss, the mandarin – flung
chunks of sententious philosophy over his left shoulder at his impassive
hearers.

'You are now,' said Corp, as we swerved eastward from the tram track,
'within a hundred yards of the "joint" where one Chink plugged a nickel
bullet right into the heart of a brother Celestial over a game of cards. The
murderer was hung by the neck in Liverpool gaol, and the Chinese
community rose as one man in favour of his extinction as an undesirable
alien.'

HITTING THE 'FLUTE'

Personally, I had some doubt about our chance of 'hitting the flute' in a
locality where Orientals chiefly prevailed, but my guide knew the ropes.
Corp admitted that white men were not usual in a 'joint' but they were not

uncommon enough to provoke remark, and were guardedly welcome when they looked like prosperous persons who could pay for the pleasure of 'chandoo' in the pipe, or stand their corner at fantan, whether that alluring game be played in cards or cash. My friend had no doubts about the matter. His flirtation with the opium 'flute' was frequent enough to make the effigy who opened the door to us as friendly as a porcine grunt might indicate.

The building, three storeys high, and one of the tiniest 'joints' in all Chinatown was in absolute darkness but for the glimmer of a gas-jet in the passage. Two quick knocks on the upper panel of the door and one strong rap on the shutter brought a startlingly swift response. Through the keyhole my guide huskily whispered a word, and the door swung back, revealing no janitor to us in the impenetrable gloom which the wretched burner only served to accentuate. When we had crossed the threshold into the passage where the sprinkled sand made a crunching sound, an invisible hand closed the door and shot the bolt almost noiselessly into the slot, and the same ghostly hand heightened the light.

BURNING THE 'CHANDOO'

Going to a tube, the mouthpiece of which hung against the wall, Corp blew softly twice, and we sat down and waited a response. The door in a second or two swung noiselessly open. Everything and everybody went on the silent principle. The noisiest thing in the whole caboose was the soul-destroying smell of burning opium.

In the doorway stood an aged Chinaman – how old, heaven only knows. His flat, lack-lustre eyes were set in a face of yellow parchment, stretched to cracking point over the bones, unrounded by any visible ligament or muscle. This apparition wore a pigtail, a vestment of what looked like flannelette dyed in ochre, and a pair of felt slippers.

He carried two wooden trays with a smoking 'lay-out' for each of us – a pipe about 20 inches long with the bowl fixed about four inches from the far end, a metal dipper like a lady's hatpin, a villainous little lamp that stank atrociously, and the treacly-looking opium in a sort of cockle shell. These interesting appurtenances, or, rather, the hire of them, cost half a crown a set, in acknowledgment of which Confucious [sic] stretched the lower part section of his features until, I am sure, I heard part of his cranial mechanism snap under the strain.

He led the way to a room on the next floor, set the tray on the floor, and vanished as soundlessly as he came.

There were three persons in the room already. All three were Asiatics – one a close-cropped son of the Prophet, another a pilgrim from the

Flowery Land, and the third a coolie. The Mohammedan with the shaven head lay on a mattress in the corner, his eyes wide open, his lamp still burning; but he was far away in other realms, dreaming strange dreams and seeing celestial visions, and his lips were moving as if he held speech with creatures all unseen of us.

The other two seekers after ecstasy were on the floor, one lamp between them, twirling the treacly drug around the pin, burning the 'chandoo', or pellet, in the flame, and inhaling the vapour through the bamboo tube as if it were a breath of fragrant incense.

Corp and I pulled off our boots, arranged our cushions and mats, and fell to the task of inducing the heavenly hallucinations which are said to be the result of opium smoked in the right way. Corp was an expert at the business, and could conjure the semi-fluid drug into a neat little pellet five times while I was doing it once. He fell asleep in the space of half an hour.

A SIGHT OF STARS

The only effect which the infernal stuff had on me was to [make me] wish I was dead. I don't believe all the poppy juice extracted east or west of Suez could do more than violently upset a good Scotch stomach. At any rate, I got less spiritual exaltation than a smile from a *People's Journal* prize beauty would have produced any day of the week. I certainly did see stars, but that was just before daylight, when the man on the mattress – in an excess of spirituality, I suppose, let out a yell, and swinging his pipe through the murky air, caught me neatly on the bridge of the nose.

I sprang to my feet, struggled into my boots, and after rolling Corp over and failing to awaken him went down the three flights of stairs in a hurry, boarded a car in Lord Street – a solitary passenger – and had the happiness of hearing the guard tell the driver at the Pierhead that there was 'a young spark inside' who had been ''avin' a 'igh old time on 'is own!'

Casualties

For three weeks the working hours of the unit had been sixteen out of every twenty-four, and at length, in the centre of that sloppy and muddy field, appeared what was to be known to the Army as the Nth Casualty Clearing Station.

Tired enough from the strain of continued and unremitting road-making, tent-pitching, and the innumerable heart-breaking tasks incidental to the shifting of stoves and equipment, and the improvision of those diversely essential things which cannot be secured except by indents which take many weeks to circulate through the chain of offices, the unit disposed itself, as units do, to snatch some sleep before the first rush should begin.

None too soon, it shortly appeared, for as we stumbled to the Fall-In, headlights began to appear on the road from Albert, a long trail of ambulance cars stretching back into the rainy dampness which hid the tremendous business so casually referred to as 'The Big Push'. The turn of the first car into the little road found a quietly active camp, for hasty preparations had been carried out in just such improbable corner-grounds many times before.

Here, as always in the track of armies in the Somme region, the salient element was mud – thick, deep, insistent and clinging mud that the strongest will could not treat as negligible. There it was and it made the smallest errand an exacting fatigue. The cars manoeuvred through it with the casual air that comes of much experience. Even London taxi-drivers might have learned something from the dexterous and undelaying way in which Red Cross cars were juggled over that boggy land. One by one the cases were slid out by stretcher-bearers working deftly and surely with a sort of tired ease. Car after car rolled up – just the price of 'strengthening the line and solidifying positions in the neighbourhood of – ', as it would appear from the day's official report. Men of all units, tired, pale and dirty, were carried into the hut that a party of engineers had finished feverishly that very day. Their khaki barely showed through the encrusting mud save where it had been slit to rags to allow of temporary dressings being put on at Field Ambulances and First Aid Posts and now showing in curious patterns of white and red. Among them were some to whom this station would be something more than a wayside resting-place, men to whom the doctors up the line, working in dug-outs where immediate attention to all could not be given, had given a desperate last chance. They died on the way or slipped off without fuss in the Receiving Room, but one or two were pulled through by efforts and methods that would stagger civilian practice.

All night the slow heavy labour of stretcher-bearing went on. And great grey cars pulled up with loads of less seriously wounded who straggled brokenly into the room, muddied and shivering, hatless and coatless often, and with that complete apathy of look and bearing which tells of strain that has gone beyond endurance.

The detached onlooker might have found it moving enough, but here, fortunately, there were no detached onlookers. Lady friends, of the type we all know, were compelled to find stimulants for their sentiment somewhat farther down. But, here, a man who had been shovelling mud from the road during a back-breaking afternoon was now booking particulars of the arrivals. But some stared blankly through the interrogator, deaf and speechless, shaking and quivering, and that matter-of-fact fellow entered them as 'Shell-Shock. – No particulars available', and they were led off in that new world of theirs to a mattress, and ultimately who shall say to what strange and undesirable destiny.

The slightest cases walked or limped casually up to the keen deft-handed doctor and his alert assistants with the air of men to whom this was but one more incalculable phase of a business whose immensity made all impressions unseizable. To them, indeed, it had been overwhelming, and many of them were so youthful that one felt that the first instinct of their mothers, could they have seen them, would have been to reprove them for being out without overcoats on such a night!

The lashed rows of marquees that had been dignified by the name of 'wards' received these exhausted men on straw paillasses and blankets, and even, for serious cases, cot-beds. Casualty Clearing Stations belong not to any particular division but to an army, and therefore hither came representatives of most of the troops of any Army – Canadians, New Zealanders and South Africans, as well as famous British regiments and new raised battalions, and sick from locally quartered West Indians, Artillery, Engineers, and billeted troops. And there were men in mud-stained grey, stoical as our own, who somehow seemed mere ordinary men again and enemies no longer!

Serious cases speedily filled every available cot and an overflow lay around on stretchers. From all sides came the accustomed moaning for water and the close and heavy breathing of those past even moaning. A strapping sergeant of New Zealanders, gasping out his last unconscious moments, was the first to go. There was no more than time for a quick laying-out (with the boot which was hanging so unnaturally to one side, the foot came off too, despite bandages). His transit must have been a desperate gamble from the start – a wrapping in a rough blanket with scrawled particulars attached, and the big fellow who had travelled so far to his fate was taken on a stretcher to the marquee that served as mortuary.

Many joined him that night. With these hopeless ones there was no time even to stop to watch by the ebbing life, so many bedside fights there were where a forlorn hope still remained. Work went on without respite, changeless save for the occasional sudden appearance of officers who would leave a few hasty directions for the special treatment of cases which

had just left their hands in the operation theatre. Those worst hours before
the dawn passed in hectic attendance – the tiredness of the body had
perforce to be treated merely as a clogging dream – and the day-staff came
to the relief of worn-out men.

The peaceful dawn-wind smote the workers as they stooped to pass
through the low canvas doorways and the first faint flush of red showed
behind a tree on a far ridge.

Up to that ridge wandered the indescribable waste of the countryside,
trenched and pitted and ploughed until it had become a fantastic and
nightmarish wilderness. On this dreary tract nothing remained of the gifts
once showered by nature. But the grim legacies of man at war were
countless – chaotic and half-buried heaps of his machinery, munitions and
equipment, and the remains of his hasty meals. And he himself lay there,
shattered in thousands, to give a lurking horror to a treacherous and violent
surface of mud and slime and unlovely litter. The very weeds which might
have graced the desolation refused such holding-ground.

Pale now beside the compelling splendour of the reddening day showed
the yellow stabs of our guns, flashes that had lit the sky in the night watches,
and only the long road, never varying, told that the unspeakable harvest on
the Somme was still being gathered in.

Nisbet, an Interlude in Post War Glasgow

(Scene – A Street Corner.)

Duthie: Hullo! Fancy running into you of all people and here of all places!
  *(Draws back a little, still holding Nisbet's hand, but speaking as if to
  himself.)* What made me add that now? I run up against thousands of
  all sorts of people every day in life. Why should I feel it funny to run up
  against you, and why should I feel it particularly curious to find you in
  Glasgow? It's a tribute to your personality in some way…

Nisbet: But one it is difficult to know how to take.

Duthie: No more difficult than to imagine what prompted me to make it.
  I've no reason for such a feeling. But that's how one does form personal
  opinions, isn't it? No rhyme or reason. Yet these things strike deeper –
  right to the roots, I believe. What breeds likes and dislikes? Inexplicable.
  The mystery of Life. That you and I should know each other at all in
  such a world is incredible, even more incredible than if we didn't. (And
  yet I don't know. It is such an extraordinary thing to meet people one

doesn't know, never will know, is constitutionally incapable of knowing, and it happens a thousand times a day. Appalling!) But what are you doing? Where do you live? How long are you to be in Glasgow?

Nisbet: One at time – one at a time! I live in Glasgow – been here for six months.

Duthie: Stupendous! You don't say so.

Nisbet: Why?

Duthie: Oh, go on! We'll take it for granted. I feel you shouldn't be here, that's all, in fact that you're not here except physically.

Nisbet: Now, you strike me as part and parcel of the place. It's people like you that are Glasgow. But for you and such as you it would be simply any old city in Scotland, or a rubble slide. Except when I analyse what you're saying I feel that I am speaking not to you in particular but to almost any Glaswegian. You look composite. And yet your conversation is all wrong. The tone or rather the tune is perfect, but the sense is utterly out of keeping. You speak Glasgow, but seem to think – Chinese. You've already said things that I am perfectly certain only a small minority of Glasgow folks could ever either think or say.

Duthie: But you've no grounds for that conviction. You've only talked with the smallest fraction of Glasgow folks. No matter how stupid a chap looks – and probably is – you can never tell what he'll get mixed up with in the course of talk. A crowd's a curious thing – impossible to form any opinions but false ones about. Nothing easier than to say, 'What a lot of sheep.' But are they? If you could only hear what they are saying individually Babel isn't in it. The miracle of pentecost is repeated on an ever increasing scale every second. Their topics are a hundred times more numerous than themselves and far more interesting…

Nisbet: Diversity of topic is nothing. The most impecunious minds generally have enough conversational small change to make some sort of rattle. Only corpses are absolutely stoney broke. What I mean is that your turn of talk is unusual. You look so typical to me that I am all the more struck by the peculiar run of your ideas.

Duthie: Hasn't every man's mind a move of its own in this super chess?

Nisbet: No! Within certain limits I am sure that 99 per cent of Glasgow people think in the same way – no matter how the things they think about, or think they think about, or at any rate talk about, vary. You belong to the odd 1 per cent. You select your subjects and not only your sentiments about them. Everybody says things – you are one of the few who…

Duthie: You've nothing to go upon. You're like a snake. You haven't a leg to stand upon.

Nisbet: Haven't I? I feel different. You say I strike you as different. I am different. I can't talk to the majority of Glasgow people at all – except in the way that a ventriloquist talks to his dolls. But I can talk to you. I haven't found any other Glasgow person I could talk as much to as I have talked to you already. So you must be different too.

Duthie: What does it matter? I do belong to Glasgow in any case.

Nisbet: The devil belonged to Heaven.

Duthie: I shall stay in Glasgow. I'll be the last person to rebel against the Lord Provost. Believe me or not, I am the roundest of pegs in the roundest of holes – but what are you doing here anyway?

Nisbet: Nothing.

Duthie: How long are you going to stay here?

Nisbet: I don't know.

Duthie: Where do you live?

Nisbet: Partick.

Duthie: Good God. Married?

Nisbet: No.

Duthie: You look pretty fit – now.

Nisbet: I am.

Duthie: Then what the devil's the matter with you. You're a fish out of water. A blind man could see that if he heard your feet. Don't people turn round in the streets to look at you?

Nisbet: I don't know and don't care.

Duthie: Hmm.

Nisbet: How long have *you* lived here?

Duthie: All my life bar the Army.

Nisbet: You look pretty fit.

Duthie: I am.

Nisbet: Then what's the matter? You look like an outside without any inside – as if you'd lost your personality.

Duthie: Probably I have. Did I ever have one? Does it matter?

Nisbet: In my opinion it is one of the few things that do matter – for ordinary individuals.

Duthie: That's it. That's why you look so disturbingly odd. You're still a mere individual.

Nisbet: While you've lost your soul and gained the whole of Glasgow.

Duthie: A bargain. I was never proud of my little peculiarities.

Nisbet: You're a Socialist?

Duthie: Of course! Aren't you?

Nisbet: I suppose not. We couldn't both be, could we – or it wouldn't mean anything, would it?

Duthie: That's why you look so desperate. Glasgow is enough to turn anybody but a Socialist into a gibbering lunatic. But Socialists are at home here; you see it takes places like Glasgow to make them. 'Socialism is not an antithesis to, but the crowning stage of, the one-sided bourgeois civilisation.' (*Aside* – It's no use trying to make a good collectivist of a fellow like this – like sending Christ to the YMCA.)

(*Silence for a little.*)

Duthie: You used to write? (*Nisbet nods.*) Poetry wasn't it? Ever do any now?

Nisbet: No. I keep trying – it's no go. Brainlock.

Duthie: Bad business! I do yards. Verse too. In the Ham and Meat Column. (*Fails to create any impression: and adds a little defiantly*) They pay jolly well too.

Nisbet: (*Ironically*) Do they?

Duthie: You despise money? (*As if he had solved the secret.*) Excuse me for saying that you're in a critical condition. If I were you I'd toddle right off home and do a love story the *People's Friend* could accept – or die in the attempt. You might as well die that way as any other. You've just a bare chance. If you don't try for it you'll burst. You're bottled up. A set of verses in the Column…at 7/6…is better than a score of epics in the head. You haven't even written your war book, I suppose? That's fatal. Like internal bleeding. The only cure for modern war experiences is to write a book about them. An inexpressible emotion must be Hell… who's a b— fool?

Nisbet: I said it to show you that my case isn't quite so hopeless as you make out. I can express myself all right – but what I am concerned to say isn't printable, that's all – and what I feel I'll be compelled to try to express soon won't even be intelligible – to the sort of people you resemble.

Duthie: Hmm! I never try to say anything that could possibly give me dental hernia… Oh! Here's Young! We'll ask him. He'll know – if he's sober. (*Grabs him.*) …This is Nisbet, Young. (*Aside:* It's like saying Jesus… Judas.) Nisbet and I were together in France. He was gassed. (*In a whisper:* Body and soul.) But he's not like me. You're not a Territorial, are you?

Nisbet: No.

Duthie: Would you join up if there was another war?

Nisbet: I'd see the King… (*The clatter of a passing motor van makes the remainder of the remark inaudible.*)

Duthie: (Sarcastically) Spoken like a comrade. Young, thank me. You get him on the rebound. And he's a virgin – doesn't know the difference between Blatchford and Lenin. Doesn't want to.

Young: Shut up. You're not a human being. You're a mere sorting house for mixed motives. That letter of yours in the *Herald* yesterday on the necessity for caution and method in the disbursement of doles was the work of a mental degenerate.

Organised charity, measured and iced.

In the name of a cautious, statistical Christ.

(Duthie laughs unconvincingly. Young turns to Nisbet.) You mean it? *(Nisbet looks puzzled.)* What you said.

Nisbet: Absolutely. I am constitutionally incapable of rendering any more to Caesar. Nothing is his and that's all he'll get from me.

Young: Constitutional inabilities of that kind constitute dungeons in the present state of society.

Nisbet: I know.

Young: Do you like it?

Nisbet: No.

Young: What are they giving you?

Duthie: Solitary confinement – the straight waistcoat.

Young: Why?

Duthie: He's utterly intractable.

Young: Where does he live?

Duthie: Partick, poor blighter.

Young: What does he do?

Duthie: Nothing.

Young: How long has he been doing it?

Duthie: Ever since he was demobbed.

Young: Choice or necessity?

Duthie: Choice, in a way… But he's quite unfit for civilised life.

Young: What is he to trade?

Duthie: A poet – but he complains that modern Scottish acoustics are so bad that it isn't worth while trying to make himself heard. He's trying to invent a new insubmersible sort of song… But tell him all about your sad case, yourself!

Nisbet: Verhaeren visited Glasgow. He didn't say anything about it.

Duthie: Its modesty's at the root of his disease.

Nisbet: It's all so hopeless.

Young: What?

Nisbet: This. *(With an all-embracing gesture.)*

Duthie: He means that he can't tuck it all away neatly into a sonnet, like I can. It's the old problem – what happens when an irresistible force comes up against an immovable object? He hasn't found the answer yet. All that he knows is that if he's the irresistible force he's getting the worst of it – but he isn't quite sure any longer that he is... He'd have been all right if he'd stayed in Nazareth or Auchtermuchty or whatever his native village was. But he would come to Jerusalem – and he'll be crucified on Gilmorehill.

(They watch a dog-fight which commences near-by and develops into a battle-royal between a drunk Irishman and a pregnant woman. Police come up, and drag the struggling, cursing combatants away.)

Nisbet: How can a fellow see that sort even once – all that despair of humanity – and then go home and write verses?

Duthie: And yet you would if you could. What's wrong with you is that you can't.

Nisbet: (With savage inconsequence) I agree with MacGill – Glasgow's a RAT pit.

Duthie: (Indulgently) Tuts! Adam and Eve would feel perfectly at home in Rouken Glen.

Nisbet: (Doggedly) Sodom and Gomorrah weren't a patch on this. Sin isn't even original here: it's mechanical.

Duthie: (With an effect of triumph) Harry Lauder's here next week.

Nisbet: (Blankly) Who's he?

Duthie: Eh – oh – um – quite! *(Obviously staggered: one to Nisbet, who knows it, and preens his brain tantalisingly: but recovers adroitly and proceeds with increasing rapidity.)* Our High Priest – eat-drink-and-be-merry-for-tomorrow-is-another-pig-by-the-ear-old prophet. Laugh and the world laughs with you; weep and you wet your hanky sort of thing, don't you know.

> I have covered up with laughter
> More than you have drowned in tears.
> Let Glasgow flourish...but there's no fear.

Nisbet: (Brutally) There doesn't seem to be. What's the emblem – a what-d'you-call-it rampant?

Duthie: Tut, tut! There's quite as many decent married women in Glasgow as... the thingummyjigs you say... despite the police. *(Laughs solicitously.)*

Nisbet: (Taking no notice of the invitation, and reverting to mock-sententiousness.) Glasgow, like every other city, is a cannibal that feeds on its own children.

Duthie: You quarrel with the nature of existence – and you've precious little room to speak. You're eaten up with your own thoughts.

Nisbet: Ever been to Clydebank?

Duthie: I've passed through it several times – on the way to Baloch.

Nisbet: You know the song 'John Brown's body'?

Duthie: (Enthusiastically) Yes, and 'Wash me in the Water' and 'One Grasshopper Leaps' and...

Nisbet: (Austerely) It's Clydebank's soul that lies mouldering in the grave while John Brown's body goes marching on. He never had a soul.

Duthie: (Pityingly) But Clydebank isn't in Glasgow.

Nisbet: (Not quite over-emphatically enough) No! It's in Hell.

Duthie: (Severely) Look here! This has gone far enough. I'm a member of the University Fabian Society and the Scottish Home Rule Association and half-a-dozen other things...keep me busy...Satan still... *(Turning to Young, who has been standing in patient puzzlement)* but they'd suit him about as well as an eldership in St Columba's would suit Jesus. You can see what he needs just as well as I can. Take him away to your lair... *(Reverting to Nisbet)* Young's Propaganda Secretary of the Glasgow Branch of the Communist Party of Scotland! You know – bloody revolution, hacking a way through, dictatorship of the proletariat, deeds not words, propaganda of action, all that sort of thing. No pink politics for pale people about him. He's the man for you. There's no satisfaction for your type except in active political propaganda... Out of the mouths of miners and dock labourers...

Nisbet: I'm not interested in politics.

Duthie: Oh, yes, you are! But you don't know it. You soon will... It's the only way. I'm a mere conventional worm, quite pleased to become another Neil Munro or Wee MacGregor. But it's different with you. That's why you look so – so inappropriate, here. It's an axiom that our agitators are always foreigners, Jews and so forth – like Shinwell and Christ. We crucify them all if they give us half a chance – even when the only thing foreign about them is that they agitate, or the only thing agitating is that they are foreign. Don't disappoint us. Go and become the prophet you are. There's nothing more foreign in Glasgow today than a real Scotsman. Young will betray you at the psychological moment. He has had sufficient experience now as a labour leader to know that the only way to give the People the bread that doesn't exist is to give them circuses. That's his job – to make dummy-bombs and get fools who think they are real to hurl them at us; and we treat them as if they had been. It's a great game. – Yes. Dummy-tits and dummy-bombs.

Young: (Impatiently, to Nisbet) What's *your idea*?

Duthie: (Triumphantly) There you are! What did I tell you? *(Admiringly)* You're the chap to size them up, Young... 'Strordinary! *(To Nisbet)* He notices right away that you're an embodied idea. People like me have only opinions and he has no use for us, but to you it's 'What's your idea?' He's looking for a Man – a Messiah. 'I am not he, though few feel the curse as I do.' He stands before you like a sculptor before a mass of marble, and he'll chisel out the figure that's hidden in you with his questions. He's a maker of men, is Young. Don't be frightened when he begins to chip you up. He knows his job – although he made a botch of me. Puzzled you ever since, hasn't it, Young? – My veining's all wrong. Every now and then he thinks he sees just how to give me the finishing touch and makes a dive at it, but his chisel slithers, and I am transformed into something quite different from what he intended. I am continually being born again, but – I always distress my proud parent by turning out an illegitimate child, don't I, Daddy?

Young: (Fiercely) For the love of Mike, shut it!

Nisbet: (Solidly) Our literature is bankrupt!

Duthie: (Sotto voce) Not quite sepulchral enough.

Young: (Indifferently) Indeed.

Nisbet: (Passionately) But yes, I say! There's no arguing about it. All forms of literary and artistic expressions, equally with other phenomena of intellectual and spiritual activity, have reached in our Western civilisation the point beyond which they can go no further. Western Europe, with America, has exhausted her energies, as Greece, Rome, Assyria, Babylon...

Duthie: (Anxiously) Don't forget Peru!

Young: (In a bewildered but hopeful way) Leave him alone. He's finding his voice.

Nisbet: ...exhausted their energies before her. She can add nothing more to the sum of vitally new human knowledge, of fresh and adequate channels of self-expression. We must wait...

Duthie: (Sadly) ... for the inevitable end?

Nisbet: (Austerely) Or rather the new beginning which will come from a civilisation other than ours.

Duthie: Rats! There isn't any.

Young: (With immense relief) I don't know a great deal about literature and art; but I believe you're right and that if you care to go into the matter you will find that the renewal is coming, has begun to come, from

Russia. I have been told – by Moira, I think – that in Dostoevsky, if that is the correct pronunciation…

Duthie: An open sesame to the great inane!

Young: … is to be found the first delineation of that new world.

Duthie: That's just the sort of thing Moira *would* throw out in passing. A wonderful lassie! Chokeful of world-intuitions of the most concise and comprehensive kind. It's ages since I saw her. How is she?

Young: Full of Sinn Fein!

Duthie: Go on!

Young: Fact! No balance. Brain's like quicksilver.

Duthie: Thinks a rebellion in Ireland is worth two revolutions in the bush?

Young: Can't see beyond her nose!

Duthie: I shouldn't want to myself if I'd half such a pretty one. I'd spend all my time crinkling it and counting my freckles. Hot stuff Moira!

Young: Not a bit. Mere red paint!

Duthie: She hasn't set fire to you, eh? You Marxians are made of asbestos.

Young: Bah! The Celtic fire is only pyrotechnics. Moira looks the real thing – but her politics are crackling tinsel. She's a flash in the pan – a myth in motion.

Duthie: The poetry of motion! *(To Nisbet)* You must meet Moira. She's the Dark Rosaleen in the flesh. Young cast her for one of his Red Virgins, but he's just discovered that he's colour-blind… She's some bird: but no Phoenix. Too downy, eh Young? You've discovered that she's not only a force but a female… How about Ireland, Nisbet? There's an opening for you there perhaps.

Nisbet: My soul is no shillelagh. Deirdre was Mrs Grundy's maiden name.

Duthie: (Impatiently) Sigma all that, but you haven't seen Moira… You're not built on Young's foundations. Utopia may withstand her, but Moira's the trumpet for the Jerichos. I think you'll turn out a mere Jericho after all!… Perhaps not! Pearse and Plunkett and MacDonagh were only minor poets – only a half-size bigger than me. 'I see his blood upon the rose' sort of thing – 'winds trampling and militant upon the hill'…

Young: Come on then! *(With deliberate asininity)* All men are sinners, but it's better to be a Sinfeiner than a cynic. *(Pretends to laugh at what he pretends to regard as his delightful wit.)*

Duthie: By-by, Nisbet! I look upon you as two of the ten just men of Glasgow…full of the saving grace of tragedy; Young'll straw the deserts of your impotence with the guano of Bolshevism till they bloom with beauty and bloodshed and bunkum. There's no hope for a man who isn't full of despair….Remember me, poor thief of *vers-de-société*….But what can you expect of a *nouveau pauvre*? *(Exit Nisbet and Young.)* Poor souls! It's easy enough to say that little else is worth studying than the development of a soul: but the trouble is to tell just whether it's a soul or not that you're looking at, and then to discover what constitutes development, and so whether there's any to study or not. *(Looking round dissatisfiedly)* How can one be sure of anything in this light?

The best of what we do and are

Just God, forgive!

They go one way and I go another, but we're all going the same way – further and further away from home! *(Exit.)*

Following Rebecca West in Edinburgh: A Monologue in the Vernacular

Whatna fearfu' image is that like a corpse out o' a tomb, that's makin' a' this rippet for the cheatrie instruments o' pen an' ink?

'Yech! *(contemptuously)* A cockalan!....She's made a silk purse oot o' a sow's lug, an' *(with an effort towards gaiety)* I dinna haud wi' vivisection – the sow's alive. Forbye, – there's nae ca' for sic baffles. It's what they lads at the Mound ca' "luxury production" an' a' art worth the name maun be "production for use".'

It was a brave effort; but his attempt to carry it off lightly was pathetic. I had set him off, and we both knew it. He could not help himself. He had Edinburgh on the brain – pondering and re-pondering its great black problem for ever. I could see the passion crowding into his face. Perhaps it was cruelty on my part. He looked at me as though to say 'I ken weel eneuch what yer ettlin' efter – dinna! – Ech ye deevil!' For the thing was done and could not be undone. I had no more to do – no need to force the pace – he was silent awhile. I looked anywhere but at him. I knew the struggle that was going on – but he was never the man to say the first thing that jumped into his head. At last he rose, quietly enough, yet most dramatically, crossed over to the window, pulled the curtains aside, and shot up the lower half. A rough, black lump of Edinburgh was visible, hairy with light.

'Look!

"Thou scowry hippit, ugly averil,

Wi' hurkland banes aye howkand throu' thy hide!"'

I had to admit the grisly exactness of the description. He shut down the window again and came and sat opposite me, leaning towards me as if about to give a confidence – as he was.

'She's an allagrugous auld city in this allerish licht!... I'm no blamin' Miss West – but ye canna play Beethoven on an Almanie whistle! It tak's an almark like Joyce* tae write aboot Edinburgh. The lassie never gets amidward. She canna be fashed wi' a' its amplefeysts – she hesna' got the necessary *animosity*. Mebbe Edinburgh

> "Wes in his yhowthyede
> A fayre, sweet, pleasant childe,
> At all point formyd in fassoun,
> Abil, of gude condityione."

But ye canna analite it tae Arcady noo….Na! Na! It's black abies that, an' crookit an' croodit. (*He was obviously thinking of sundry pretty little descriptions of Edinburgh in* The Judge.) This michty coutribat o' stanes an' souls!...Mony's the ablachs glowrin'...An' ankerly auld toon, spyrin' a' airts, filed wi' the bachrams o' the ages, wi' its cranglin' streets whastlin' like stirks i' the backdraught, an' its mochy startle-o'-stobie o' life an' death, its chowkin' guff o' humanity. Look at the ca' o' the stanes, man! Shoggin' frae the flair o' the sea tae the crap o' the earth?....It's a' assopat aneath her style. Corbaudie ne'er comes in at a'. Her wark's clean-fung eneuch in a way, but she's far owre clocksie, wi' her tongue gae'n like the clatter-bane o' a goose's hass! Edinburgh's black wi' fleas that there's nae clapper-clawin'….Man! It's a fearfu' thing for a bit lassock like yon tae wee an' wale a toon like Edinburgh, makin't *incidental* tae a gowpenfu' o' bodiless bodies – a toon that has *poodered* its hundreds o' thoosands o' leevin' souls….A' her bleeze an' busk o' words, as if she was bagenin' wi' the Almichty. It's a disease, is Edinburgh. An' *(his queer wild humour breaking out again – laughingly!)* the kind o' the disease, if ye'll observe, is an attrie bile strikin' oot i' mony heids an' plukes. (*Waving his hand towards the window.*) An attrie face a' boundened up wi' wrath!...'

He was purposely using many obsolete words, partly to despite me for forcing him to talk of Edinburgh, and partly because they acted as a brake on his utterance. In any case, he was deliberately inconsequent, allusive, and obscure. As keen students of the Vernacular will appreciate, he was making scores of little experiments in Doric composition and style even as he spoke – subtle adaptations of ancient figures of speech to modern requirements, finding vernacular equivalents for Freudian terminology –

---

* James Joyce's *Ulysses*, published in France by Sylvia Beach.]

all infinitely difficult work but infinitely necessary if the Doric is again to become a living literary medium. His perfect knowledge of Ross's 'Helenore', Duff's Poems, the Maitland Poems, Douglas's Vergil, and the like, stood him in splendid stead; and the dexterity with which he drew upon them delighted me immensely. If any Doric enthusiasts think this is easy enough let them try to translate a paragraph or two treating of introverts, extroverts, complexes and specific aboulias into 'gude braid Scots' – and if they do not think this necessary, let them cease to talk of reviving the Doric. Such a revival depends upon the Doric being brought abreast of modern civilisation in every respect and detail. There is no other way....He was silent again for a little; then broke out, speaking somewhat more rapidly, as if excited by his notion.

'Edinburgh Castle is Scotland's Abbote Unreassone.

"Abbotis by rewll, and lordis but ressone
Sic senyeoris tymis ourweill this sessone
Vpoun thair vyce war lang to walk
Quhais falsatt, fibilnes, and tressone
Has rung thryris oure this Zodiak!"

Look at it again!'

He flung up the window again; and standing in the corner we could see the Castle over the chimney cans.

'See!....A' the wild contours an' cullages an' a' the orra outlines o' the stormy geometry o' Scotland, flockin' thegither, chuse them a graund Captaine o' Mischief....an' him they croun an' adopt for their King....The King, anointed, *(and just then a ray of the sun escaping from the clouds put a greasy gold upon the Castle)* chooseth forth a hunder steeples an' chimley-stacks an' muckle roofs to wait upon his lordly majesty. Every one of these he investeth wi' his liveries o' greene, yellow or some ither licht wanton colour, an' as tho' they werena' gaudy eneuch, they bedeck themsels wi' plumes o' reek an' sparklin' fanlichts an' chackit tiles. This dune, they tie aboot the air a mony bells, wi' electric signs an' winkin' bulbs, an' muckle standards wi' bleezin' taps; an' tangle the haill closeevie wi' upper an' nether nets o' polisht wire. Thus a' things set in order then hev they their hobby-horses, their dragons, an' ither antics...to strike the devil's daunce wi' a'.'

I have no notion what old description of the Liberty of December he was adapting to his purpose; but look over Edinburgh from the window of an upper room at certain times, and you will see the amazing relevance of it all.

'This heathen company, their pypers pyping, their drummers

thundering, their bells jingling, their handkerchiefs fluttering aboot their heids like madde men, their hobbie horses an' ither monsters skirmishing amongst the crood…dancin' and singin' wi' sic a confused noise that nae man can hear his ain voice, an' thus these terrestrial furies spend the day. *(Down below in the street a newsboy was crying 'Special Edition'. I saw the light of his reckless humour spring into his eyes again, but he continued without a change in his voice.)* Then they have certaine papers wherein is painted some babelerie or other of imagerie worke. These they give to everyone that will give them money to maintain them in this their heathenish devilrie; an' who will not show himself buxome to them and give them money, they shall be mocked and flouted shamefully….'

This came so extraordinarily pat that we burst out laughing together.

'*Larvatis faciebus,* they incense wi' stinkin' reek frae the leather o' auld shoon…an' "*in choro cantilenas inhonestas cantabat!*"'

The strain of a music hall ditty floating up made him add that last parallel. Then he became very grave all at once, consumed as it were with the tragedy of it all.

'I dinna blame the lassie. Let her scuttle aff intae the appen furth. This aidle-hole's nae place for the likes o' her. It'll tak a *man* tae write aboot Edinburgh, as it sud be written aboot, an' he'll need the Doric tae get the fu' aifer. Wemmen are a' verra weel i' their way…but Edinburgh'll tak an almark like Joyce – a scaffie like Joyce. There's aye explosions i' a' thae hooses that ye canna acoont for but by the clyres o civilisation. It's nae wunner sic clowders o' suppression are aye bealin' an' brakkin' oot. There's far ower muckle *chapling.* It needs a Joyce tae prick ilka pluke, tae miss nowt…aye even tae

"The Kinkhost, the Charbuckle, an' worms i' the chiecks!"

A wheen o' us…no' the feck mebbe…hevna' ony richt at a' tae lat oorsels be brubbed, tae hide frae the truth because it's laithsome.'

I nodded to show that I understood. *Ulysses* is not staple fare – but it has made cleanliness and beauty more precious to us hasn't it? The dismally dirty and giggling sexual novels will continue to roll out under a thin pretence of psychological treatment. But Joyce!…Somehow that stupendous uprising of the *vis comica* in his work seemed to be reflected, as I looked in the 'breengin'' masonry of the grey Metropolis.

'The verra last thing Scottish literature needs is *lady-fying.* Gillespie's an idiot!* It needs an almark like Joyce…I'm no' cock-bird-high yet. I'm like a Lilliputian courtin' a Brobdingnagian Queen. Ae glisk o'r

---

* See Martin Gillespie's review of *The Judge* in the September *Chapbook.*

emasculates me. A mannikin's nae use tae the likes o' yon – a buist o' a wumman! But I'd glammoch her if I'd Joyce's virr….Look at her!

> "If she could get hersel' but carl'd
> In time o' need…."

(Changing his metaphors carelessly.) See her carvortin' in a licht like this, like yin o' the Fower Horses riderless!

> "Whene'er her tail plays whisk
> Or when her look grows skeigh,
> It's then the wice auld man
> Is blythe to stand abeigh."

But I'm nae wice auld man. God forbid! Scottish literature's had far ower mony o' *them*. I'm nae aulder than Edinburgh at ony rate an' juist as young an' allryn – if I was only a wee thingie bigger….*(Waving his hand castle-wards.)* The Apocalyptic Beast wi' her black hoofs o' a Castle pawin' i' the air an' yon shaggy mane o' cloods hodin' the starnies like nits.

> "Auld Reekie cavie't back an' fore
> An' flapt her sooty wings."

Puir Rosenberg's poem is juist how I feel when I look at this camsteerie toon –

> "No slim form work fire to my thighs
> But human life's inarticulate mass
> Throb the pulse of a thing
> Whose mountain flanks awry
> Beg my mastery, – mine!
> Ah! I will ride the dizzy beast of the world
> My road – my way!"

….I'm by wi' clotchy novels. They're a delusion and a snare. Their effects have nae lastin' i' them. Lichtly come, lichtly gane. If fiction's the modern reader's University it's a schule whaur he learns owt an' minds nowt – a literary blin' alley….Look at yon curn o' camla-like tenements! A cary-tempered cratur's nae use. Yon mannie Synge was richt: 'It may almost be said that before verse can be human again it must learn to be brutal.'….The like's true o' a' forms o' literature. Novels are juist bletherin' bagrels. Joyce has chammered them a' for the likes o' us…Ech! It needs an almark like him tae claut a city like this. Na! na! I'd leifer be cuckold than capstridden but…this *aigre*?…*(with intense anguish)* I canna dae't. I canna begin tae dae't…I dinna blame the lassie…but *(with the bitterest smile of self-contempt)*

> "Oh had I but ten thousand at my back
> And were a man I'd gar their curpons crack.'"

In the Fulness of Time

'She had the foul disease of animal existence in its most enfevered and terrible form, complicated to an unthinkable degree by that quality which men, baffled by their blood, miscall beauty,' he said quietly, and then, with a note of exultation, almost of gloating, added, 'I do not remember a more radical cure. Peace to her bones!'

As he spoke a dark ray seemed to accentuate 'the strange superfluous glory' of the autumn air. Looking up at him, momentarily silent, I remembered these lines:

> Then did Ormuzd stand
> Silent, the monstrous silence of the sky
> Dwarfed by his own. Fathomless was his eye,
> His face the cloister of his thoughts, his head
> A still lone summit.

I recognized that our acquaintanceship was for me an Alpine adventure.

'She is driven hither and thither no longer – her real nature obscured – by the lusts of the flesh with its shivers and heats,' he continued. 'She has entered into the antique order of the tongueless dead. She is set in silence, a prey no more to the sickening pulsations of life. Her incredible courses have at last exhausted themselves, and she has come to the peace that passeth understanding. You remember what the Amida-Kyr says? "All who enter into that country enter likewise into that state of virtue from which there can be no turning back."

> Flesh fade and mortal trash
> Fall to the residuary worm; worlds wildfire leave but ash,
> In a flash...
> This jack, joke, poor potsherd, patch, matchwood,
>   immortal diamond
> Is immortal diamond.

' – I am afraid I do not make myself quite clear.' As he looked at me it was as if a great bird had swooped down from the height of the heavens and sliced my sight with the points of its pinions.

'If cleanliness is next to godliness,' he proceeded, 'how high now is her estate? Her bones are free of the toils and torments and embroilments of the flesh. The cannibal clay has picked them clean as starlight on a night of frost. A miraculous reduction to ultimate reality! They have thrown off for ever and a day with one swift white gesture the restless tyrannical burdens which battened so unendurably upon them – the insatiate flesh that lives upon itself and the flesh of others, shapeless and impotent but for these! – shifting and straining upon them, from birth to death, this way and that, now surging to incontinent heights, now sagging in the troughs of delusory deliverances – and have sprung out, for the first time, into their free and natural shapes, white, inveterate, turned on the lathe of Eternity, unsearchable, compact with silence. What artistry has wrought such sculpture from such chaos, with this finality of form, this economy of means, this undeluded surety of touch? Think of the antiseptic vision, the unnerving eye for essentials, the ruthless mastery – the consummate finish! No mawkish sentiment here, no pandering! He has probed his subject and come to unanswerable conclusions, profound, exclusive, universal! No straining here after originality, no needless elaboration of the theme, no moralizing! His work has the impersonality of all great art. It lies before us, stark, simple, pitiless, unpalliated. A bone taken away – a missing rib – and you would have realism; a bracelet loose on the wristbones or a pendant garish on the sternum, and you would have sentiment; as it is you have reality. As a study in the elimination of unessentials it is incomparably successful, an inexorable victory, accentuated by the one wild flourish of her living hair, a virgined and vehement art voiding without compunction all that most men praise as beauty, fulness and fertility! Cold, controlled, complete, bladed and pointed with cardinal justice, it is the final tribute of time to eternity, the loneliest masterpiece of human art....Who that knew her unstable, bright, voluptuous life could have dreamt that it lay in her to sign her forced renunciation with a signature such as this in the page of fate, decisive, neat, unalterable? She had such a volatile, enticing and exciting concupiscence that even I bad difficulty, looking upon the living woman, in determining her morphic values. She always brought to my mind Meredith's:

> Ravishing as red wine in woman's form,
> A splendid maenad, she of the delirious laugh,
> Her body twisted flames with the smoke-cap crowned
> … who sang, who sang,
> And drew into her her swarm
> Revolved them hair, voice, feet, in her carmagnole!

But now – this! hard, intrinsic, whittled down to the last essentiality and directness, cruel yet so unswervingly sure in its concentration, so distinct in its surety! Who would rather have diffuse heats, blind hot livingness, than this keen hard separateness? Does it not make you aware of another freer element in which each fate is detached and isolated? Here is no confusion. Is not this our natural element? Who does not envy such a faculty of sharp incontrovertible response to all the lapping, suffusing, swamping, endless conspiracies of life?... Complexity has laboured and brought forth the most signal of all the simplicities. The last gaunt midwife has delivered this travailing creature of the final issue of her ravelled womb – this naked and incorruptible offspring, building in ivory, the heir of Time!

> Wanderers eastward, wanderers west
> Know you why you cannot rest?
> 'Tis that every mother's son
> Travails with a skeleton.

'Whenever I think of a section of flesh, I remember that indispensable phrase "bizarre, compliqué, nombreaux et chinois". Ah, that flesh of hers, blazing and blurring, full of malady and murmuration! Perhaps you do not understand. Did it never strike you as horrible, as intolerable, that these slim, shapely bones, so calm and clear and capital, that these immaculate blades, these cups and balls of polished ivory, should be so grossly overlaid, beslimed, befouled, and bloodied, by the abominations of the body – hemmed in so noisomely by masses of clogging corruptible flesh, rank with blood, raging with carnal lusts, hideous with livid rioting muscles (lightnings in the oppressive thunderous atmosphere of animal being) instinct with incipient death – tugged this way and that under the incessant drumming of the pulses – obscenely put upon? Do we not know it all – "the brute betrayal, the dead load, the cry of worlds, the laughter of the pit?... "

'All the vain violence is over. No trace remains of the stenchful ichor of her lustful life. No memory of passion confuses or corrupts these incontestable symbols of purity. Only the clean cold light of death streams straitly through her liberated, bare, and unvibrating bones, ranking in silence here, radiate in finality, cradling the invisible, unpulsating heart of eternity, "the general gender", the organs of oblivion, the largest rhythm, the inviolable spirit... dominant upon her little satiate teeth...proclaiming in sheer white accents on the glittering edges and in the opalescent hollows of her pelvis (emptied of that little hot incontinent belly we knew) – set, as it were, like the ivory wings of an immortal bird immobilized on the very bit of passion! – that out of corruption cometh forth incorruption.'

His voice fell. 'The awful devices of her breasts are shredded away. Level and starless lie the bones of her passioning thighs. The fingers caressing are fingers of naked bone. The slant green eyes conjure no longer. The red enchantments of her lips and quick, exciting tongue are flames that have faded and fled. The smile is the smile of fleshlessness and the places of her eyes are darknesses and voids... Only her hair streams still like seaweed over the alabaster shell of her head, decorating her cervical

vertebrae with the remnants of ravishment, the impotent lustre of this last
sexual symbol life's ghastly tribute to the stern omnipotence of death...
    'And it is well with her now as it was in the days ere she was born.

> So let this fire of sense decay,
> This smoke of thought blow clean away,
> And leave with ancient night alone,
> The steadfast and enduring bone.'

He fell to silence, pulling upon his pipe, and was lost in clouds of smoke;
and, lonely upon this withdrawal, meditating eyried as it were in inhuman
resignation, I recollected another passage of verse:

> Were you to see
> The graves gape wide asunder
> Cracking with noise of thunder
> The marble monuments and thenceforth rise
> Strange things with cavernous emptiness for eyes
> And wormy horrors in a ropy mesh
> Where there should be round limbs and veined flesh
> Your brain would reel and spin –
> Turn you your eyes within
> On us – even such, even such as these are we.

Some Day

*Scene: A winter afternoon. An ordinary Scots lower middle-class kitchen.
Round the fire are John Macfarlane, a rugged middle-aged man whose
natural bluffness is overclouded by a mixture of awe, bewilderment and
humility: his elder daughter Polly, thin-lipped, severe-looking, in the
thirties: his younger daughter Jeannie, a fine lively girl in her late teens,
obviously excited. Both are intent on their father's cautious, hesitant
narrative: but while Jeannie is obviously all agog, Polly affects a sort of
disdainful impatience, and knits away as if to say 'Talking's all right – and
I suppose the thing's got to be discussed – but one can talk and work. But
in this house I've got to do anything that's done. Jean never puts her hand
to a mortal thing: and Father's too soft to notice how idle she is. If Mother
had been alive...'*

Macfarlane: Mony's the funeral o' man an' wumman an' bairn I've seen at
    Sleepyhillock i' the past forty or fifty years. There's a gey population

there noo. A' kinds – auld an' young – deein' in a' kind o' ways. Maist o'
them i' the ordinary coorse o' natur' – an' yet ye'd wunner…accidents,
suicides, aye, an' even murders. Twa at ony rate. Na, three – i' my time.
An' that's no mentionin' auld Mrs Peters, puir body. But the richts or
wrangs o' that were nivur fun oot – or made public. Some thocht ae
thing, an' some anither…But a' through I've seen nocht tae approach
the day's ongangans, no' even the biggin' o' auld Granny Nisbet's airch.

Jeannie: Oh, what was that faither?

Polly: Ye've heard the story owre and owre, Jean.

Jeannie: What aboot it? I've nivur heard Faither on't.

Macfarlane: Deed, there's no muckle tae tell. She was a bit lame body, an'
as perjink as they mak' them. 'Ears afore she dee'd she had the airch
made – an' it's there to this day, but gey ill to see unless ye ken juist
whaur to look, owin' to the way the plantation's grown fornenst the
wa'…I juist min' o' her an' nae mair, gaen' hirplin' aboot, an' a tongue
that wad clip cloots. But the biggin' o' the airch made a gey like stir at
the time. Ye see she's a lair next the wa'. An' she wad hae an airch biggit
i' the wa', aye, an' steepulated i' her wull that she sud be buriet wi' her
feet pointin' that airt…She didna' mean tae be behindhand whan the
Resurrection comes. 'I'm a wee wommun,' she yaist to say, 'an' a
crippled ane at that, – an', seein' whaur ma bit grun' is, the feck o' the
folk'd be up an' oot and owre the hill afore I kent whaur I was. I'm a
lang wey frae the yett, an' I could never sclim' the wa'.'…So she'd her
airch put intae the wa' to gi'e her a fair chance wi' the lave. It cost her
a braw penny. An' the Pairish meenister mad' a sermon o't – takin' for
his text 'The Deil tak' the hindmost.' Opeenion was sair divided wi'
regaird to the maitter. Fowk didna ken whether to lauch at the auld
wumman or gin there michtna be somethin' in't efter a', or gin it wasna
juist eindoon supersteetion. She yaist to talk in a silly kind o' way aboot
the Last Day: 'It'll be a sair how-dye-doo, I'm thinkin',' an' her remark
was lang debatit i' the Pairish. It seemed to thraw a kind o' queer licht
on the Resurrection. It was deeficult to ken what to mak' on't…

Jeannie: Aye. It mak's yin think.

Polly: It depends what she meant. But as for the airch the deid'll rise in a
different frame o' min', I'm thinking. There'll no' be ony siccan rush.

Jeannie (seriously): Ye nivur ken.

Macfarlane: But I've nivur seen onything the equal o' the day's ongangin's.

Polly (impatiently): What juist did tak' place?

Jeannie: The warst o't was that naethin' happen't – as it sud. Wasn't that
it, faither?

Macfarlane: Weel, yin micht gae the length o' sayin' that, Jeannie, yin micht say that…*(turning to Polly)* – Whan the coffin was lower't into the grave, Hugh an' Alick kneelt doon by the gravemou', an' baith cried oot in a muckle voice, 'I' the name o' Jesus, Arise!' Ye could ha'e knocked doon the hale jing bang o's wi' a duster. It was sic' an unlooked-for thing. We didna' ken whaur to look or what to dae. There bein' nae meenister there made it a' the waur. There was naebody ye could look to – naebody to gie's a lead, as 'twere. Sprung on's suddenly that wey, it was deeficult to ken hoo to tak' it – whether to approve o't, or to regaird it as pure blasphemy, or to keep an open mind. I was fair at sixes an' seevins wi' mysel'…No' that I didna sympathize wi' the lads, of coorse…but, somehow, it wasna canny. It didna seem richt.

Jeannie: Why ever no'?

Macfarlane: (confused) Weel, it's no easy to say. We a' believe i' redemption thro' the grace o' the Lord Jesus Christ – every yin o's – an' in the resurrection frae the grave. But still an' on…

Polly: (roused) It was an awfu' like way o' daein'. Silly laddies like Hugh an' Alick sud nivur hae been allo'ed to hae their way i' a maitter o' that kind. I dinna ken hoo they'd the hert…their ain mither! I dinna suppose either of them shed a single tear. It's no' natural. Fowk that's makin' the best o' this life dinna worry muckle about the neist. Hugh M'Taggart'd be better employed playin' fitba than prayin'… an' as for seekin' to perpetuate his puir auld mither, wha's she that he sud ha'e nae een i' his heid for the lassies he'd be coortin' gin he was a man ava…Can you really imagine RESURRECTION DAY at Sleepyhillock…a' the graves crackin' open an' the fowk loupin' oot. No' me… There'd be some gey objects amang them. Mony o' them wad be better bidin' whaur they are…aye, an' kent it themsel's when they dee'd.

Macfarlane: Weel, they were baith deid calm an' as confident as ye like. A' the rest o's were verra far frae either, I can tell ye.

Jeannie: But they believed in what they were daein'!

Macfarlane: Oh, aye. They were baith i' deid earnest. There was nae doot aboot that.

Jeannie: An' efter a' if miracles could happen i' Palestine lang syne what's to hinder them happenin' i' Scotland noo?

Polly: But it was Jesus wha performed the miracles himsel'.

Jeannie: But the Bible says gin ye've as muckle faith as a grain o' mustard seed ye can move mountains. An' I believe baith Hugh an' Alick had as muckle faith as onybody ever could hae. *(Turning to her father)* The rest o' ye were confused juist because ye didna believe richt thro' an' thro', beyond a shadow o' doot the way they did. It's a kind o' death in itsel' – this sayin' 'I believe, I believe' until yin really thinks yin does, an' hasna an honest doubt or a real live hope left. If I didna believe onything micht happen ony meenut I'd become a doonricht atheist.

Macfarlane: I dinna ken. But juist suppose for the sake o' argument that their faith had been rewarded there an' then. Suppose a bit cry had come frae Mrs M'Taggart's coffin doon there – what then? An' they'd hauled it up an burst aff the lid, an' she steppit oot again as large as life?…Half the population o' Scotland would ha'e been here the morn. An' the rest o' the warl' afore the en' o' the week. The papers would ha'e been fou' o' nocht else. The hale coorse o' history would ha'e been changed… I'm no' sure it would ha'e bin for the best.

Jeannie: (in sharp protest) Faither!

Macfarlane: (doggedly) Weel, I'm no'. I believe i' Heaven an' i' reunion there wi' oor loved yins. But I honestly confess I wadna' like to ha'e seen Mrs M'Taggart brocht back to life…an' yer mither lyin' there a' thae years…an' my faither an' mither…an' a' the ither deid men an' weemun an' bairns I kent. But, mind ye for a meenut or twa, every yin o' us felt that something wad happen. In a way we were prepared for't. We wadna ha'e been surprised at onything. There was something in the way it a' happened, in the way Hugh and Alick behaved, that fair took awa' a' oor poo'ers o' thocht. Their voices rang oot like commands that couldna be ignored.

Polly: It was takin' the Lord's name i' vain. Neither mair or less. There's a hantle difference atween a prayer an' a command. Hugh M'Taggart's no' in a position yet to gi'e his orders to Almichty God.

Jeannie: They didna mean't that way, as ye weel ken. They had faith. An' noo they've lost it, it's mair than likely. Ye couldna blame them if they've turned into pure atheists. It's a lang time sin' Jesus raised Lazarus. It's high time it was happenin' again. Even yae case 'ud gang a fell long way. Fowks losing faith, an' nae wunner. The kirks are a' gaen back an' back. It wad ha'e dune a pooer o guid. I'm deid sorry for Hugh an' Alick. If there's a man I ken guid eneuch to perform miracles it's Hugh M'Taggart *(blushes as Polly looks at her)*. It's true.

Polly: Muckle learnin's made him mad. I dinna haud wi' this faith-healin' ava', an' neither does God apparently. It's fair fleein' i' the face o' Providence. Hugh's got his heid swelled at the College. He'd be better advised to be studyin' the things he needs to study. Christian Science'll no tak' him fer i' the teachin' profession, even as things are ga'en noo-a-days. An' he's leadin' Alick fair aff his feet tae…Noo look here, faither,

gin I was to say to ye, ye'll no' dee. Ye're gaen to be the a'e exception.
Ye'll leeve for ever...ye'd think I was oot o' my heid a'thegither... An'
I wad be tae...but gin it was true, an' ye kent it was true, wad ye like it?

Macfarlane: Weel.

Polly: Feint a bit. Ye'd be the maist miserable man the warl' ever saw. Ye
ken yersel' ye'd be far better deid...It's got to be a'body or naebody, an
a' the same time, if there's to be ony Resurrection at a'. An' even then
it'd be a fell queer mix-up. Eternal life'd be a gey puir thing compared
with this. If it wasna for disease an' death life wadna be worth
leevin'...Och, I believe in a life beyond the grave...but I canna imagine
ony that'd be worth ha'en. An' I dinna think onybody else can. I've nivur
heard ony Heevun described yet that ony sensible body could tolerate
for a...

Jeannie: (who has been following her own thoughts) It's my belief Mrs
M'Taggart wad nivur ha'e deed at a' if Hugh had been at hame. The
doctors expected her to dee months an' months syne. They canna mak'
oot hoo she kept on leevin' ava'. But she wadna let Alick sen' for Hugh
i' time. She did improve wonderfu' efter Hugh cam'. The doctors were
fair dumfoonert. If Hugh'd come a day or twa sooner he'd ha'e pulled
her thro' a'thegither. But she'd let things gang owre far afore she sent
for'm. She didna gie'm a chance... It's a puir kin' o' God that canna
reward faith like that yince in a while.

Polly: Jean! Faither! D'ye hear her – but ye're as bad yersel'!

Macfarlane: (who has been sitting completely bemused) Ech! Oh, it's
deeficult to ken what to think. Weel, as I say, we waited in complete
dumfoonerment. Naethin' wad ha'e surprised me – mair than the fac'
that naethin' did happen. It didna seem richt that naethin' should
happen. Everybody meltit awa' as soon's they could – scared-like. Ye
can tell what like it was, when even auld Tom, the gravedigger, hung
back an' daurna pit his wisp o' hay doon an' begin fillin' in... He was
still staunin' switherin', loathlike, when I lookit roon frae the yett. An'
the twa laddies were still kneelin' by the grave-mou' prayin'...As Jock
Greig said to me i' the road back, 'There's only twa ways to't – either
Mrs M'Taggart sud ha'e been brocht back to life there and then – or
Hugh an' Alick sud ha'e been struck doon. As it is it's almost as if there
wasna ony God ava' – if ye ken what I mean.'

Polly: (deliberately) I'm no' sae shair that ye dae yersel', faither.

Macfarlane: I'm no' sayin't i' ony irreverent way... Jock Greig was very
bitter about neither o' the meenisters attendin' the funeral juist because
they waurna asked to offeeciate. Of course, ye couldna wunner at a

stickler for form like auld M'Queen – but Latimer's different. He mak's oot to be sae unconventional – an' oot-an'-oot evangelical. Hoo did they ken onyway that God wadna side wi' Hugh an' Alick? What a drap that'd ha'e been to them. An' they could ha'e dune wi't. The reeligious life o' this toon's a' ga'en to wind and stour. A miracle yince in a while wad quicken the souls o' the folk. Sic patient believin' an' believin' year in an' year oot, wi' naethin' ever happenin's no' natural. Fowk believin' even on like that's nae incentive to God. Still an on God micht weel tak' a thocht…

Knock at the door, and, opening it, a woman thrusts her head round the corner.

Polly: Come awa' in Mrs Thomson.

Mrs Thomson: (coming forward a little in great excitement) Na! na! I ha'ena a meenut to spare. Ha'e ye heard the latest?

Polly and Jeannie: (together) No!

Macfarlane: (amazed – half-rising from his chair) – Ye dinna mean…?

Mrs Thomson: (portentously) Alice M'Taggart's had a veesion.

Polly: A what?

Jeannie: Oh, ye dinna say so! What? When?

Mrs Thomson: (with unction) Aye! Her mither appeared to her, no' quarter o' an 'oor syne, an' said her speerit'd return to her body at fower o'clock. The news has run like wildfire. Half the toon's up at Sleepyhillock, an' Hugh an' Alick are fair garin' the dirt flee.

Macfarlane: Puir laddies!

Mrs Thomson: I'm juist on my way up mysel'. Yin nivur kens. An' maister M'Queen's had a shock, a' doon the left side. It's like a judgment.

Polly: I wunner at ye – a wumman come to your time o' life. Ye can spare yersel' the trouble. Nocht'll happen.

Jeannie: Ye mean ye hope nocht wull. Ye dinna ken mair than the lave o's. Faith's no' that common that God can afford to squander't, an' gi'e mean wee souls that ha'ena the strength to haud a decent hope leave to craw owre their betters. *(Jumping up and grabbing her hat.)* Oh, I hope it's true, I hope it's true. *(Suddenly drops onto her knees.)* O God, answer this prayer. We believe ye wull. Fulfill the veesion. Gi'e back this mither to her sons an' dochter. Amen!

Macfarlane: Amen!

Exit Mrs Thomson and Jean.

Macfarlane: (squirming under Polly's look) It's bound to happen some day
  – an' as weel the day as ony ither…
Polly: (unrolling a bundle of knitting wool and passing a cut to her father)
  You'll mebbe gi'e's a haun' wi' this i' the meantime.

*Macfarlane puts the cut round his wrists and Polly begins briskly winding
it into a ball.*

The Purple Patch

*Scene: Summer evening. Beside gate in wall leading through churchyard
to church. Congregation 'skailing'. Three groups, comprised each of six or
seven persons, form themselves near the gate. All the people seem in an
unusual state of excitement. Speakers in each of the three groups are heard
simultaneously. The side letters indicate roughly the various speakers
heard at the same time – although, for reading purposes, it is impossible to
do this accurately (and so secure the exact counterpoint), since the different
speakers speak at various rates, and the incidence of interjections,
movements, etc., of the other component members of the groups varies
incessantly. Occasionally a particularly striking phrase from the speaker
in one group makes the eyes of the members of the other groups turn thither,
away from their own speaker; an odd member is first attached to one group
and then to another; inside each group others are always vainly
endeavouring to get their word in, and move about; side conversations
develop inside the groups, sometimes threatening to disintegrate them into
smaller groups of trios or couples, while a certain amount of inter-activity
by an occasional remark shouted over and the like is maintained between
members of the different groups, which occasionally tend to fuse into one.*

Dramatis Personae
GROUP I. *William Beedie, an alert old chap with restless eyes and a thin
sandy beard; a retired village postmaster who writes verses for the 'Poet's
Corner' of the local paper. His crony, David Dunbar, a buirdlier and more
genial-looking old fellow. Charlie Mearns, a long, thin old man with a lean,
wrinkled face but twinkling eyes. Johnny Soutar, a little bow-legged man
with an obvious 'want' and a sort of 'nihum-nahum' utterance.*
GROUP II. *Miss Frew, a tall ungainly, harsh-featured spinster. Mrs David
Dunbar, a pleasant-faced little body, but with a sharp enough edge at her*

tongue at times, especially in conversation with Miss Frew, whom she intensely dislikes. Mrs Roebuck, Miss Frew's harassed-looking married sister, with a couple of girls about six and eight years old respectively. Her mother-in-law, Old Mrs Roebuck, far gone in senile decay. ·

GROUP III. Tam Stoddart, the village storekeeper, a stout man with a kindly aspect and an insisting way of speaking. Adam Pert, the shoemaker, a caustic-tongued little hypocrite who plays up to his wife by 'digging' at those who are his cronies behind her back. Mrs Adam Pert, who 'wears the breeks', a 'managing' matron.

The Rev. John M'Ilwraith. Heb Duncan, the veteran beadle.

A. *William Beedie:* It was a peculiar utterance – a maist peculiar utterance – there's nae gettin' awa' frae that; an' the wey he delivered it, an' the wild lichtnin'-like fleer o's een! It fair grippit me (*aside* – an' I'm nae green member noo); made me feel like a puppy held up by the slack skin o' its neck an' scaired to death for what bood to happen neist. I'd a dwamie feelin' o' pawin' oot a' airts an' fin'in' naethin' to claut at. If he'd made it mair precise – gi'en time an' place, an' ony sort o' clue as to his real meanin' in introducin't whaur he did, yin 'ud ha'e felt different. Auld Dr Gilruth's sermons were aye a' o' a'e piece – a' a'e 'oo' – an sittin' a' thae years unner him has mebbe made us look owre muckle for the pure logic o' things. There were never ony doots aboot onything *he* said. But this new meenister o' oors is a different sow by the lug a'thegither. That's plain! Gosh, the thing fair ploupit oot there frae the maist innocent settin', like a twa-heided eagle hatchin' frae a bantam's egg unner yin's very nose. It's no' natural. It had nae conceivable connection wi' onything else in the haill sermon. A canny eneuch sermon…tho' in an uncommon kind o' strain, but ye'd as soon lippen to meet a reid Injun in a' his wigwam an' warpaint i' the Market Place yonner i' braid daylicht as ha'e a hearin' like yon i' the middle o' a discoorse that was mebbe a bit ajee frae what we've come to consider plumb hereaboots, but was suffeecently straucht-gaen for a' that to fa' weel eneuch… frae a beginner, at ony rate, compared wi' the auld Doctor… on lugs used to discriminatin' a wee…between decent limits…

A. *Miss Frew: (fairly flustered and not knowing what to do with her umbrella in her anxiety to gesticulate effectively)* Losh, preserve's! I'm nae witch an' I've nae notion i' the warl' wha the mannie was aimin' at; but – mark my words! – he'd *somebody* in his mind's e'e wi'oot a doot. An' no' wi'oot cause! Weel, he's gi'en them fair warnin'. He's no' a man that'll stan' ony nonsense frae high or low. He hasna been lang here, but lang eneuch, seemin'ly, to ken that it's no' a' gowd that glitters even in Blawearie. He's a young man, but his heid's screwed on the richt side up, an' wi' yon twa glowerin' een o' his – like twa burnt hools in a blanket – ye can rest assured that he'll see richt through the whitest sepulchre i' the place to the abomination o' desolation inside. An' he's no' feart to speak. Auld Gilruth, canny man, daurna let his jaws snap, but even or he got owre auld he could never rise to sic heights o' richteous indignation. It was never in him. He was fer owre saft for Blawearie. But we've got a man at last *(sees her unfortunate phrase in time and quickly adds – not too quickly, however, to escape Mrs Dunbar's meaning smile)* – a man efter God's ain hert! Some o' the mair freevolous dinna like it. I saw Missus Graham an' Missus Lowrie *(aside – in her new hat, maist likely afore her auld yin's peyed, an' sic a contraption at that!)*, flushin' up like a couple o' beetroots…I'd like fine to ken juist *wha* an' *what* he *was* aimin' at, tho'. But murder'll oot, an' it's nae mare's nest 'ud gar him speak oot like yon, an' it's high time there was less smooth talk an' mair o' the fire o' God i' the pulpit. God micht be a rubber doll for the wey some meenisters ha'e him bobbin' aboot – stottin' frae a'e thing to the tither as if fleggit to touch owt. It's a real relief to hear yin again wha probes richt doon to the hert o' things. His een fair loupit oot like the claws o' an eagle, an' whaever he meent 'll no' get oot o' yon grip in a hurry. I'd a feelin' that the poo'er o' God until salvation had clean swoopit doon through him an' catched up oot o' oor verra midst some hidden monster o' uncleanness…I gied a kind o' side-scance at the seat neist mine, half-expectin' to see a vacant pew. I daurna look up when his een were at their fiercest, but I thocht that gin I could I'd see a damned soul wrigglin' half-way between the flair an' the ceilin' in the grip o' its maister…

(Both little girls have been listening in fascination, but at the words 'damned soul wrigglin',' the elder bursts out giggling. The younger is extremely solemn of face, as if excogitating deeply, and tugs at her mother's skirt; but her mother is too busy slapping the elder's head and telling her what she'll get when she gets hame – lauchin' like that, an' on the verra Sawbath evenin'.)

A. *Tam Stoddart:* It'll no' dae. It'll no' dae ava. I dinna haud wi' hintin' an' hidin'. Nae guid ever cam' o' that. Playin' a kin' o' kee-a-boo wi' fowk's souls. Let a man either lash oot wi't or haud his tongue. Ye dinna win

souls by tricks o' talk an' playactin' i' the pulpit. It does an immense
amount o' hairm – the fowk it's meent for 'ud be the verra last i' maist
cases to tak' it to themsel's, but it sets a' the silly craturs i' the
congregation fair bizzin' wi' excitement an' terror. It's the humble an'
contrite o' hert that are easiest made believe they're verra deevils o'
ineequity, singled oot for the wrath to come. But the hard nits can sit
like lumps o' asbestos through the hettest harangue. Na! Na! The man
hasna bin five minutes i' the place, an' can only ha'e been talkin' at large,
shootin' oot his neck at random i' the hopes o' fetchin' doon somethin'.
But he's owre big for his boots – an' fer owre wee for the boots o' the
auld Doctor he's tryin' to fill. Heck! It's eneuch to mak' him turn in his
grave – sic a sermon as that frae his auld pulpit. We're no' leevin' in Auld
Testament times noo, an' he mauna come to Blawearie thinkin' to stalk
muckle big game i' the sin line. I question verra much if there's a crime
i' the haill community bigger than a bit poppin' flea (an' we've a' got
plenty o' them), an' yet here's him bendin' the bow o' Ulysses by his wey
o't, an' knockin' oot the feck o' the congregation wi' an arrow fit to smash
a rhinoceros, juist like yon fool shootin' tenant o' a Yankee at the
Todheid last back-en' wha took the auld mare for a stray stag an' shot a
haill hirsel o' sheep in his attempts to pot it…

B. *William Beedie: (still at it, and going strong)* I dinna think he kent it was
comin'. Something took possession o'm – but it was for a' the warl juist
like gettin' the rick end o' the wool an' ripplin' oot the haill stockin'. It
made threads an' stour o' a' the rest o' his sermon, an' left us wi' nowt
but a muckle hool – an abyss o' flame an' fury. The mair I think on't,
the mair I'm shair the man couldna help himsel'. There was a superior
foorce at work. It made his een lowe like a pair o' beacons on a pit-mirk
nicht. Ye wadna ha'e thocht a wee bit white-faced shilpit cratur like yon
could ha'e held sic a bleeze wi'oot burstin'. It turned the haill kirk an'
a'body in't into a swirl o' stour. When he cockit his een up to the gallery
I ventured to keek that wey tae, an' a' the fowk i' the line o' his veesion
were juist like a parcel o' motes reelin' in a beam o' licht wi' ooter
darkness on baith sides. Man an' boy I've sat i' this kirk twice every
Sawbath for five and sixty years, an' never saw or heard the like o't.
There was mair than human poo'er in there the day, but whither it was
the poo'er o' God, or…

B. *Mrs Dunbar: (with acerbity)* Weel, it didna' affec' me that wey, at ony
rate. Quite the contrair! It's a hantle easier for some fowk to picture
puir souls wrigglin' between the grun' an' the lift than to imagine the
kin' o' reeligion that could mak' ye feel that Jesus himsel' had slippit into

the same pew wi' ye an' was shairin yer hymn-book. An' I've nae doot
it comes mair natural to Mr M'Ilwraith to steer up the fire an' brimstane,
an' flap aboot wi' his goon like a figger o' fate, condemnin' fowk to the
pains o' hell forever, that to show them the roads to Heaven. It's no'
mony meenisters that can look baith ways at aince like auld Dr Gilruth,
an' that bein' sae, I prefer them that look up, no' doon, maist. It ill
becomes the like o' him – a mere herrin' o' a man! – to threaten to dae
owt he canna undae, an' to talk o' bringin' doun the wrath o' God in a'
its veesibility on the heid o' somebody present 'ud carry mair wecht wi'
me, at ony rate, if I could feel that the prayers o' sic a man were juist as
lief to be the savin' o' ony puir cratur…An' as for the seat neist ye, I'd
ha'e ye recollect that my puir auld mither sat there a' her marriet life,
altho' she's been deid an' gane these fifteen years come Candlemass,
an' naebody's ever sat there since…unless it was mebbe yersel' when
ye'd freens stayin' wi' ye, an' yer ain seat wasna quite eneuch to haud
ye a'…

*(Younger of the two girls now succeeds in attracting her mother's attention,
and the following colloquy is heard:)*

Whit are ye tug, tug, tuggin' at my skirt for? Keep still, wull ye?
Mither – mither!
Whit is't then?
Wad it no' be faither the mannie meent?
Losh! Whitever pits that in yer heid, lassie?
Weel, ye ken whit he said on Setterday nicht when ye ca'd him a great
    muckle druck…
Can ye' no' haud yer tongue when yer elders are speakin' *(slapping her
    over the hand)*. An' as for you, teeheeing like a peahen *(as the elder
    sister bursts again into a wild giggle)*. Juist you wait till I get ye hame…

(Meanwhile Miss Frew has joined issue with Mrs Dunbar.)

B. *Miss Frew:* Och, if the cap fits…but I didna mean onything personal,
and *(very snippily indeed)* ye needna be sae snippy. But I'm shair there's
mony forbye mysel' ha'e been lang tired o' the wishy-washy stuff that's
maistly served up i' the name o' releegion nowadays. It tak's a guid nerve
to be a *real eindoon* Christian. Yin canna but wunner hoo some puir bits
o' things'll stand the shock o' the last Day an' Judgement. A clean
conscience is nae great help, if it's as nesh as a' that. But tastes differ,

an' I maun say I like releegion 'neat', as my auld faither used to say, if I'm to ha'e it at a'. Heaven an' Hell's no' nice eneuch for some fowk. They want a sorts o' half-wey hooses to suit their particular requirements... What I meent was that I felt that a verra prophet o' Israel, a Daniel come to Judgment, was i' the pulpit the day, an' that whatever was said was in God's ain voice.

B. *Mrs Dunbar: (sardonically):* Wi' sic a Peterculter accent as yon!

B. *Miss Frew:* He disna belang Fife in particular either. He's a' things to a' men, an' no' aye indulgin' in buttery compliments an' pleasant promises...

B. and C. *Old Mrs Roebuck: (in an uncanny voice)*

> The sumphish mob, o' penetration shawl,
> May gape an' ferly at your cunning saul,
> An' mak' ye fancy that there is desert
> In thus employing a' your sneaking art.

(Everybody looks at her in astonishment, afflicted by the recognition of some obscure pertinence in the verse. Frightened by the attention she has drawn upon herself, the old wife cunningly pretends that she has been trying to amuse one of her granddaughters, and, bending towards the youngest engagingly, in her way of it, continues –)

> Red, blue, an' green, an' likewise pearl,
> I hae to fit the little girl:
> Wi' mony a bony tirly-wirl
> Aboot the queets.

Mrs Roebuck: Wheesht mither, wheesht!

(Old Mrs Roebuck blackens with rage at being found out. She waits for her revenge till Mrs Dunbar begins speaking again, and then, pointing a skinny forefinger at her daughter, and executing a sort of obscene movement in front of her, shrills out with a sort of vicious glee –)

> Her nainselle shook her naked breeches,
> For she was tyred with his speeches;
> She would far rather had a tirrle
> O' an aquavitae barrel.

(It takes a few minutes for Mrs Roebuck – terribly flustered with shame

*and frightened for what her mother may say next – to force her back into
sullen impassivity.)*

B. *Adam Pert: (hypocritically)* I'm surprised at ye, Tam Stoddart. It's nae
lauchin' maitter. You an' yer Yankee shots. Men o' your kind seem to
think that the fates o' immortal sauls are decided in a sort o' auction
mairt, an' that God an' a wheen o' yersel's can sit doon an' discuss the
run o' the business owre a tappit hen i' the back pairlour o' the 'Black
Swan'…

B. *Tam Stoddart:* An', faith, there was nane better kent there than yersel',
Adam, till ye went an'…

B. *Adam Pert:* An' what?

B. *Tam Stoddart:* Weel, ye ken what I was gaen to say – lost yer rib a second
time, for it's weel kent that yer first wife had a braider an' kindlier view
o' things, an' second thochts…

B. *Mrs Adam Pert: (with a warlike gleam in her eyes)* An' second thochts
means me, I suppose, Maister Stoddart. I hadna the pleasure o' kennin'
my predecessor, as ye ken. But she was a kind o' cousin o' yours, I'm
gi'en to understand. Weel, a'body's entitled to their ain opeenions, nae
doot, but it wadna dae you ony ill to think mair an' jaw less, an' ye micht
dae a heap waur than juist pop back into the vestry an' discuss wi' Mr
M'Ilwraith hoo the puir misguided lassie's opeenions may ha'e changed
since she deed. If she's lookin' doon on's noo, I'se warran' she kens that
Adam was owre big a handfu' for the likes o' her, an she'll be gey an'
glad I took him owre when I did, for her ain sake, if no' for his, for if
he'd gane to utter destruction wi'oot kennin't, like some ithers he used
to mix amang in his unregenerate days, she'd ha'e had to thole her share
o' the blame an' her condeetion the day…

B. *Tam Stoddart:* Some fowk ken mair o' ither fowk's business no' only i'
this life, but i' the neist, than's canny.

B. *Mrs Adam Pert:* Aye! an' some fowk ken the real facts o' their condition
here an' chances hereafter sae little that we'd fain hope the exemption
o' born eediots frae the operations o' free wull an' choice may ha'e a
wider application than it 'ud be compleementary to indicate. But, mark
my words, a tappit hen'll no' keep onybody's stammack lang on the Day
that is to come…

C. *David Dunbar:* That's juist it. Ye hut the nail on the heid. I canna say
that I'm fair convinced it *was* the real Mackay – I mean, the poo'er o'
the Holy Ghost – mysel'. The de'il plays some unco tricks. But at ony
rate, if it wasna the genuine article, it was a marvellous imitation, an'

the maist impressive thing o' the kind I've seen since auld Dr Nixon afore Gilruth's time, said, 'Let everybuddy sing,' wi' sic emphasis on the everybuddy that we'd nae sooner sterted than puir Jimmy Carruthers, who was born deef an' dumb, joined in wi' sic an unearthly timmer that half the congregation lost their voices wi' shock...

C. *Charlie Mearns:* An' it minds me o' anither occasion when a verra peculiar effec' was conjured up – a verra peculiar effec' indeed. A veesitin' meenister – a long drink o' water frae Paisley wey – had just gi'en oot his text, when a cock outside gied affwi' a tremenjous 'Cock-a-doodle-do!' The haill congregation gapit like a'e man; like a boxin' referee or an auctioneer, somehoo or ither there was nowt i' their heids but the coont – yin – twa – three! When the cock crew thrice a sort o' spasm o' fear ran through the haill buildin'. Naebody kent whaur to look or what to dae. Then, daggont, if the doited fowl didna craw aince mair, an' the tension brak' an' we a' burst oot lauchin' in a helpless kind o' way, the veesitin' meenister leadin' off wi' a howl like a hyaena .

C. *David Dunbar:* But what did the man *mean?* That's the thing. It was like seein' something that was naither flesh, fowl, or guid reid herrin'.

C. *Charlie Mearns:* Like the beast in Revelations!

C. *David Dunbar:* Ye canna gi'e ony name to it. Tak'n word for word, it was a rigmarole o' nonsense – every phrase seemed chosen because it was the unlikeliest possible phrase to tack on to the yin that gaed afore it. An' yit there's nae gainsayin' the terrific effec' he somehoo or ither produced...

C. *Charlie Mearns:* It was something like the kind o' grand paralysin' feelin' that can sometimes be created by brakin' oot, wi'oot ony warnin', frae a plain everyday kind o' passage into a crashin' bit o' French or Latin...only fer stranger.

C. *William Beedie:* Aye! It was stranger than French or Latin. It was a language that has lost a lot in Blawearie for mony years i' the coorse o' translation into what passes for English. It was the language o' God...

C. *Johnny Soutar:* Ye dinna mean he was speakin' i' Braid Scots?

C. *William Beedie: (savagely)* No! ye gowk !

C. *Johnny Soutar: (anxiously)* Oh, I didna ken. Dinna get angry wi' fowk less gleg i' the uptak' than yersel'! Only, if it had been Braid Scots, nae maitter hoo auld-farran', I'se warran' I'd ha'e kent a wird or twa here an' there at ony rate.

C. *William Beedie: (disregarding Soutar)* Ye ken the text, 'My words are not as your words.' Weel, there ye are. God tak's oor words when he speaks to us, but he fills them wi' his ain meanin's, which are quite

different to ony we gi'e them oorsel's. An' that's the wey they soon' half-
familiar, an' yet entirely strange an' beautiful an' terrible... *But here he
comes!*

C. *Mrs Dunbar: (returning to the 'muttons')* A prophet o' Israel wad ha'e
been sair oot o' plaice an' a maist unprofitable objec' in Blawearie pulpit
at this time o' day! We've made some progress dunn' the past twa-three
thoosan' years – although ye wadna think sae to hear some fowk talkin'!
It used to be thocht great sport hereaboots to gang an' see a public
hangin' an' it strikes me the feelin's no' deid yet, an' some fowks gang
to the kirk to enjoy the thocht o' some o' their neebors bein' fried to
death in hell. But I dinna think that Christ himsel' had muckle
stammack for that kin' o' spectacle...

C. *Miss Frew:* Christ came to earth to seek an' to save.

C. *Mrs Dunbar:* I ken *(tartly)* – an' his meenisters 'ud dae weel to follow
his example while the time lasts. They'll need it a'.

C. *Miss Frew: (completing her sentence with ostentatious patience)* But
God'll judge at the hinder-en'.

C. *Mrs Dunbar:* It s'ud be left to God an' to the hinder-en' then. Mr
M'Ilwraith (an' him an unmarriet man that disna ken what every man
an' wumman born has meent to some mither) spak' wi' as muckle
assurance the day as if he were God himsel' dividin' the sheep an' the
goats at his appinted time. I wunner *(her temper rising)* God didna...

C. *Mrs Roebuck: Wheesht, here he comes!*

C. *Tam Stoddart:* Christ himsel' wisna averse to a wee drappie noo an' then,
for his stammack's sake.

C. *Mrs Adam Pert: (scornfully)* Ye're no' the only elder o' the kirk wha's
mair fu' o' Paul's clash than the gospel o' the livin' God.

C. *Tam Stoddart: (patiently):* Weel, if that was Paul an' no' the Lord
himsel', at ony rate it was Christ that cheenged the water into wine...

C. *Mrs Adam Pert:* To suit some fowk he'd ha'e ha'en to aboleesh water
a'thegither – an' then ye'd ha'e been aye dookin'.

C. *Tam Stoddart: (losing his temper)* Hyech! I expec' a wumman'll ha'e the
last word at the verra Judgment itsel'.

C. *Mrs Adam Pert: (victoriously)* Nae doot; but mair than likely if she has,
it'll be to plead for some sumph o' a man.

C. *Adam Pert: Wheesht, here he comes!*

*(The Rev. Mr M'Ilwraith and the veteran beadle, Heb Duncan, come slowly
down the path from the church to the gate. All eyes are turned towards
them. Coming alongside the folk:)*

Mr M'Ilwraith: Well, how did you like the sermon?
In Chorus: A searchin' utterance.
                     Aye, sir, yon's the stuff to stir fowk up.
                     A whiff o' the pure Jerusalem, etc., etc.
Mr M'Ilwraith: (patting little Roebuck girls' heads, and going off) We must
   try all kinds of methods.

*(The old beadle stands giggling away into his beard at a great rate,
incoherently amused.)*

Several Voices: What are ye lauchin' at?
The Beadle: (at last) Lauchin'! It 'ud mak' a cat lauch. The method was
   mebbe his ain, but the sermon wasna. Dr Gilruth gied it frae the verra
   self-same pulpit here close on twenty years ago, an' I've heard it fower
   times since to my shair an' certain knowledge, an' bits o't at orra times
   forbye...Ye ken that muckle purple passage in the middle o't. Weel,
   when Dr Gilruth was writin't he found yin o' his bit sheets o' paper half-
   fu' to start wi' – wi' a passage he'd been copyin' frae that fantastical
   divine, Dr Donne – a great Yankee revivalist, if I remember rightly! –
   an', absent-minded-like, thocht that he'd juist written it as pairt o's
   sermon. So he tacked on the rest to the end o't. He never noticed it the
   first time he delivered it; but I spotted the cuckoo i' the nest, an' when
   he gied it a second time, I spiered why he keepit in a passage that had
   nae connection wi' the rest o' the sermon ava! 'Man, I never noticed it,'
   he said, an' then he tell't me hoo it must ha'e happened. 'But I'll juist
   leave it there,' he added. 'It may be an accident, or it may be the hand
   o' God. It'll no' dae ony ill in either case. Them that comes to the kirk
   i' the richt frame o' mind'll never notice that onything's amiss, an' them
   that dae notice'll be puzzled to death to ken what to mak' on't...

(A Study in Faces.)

Old Miss Beattie

It's as faur back as I can mind. I maun hae been a gey wee laddie at the
time. I aye gaed wi' my mither on her veesits to the seek and the deein',
and whiles wi' my faither tae. My brither didna. He juist point-blank
refused. I kent I sudna want to gang either – but I did. I didna let my faither

and mither ken hoo keen I really was. No' that I was ony feart o' them jalousin' that it wasna naitural for a boy to want to see auld dottlin' craturs o' men and wimmen leevin' their lane in a'e-room hooses in out-o-the-wey corners o' the toon, and stertin' to think oot my real reasons. But I kent that ither folk (includin' my brither) had different opinions and wadna be lang in expressin' them. My faither, and still mair, my mither were different frae the feck o' folk – they were mair religious. That was hoo they'd aye sae many silly auld folk to veesit. And they thocht their sons sud be different tae. As a maitter o' fact they were puzzled owre my brither; he took life that easy. He was aye oot playin' wi' a pack o' ither loons. It took my faither and mither a' their time to get him to bide in long eneuch to dae his lessons at nichts. I wasna like that. I had to mak' the best o' lads and lassies aboot my ain age in the schule – I managed no' sae bad wi' the lassies. But outside schule 'oors I'd nae use for the lads ava', and nane for the lassies either unless I was fair stuck for something better. Folks that saw e'e to e'e wi' my faither and mither used to say I'd an auld heid on young shouders. I'd learned the knack o' sayin' byordinar' pious things – in the richt company. I could gar them forget I wasna as auld as themsel's. And I could dae't withoot lookin' the least bit self-conscious tae. 'Losh me,' folk used to think efter a bit when they mindit again that I was only a wee laddie at the schule, 'the boy's lost his ain mooth and fund a minister's.' But it was only the kind o' folk that were mair or less like my faither and mither themsel's that I could strike in that way. Ithers took a vera different view.

And they took a vera different view o' my faither and mither tae. A' they did for auld folk and badly folk never brocht them a penny piece, and whiles it brocht them nae end o' ill-wull – but ither folk got it into their heids that there was 'mair in't than meets the e'e'. Noo I ken vera weel that it was naethin – sae faur as my faither and mither kent – but eindoon Christianity. My faither's wages werena abune the average – but mither and him seldom gaed onywhaur empty-haundit. And the funny thing was that the mair they gied the better they got on themsel's. That's what took folk to the fair. It was aye a couple o' oranges or a quarter o' tea, or twa three scones, or, in the warst cases, a bunch o' grapes. And mony's the auld cratur, as it cam' near the end, they sat up wi' nicht aboot, and weel they kent it was a thankless job. Even the bodies themsel's were fell suspicious and ill-to-dae-wi'. Tho' they'd naething in their bit hooses worth a bodle they followed your every move as tho' you were a thief, and every time you gied them their drap o' medicine you micht hae been poisonin' them. Whiles, gin the illness was lang-drawn-oot or o' a delicate and fiky kind, the mair you did for them the mair they hated you. They couldna help needin' you tae handle them – but the mair they needit it, the mair they resented it. And abune a' they hated deein' and you watchin' them. Afore the end cam' they'd send their een through you like reid hot needles. It was a' vera weel for you to want them to tak' it easy and to pass oot quiet – a' vera easy for you – when it was them that was daein' the deein'! You were fell clever – but no' clever eneuch to help them – even if you wanted to, which was questionable. Hoo can onybody ever be deid shair o' onybody else's motives? Few o' thae folk were when they cam' to dee. Suspicion and dislike were uppermaist. It's fine for doctors and ither folk roond a bedside to keep a calm sough, but it's no' sae easy for the cratur in the bed.

Noo I'm no' gaun to probe into the real reasons that gar'd my faither and mither tak' up sae mony cases o' that kind. I ken what they themsel's thocht. I ken that that didna juist exhaust the maitter. But they had baith ony amount o' patience, and naethin' was owre muckle bother for them, and, for a' that was thocht and even said to the contrary, they never got a brass farthing or a stick o' furniture for their trouble. Mair than aince when there was onything o' ony consequence left it was claimed by relations that had taen precious guid care no' to come near as lang as there was onything to dae, and they werena slow in suggestin' that faither and mither had poked in their noses whaur they werna needit, and hintin' that there micht be reasons for't. Mither used to get fair in a wax when onything o' that kind happened, and the angrier she got the mair colour attached to the suspicion.

Speakin' for mysel', I dinna think I was ever the least bit concerned owre ony o' the craturs. A' that I wantit was to see what happened and hoo. And to watch my faither and mither 'in action', as it were, and speculate owre the sense o' pooer – or, as the case micht be, pooerlessness – a body feels at somebody else's daith-bed. Yin got a' kinds o' eerie thrills. I used to watch a' that my faither and mither did and listen to a' that they said – but ahin' the twa three oranges, or the bit prayer, or the medicine, or the talkin' aboot things, or the 'wheesht, wheesht noo, an' no' tire yersel' oot – ye're bringin' on the cough again' – ahint a' the Christianity and humanity, as it were, I saw an eindoon animal drama. Whiles I thocht that, though they keepit up the surface play, my faither and mither got a blink o't tae, but nearly aye I kent the body that was deein' saw naething else. A' that was said to them or dune for them then seemed to gang alang a different plane a'thegither and never came into contact wi' them ava'. It made you feel that the Doctor and whiles the Minister, and your faither and mither, had made a queer mistak', and were treatin' a beast juist as if it had been a human bein'. It was like bein' at the theatre – only me and the body that was deein' mindit that we were only watchin' a play; a' the rest were like the silly wumman at the pictures that whiles forgets they're no real and bawls oot a warnin' to ane a' the characters.

But the craturs were generally owre faur gane when they got to this stage, and it didna last lang eneuch for me, besides bein' maskit maistly by the effect o' the medicine or me no' bein' there at juist the richt time. Auld Miss Beattie was an exception. She was in that state frae the vera beginnin' – lang afore she was bedridden even. She lookit like a monkey to stert wi' – and had the brichtest and broonest pair o' een imaginable. As a rule, there was naething else in them but juist pure glossy broon. But whiles they seemed to slip and slither aboot and syne to reel in her head wi' excitement, and whiles they narrowed to the thinnest slits and syne you'd see eindoon malice keekin' roon' the corners o' them. She wasna to be trustit. My faither and mither used to whisper to each ither aboot her – when they thocht I wasna listenin'. I dinna ken juist what they said, but she wasna to be trustit, no' even wi' hersel', and I kent better than let mysel' be left alane wi' her. Yince we were in her parlour and my mither had to gang into the kitchen to get something or ither. She was nae suner i' the lobby than I saw Miss Beattie movin' – as if she wasna' movin' ava', and wi' the blandest and maist benevolent licht in her een – to get atween me and the door. I made a dive for't juist in time. Sic a snarl o' rage she gied! I dinna ken what 'ud hae happened if she'd got me, and I dinna like to think. I was mair carefu' efter that; sae were my faither and mither. We never turned oor backs an her again. You couldna move in that hoose but the auld cratur's een were on you – like a snake's, waitin' to strike. There was a queer atmosphere about it – as o' something no' human ava'. You couldna pit it doon to onything in particular, but it was a' roond you. Uncanny wasna the word for it. And nae maitter what she said, or what anybody else said, in that hoose it soondit unreal, as if it was juist a pretence, a disguise for something else that didna bear thinkin' aboot. Whatever was wrang wi' her made a'thing but itsel' seem wrang. A big book o' texts hung on the kitchen wa' and it was aye open at the same page. 'Ho, all ye that thirsteth.' I wadna hae taen anything to eat or drink in that hoose for love or money, but I never lost an opportunity o' gangin' there a' the same – especially efter the time I've juist tell't ye aboot – and it's little my faither or mither ettled the kind o' stimulant I was aye imbibin' there. But auld Miss Beattie kent – and 'ud fain hae gi'en me a stronger dose!

The Common Riding

'Ambition's a queer thing,' he said, 'and grows in the maist unlikely places and tak's the maist unaccountable shapes.

'The queerest case o' ambition I ever kent o' here in the Muckle Toon was that o' puir Yiddy Bally (Bally for Ballantyne). Yiddy was a puir bit eaten-an-spewed-lookin' cratur a' his days; but even afore he left the schule he was Common-Riding-daft. He seemed to leeve for naething else. This year's was nae suner owre than he begood talkin' aboot next year's. Ye could scarcely get him to say a word aboot onything else – but mention the Common Riding! But at first he hadna muckle to say aboot that either – only if onybody mentioned it ye could see that he was a' lugs. And he was aye spierin' whenever he got a chance at auld folks aboot Common Ridings lang syne. It sune becam' a standin' joke – Yiddy Bally and the Common Riding. And at first he didna' like bein' lauched at, and ye could see him pretendin' no' to be interested if it was mentioned, and even gan' oot o' his wey to cheenge the conversation. But that didna last lang, and he sune got used to bein' lauched at – and, aiblins, to like it. It gied him a kind o' distinction o' its ain, and he was sherp eneuch to ken that folk are apt to be gratefu' whiles to the cause o' their amusement. For a while, tae, he used aften to get his leg pu'd – some o' the wags 'ud mak' up the maist ludicrous fables o' past Common Ridin's and puir Yiddy swallowed them a' like lamoo. But a' the same his real knowledge o' a' the oots and ins o' its history was growin', and it wasna lang afore he kent the guid coin frae the fause.

'Naething could stop him. He even got at the files o' the local paper and read every line aboot the Common Ridin' that had appeared in't since the year one. And, forbye, he kept a' that ony leavin' body cud tell him. And the mair he learned the mair thrifty o' his lear he turned. He wasna aye talkin' aboot the Common Ridin' noo, tho' a'body kent he was aye thinkin' aboot it. No. It was only as a special favour he'd talk aboot it. And syne it was only to a wheen carefully-selected cronies. In ord'nar company if Common Ridin' was mentioned he'd never let cheep unless he was appealed to to settle a knotty point. He was the final court o' appeal. Whatever he said was richt. Frae the time he was oot of his teens he was never kent to mak' a mistak'. He was like that memory man in the papers – only the Common Ridin' was Yiddy's a'e subject. On a'thing else he was as toom as a cock's egg. But ye couldna riddle him wi' the Common Ridin'. He'd the names o' a' the Cornets aff by hert frae A to Z, and no' only the Cornets, but the dogs that wun the hound trail; the horses that wun the races; the men that wun the wrestlin' and wha cairried the Croon o' Roses and the Thistle and the Bannock and Saut Herrin', and wha cried the Fair, and hoo mony horsemen followed the Cornet, and wha was his right-hand man and wha was his left-hand man, and whatna year saw the first wumman rider, and what like the weather was – and dod! I'm no shair that he didna ken the name o' ilka bairn that ever toddled wi' a heather besom and got a thripp'ny bit. He was a fair miracle. And forbye, he was an authority on the rites themselves – the size o' the Thistle, the bakin' o' the bannock, the twal' penny nail that hauds the saut herrin' to the bannock, the order o' precedence in the procession, the exact wordin' o' the Cryin' o' the Fair, and a' the ancient details o' the burgh boonds and the rights o' the freemen.

'But he hedna wun on the Committee yet. Ye ken what a Committee is in a place like this. It's aye in the haunds o' a certain few, and if ye dinna belang to their cleek ye've nae mair chance o' gettin' on to't than a rich man has o' gaen' through the e'e o' a needle. But Yiddy's cheenge o' tactics showed the steady development o' his ambition – his maister-passion, as the meenister ca's't. It was a move in the right direction no' to be owre free wi' his information to Tom, Dick, and Harry, but he took guid care no' to disoblige ony o' the Committee if they did'm the honour o' askin' his opinion on ony point. He played his cairds well. The Common Ridin' Committee was like a'thing else in the Muckle Toon – kirks, the Masons, freen'ly societies – it was composed o' individuals you never heard o' in ony ither connection. And apart frae the Committees they specialise in, their opinions on onything else arena worth tippence. It only met in public aince a year for the choosin' o' the Cornet. The committee were chosen tae, but naebody ever thocht of no' juist re-electin' the auld haunds again unless there was a vacancy by act o' God or ane o' them leavin' the toon; and a' the ither arrangements were made by the committee. And, to tell the truth, although the Cornet was chosen by the meetin' to a' appearances, the committee aye had it a' cut and dry aforehaun'. For a' his knowledge it wasna until he was in his twenty-third year that Yiddy was elected a member o' the committee. Twa years afore that some bletherin' fule proposed him when there was nae vacancy. If it had gane to the vote there's nae doot he'd hae been elected a' richt and some ither body knocked oot – but Yiddy up and said he couldna allow his name to gang forrit under sic circumstances. Ye should hae heard the applause. It was an understood thing efter that that Yiddy would fill the first openin'.

'And when he did he said that as far as could be ascertained he was by at least ten years the youngest member that had ever had the privilege o' servin' on that committee, barrin' Cornets. Ye'd ha'e thocht that that would ha'e been eneuch for the maist ambitious man. But Yiddy was cast in a different mould. I aye had the reputation o' bein' a gey lang-sichted customer, and I kent weel eneuch that Yiddy had fish to fry naebody else had seen. But what kin' o' deep sea craturs they could be was anither question. Somebody asked me what I thocht he hed at the back o' his mind, and it was on the tip o' my tongue to say, – "What price Cornet!" By guid luck I was juist in time to check mysel' frae sayin' ocht sae foolish. Yiddy was young eneuch and licht eneuch in a' conscience to be Cornet, but he'd nane o' the ither qualifications. Apairt frae the fact that he didna' ken a'e end o' a pownie frae the ither, the Cornets are aye drawn frae the sprigs o' the gentry or young bluids o' fairmers – no' factory haun's. It tak's a bonny penny to be a Cornet, and Yiddy was the last man on earth to want to lower the dignity o' the Standard-bearer and ha'e the committee at their wits' end for the cash to cairry oot the programme in proper style. Sae I juist said: "Yiddy kens what he's efter – and it'll no' be common property till he says the word," and, juist to keep up my reputation and forgettin' that mony a true ward is spoken in jest, I addit, "And ye can guess till ye're tired, but ye'll no' fin' oot."

'It sune becam' perfectly obvious that Yiddy was playin' a deep gaim. Ye'd hae thocht he'd hae dominated the committee aince he got on t' it. But no' him. He did the lion's share o' the donkey wark – and gied the credit to the ithers. Ye never heard his voice in the public meetin's. Even in the committee meetin's he let the ithers dae a' the talkin' – but he'd talked tae each o' them singly first (or as many as he needit tae talk tae wi' a particular end in view), and maist a'thing they did and said had come frae him in the first instance. Yiddy had them a' on strings withoot them, or onybody else, haein' ony idea o't. And as time gaed on it seemed clearer and clearer that he'd nae axe to cairry the croon o' roses or to mairshal the bairns wi' the heather besoms or gie oot the thrippeny bits or get ane o' their freens on for this or that or the ither thing, and naebady was better at smoothin' oot the runkles and seein' that everybody got what they wantit or as near haund it as possible, than Yiddy. But he aye kept in the backgrun' himsel' – the poo'er ahint the scenes, as the minister says. Aft an' on he got the chance o' maist o' the plooms, but he aye said 'No,' like George Washington – till he had refused sae often and yet dune sae much and obliged every one o' them in sae mony ways that they simply couldna refuse him whatever he did want. Noo ye ken what Yiddy was like – juist a rickle o' banes wi' the thews o' a maggot. The thistle for the Common Ridin' was grown doon at the Toonfit. A plot o' grun was set apairt for the purpose, and mebbes half a dizzen thistles were grown each year, and for weeks aforehand croods used to gang doon on Sunday efternunes to see hoo they were comin' on. The biggest and shapeliest was chosen, but it was an unwritten law – and a point o' honour wi' the gairdener – that it had to be at least aucht fit high wi' the tap aboot as muckle in diameter. Tied to the tap o' a flag pole it made a bonny sicht, wallopin' a' owre the lift, an' a hunner roses dancin' in't, a ferlie o' purple and green.'

Like the suffragette colours, I thocht.

'It was mair than ae man could cairry, of coorse, for mair than a few yairds at a time. There were aye fower or five hefty chiels tell't off to gie a hand wi't, but the principal carrier for mony a year had been Neen Ferguson. Ye mind Neen? A buirdly figure o' a man he was, sax fit three in his stockin' soles and braid in proportion. It used to be said that he could hae felled a bull wi' a single dunt o' his nieve. Well, it was aye Neen's pride to cairry the thistle single-handed frae the fit o' the Port into the Market Place – a distance o' mebbe a hunder yairds – and auld folks used to say that mair than ae cairrier afore him had tried the same dodge, but he was the first that had ever succeeded. Weel, juist three weeks afore the Common Ridin' puir Neen was cairret aff wi' the 'flu, and there was a rare howdy-do as to whae was to tak' his place.'

I jaloused it richt aff the reel. 'Yiddy,' I said. He lookit me up and doon and then he gaed on:

'Aye, Yiddy it was. The cat was oot o' the bag at last. There was nae gainsayin' him. He was deid set on't, tho' ye'd as sune hae thocht o' a rabbit settin' in to worry a beagle. And mind you, tho' as I've tell't you, he'd pit them a' in sic a position that his word was practically law, they tried their utmaist to get him aff the notion. They lauched at him and pled wi' him and pointed oot hoo important it was frae the general standpoint o' the programme that the Thistle should be weel and truly cairrit. But it was nae use. "I'll cairry the Thistle," he said. "I'm no' muckle to look at but I've never let the Common Ridin' doon yet through onything I've either dune or left undune – an' I'll no' let the Thistle doon either. I'm mebbe no a Hercules athegether – but guid gear gangs in little buik, and ye'll aiblins be surprised to see what I can dae when I set my mind to't." "It disna' maitter aboot settin' ye'r mind to't," somebody said, "Ye're no asked to balance't on yer heid. If your back was as strang as your will there'd be nae question aboot it." "I'll cairry it," said Yiddy. "I'll hae my helpers, but frae the fit o' the Port to the centre o' the Market Place I'll cairry it mysel', and nae ither man'll pit a finger on the pole." Excitement ran high when the news leakit oot; and shair eneuch when the day cam' there was Yiddy wi' the holder strappit roond his middle, at the howkin' o' the thistle, wi' his helpers roond him. It was a whopper tae.

'It took them a' their combined strength to lift the pole aince the Thistle was tied on and fit the end o't into Yiddy's holder. It was perfectly clear then that they'd made a big mistake. The rest left gae o't juist for a meenit, and Yiddy fair doobled up under the load. They'd to tak' haud again at aince. Yiddy never said a word but juist gied reid and white by turns like – like a signal. Aff they gaed to join the procession. The helpers raxed themsel's for a' they were worth tae mak' it as licht for Yiddy as they possibly could – but even then as ane o' them said. "We expectit tae hear his spine crack at ony step." Yet it was wonderfu' tae see hoo the wee cratur braced himsel' up. Heaven only kens what he maun hae been sufferin'… Still they got to the fit o' the Port a' richt, and then Yiddy said: "Noo, haunds aff. I'll manage the rest mysel'." No' a haund slackened, but Yiddy lookit at his helpers first on the ae side, then on the ither with sic a glower in his een that they let gae afore they kent what they were daen. They said efter his een were juist like twa slaps into Hell itsel'. And he moved – cairryin' the Thistle by himsel'. The first twa-three steps maun ha'e shown him that nae maitter what unheard o' strength he'd summoned to his assistance he'd never manage to the centre o' the Mairket Place. That maun ha'e been an awfu' moment for him – for this is hoo I figure it oot. It was the pride o' the Common Ridin' versus his ain. Could he maintain them baith? The first wadna suffer materially if he let his helpers tak' haund again – but the second, wad, mortally. There was only a'e way oot it seemed. Sae he sterted to rin'! Guid alane kens hoo. A'body else stude stock still, their een stelled in their heids and their herts in their mooths; ye could ha'e heard a peen fa'. He reached his goal. The Thistle swung for a meenit in the air. Syne he seemed to crumple juist as if he'd gane fair through himsel', wi' the thistle hidin' the hole. In the deid silence it was the eeriest thing ye could imagine. Then, as sune as he was doon, sic a hullabaloo! I was as near him as you are to me noo, and a wheen o's pu'd the thistle affin'm, and had him up in oor airms afore the crood had time to surge in. We were like herrin' in a barrel noo. "Gangway," somebody shouted – and a lane opened up to the door o' the chemist's shop as if by magic. "Haud on," cried Yiddy: "Alick," he said, turnin' to ane a' his helpers, "Tak' the Thistle. I dinna ken what possess't me – but the Common Ridin' maun go on. A'e man can cairry me – I'm nae great wecht – and I haena faur tae gang. Let naebody else move." Sae ae man cairret him to the chemist's shop, while a'body else stude like stookies and Yiddy made him halt on the doorstep.

'"Gang on wi' the Common Ridin'," he cried, in a voice that soondit richt owre the Market Place. And we did. But Yiddy was deid afore his voice had stappit echoin'! – and whiles I think it hesna stoppit yet.'

Murtholm Hill

'The warld's like a bridescake in a shop window the day,' he said.

'Weel, see and tak' care o' yersel' noo,' said his mither, 'and no' be comin' back killt.'

'Nae fear o' that.'

She was smilin'. The things that boy said! She'd see him waggin' his heid in a pulpit a' richt – if naething cam' owre him.

He was pleased that he'd gar'd her smile, and wonderin' what had pitten that in his heid – 'the warld's like a brides-cake'. No' bad far a boy of twelve. There wasna' anither boy in the toon could hae said onything like it. He was wishin' he could follow it up wi' anither. It had never really been in his heid ava. It had juist louped frae naewhaur to the tip o' his tongue. He micht sit in the hoose a' day and no' think o' anither to gang wi't. Forbye, for his age, he was as tall and weel-built as ony o' the boys in the toon, tho' he'd never been allowed to rin wild like maist o' them. Sittin' in the hoose and thinkin' o' things like that was fine; nane o' the rest o' them could dae that – but he wanted to show that he was as guid as them at ither things tae. If they could dae things that he couldna that took awa' frae the things he could dae and they couldna. 'Aye, he's clever, but he's no' strang.' That took the gilt aff'n the gingerbread a'-thegither. It made brains nae mair than the result o' bein' silly; a thing naebody envied.

Of coorse, he kent it 'ud be a' richt aince he was a bit aulder. It was only for a while he'd to thole it. He'd grow up into a banker or a lawyer, or, at the vera least, a teacher, and they'd be mill-haunds a' their days; and nae wicer, the feck o' them, at forty than they were at fourteen.

Seein' him dackle, his mither swithered tae. She wanted him to enjoy himsel', of coorse; yin's only young yince, but, a' the same... She thocht she'd try again.

'I wish ye werena gan' to the Murtholm tho'. The Lamb Hill 'ud dae ye fine. Ye'd enjoy yersel' as weel there, and it's faur safer.'

'I'm owre big. It's only the infant schule that gang there.'

'Weel, there's lots o' ither places – up Ewes or awa' oot the Capshawholm Road or the Wauchope, and ye'd hae them a' to yersel' and could dae as ye liked.'

'They're a' richt for sli'in', but no for sledgin'. There's naething worth ca'in' a brae till ye gan' miles oat.'

'Havers! The Copshawholm Road....'

'The Copshawholm's no' steep eneuch to stert wi' – and syne it's owre steep. It 'ud be the best o' the lot if it began suner and endit better – and besides, the bobbies'll no' let ye sledge there. It's a blin' corner and bad eneuch for a bike let alane a sledge. There's been plenty o' accidents there already.'

His mither had had nae thocht o' that end o' the road – and it aboot took her braith awa' him thinkin' she had! – but o' the heichs and howes awa' oot by the White Yett. There wadna be ony danger oot there, and it was quite steep eneuch for him, besides gan' up and doon like the switchback at the fair, but it was juist as weel to say nae mair aboot it. He'd shairly never think o' attemptin' the Lang Brae – but the bare idea o't hadna' been sae impossible to'm or hoo could he hae thocht she'd actually suggested it? The idea fair gar't her shiver.

'The Murtholm's fell dangerous tae,' she said. 'The bottom hauf's steep, and if ye dinna tak' the corner ye gang richt into the water.'

'It's frozen owre,' he said, 'and what's mair, it's as shallow as a saucer juist there. It wadna' come owre your taes, even if there was nae ice.'

'Weel, it's narrow between the wa's. Some o' the bigger yins'll mebbe rin ye doon and coup ye. See and let the ithers awa' first. Ye'll be safer if ye come doon last wi' naebody ahint ye.'

He gied a crookit kind o' lauch. Weemun didna' understaund. Hoo could ye wait till the last when there was nae last? They were gan' up and doon a' the time. He kent weel eneuch what she was hintin' at tho'! Twa winters syne he'd been on the Lamb Hill, when some o' the bigger yins cam' up and chased the youngsters awa' and took his sledge frae him. It was the finest sledge o' the lot by a lang chalk, wi' lang steel rinners – the roond, narrow kind, no' the braid, flat yins. Maist o' the ither bairns had been on bits o' boxes withoot rinners at a'. Pride gangs afore a fa' – and he'd been fell prood. He'd been ane o' the biggest yins there, and wi' the best sledge he'd been nane owre canny aboot claimin' the croon o' the hill and hustlin' some o' the wee'r and less forritsome yins into the side. What a stound he had at the stertin' place! 'Na, na. You gang first,' said the ithers that were there. And as he flew doon he saw the envious looks o' the ithers that were climbin' back. The best sledge on the field! Gosh! it could gang! Like greased lichtnin'! And aince or twice that efternune as he was near the top climbin' up he saw ithers stertin', and, by rinnin' as hard and launchin' off as quick as he could, he was able to mak' up on them hauf way doon and send them whirlin' and whummlin' into the wreaths at the side. Nae end o' fun. And he was juist in the middle o't when a wheen o' the big yins cam' alang the tap road frae the heid o' the Kirk Wynd and clam' the palin' and ordered them aff the coorse. He was climin' up at the time – and heard them. But they didna' mean him? It 'ud be some o' the sma'er fry; and they *were* a bit o' a nuisance and 'ud be apt to get hurt if the big yins were usin' the coorse as well. It 'ud be for their ain guid to keep oot o' the road; but he was a' richt – he could look efter himsel'. Abune a' wi' a sledge like that. Sae he paid nae heed, but trudged on to the stertin' place and clappit himsel' doon on his sledge – and was off. The big yins were still a yaird or twa away. The coorse swoopit doon and then there was a hump, and as you gae'd owre it the sledge flew clean in the air and landit again a yaird or twa doon, and then there was a glorious lang swoop wi' a curve-up at the end that brocht the rin' to a fine finish. But juist as he was toppin' the hump a muckle snawba' dung him clean aff the sledge and sent him whizzin' heid first inta the bank at the side. When he pickit himsel' up and got his e'en and his ears shot o' the snaw his toom sledge was birlin' awa' doon near the fit o' the coorse. And, a' at aince, wi' a shout that gar'd his hert stan' still and made him forget the stoundin' pain in the side o' his heid, ane o' the biggest o' the big yins – Bobby Price – gied a rin' and a jump at the stertin' place and brocht his feet thegither and was off – swoopin' and soarin' owre the hump and swoopin' again like a bird wi' his airms ga'en up and doon as if he'd been dancin' the Hieland Fling, and whiles he coo'ered till his doup was level wi' his heels and up again. By sang! That took some daein'. It wasna mony could dae that. Hoo he wish'd he was as big as Bobby Price!

Bobby Price was at the bottom a' the coorse; and was comin' up again trailin' *his* sledge.

He felt like shoutin' to'm 'Wha cut the yorlins' throats wi' the roostit nail?' and rinnin' awa' as hard as he could. He was a bad yin, Price – up to a' kinds o' ill. Him and his gang used to gang alang the waterside, and when they saw a cat they'd 'Cheechie, cheechie, cheechie,' till it cam' wi'in reach and syne grab it and whirl it roon' and roon' by the tail in cairtwheels – and let gae. And syne there was a splash hauf way owre the water. He'd let them see. He'd…!

But a' at aince he pit his haund up to the side o' his face and brocht it doon again reid wi' bluid. The hert gae'd oot o'm, and he was as seeck as a dog. There maun hae been a stane in the snawba'. That was like them. He never kent hoo he got hame. Naebody gaed wi'm. He kent them a', juist as they kent wha he was – but he hadna a chum amang them. And he gaed hame withoot his sledge. Bobby Price had it. He grat in his mither's airms as if his hert 'ud brak.

'Never mind', she said. 'Your faither'll gang and get it when he comes in – and gi'e them what for, that's mair. That Price needs a sing an the side o' the lug.' He'd picked up eneuch by this time to say: 'Aye. It 'ud be the price o'm.' He smiled even yet inside himsel' when he minded that pun.

But that wasna the warst o't. When his faither gaed to get the sledge there was nae sign o't. Price denied point blank that he'd ever seen it, and the rest backed him up. It was only when his faither was comin' awa' again that he fund a wheen broken sticks lyin' in the corner aside the yett. It was a' that was left o't. The brutes had kickit it to bits when they were dune wi't. But the rinners werena there. He kent naething o' that till the following mornin', and syne he'd anither greetin' match.

'Wheesht, wheesht,' his mither said. 'Your faither'll mak' ye anither yin – and a bigger yin at that.'

'But the snaw'll be a' awa' again afore its ready. Boo-oo.'

'Nae fear. He'll stert to't the nicht, and mebbe finish't tae, and ye can tak' it doon to the smiddy and get the rinners on't the morn's forenune.'

And his faither did. It was a beauty. But he wasna allowed to gang sledgin' again unless his faither was there to watch. And there had been nae real sledgin' weather last winter at a', and he'd never had it oot. That was the sledge he had noo. It was a real grown-up sledge. But, of coorse, he was big eneuch for't noo.

'Oh, I'll be carefu',' he said. 'Ye needna' be feart. I dinna want *this* sledge broken.'

But he wasna sae shair in his ain mind. He was big eneuch and strang eneuch – but he was only yin. The rest hung thegither in cliques. They micht mix as free as ye like: and they were a' freenly eneuch wi'm on the surface; but if ocht gaed wrang – if there was a row or ither – the rest 'ud split up in their different groups as quick as lichtnin', and he'd be left on his ain. And it wasna only that. He couldna' fecht. He'd never had a fecht wi' onybody. Fechtin' wasna' sae muckle a maitter o' strength as juist kennin' hoo. Ye'd to be used to't or ye were nae match for them that were. And it wasna only in regard to fechtin' that he was at a complete loss as compared wi' the ithers. They had an' understaundin' – ways o' sayin' things, and o' lookin' at each other, and twistin' their faces, and a' the rest o't, that meent faur mair than they could ever hae pitten into words – that he couldna' faddom. It cam' frae a' kinds o' experiences and appetities that he didna share wi' them. Ye needit to be leevin' amang't day and daily, to pick it up. He'd never been let rin' aboot the streets or play wi' the ithers oot o' sicht o' his mither's windas. He kent that he was cleverer than them – but only in his heid; he could think a' kinds o' things – but they did a' kinds o' things they couldna' even think aboot, as quick as lichtnin' afore he'd had time to ken what they were daein'. They couldna follow his thochts; but he couldna follow their actions. Though he was as healthy and as strang and as guid-lookin' as ony o' them – and better fed and better clad than maist o' them – somehoo or ither his body didna' seem as quick and as shair o' itsel' as theirs; or, raither, his body and his mind were disconnected somehoo. What they thocht, when they thocht at a', aye depended upon what they were daein'; their minds and bodies worked thegither. And often the bodies were the quicker o' the twa. No' his. His thocht was aye first, and mair often than no' owre fast and fankled his actions – it made him dackle. He lacked self-confidence. It gied him a miserable feelin' – as if he was shut up inside himsel' and couldna' get oot. There was naething the maitter wi' his thocht if only his body 'ud answer to't. But, as the meenister said, 'the spirit was willin', but the flesh was weak'.

And then there were a' kinds o' things that he daurna even attempt for the sake o' his faither and mither. He didna' really want to – except that the ithers did them, and he juist wantit to show that he could tae. There were some o' the things they were aye sayin' – he could say them tae, but he kent that if he did they'd simply roar and laugh, because it 'ud be perfectly plain he'd nae idea o' what they meant. And he'd nae way o' findin' oot. They were things ye couldna ask onybody. Nane o' them had learned them by spierin' – juist by listenin' and lookin' or aiblins some kind o' instinct he hadna' got. You'd to live in a certain kind o' atmosphere to learn things o' that kind – and he didna, and a'body else did. It gied him a queer feelin' that he was naethin' but a pair o' e'en and a brain lookin' on at life – but withoot ony share in't. This was especially the case wi' lassies. A' the ither lads were aye daffin' and cairryin' on wi' the lassies. Of coorse, maist o' them had sisters o' their ain, or were aye wi' chums that had sisters. He hadna. And in dealin' wi' lassies there was a haill complicated way o' gan' on he didna ken the vera first letter o'. Lassies took nae mair notice o' him than if he wasna there. Or, if they did, it was to cry names efter him – 'Lassie-boy', and the like – or pu' his leg and roar an' lauch at the funny way he acted wi' them – no' like ony o' the ither boys ava.

And (he had crossed the wee brig owre the Wauchope noo and gane alang the side o' the burn and was turnin' up the brae between the wa's: and sledge efter sledge was whizzin' past him and landin' its riders on the bank at the corner, lauchin' and shoutin' in the height o' delight) this was the rub. Ye needed a lass ahint ye on a grown-up sledge to get the best fun oot o't. He hated comin' doon by himsel' and a' the ither lads wi' lassies sittin' on ahint them wi' their airms roond their necks. What was the use a' ha'ein' the best sledge on the coorse if a' the rest were gettin' twice as much fun oot o' sledges hauf as guid? And, besides, ye gaed quicker wi' somebody on ahint. Wecht for wecht, naebady could pass him. Stertin' level he'd be at the fit afore they were hauf-way doon the last brae. But if there was twa or mair on their sledges and only him on his, it was a different story. And nae maitter hoo quick he gaed or hoo fine his sledge was rinnin' or hoo weel she took the corners, he'd naebody to share his pleasure and pride – unless a look noo and then frae somebody climbin' up (but then a'body climin' up envied a'body comin' doon), or wi' a much puirer sledge, or less nerve than he had. But it was different wi' a pairtner! He'd an idea that to ha'e a lassie on ahint was only the last proof o' bein' grown-up – a man in the fullest sense o' the term – and wi' a queer thrill o' its ain owin' to he didna' ken juist what; but, apairt even frae thae twa considerations a'thegither, it mair than doobled your enjoyment.

The wa' at a'e side stopped and a hedge began, and, huggin' the ditch, and keepin' a gleg lookout – for every noo and then a sledge wi' its shoutin' riders cam' swishin' by (and there were some whoppers oot, though his ain could compare wi' ony o' them, even in point o' size, and for beauty o' design and its thick reid cushion he hedna seen its marrow yet), he got to the top o' the first brae and on to a wee level stretch. The second brae curled awa' frae his taes like the letter S, hauf o't atween a couple o' slopin' fields, and the rest roon' the side o' a wud to the yett to the hill. Crickey, what a lot were oot. The haill way up was dottit wi' knots o' folk climin' back up, and there was a fair crood at the stertin' place. He'd been ower busy thinkin' to dae mair than notice that maist o' the sledges that had passed him were fu' o' young men and wimmen nearly dooble his ain age. There werena many as young. Up to noo, for a' his doots and difficulties, he'd felt big eneuch and strang eneuch at a' events – but this wasna the Lamb Hill. Frae top to bottom it was nearly a mile and a hauf lang – and tho' it was heavy gangin' on the snaw, an' it took ye the best pairt o' hauf an 'oor to spiel to the stertin' place, ye gaed to the bottom in five meenits. He'd need a' his wits in a press like this. 'See and let the ithers awa' first.' Gosh, that wadna be afore midnicht.

A wee sledge cam' whirlin' roon the first bend o' the S. He saw at a glance that it was a boy in his ain class at the schule. Tam Montgomery, a cocky wee buffer, wi' ane o' the Fletcher lassies on ahint. But he hadna got to the straucht afore twa big tobaggans – bigger even than his ain – wi' four folk on each o' them – shot oot roond the curve ahint him. They were racin' each ither. The lassie Fletcher lookit roon' and the toboggans were fleein' abreest and no' mair than a wheen yairds ahint them, and she whispered something to Tam. He should ha'e steered the nose o' his sledge into his left side a wee and then strauchtened her – and aiblins baith the toboggans 'ud ha'e had room to pass him or ane o' them micht ha'e pu'd up a wee and let the ither aheid. Mebbe he did mean to dae that, but gied owre sudden a jerk, for he coupit richt in the middle o' the coorse on the tap o' the Fletcher lassie. The toboggans were still abreest; but the drivers were leanin' awa' farrit – each wi' ain o' his airms oot, and as they cam' up (it was eneuch to steeve their wrists) they gied Tam and the lassie a shove that sent them skitin' – ane to the ae side and ane to the ither – richt into the ditch. But the steel-shod rims o' the toboggan catched the wee sledge fair and square and dung it to splinters... He didna even lauch as he cam' up past Tam, scramblin' to his feet.

'A narraw escape that time,' he said. 'You're no hurt?'

'No. But there's owre mony big folks', said Tam, 'and they shouldna gang twa abreest. I'd keep aff if I was you. It's no safe.'

'Och, I'll be a'richt,' and then, on a sudden impulse, 'Noo that you've nae sledge, you can come on wi' me if ye like. There's plenty o' room.'

'Na!' says Tam, nesty-like, 'unless I was drivin' mysel'.'

That was owre muckle to ask. And besides, he'd wantit him to refuse. That gied him his chance. 'Weel, if you're gaun hame, and Jeannie's no' tired o't, she can come wi' me.'

Jeannie lauched like to burst – in a kind o' way that needit nae words to complete her answer.

'I'll show them,' he thocht as he trudged on.

He heard them sniggerin' ahint him, and Tam sayin' he hopit something or ither – he didna hear what, but he'd an idea. He'd show them – and yet he kent he'd pit his fit in it again, even offerin' Tam a ride as if he was tryin' to 'come it' owre him, and waur, in regaird to the lassie Fletcher. It was ane o' the kind o' things that werena' dune – except by him – and he didna' ken why he'd dune it. She was nae beauty – wi' a face like a suet puddin'. It 'ud be fine to gang sailin' past them – if the same thing didna happen to his sledge. He hadna' bargained for sae mony big folk. Tam was richt eneuch. It wasna' safe – and a' the less safe him bein' himsel'. Pride gangs afore a fa' – but he wisna prood. Only he'd show them. He'd let them see. The sniggering...

He was nearly at the top, gan' roon the last curl o' the S. He'd been that thrang thinkin' that he hadna' noticed the sledges flashin' by. Sic a crood at the stertin' place – a dizzen or mair at least. But naebody had passed him on the way up and a fell lot had gane doon. He'd aiblins get a clear field efter a' – tho' sometimes that wasna' sae safe either. Some o' the big yins climin' up micht try pranks to whummle him or pelt him wi' snawba's. They were less likely to dae that if a wheen different sledges were comm' doon ahint each ither. Och weel, what did it maitter! He couldna' clim' up and syne walk doon! But he wished there had been naebody at the stertin' place. There was sic a banterin' and cairry-on whiles.

Then juist as he was comm' forrit he saw that the nearest to him was the new minister and his wife, and a lassie wi' them aboot his ain age. It was the minister's niece. The minister had been in his hoose the nicht afore last – his faither was rulin' elder o' the kirk. The minister kent him again: and said, afore them a', 'Hullo, Peter.'

Peter touched his hat and grinned.

'That's a fine sledge you've got.'

'Aye.'

'It's the prettiest I've seen yet,' said the minister's wife.

There was juist a wee thing lackin' here tho' – he didna want them to think that his sledge was owre bonny. That was kind o' Jessie-like.

'Aye,' he said, 'and it can gang like lichtnin'!'

He blushed as he said this, far it had been on the vera tip o' his tongue to say 'like the vera deevil'. No' that he was in the habit o' sayin' things like that. He didna ken quite what had gar'd him think o't, juist at this particular time: and he hadna time to fin' oot. The stertin' place was clear. The last sledge had left juist as the minister spoke to him first.

He whirled his sledge roon wi' an expert air and clappit himsel' doon on't, diggin' his caukered heels in sideways a wee till he was richt to stert.

A'body was watchin' him. He lookit up and was juist gan' to touch his cap to the meenister and be aff when he catched the niece's e'en. There was nae mistakin' her look. Up he jumped and afore he'd time to think, he'd asked her if she'd like to come wi'm. Afore the words were weel oot o' his mooth he was thinkin', 'What a fule I am! What if she winna?' And he kent hoo a' the folk 'ud lauch and say what a cheek he'd had. It 'ud be a' owre the toon; and his faither and mither would be shair to hear o't, and wadna like it. Forbye, it was sae unlike him'. And mair than that, a' at aince, he'd a horrible picture in his mind o' them coupin' and her lyin' deid wi' her heid twisted under her oxter and her neck broken like a stick. He'd never hear the end o' t. It 'ud juist be like his luck.

But the lassie was beside hersel' wi' joy. 'Oh', she said, 'Will you?' 'How kind,' and she was dancin' roond aboot her auntie seekin' permission. 'Please, please!'

He could see that her aunt wantit to let her gang, but was feart and yet didna ken hoo to refuse withoot disappointin' her and withoot hurtin' his feelin's tae.

At last – efter what seemed an eternity – she turned to the minister.

'What do you think, Dick?' she said. That was a'. Left it to him. And 'Dick' to the minister! He lookit at him. Nae doot it was something in his e'en – for he was shair the minister was juist aboot to shak' his heid, when a' at aince he grinned.

'I think,' says he, 'if Peter'll be so kind – and (to his wife) if you don't mind, my dear – there's room for three – tho' what the guid folks'll think o' their new minister now I dare scarcely think.'

Peter jumped at the chance. This was different frae Tam wantin' tae drive. The minister! And in twa three seconds there they were – the minister, then him, then the lassie wi' her airms roan his neck. His sledge juist held the three o' them neat.

'Now, hold on tight, Barbara,' said the minister's wife. 'Barbara!' What a wonderfu' name! Barbara! Barbara needed nae second tellin'. She tightened her grip till he was near chokin'. It was rare to feel the lassie snugglin' in: she'd a wee fur coat on – and the sleeves o't were as soft as silk aboot his neck. and had the bonniest smell – like – like a chemist's shop.

'Keep your legs well up,' said her auntie.

And she stuck them oot alangside his. Fine trig legs wi' lang-laced boots.

Juist as they were shootin' oot o' the first curl o' the S, they met Tam and the Fletcher lassie gaen up again – tho' what for, when they'd nae sledge? He didna let his een licht on them, but juist turned his heid roan, lauchin' to the minister's niece. Her een sae close to his made his tail-end views o' the snaw and the sky like farles o' soot – and aince they were past he saw Tam and the Fletcher lassie stanin' gapin' efter them wi' their een like saucers. The sledge was gan' at a terrific rate. It soared oot o' the S like a swallow, juist rocked for a minute on the wee bit level at the tap o' the first brae – then swoopit doon atween the wa's, wi' the folk climin' up, skippin' in the side like a puckle rabbits. He kent he was missin' a' kinds o' looks on the folks' faces – he hedna even time to tell himsel' that he was seein' this body and that body – but it 'ud a' come back to him efter; he wisna really missin' onything – his een were takin't a' in; tho' his brain was owre excited. But he'd mind a'thing later on. It 'ud bear thinkin' aboot for days an' days, and aye he'd mind something new. As the sledge gethered speed – an' there were mair and mair shadows o' folk skitin' oot o' the road – there didna seem to be three folk, but only yin. He was famous as the minister in front, and as bonny as a picter (no like yon suet-puddin' o' a Fletcher cratur') in the lassie ahint, but, still and on, he was himsel', Peter, the seen o' a' een, the owner o' the sledge, here in the middle, feelin' that the minister and his niece were naething but pairts o' himsel' that he'd been able – hey, presto! – to flash oot to impress the folk and show the reenge o' his personality. Of course, the ithers micht tak' it oot o'm efter. He mauna look owre cocky... Bother sic ideas! He was leevin' for the meenit like a bird on the wing...

The minister took the corner at the fit dandy – as clean as a whustle, and they shot alang the level as far as to the wee brig itsel' afore 'the cat deed'.

The Waterside

There was faur mair licht and life – o' a kind – in the hooses alang the Waterside than onywhere else in the toon. The front windas lookit richt into the water wi' nae trees to daurken them, and the lift was clearer and braider there than owre ony ither pairt o' the toon. There were juist twenty hooses frae the Stane Brig to the Swing Brig, and the toon gaed abruptly up ahint them through a patchwork o' gairdens wi' grey stane wa's to the muckle backs o' the High Street hooses and on to the terraces on the face o' the hill. And on the faur side o' the Water there was naething but the Factory. But the river was braid and a' broken up and fu' o' movement there, and, tho' some o' the loons could thraw a stane frae a'e side to the ither, the Factory seemed faur awa' and could dae naething to impose itsel' on the Waterside windas or oppress them in the least. Abune the Stane Brig lang gairdens, dark wi' auld trees, ran doon to the river frae the backs o' hooses that lookit the ither way and formed a continuation o' the High Street, and aneth the Swing Brig there were the heichs and howes o' a lump o' waste grun' in front o' the New Mill that the Toon Cooncil were usin' as a cinder dump, and owre frae them the Murtholm Woods spielin' the braes o' Warblaw.

Juist abune the Stane Brig there was the meetin' o' the waters whaur the Ewes clashes into the Esk and alow the Swing Brig the Wauchope cam' tumblin' in. But in front o' the Waterside hooses the bed o' the river was fu' o' muckle flat shelfs o' rock they ca'd the Factory Gullets that cut up the water into a' kinds o' loups, and scours, and slithers, and gushes, wi' twa-three deep channels in atween them through which the main flows gaed solid as wa's. Gulls were aye cryin' there and whiles there was a heron standin' on a rock when the water was low, or a kingfisher even. Sae, in the simmer time, or bricht winter days, the hooses alang the Waterside were aye fu' o' a licht and life that made the ongauns o' their inhabitants o' as little consequence as the ongauns o' the rats in the cellars were to them, and the dunt and dirl o' the river was in them like the hert in a man, and they had shoals o' licht and the crazy castin' o' the cloods and the endless squabble o' the gulls in them faur mair even than the folk talkin' and the bairns playin'. It wasna sae much a case o' leevin' your ain life in ane o' thae hooses as bein' pairt and paircel o' the life o' the river. Your hoose wasna your ain. It was wind-and-water ticht in a'e way bit no' in anither. A' the ither hooses in the toon were sober and solid in comparison. And the folk that leeved in them had a guid grip o' their lives. But alang the Waterside they were windy, thriftless, flee-aboot craturs. The sense was clean washed oot o' them. A' the sense – and a' the stupidity tae. It's only some kinds o' birds that ha'e een like what theirs becam' – cauld and clear and wi' nae humanity in them ava.

The folk up the hill lookit doon on the toon and some o' them pitiet it and some o' them felt clean abune't, but the taps o' the hills a' roon aboot that they saw frae their windas kind o' steadied and silenced them. They werena like the Waterside folk; there's a queer difference atween ha'en taps o' hills and taps o' waves aye in yin's life. And the folk in the tree-daurkened hooses were different again – they were slow and secret and aften kind o' sad. And the folk on the High Street had naething but themsel's and ither folk in their lives – they were clannish and fu' o' clash and conceit, and aye comin' an' gaen throughither. But the Waterside folk kept skitin' this way and that. There was neither peace nor profit in the lives. They couldna settle. Their kind o' life was like the dipper's sang. It needit the skelp and slither o' rinnin' water like the bagpipes' drone to fill oot the blanks. Withoot that it was naething but a spraichle o' jerky and meaningless soonds.

There was only a narrow cobbled street between the hooses and the water wa' that stude aboot twa feet high, and was aboot as braid on the tap and syne fell frae aucht to ten fit to the riverside rocks. And dae what ye wad, naething 'ud ever content the bairns but to be scramblin' up on the wa' and rinnin' alang't, and their mithers were aye at their doors wi' their hearts in their mooths. They never kent a meenit's peace.

It was only in the winter time that the water exercised its poo'er owre the haill toon. The hills were hidden in mists then and the folk that were aye accustomed to them were at a loss. They were like a puckle water when a jug braks; they'd tint the shape o' their lives. And the folk in the High Street couldna talk lood eneuch to forget the roarin' o' the spate. It seemed to be underminin' the toon. It was level wi' the tap o' the water wa'. Trunks o' trees, hayrucks, and whiles sheep and kye, cam' birlin' doon on the tap o't. The Waterside folk lived in their doors or windas as gin their hooses had nae insides. They could dae naething but look, or raither be lookit at, through and through, for it was the water that did the lookin' and no' them. There was nae question o' thinkin'. It was faur owre quick and noisy for that. It fair deaved them, and every noo and then a muckle wave loupit in through their een and swirled in their toom harnpans and oot again. That's what I mean when I say that the Waterside folk were brainless craturs. Brains were nae use there. To dae onything ava they'd to use something faur quicker than thocht – something as auld as the water itsel'. And thocht's a dryland thing and a gey recent yin at that.

The Waterside folk couldna stop to think. The High Street folk thocht aboot naething bit themsel's, and a' they did was the outcome o' that. The folk on the hillside were like the sailor's parrot – they didna say muckle, but they were deevils to think. The Waterside folk micht ha'e managed to dae a bit thinkin' in the simmer time when the water was low, but low water, they said, gied them a queer feelin' as if the fronts o' their faces had fa'n aff, that fair paralysed them. They were like the man that tell't the wumman he wanted nane a' her damned silence; and sae they juist stottit aboot like a wheen hens wi' the gapes.

I mind a'e Sunday when the water was higher than onybody had ever seen it afore. They were frichtened for the Swing Brig. But it had stoppit rainin' a wee by dennertime, and the fules o' High Street folks, and a wheen o' the Hillside yins tae, wad send their bairns to the Sunday schule. To get there they'd to cross the Swing Brig. It was weel named Swing Brig that day. It was as crazy wi' unexpectit movements as the flair o' the Hoose o' Fun at the Glesca Exhibition. Every noo and again the rusty contraption wheenged richt abune the clammer o' the spate. Ye could hear nae ither soon' but the roar o' the water and whiles the whine o' the iron.

Juist at skailin' time for the Sunday schule the rain cam' on again waur than ever. It fell haill water. Faithers and mithers cam' rinnin' doon wi' umbrellas and waterproof coats juist as the bairns were croodin' on to the Brig. And a' at yince it brak in twa haufs and skailed a'body on't into the river like a wheen tea leafs in a sink.

The news spreid like lichtnin'. Afore the bairns struck the water the banks at baith ends o' the Brig were black wi' folk. Men that could soom, and some that cauldna, dived richt in and brocht bairns oot. Ithers had run to a tongue o' rock that ran oot into the river a bit faurer doon, and were in time to grab a wheen o' the weans there as they gaed whummlin' by. Atween the Brig and the end o' the cinder dump a back swirl had scoopit oot a hole for itsel', and by guid luck maist o' the bairns were spun into that. Men jumpit in wadin' up to their oxters to rescue them, and a wheen wimmen tae. Human cheens were made frae the tap o' the dump to the middle o' the pool. A'e wumman, in particular, was fair awa' wi't; her bairn had been on the Brig, and she slid doon the cinder brae on her hunkers richt into the pool. She grabbit a wee lass frae a man a bit faurer oot, but when she saw it wasna her ain bairn the doited cratur, withoot kennin' what she was daein', pitched it into the water again. She was frae ane o' the hooses on the Hill – a' thocht and nae sense! Nane o' the High Street folk ventured into the water tho' a' their bairns were rescued; and nane o' the Waterside folk's bairns were on the Brig when it brak. Catch them! But they did the feck o' the savin' wi' an air as muckle as to say: 'If the fules 'ud keep their brats at their ain gate-en's they'd be less nuisance to ither folk.' If it had been the faithers and mithers instead o' the bit bairns, I question whether the Waterside folk 'ud ha'e bothered to rescue them, and even as it was I'm no shair they felt in their herts they were daein' richt – especially on a Sunday.

A'body's Lassie

She turns up at a' kinds o' odd times and in a' kinds o' odd places. Whiles she's dressed in rags and whiles she's in the vera height o' fashion like ane o' the coonty gentry. Her age varies. She may be nae mair than a lassie wi' her hair hingin' doon her back, or she may be a braw figger o' a wumman ye'd tak' for onything atween thirty and forty. But as a rule she looks aboot nineteen. Whatever her age she's as bonny as a dream. And there's nae end to her tricks. Mrs McVittie, the baker's wife, was juist sayin' to me yestreen that ye never ken wha's turn it'll be next wi'r. Ye'll hear a chop at the door and there's a split image o' yer wee lassie that deed o' the diptheria. Ye ken that it's owre guid tae be true and yet ye can hardly misbelieve yer ain een. And it's no' juist yer een. 'Mummy', she'll say, that lifelike. A'e puir wumman I ken that's aye in a natter wi' her big faimily kent there was something wrang and yet she wisna in time to keep back the words. 'What gars ye knock, ye wee limmer?' she said, 'haudin' me rinnin' to the door when I'm thrang.' She cud hae pu'd her tongue up by the roots efter.

And there's mair than ae mither in this toon has been ca'ed tae the door in the same way to fin' a wee white-faced, waesome bit critter stannin' on the steps. 'Weel, what is't?' or 'What ails ye, lassie?' – but never a word oot o' her heid. 'Ha'e ye lost yer tongue? Noo, noo, nae mair greetin'. Rin awa' hame to your mammy. Whaur d'ye bide?' Or whiles ane o' her bairns 'ud come to the door wi' her or she'd cry ben to see if they kent wha' the streenge lassie was. But they'd nae idea. And it wasna till later on – mebbe efter she'd gane till her bed and hed a meenit to think – that the wumman 'ud say to hersel', 'Losh, but it was fell like my puir wee Jeanie,' or Lizzie, as the case micht be, and begin worryin' hersel' till her man said, 'Toots, wumman, what're ye rowin' aboot at? Can ye no lie still? Ye're like a hen on a het girdle. This is no' a soomin' pond.'

I'm namin' nae names, but I was tell't aboot a'e wumman that lives up the brae, and I hope there's no anither like her in the toon. The chop cam' to her door a'e forenune, and when she gae'd to't there was the bit lassie on the step. 'What d'ye mean stannin' wi' yer clarty feet on my new-cleaned step?' says she. The lassie juist hung her heid. 'What d'ye want, onyway?' said the wumman, but the lassie juist swallowed in her throat and couldna get a word oot. 'D'ye think I've got a' the mornin' to plaister wi' the likes o' you?' says the wumman, 'clear aff oot o' this!' And slammed the door in her face. An 'oor efter, she happened to gang to the door again and there was the lassie aye stannin' on the step. Ane o' the bobbies was gaen by at the time, sae the wumman cried him owre and tell't him aboot 'this silly wee brat that disna ken what she wants and'll no' gang awa'.' The bobbie was a great muckle fat reid-faced man that was a favourite wi' a' the bairns, and he pit his haund doon neth her chin and tilted up her facey. He'd juist time to see her afore she disappeared as gin she'd never been. Neither him nor the wumman saw which airt she gaed. 'Missus,' he said, 'It's your ain bairn.'

By jing, there was a row owre that. The wumman gaed richt in and pit on her bunnet and gaed doon to the Polis Office and reportit the maitter; and the Superintendent held an inquiry int't. The bobby stuck to his guns, and by guid luck the wumman neist door had seen the lassie and said she thocht nocht o't at the time, but later on it struck her that the lassie on the doorstep was the verra image o' the wean that deed. And she said she wisna surprised a bit that her ain mither didna recognize her. 'She's like that,' she said. 'She's forgotten she ever had her – tho' it's nae mair than three years come September that she deed.' But ye ken what neebors are; and besides, wha ever heard o' a deid bairn comin' back hame and stannin' on the doorstep? The Superintendent gaed the bobby a gey tellin' aff in front o' the wumman – but, after she was awa', he spoke to him and the next-door wumman in a different way a' thegither. As weel he might, seeing that he wisna only Superintendent o' the Polis but o' a Sunday schule, and the faither o' a faimily himsel'!

Whiles the critter's ploys had a different endin' frae that tho! There was the case o' the druggist's hoose-keeper that was engaged to Wilson the plumber and had gien notice to quit at the term to be marriet. Guid kens what she saw in Andra Wilson, the muckle sumph. He wasna fit to clean her shoes to'r. Weel, he was stannin' lauchin' and talkin' wi'r at the druggist's door a'e nicht when a wee lassie cam' fleein' in frae naewhaur into her airms cryin' 'Mummy, mummy'. Afore the wumman kent what she was daein' she was doon on her knees cuddlin' the wee cratur for a' she was worth and lauchin' and greetin' at the same time, but in the verra middle o't – whisk! and the lassie was gane as if it had been a' a dream. Wilson ca'd her a' the names he could lay his tongue to, and rived the engagement ring aff her finger and pitched it into the gutter whaur it rowed doon the cundy. The scaffy had a gey job graipin' in the glaur for't the followin' day.

Sic a crood had gethered. It cam' oot that a gey wheen years afore when she was a young servant lassie she'd had a bairn to a son o' the hoose. Her auld mither brocht it up and it was the bonniest wee thing imaginable. But it deed when it was aboot nine. The wumman was still on her knees a' this time wi' a face like the day o' Judgment, but the druggist – his shop was juist owre the way – cam' elbowin' through the crood and liftit her up withoot a word spoken and took her into the hoose and banged the door on a'body's face. She's still wi'm; and I heard a rumour the ither day that they're gaun to be marriet. He's a guid bit aulder than her, but he's no' juist sic an auld man either.

Then a'e nicht juist efter dark there was a wheen bairns playin' ring-a-ring-o'-roses at the heid o' the Factory Entry, when anither lassie cam' rinnin' oot frae the shadow o' the hooses into the ring o' the lamp to join them and twa o' the bairns let gae to mak' room for her. And juist then they saw what it was and the dance stoppit as if they'd been struck.

'Jeannie Morrison', said ane a' the auldest o' the bairns aince she fan' her voice, 'whaur hae ye sprung fra?'

'Whaur d'ye think?' said the lassie lauchin' and tossin' her curls.

'But ye're deid,' said the other.

'Deid?' says she, 'What's deid?'

The bairn lookit roon' at the rest for help, but they'd nane to gie.

'Deid's juist deid,' said she.

'You mauna believe a' that the big folk say,' said the lassie.

'Then you're no' deid efter a'?' said the ither.

'Ee!' said the ither, 'Sic a fraud! A' the rest o's in the class had to gie money to the teacher for a wreath for ye.'

'Dinna let's waste time,' cried the lassie, stampin' her feet. 'It'll sune be bedtime and it's a while sin' I'd a game.'

Sae they a' forgot what they'd mindit and clasped hands and danced roon' and roon' in the licht o' the lamp shoutin' and singin' till they were fit to drap. Syne twa-three o' their mithers cam' cryin' to them to c'wa hame and get to their beds and off they ran this way and that. But them that mindit that Jeannie Morrison had been supposed to be deed, and tell't their faithers and mithers aboot her, thocht they took it in a gey queer way and Jeannie didna turn up at the schule the next day or ony ither day, and she never cam' to play wi' them again.

That's sae muckle for a'e side a' her pranks. I could keep on tellin' ye ither stories a' nicht. Nearly a'body else in the place kens them as weel as me; but naebady need think: 'If she comes to my door, I'll say "Ho, Ho! Y'ere no' gan' to play ony o' your tricks on me."' Ye canna gaird against her. She does things that naitural-like you're taen in against your ain judgment. She's mair alive than Life itsel'.

It's a queer body that hasna some unsatisfied desire or some skeleton in the cupboard, or doesna wish that something or ither hedna' happened – even if it's only gettin' auld. If you're a decent kind o' soul at a' she sets your hert agin' your heid (and you're nane sorry efter that it won); and if you're no', your conscience mak's a fule o' you, juist when you're least expectin't. Tak' Mrs Dunbar, the banker's wife, for example. She was walkin' doon the High Street in braid daylicht. And by the time she got doon to Cunningham the shoemaker's, there was the bonniest wee lassie, walkin' alangside her, her hand in hers. And Mrs Dunbar and her was lauchin' and talkin' to each ither as happy as ye like! But juist at the fit o' the Kirk Wynd – whisk! – the lassie was gane. Mrs Dunbar lookit a' roon' aboot and gaed doon juist like an umbrella when the shank comes up through't. She'd to be carriet hame, puir body. She's kinda got owre it noo. 'D'ye ever hear onything sae stupit?' she says, when she's tellin' aboot it. 'I've aye wanted a lassie, and, ye ken, I clean forgot that a' my bairns are laddies.'

Ye ken auld Bauldy, the milkman? They say he hesna been able to see his ain feet this forty year an' mair. He was makin' his mornin' ca' at the Manse no' a month agone, when oot she trippit. Auld Bauldy cocks his een when he sees her, as wild as a turkey cock. 'Ye didna turn up last nicht,' says he. 'I did,' says she, 'but I didna see *you* there.' 'What!' says he, 'Ye leein' besom!' And in his anger he turned on the spigot wi' sic ajaw that he splashed himsel' wi' milk frae heid to fit. 'Noo it seems it's your turn to droon,' says she, and disappeared aff the face o' the earth.

He opened his mooth like a fish and couldna shut it again, and he was stannin' like that and no' a drap o' milk left in his ten-gallon can when the meenister's wife hersel' cam' oot. She'd been withoot a servant for a month – and I dinna wonder at that; wha'd bide wi' a critter like yon. It turned oot that twenty or thirty years back, Bauldy had been keepin' company aff and on wi' a servant lassie at the Manse (and as pretty as a picture she was, they say), and ae nicht he trysted her to meet him near haun' the Wauchope Brig whaur the road turns up to the Bex. Bauldy fell in wi' a wheen ithers doon the toon and got as fou' as a puggy an' forgot a' aboot it, but the lassie keepit the tryst. It was a pitch black nicht and somehoo or ither she had faun into the pool at the Brig and couldna win' oot... Bauldy was in an awfu' state the followin' day. But it's queer he should hae mindit juist what she lookit like sae mony years efter, and him marriet and a widower and marriet again and wi' a dizzen o' a family. Tho' they say the seecund wife's a tartar – he hesna had her lang – and nae doot the puir man whiles wishes things had fa'n oot different. It's haurd to tell.

Then there was the case o' the Provost himsel'! A mair dignified auld josser ye wadna meet in a day's mairch, wi' his white fish-tail beard and his lum hat. He was crossin' the Square a'e day, noddin' to this body and that body, and liftin' his tile to the ladies, when, a' at aince, she steppit oot o' Myrtle's fruit shop and gaed a whistle. He whirled to the richt aboot like a young ane and sterted rinnin' to meet her. Of coorse, he flew heels-owre-gowdy and knockit in the croon o' his hat and broke his siller mounted nibby in two into the bargain.

Then there was the time she put her airm in puir Jim Tamson's. And there was Jim, feelin' twenty years younger and fair forgettin' a' aboot what had happened in the interval, and lauchin' and cairryin' on wi' her, and back in the daft days. But when they turned the corner o' John Street, wha did they rin into but his wife? At the first glance he didna even ken her, but she sune enlightened him. She lookit auld eneuch to be the mither o' the bonnie cratur' swingin' on his airm and it was nae use him sayin' 'We used to be great chums – we were in the same class at the schule.' 'Schule!' said his wife, 'It's easy seen ye're in yer second childhood.'

Och, ye can explain it hoo ye like – but there it is. Mebbe it'll be your turn next.

The Moon Through Glass

'Ee!'…She felt she'd been owre late to haud the exclamation back: but, scansin' owre her shouder at her mither and sister she saw that she hedna gien hersel' awa' efter a'. Wi' a shakin' haund and flutterin' hert she gaed on clearin' awa' the tea things. Should she say onything? It 'ud ser' them richt if she cried oot and gar'd them look up and see the new mune through the winda' tae. But she'd never hear the end o't. No' that either o' them believe't in't the way she did. If they'd seen it themsels they'd never hae thocht twice aboot it, or the ane micht hae drawn the ither's attention to't and made some joke aboot it, prood o' daurin' the auld superstition and kennin' the ither 'ud feel the same way or mebbe pretend to be angry for the sake o' hae'in a row and pittin' the hoose in a steer. Especially if she was aboot, for she hated rows and her no' kennin' which o' them to side wi' for peace's sake aye amused them and suner or later they kent they'd draw her into the row tae and syne they'd baith yoke on her and blame her for the haill todo. If either her mither or sister had seen't they wadna hae swithered a meenit aboot trappin' her into seein't tae and lauchin' thegither at her. But she daurna try ony sic pranks wi' them. They'd mak' the maist o't, tho she kent weel eneuch – and they kent she kent – they thocht naething o't really and were only makin' a sang because it was her or for the sake o' makin' a sang. If it wasna ae thing it was anither. They'd aye to be wranglin'.

She could hear them and a' the turns and twists they'd gie't. 'You sud think o' ither folk.' On and on and on, as if she had dune it on purpose or, if no', oot o' eindoon want o' thocht which was even waur. 'What were ye glowerin' through the winda at onywey? Dreamin' aboot that muckle sumph o' a man o' yours? Mebbe he'll propose the nicht at last. If he does ye can tak' it the auld sayin's come true for aince.' That 'ud be her mither: she could hear her – and syne her sister 'ud follow suit. 'But cheer up, Meg. It's no' you that need be hingin' the fupple – unless it's wi' disappointment at the kind o' man you've got efter a' your fancy notions (no' that he'll no' be guid eneuch for you whatever he's like) – for it's him that'll hae the feck o' the ill luck, wi' you for his wife.' And on and on and on.

She daurna say onything aboot onything. They were aye doon on her, aye raggin' her. She could dae naethin' to please them. She wished her haund 'ud stop dirlin'. They'd baith sic quick een. Yet she was feart to gang to the back kitchen – she'd mak' sic a rattlin' as 'ud gar them look up, or she'd let the dishes fa'. It 'ud juist be like her luck. What a how-d'ye-do that 'ud mak'! She'd hae to pay for them – and it was Jack's birthday in a

fortnight. She'd be tell't her fingers were a' thooms – pity the man that
mairriet her! – but nae doot she'd be mair carfu wi' her ain things. Aye gan'
dreamin' aboot! That was the main burden o' their complaint – she was
aye dreamin'. That was the trouble atween them. They didna' ken what
dreamin' was, what onybody could get to dream aboot. And the mair she'd
tried to tell them (when she was younger) the less they'd understood and
the mair they'd made a fule o' her. Her and her dreamin'! What did she
think *she* was? Better than ither folk? Aye moonin' aboot!

And, in the middle o' flytin' at her owre the broken dishes, her mither
looks at the winda, and whups roond waur than ever wi' her haunds on her
hips. 'Ho! ho! Sae that's the cause. You and that damned mune. The ill-
luck's no frae it, but frae you believin't.' And her sister 'ud chip in: 'And
she wasna gaun to say a word aboot it. She wanted us to see it tae! O' a' the
mean, dirty, underhaundit – 'On and on and on, the pair o' them! What
could she say or dae? Suppose she tried to warn them. Nae maitter hoo
quiet she spoke, Jean at onyrate was facin' the winda and 'ud lift her heid
and see't – and blame her for no' warnin' her quicker. Even if she did get
the warnin' oot withoot either o' them see'in't first, they'd juist lauch at her
and look at it to spite her. And syne cairry on aboot her superstitiousness
and the curse it was to a hoose, and to a'body connected wi' sic an afflicted
cratur. Her best plan was aye to haud her tongue – tho' when she did they
ca'd it bein' 'in the dorts' and ranted on aboot her perpetual ill-natur' – she
was as blithe in a hoose as a thunder clood – and she kent as a maitter o'
fact that no' bein' able to speak to them – to open her heart to them – had
made her feel dour and tongue-tacket eneuch in the coorse o' the years.
Thank God, she had Jock.

But at the thocht o' Jock the fu' tide o' her ill-luck in seein' the mune
through gless – this nicht o' a' nichts – poored owre her. It micht mean…
This was the first time her thocht o' Jock had had a tinge o' doot or fear.
This was the first time that she hedna kent for shair that nae maitter hoo
miserable things micht be at hame, she 'ud find naething but joy wi' him.
He was her only ootlet. Only wi' him could she be hersel'. She wasna hersel'
wi' her mither or her sister or ony o' the rest o' them. This wasna her life
– this wranglin' back-bitin' miserable way o' daen'. But ilka noo and then
she won clear o't for a wee – wi' Jock: and she'd been hopin' to win' clear
o't a'thegither sune. In fact she'd expectit him to say the word that vera
nicht – if she hedna seen the new mune through the winda. Whatna price
to pay for a pure accident! And even as this thocht gaed through her heid
she kent that there was a waur yin dodgin' through ahint it that she wasna
able juist to see richt. It was that mebbe he'd still say the word this vera

nicht! The ill-luck 'ud be in her bein' disappointed wi' him – or him wi' her – efter they mairriet; or, frae ae cause or anither their mairriage no' turnin' oot as they expectit. It was the first time *that* had ever entered her heid. Nae wonder it gaed slinkin' through it, she thocht in an effort to tell hersel' that it was oot o' the question – but even as she tried that, it cam' back in again, bigger than ever, and blacker. She sterted to bamboozle hersel' sae that she could imagine it wasna there (altho' a' the time it was gettin' bigger and bigger and blacker and blacker) by tryin' to lauch at hersel' for forgettin' that the ill-luck only lasted for a month sae it couldna affect her mairriage (and, by jings', she'd be mair carefu' in the future in regaird to new munes) and syne, when that didna' work, by tryin' to mind whether or no' the ill-luck couldna' be averted frae something o' consequence to something o' nane by brakin' a plate or some sic thing: and noo she was in sic a state that she was in twa minds either to let the tea things fa' and pit up wi' a' that her mither and sister micht say, or juist tell them what had happened and ask them if brakin' a plate 'ud ward off the ill-luck. But if she did this last they wadna tell her – or they'd tell her wrang; and yet it was an awfu' pity to brak' a' the dishes if ane 'ud dae! She was fair in a swither.

It took her a muckle effort movin' into the back kitchen (it was a God's wonder her mither and sister hadna been at her for takin' sae lang to clear the table as it was) and the dishes jiggle-jiggled in her hands to sic a tune that aince she sterted (near-haund trippin' on the mat) she'd to rin to get them safe to the sink. And the warst thocht o' a' struck her then. What if the ill-luck concerned Jock? What if onything had come owre him? What if he jilted her? Or if he'd had an accident and was deid! She catch't sicht o' hersel' in her faither's lookin'-glass at the side o' the sink. Jock hadna missed muckle onyway. What had he ever seen in her? She didna look the least like what she'd been feelin' inside hersel' afore she saw the mune. She was faur mair like her sister or her mither than she'd ever imagined. If Jock had been a' that she'd thocht he'd never hae gien the likes o' her a second look. But if love had blinded her to the truth aboot hersel' nae doot it had blinded her to the truth aboot him tae. Her sister had aince said: 'Wait till you're mairriet – he's only a workin' man and you an' him'll juist be like ony ither workin' class man and wife.' She'd had a horrid vision o' Jock as nae mair than a common ploo-man, and o' mairriage as the same auld drudgery under a different name. Had a' young couples the same high-falutin' ideas – afore they mairriet? If they'd ha' come doon to the level o' the feck o' the folk roon' aboot – o' her faither and mither say – it was a guid job he was deid. He couldna come doon then. She'd keep him the man she'd thocht him as lang as she leeved. He'd aye be the ootlet for her dreams. But in that case whaur was the ill-luck o' seein' the mune through gless...Tchah! She couldna' mak' heid or tail o't. But she'd better get on wi' the dishes or she'd be late – for what?

Maria

Maria was gaun to dee. 'But it'll no' likely be till some time through the nicht,' he'd heard his mither say. Still, that wasna lang. It was an unco queer thing to think aboot; there she was, talkin' and to a' appearances gey near in her usual – as he'd aye kent her; and even jokin' and lauchin' whiles. Did she ken she was gaun to dee? She didna seem the least bit feart. Ye'd think the prospects o' the weather and the clish-clash o' the toon wadna maitter muckle to a wumman that wadna see the morn. He wondered at his mither. She kent Maria was 'at daith's door,' and yet she was as bad as Maria – her tongue gaun sixteen to the dizzen aboot nocht o' ony consequence, and rallyin' and cairryin' on as if deein' was the maist ordinary thing imaginable. He'd expected something a'thegither different – hushed voices and lang faces, and a terrible solemn kind o' feelin' owre a'body and a'thing. He felt disappointed. To a' ootward appearances there was neist to naething oot o' the common in't ava. Maria micht be gaun to dee, but she certainly didna look like it. Yet a' at aince – accordin' to his mither – something 'ud happen, and Maria 'ud be 'nae mair'; the blinds 'ud be pu'd doon, and syne the men 'ud come and pit Maria's body in a lang black coffin and tak' it awa' and bury it in the grun', and she'd never be seen or heard tell o' again. What a queer thing! What did a body feel like, deein'? He'd ha'e liked to speir at Maria, but something tell't him that he mauna. That was hoo Maria and his mither were gibblegabblin' the way they were daein' – to keep awa' frae the thing that was uppermaist in baith o' their minds.

Mebbe he'd see Maria deein' and ken a' aboot it. His mither had to rin hame for a wee; and he'd to bide wi' Maria till she cam' back. 'Ye'll no' be feart?' she'd spiered him, and he'd said he wadna – but he'd felt feart eneuch, till he cam' in and saw Maria lookin' juist as she'd aye lookit.

But, tho' he'd felt real feart, he'd managed to smile a brave wee smile and say 'Na, na! I'll be a'richt,' for he kent weel eneuch that it wasna ilka laddie o' his age that had the chance o' sittin' by a daithbed – alane at that. It wadna be a thing to brag aboot – but to haud his tongue aboot, and that 'ud mak' him a' the mair mysterious and important. He could hear folk sayin': 'There was naebody wi' her when she deed – but Tam Mackie. His mither had had to gang hame, but Tam volunteered to bide till she cam' back. She wasna lang gane afore the cheenge cam'. Puir Maria; she'd a sair struggle at the end. The laddie did a' he could. It maun ha'e been a gey trial for him. He disna like to talk aboot it, but ye canna wonder at that.'

Sae, altho' it was a relief in a'e way to find Maria sae like hersel', it was disappointin' in anither. There was only a'e thing oot o' the ordinar'. Maria was lyin' in the best bedroom – what had been Mary's room – instead o' in the kitchen bed. It was a bonny room – a' licht colours, juist like the water-colour paintings hingin' on the wa's in their gowd frames. He mindit Mary. She'd been an awfu' lady-body; Maria had aye dune a' the wark. It seemed queer to see Maria in Mary's bed. It gied ye the same sensation as when ye crackit open a chestnut. O' a' the unexpectit things in the warl' shairly there's naething mair unexpectit than to crack open sic a pale green shell and see yon bricht broon chestnut inside it – like a muckle doonsin' e'e. Maria lookit juist as oot o' place in Mary's bed. She was that dark o' the skin. Mary had been a' pink and white – like a rose. And if Maria lookit a kennin' paler than usual it was mebbe owin' to the whiteness o' the sheets reflectin' in her face. If there had been naething but the blankets, there micht ha'e been nae cheenge at a'.

'Weel, weel, I'll no' be lang,' his mither was sayin'. 'Juist lie back and see if ye canna get a wee sleep. I wadna talk ony mair... Tam'll juist sit owre here by the winda and if there's onything ye want he'll get it for ye... Sit here, Tam.'

And she gar'd him sit beside the winda. 'Gie her a look ilka noo and then,' she whispered, 'I'll no' be lang. I think she'll be a' richt till I come back. Keep quiet an' she'll mebbe fa' owre.'

His mither was gane. As sune as the door closed ahint her, he lookit owre; Maria was lyin' back wi' her een shut. She lookit afa' faur awa' tho' and he could hardly mak' oot her face at a' for a shaft o' sunlicht that cam' slantin' in. Bairns were playin' in the street ootside. It was queer to think his brither was up on the golf course somewhere caddyin'. He wadna come and sit like this. Nae fear. 'Tam was his mither's boy.' What gar'd folk say that in sic a way as to mak' ye feel a wee thing ashamed – as if ye were a kind o' lassie-boy? Shairly it took mair courage to sit like this aside a deein' wumman than to cairry a kit o' clubs roon' the hill. Hoo quiet it was in here – like bein' cut off frae life a'thegither. He was mair feart noo; he felt his hair risin'. He wished Maria 'ud wauken again. It hadna been sae bad when she was talkin' awa' to his mither. If he moved and made a wee noise mebbe she'd wauken. He lookit owre to the bed again, movin' his heid forrit to get clear o' the sunbeam. She hadna stirred. There wasna a soon' o' ony kind. It seemed a lang time since his mither gaed awa'. Mebbe she'd met somebody an' was standin' talkin'. He wished she'd come noo.

Wheesht! Was that her? He thocht he'd heard a door openin'. Could it be Daith comin'? His hert was dirlin' inside him at an awfu' rate. He felt like rinnin' owre to the bedside for protection – but he couldna move. The bedroom door was openin' – tho' you could haurdly see it move; it couldna be a human bein' that was open'n't. His mither's heid keeked in; he'd been sittin' wi' stelled e'en, haudin' his braith – he could hardly believe it was really her and no' – no' what? He couldna conjure up ony picter o' the terrible sicht he'd expectit to see.

His mither stepped owre to the bedside. Had she seen hoo frichtened he was?

'Wheesht,' he felt like sayin', 'She's sleepin',' but something hindered him. And his mither turned roon'. He kent at aince frae the look that it was a' owre. Maria was deed – and he hadna seen her deein' efter a'. It didna seem possible. He felt awfu' disappointed. He micht as weel no' ha'e been there ava. If he'd only f'und oot afore his mither had come back – and been able to tell her, to show her he kent. Even if he hadna seen anything he could ha'e claimed to ha'e seen a' kinds o' things. She couldna ha'e contradicted him. Could he no' pretend even yet to ha'e kent? What could he say? He wished his brain didna feel sae stupid-like.

'Rin and tell your faither, Tam,' she said.

He was off like a shot – rinnin' thro' the streets for a' he was worth. Shairly folk 'ud see frae his face and the way he was rinnin' that he was cairryin' important news. That was aye something. But he was wishin' in his hert o' herts that his thochts were gaun as quick as his legs. He couldna mak' up his mind what to say.

The Visitor

I mebbe haena got the hang o't just richt. It's a queer story. But, as faur as I can mak' oot, here it is.

It seems that in the middle o' the nicht there cam' a rappin' at the door. Mrs M'Ilwrath's a licht sleeper – no' like him. She heard the first chap but wisna shair it was their door. It was a bricht munelicht nicht but fell cauld. There's this to be said for her – that if it had been ony ither wumman in the toon and they'd heard a chap at that time o' nicht, and thocht it was at

ony ither door than their ain, they'd have been oot o' bed and hauf oot o'
the winda like a shot. They wadna hae waited to wauken their men – let
alane lippened to them to find oot. It 'ud only tak' a wag to gang roond the
streets in the wee sma' hoors chappin' at this door and that in the winter
time to gar hauf the wives in the place hirple to the Kirk wi' frost-bitten
feet the followin' Sunday. But that's gettin' awa' frae the point. Mrs
M'Ilwrath prides hersel' on no' bein' inquisitive like ither folk.

The chappin' gaed on. Mrs M'Ilwrath sat up in bed. Her gude man was
snorin' for a' he was worth. She heard first a'e winda and syne anither gan'
up alang the street. The neebors were thrang. At last she cam' to the
conclusion that it maun be her door richt eneuch. Wha could it be? She
tried to think, but it wasna easy wi' the clapper gan' smack ilka twa-three
seconds. She wondered if she could lie doon and fa' asleep juist as if she'd
never heard it. Whaever it was 'ud be weel ser'd if she could. But the
knockin' seemed to be gettin' looder and looder – like to smash in the door.
The haill hoose was dirlin' – and the neebors were shoutin' to ask what the
maitter was. 'Mak' less din', she heard ane cry. 'ye'll wauken the bairns.' It
couldna gang on. She'd hae to wauken Jock. But she leuch to hersel' when
she thocht o' what the neebors 'ud say neist day. She'd never let on she'd
heard ava'. It 'ud fair rile them. They'd get nae cheenge oot' o' her.

'Jock,' she said, and gied him a dunt in the ribs. But he juist grunted a
wee.

'Jock,' she said, and dunted him again. The knockin' never stoppit. Rat-
a-tat. Tat-a-tat. Rat-a-tat. It was beginnin' to get on her nerves.

'Jock,' she said, and gied him a third dunt. That waukened him, but he
was slow in comin' to himsel', and it took a bit time to tell him what was
what.

'Wha can it be?' she spiered.

But he'd nae idea.

'You'd better gang doon the stairs an' see.'

'I'll thraw up the winda first and look oot.'

'You'll dae nae sic thing. Doon stairs and get the kitchen poker, and cry
through the door to see what it is and what they want afore ye open't.'

Aff he gaed, and syne she heard him at the door: 'Wha's there?'

But there was nae answer, and the knockin' gaed on withoot a break.

'Wha's there?' he cried again.

There was nae answer; juist rat-a-tat, rat-a-tat. Even on. Syne she heard
him open the door, and – efter a wee – speakin' to somebody.

Then the door shut. She waited to hear his fit on the stairs, but it gaed
alang the lobby and into the parlour instead.

The muckle sumph! Wha could it be? He micht hae shouted up the stairs at ony rate to pit her mind at ease. She swithered a while, thinkin' first ae thing and syne anither, and a' the time ca'in' hersel' a fule for thinkin' at a' when she'd nocht to gang by. They were takin' a lang time. It was queer that Jock hadna come up for his breeks even. She tholed the suspense as long as she could. It seemed an eternity. At last she shouted, 'Jock,' twice, but there was nae answer. Sae there was naething for't but to rise. Up she got and put her claes on. She could hear them talkin' frae the heid o' the stair. The clock struck three juist as she got to the fit o't. She gaed alang the lobby and threw open the parlour door.

Jock stude dumfoonered in the middle o' the flair. There was naebody else in the room.

'Wha' was't?' spiered his wife.

'Naebody,' he said.

'But I heard you talkin'.'

'I was talkin' to mysel'.'

'What keepit you doon here sae lang then?'

'I dinna ken.'

'Ye needna tell me naebody could clour the door like yon.'

'Ye can look for yersel' then.'

And that was a' she could get oot o'm. As a maitter o' fact he hasna' muckle mair to gie. 'When I opened the door,' he says, 'who was standin' there but mysel'? Plain as a pikestaff. For a' the warld as if the street was a lookin' glass. D'ye think I dinna ken mysel' when I see mysel'? "Guid sakes", I said, "whaur hae ye been to this 'oor o' the nicht?" "I wish," said he, "I kent whaur I've been for a lang time back." "Dinna talk nonsense," says I. "What I want to ken is, wha' I am if you're me? Ye'd better c'wa ben and let us thrash it oot." I took him into the parlour and we argled back and farrit, but neither o's could mak' heid or tail o't.

"'If you're the real me," I said in the hinder en', "hoo in a' the wide warld am I to accoont to Mrs M'Ilwrath for haen the presumption to act sae lang in your place?"

"'Accoont to wha?" says he.

'And juist then I heard the wife upstairs shoutin' "Jock".

'He jumpit as if he'd been stung.

"'Wha's that?" says he.

"'The wife," says I.

"'Then I'm far oot o' this," says he. "I'll no fash ye again. You needna be feart." "Haud on," says I. "What am I to say to her?"

'He suggested ae thing and anither, but a' they showed was that he'd nae idea o' the kind o' critter I've to deal wi' in the shape o' the wife. Ye'd ha'e thocht he'd nae idea what a wumman was, tho' he was gleggit at the very thocht o' ane.

'"Look here," says I, "I was sleepin' beside her, as canny as a lamb, when you sterted to batter at the door. You're no gan' to skedaddle noo' and leave me to tell her a cock-and-bull story nae wumman on earth 'ud believe. I'd hae nae peace efter that. Juist you stan' your grun' and let her see wi' her ain een. Then she'll no' blame me, whatever else she does."

'I got atween him and the door as I spoke, and juist then I heard the wife comin' doon the stairs and alang the lobby. Wad ye believe it – ye can either believe it or no' – juist as she opened the door the man vanished as if he'd never been there. Disappeared into naething afore my verra een. Guidness kens hoo!

'What could I dae or say? It's bad eneuch as it is, but if I'd telt her that it was my ainsel' that was chappin' at the door and syne a' oor conversation thegither, it 'ud hae been faur waur. Mind ye, I'm nane sorry the man vamoosed the way he did. If he stude his grun' it 'ud hae helpit me in ae way but it 'ud hae complicated maitters beyond a' bearin' in every ither direction. I daurna imagine what the wife 'ud hae thocht if she'd opened that door and seen me – twice. Ance was eneuch. And it's faur better she shouldna believe what I tell her than no' be able to believe her ain een. As for the neebors, maist o' them hae gane oot o' their way to get unco friendly to me sin syne. They'd been wont to imagine I'd nae spirit o' my ain – but when they saw me at the door at three o'clock o' the mornin' they drew their ain conclusions. They didna see wha opened the door, and think it was the wife. I haena thocht fit to undeceive them. Considerin' the circumstances, a' thing's fitted in nane sae badly, but, mind ye, mum's the word.'

Andy

He juist hated fishin' – but he couldna refuse. For a'e thing, his mither 'ud be on his top in a meenit wi' a voice that could clip clouts. She'd nae patience wi' him – 'aye sittin' in a corner mumpin' owre a book!' If it had been his schulebooks it wadna hae been sae bad – but poetry and novels and guid kens what! Stuffin' his heid wi' a lot o' useless nonsense. His faither was faur owre saft wi' him. 'Let the laddie abee,' he aye said; 'there's waur things than readin'!' But he'd to pey for his faither's support in a' kinds o' ways, and his mither and Andy saw that he did.

If there was a message to rin or a hank a' yarn to wind, he was aye there or thereaboots and had to pit doon his book tae dae't. He daurna complain o' bein' interrupted in his readin' tho' it was a hunner times a nicht, for his mither 'ud appeal to his faither, and his faither 'ud side wi' her then. It was only when he wasna wantit for something else that his faither stuck up for him bein' suffered to read in peace. But the mair he did for his mither, the mair she thocht him Jessie-like. And ahint it a' was Andy's influence – aye sneerin' at him, tormentin' him, eggin' his mither on. Andy was his mither's Jacob. She thocht he was that manly – aye oot fishin', or caddyin' at the golf course and makin' money. Nae books for him – barrin' his schule books, and nae mair o' them than he could help – and syne he'd to be helped wi' them. Andy – and his mither – took fu' advantage then o' his superior learnin'. But tho' his mither wanted Andy to get on, at hert she sympathised wi' his contempt for book-lear, and tho' she made him help Andy she didna like him ony the better for bein' able to dae't.

Ilka time he did gang oot fishin' it was a fresh humiliation. The fact o' the maitter was that he couldna fish. He never catched onything but auld tin cans, or the brainches o' a tree or his ain breek-bottom; and he never heard the end o't. He'd an idea that if he could gang oot aince and catch a guid fry o' troot his mither and Andy 'ud never want him to gang again.

His faither, of coorse, was a crack hand either wi' worm or fly. Andy wasna muckle better than himsel', to tell the truth, but he never got into sic predicaments and he aye managed to catch something, even if it was only a smout. It wasna his wyte he didna' catch a' the fish ever made wi' ae cast, and in ony case his mither aye said, 'The wee'r the trout the sweeter.'

His faither was wonderfu' patient wi' im. He never leuch at him – till the ithers began it. And he never lost his temper and said his fingers maun be a' thooms – or no' often! It 'ud ha'e been a' richt if Andy hadna been there. He believed he could ha'e explained his feelin's aboot the haill thing in a way his faither 'ud understand – but he haurdly ever saw his faither alane. There was never ony fishin' unless Andy had naething better to dae and got his mither to get his faither to tak' them.

Andy was aye wi' them if they were ootside and his mither if they were in the hoose. The kind o' things he wanted to say were fell ill to say – and he kent that even if he could say them it 'ud hae to be to somebody he trustit and likit, and if he tried it on wi' his faither he'd nae suner get stertit than either Andy or his mither 'ud see he got nae faurer. They kent, deep doon, the difference atween him and them – better mebbe than he did himsel' – and they took precious guid care he didna' get a chance o' expressin' it. And the things they could aye say to side-track him and pit him in the warst possible licht and gar him mak' a fule o' himsel' were that muckle easier to say than the verra first words o' ony defence he could mak'!

A' the same it was a kind o' fear that gar'd them aye chip in afore him and prevent him frae sayin' what he kent he wad hae said – whatever that was – gi'en time and fair play; and that gied him hert. He kent his faither jaloused something o' this – but no' juist eneuch. He lookit at him in a queer switherin' way whiles – and syne sided wi' his mither and Andy; it was that muckle easier. But he felt that if he could juist explain things to his faither aince he'd hae nae mair bother.

He liked bein' ootside a' richt (tho' he liked readin' better). But he'd hae preferred bein' alane – wi' his ain thochts. It was haurd eneuch thinkin' ootside onywey, even if ye were alane – haurder than in the hoose; mebbe because there was faur mair to gar ye think. What he couldna stand was Andy aye yabble-yabbling aboot things he felt sae sma' and silly in comparison wi' nature or books. The wild skelp and slither and swish o' the spate was eneuch for him – withoot makin't a' juist a side-issue to fishin'.

He could hae stood for oors daen naethin' but watchin't. But that was exactly what Andy and his mither couldna understaund or thole. Fillin' yer heid wi' a lot o' wild ideas that ser'd nae purpose – no' like fishin'! Sensible folk didna gang oot to gape and glower at the flood – they gaed to catch fish, and the degree o' their sense was determined, if no' a'thegither by the number o' fish they catched, at a' events by the evidence they gied that that was what was first and foremaist in their minds.

He kent that he was seein' a thoosan' things that Andy 'ud never see – twirly bits, shades o' colour, queer wee soonds that werena tint in the general roar, crochet-patterns o' faem – and he'd see a thoosan' mair if his mind was free.

He'd fa'n into a broon study. A' at aince he heard a yell and the birlin' o' a reel. Andy had yin on – and 'By jings, it's a whopper,' he bawled to his faither. His faither was comin' back owre the rocks as fast as his legs 'ud cairry him to help to land it. 'Gie't plenty o' play,' he cried. Andy's face was a picture – fair eindoon determination, like a thundercloud – as if there was naethin' in the warld but him and this wallopin' troot and the need to land it.

He felt he was seein' the haill truth aboot Andy noo. He'd aye be like that – deid serious aboat something that didna maitter a docken and blin' to a' that did. Puir Andy, he felt wae for him – wi a face like that, makin' a life-or-daith maitter o' something you could buy for tippence for breakfast

frae the man that cam' roon wi' the lorry. His face like that was like seein'
the flair o' the sea – a'e meenit a' jobblin' waves, and the next – naething
but dour black glaur. He felt he could gang richt through the bottom o'
Andy's mind noo to the promised land like the Jews gaen through the Reid
Sea; but it was a fell clarty road. If it 'ud only bide like that it micht dry;
but nae doot in a meenit or twa the muckle treacherous flood that generally
hid it 'ud sweep owre't again and naebody that hadna seen't for themsel's
'ud ken the horror it covered.

Whether Andy hadna heard his faither's advice or thocht he kent better
or was juist owre anxious, he'd rung in till his rod was like a hauf-hoop and
his line as ticht as the gut o' a fiddle – and there was its heid! It was a
whopper and nae mistak'! Andy wadna hauf craw owre him noo! His faither
was juist at him when – snap! – the line broke, and in the blink o' an e'e,
afore his faither could lift a haund to stop him, Andy dived into the pool
heid first – efter the troot.

It was a deep pool and a dangerous ane. There had been twa-three folk
drooned in't. His faither's mind was slow in workin'. For a second he saw
him – standin' wi' his een fair stelled in his heid. He saw as faur ben into
his faither then as he'd seen into Andy a meenit afore. Andy bobbed up in
the centre o' the pool, brakin' the bonny swirl o' the waters like a muckle
blot in an exercise-book, and still wi' the same determined look on his face
– he hadna had time to alter it. It had been that fixed. He was conscious
o' hauf a dizzen different thochts at aince – the pure comicality o' Andy
gaen in efter the troot; the fact that he'd be spared a lot o' trouble and
humiliation if Andy was drooned; a hauf-waesame, half-ashamed sense o'
his faither's flabbergasted condition – and a' at aince he dived in tae.

It was pure accident – juist the way o' the current and the angle he struck
the water at – but the next thing he kent he'd Andy by the jacket-neck wi'
the ae hand and a haud o' a rock on the faur side o' the pool wi' the ither,
and his faither was comin' splashin' through the shallower water a wee bit
higher up, and in a meenit or twa he'd hauled them baith oot.

Ane or twa ither anglers cam' rinnin' up. 'Weel dune, Tammy,' a voice
shouted frae the ither side o' the pool. 'It's the bravest thing I've ever seen.'
It was Macrae, the banker, nae less. It 'ud be a' owre the toon in nae time.
He was a hero. It was a guid job ither folk had seen it tae, or Andy and his
mither 'ud hae whittled it doon to naething. But he kent they wadna like
him ony the better – tho' for a while they micht hae to pretend to. That
micht be still waur to stand than onything he'd had to pit up wi' yet.

What had gar'd him jump in to the rescue? He couldna soom. He micht
easy hae made things waur instead o' better. That 'ud juist hae been like

his luck. A' this ran through his heid in less time than it tak's to tell while he was sittin' up tryin' to get the water oot o' his lugs and listenin' to the human hubbub aboot him and the stoond o' the spate that seemed looder than ever noo he'd had a mair intimate acquaintance wi 't. A' at aince he louped to his feet. He'd thrawn his rod doon when he dived and it had got jammed by the reel in the rocks; but – look! He couldna get owre to't. He was dancin' like a hen on a het girdle. But the banker had seen't at the same time. 'A' richt, Tammy, I'll see to 't for ye' – and he did. Played it bonny! And, by jings, it was a whopper!

But Andy aye declared that it was naething ava compared wi' the ane he'd lost – 'And, besides, ye didna' land it yersel'!'

Holie for Nags

They were crackin' aboot the auld days in the Muckle Toon when they were loons thegither (and that wasna yesterday) and o' the games they used to play in the wee grey streets when the blue shaddaws were fa'in' in them, and it got daurker and daurker till Leerie gaed roon' lichtin' the lamps and throwin' splairges o' gowd into the lift that turned a'thing else still blacker (unless you were richt inalow them), and gar'd the shaddaws skip aboot like mad a' owre the place.

You could haurdly get used to your ain shaddaw even. It was that inconsistent. Whiles it gaed shootin' oot frae your taes like a telegraph pole, and whiles it was naething but a doited dot, and whiles it crookit a' airts like a 'blotty O' or disappeared a'thegither and syne loupit oot on you roon' the neist corner like a bogey man.

'D'ye mind the twae auld Miss Beatties that keepit the Berlin wool shop in Parliament Square?' spiered Jamie.

'I mind ane o' them,' said Jock (a year or twa younger than Jamie), – 'Jenny, but no' the ither. That's juist as faur back as I can mind tae. We used to say she'd forgotten to dee.'

'Aye – but she didna in the hinder en'. Folk used to ettle she was as auld as life itsel', and 'ud live to the resurrection mornin'; but I kent better, because she could never hae come through the witchcraft days withoot being brunt, and, what's mair, I mindit her sister brawly, tho' I only saw her yince to my knowledge, and she was a hantle aulder than Jenny. Mina they ca'd her, and she was that auld that she even trett Jenny as if she was naething but a bairn. You couldna see what like she was for craws' feet.

Her face was juist like a moosewob, and she'd the queerest voice, like a scrievin' pencil squealin' on a slate, that fair set your teeth on edge. But Jenny was as bonny as an aipple, and had the brichtest and bluest een I ever saw. Nae doot it's juist my fancy noo, but when I think o't it aye seems to me as though at nicht, gin you gaed into the shop, she cam' in oot o' the back premises somewhere and lit up the haill place wi' naething but her twa een and a bit o' a smile, till it was as bricht as a dream.'

'It was a muckle dungeon o' a shop tae.'

'It was a' that. You were feart to gang in – and keepit the door wide open ahint you. I mind the time I saw Mina, afore Jenny cam' in tae: I felt juist like a flea in the presence o' the Queen o' a' the Spiders. It was the dirtiest, queerest auld shop in the warld, wi' muckle stacks o' cairdboard boxes a' the colour o' stour, but you forgot a' that when Jenny cam' in, and it was a perfect miracle to see her openin' box efter box and turnin' oot muckle hauds o' reid wool for ane and yall, frae the neist.'

'I wonder if the bairns dae ony corkin' nooadays.'

'Losh kens! I never see them at it, and haena for years and years. Nae doot they're a' motor-caur daft noo. It's the age o' machines, no' miracles. But mony a happy 'oor I've pit in wi' a pirn and fower tacks on the end o't, and a wheen ba's o' different coloured wool – and could yet!'

'And it was fine to gang spankin' up and doon the street syne wi' the brawest set o' reens in the toon, shakin' them oot like strops o' rainbows in the sunlicht, and them a' jinglin' wi' a wheen wee brass bells.'

'Anither great game was Conquerors. I haena seen a laddie wi' a decent tally o' chestnuts for mony a lang year. Fegs, when I come to think o't, I canna swear I've even seen a chestnut masel' sin' I pit lang troosers on.'

'Nor me either. It's queer. For there's boond to be juist as mony – and juist as bonny – chestnuts as ever, and juist as mony loons thrang amang them and playin' conquerors, tae, tho' we dinna see them. I whiles see the trees wi' the can'les a' owre them, but never the chestnuts themsel's.'

'I hope the loons ken aboot them, for it was great fun. Whiles I think there's naething bonnier in the warld than a muckle whopper o' a new-shuled chestnut wi' a' its mairkin's – frae cream to blood and mahogany. It's sic an unlikely thing, a chestnut – a prickly green ba', and when you crack it open what you find in't seems the last thing on earth you could possibly think o'. Sae rich and live-lookin' – like a deid man suddenly openin' an e'e!'

'Chestnuts aye mind me o' horses, and I used to love polishin' them up. Mony and mony a muckle string o' a hunder and mair I've haen.'

'There was a tree at the sawmill I used to get my best anes frae...'

'And a wheen up the langfall and in the lodge grun's. And it was great fun dingin' them doon, either by shying stanes or wi' a sling.'

'There's an art in borin' them no' to start ony cracks. I mind still o' a'e beggar I had for mair than three years. He met a' comers in his first year, and had haurdly a dent on'm at the end o't, and the second and third years he was runkled like a washerwumman's thoom and as haurd as a nail. I could pit him atween my clenched teeth and no' leave a mairk. He tint a'e corner in the lang run, and syne anither, and to end wi' there was only a wee scrunt o' a thing left didlin' at the end o' the string, but it could gang through a' the lave like a bullet through butter... '

'D'ye mind playin', "Jock, Shine-the-licht"?'

'Aye – but no' aften. Mither wadna let me oot late eneuch.'

'It had to be a nicht when the Toon Cooncil were expectin' a mune and there wasna ony. It wasna canny whiles gin you gaed aff the main streets, but it was a rare game a' the same. And bools! Ye mind playin' bools?'

'Div I no'! I used to hae some beauties tae. Glessies as bricht as Jenny's een, wi' coloured twirls inside them, and white cheeny anes, and green anes oot' o' the taps o' lemonade bottles. Clay-davies, doolies, hard-hacks, mavies, cracksie-pigs, cullies – I'd a' the kinds. I mind o' them every time I see the stars reelin', and I can haurdly look at a picter o' the globe – aye, or at the earth itsel' for the maitter o' that, as you whiles see it, no' in a toon, whaur it's a' crancrums and stour, but frae a braw brae tap, when you seem to see the haill o't birlin' clear as a penny afore you – without wantin' to cry "Holie for Nags".'

Jamie leuch, but no' for lang. 'The earth's oot o' the question a'thegither,' he said. 'It's faur owre big, and the sun and mune are no' muckle better, but a starry nicht's a great place to play daigie even yet, tho' your ain een are nocht but twa o' the bools themsel's – and aiblins the bonniest o' the lot!'

The Scab

In the very heart of these beautiful policies there is a malign piece of ground, called The Scab; and, talking with others who come here, I have been interested to discover how obscurely but overwhelmingly important it is. This is no peculiarity of my own temperament; it is shared by many others different enough from myself. Willy-nilly, all steps gravitate thither oftener than to any other part of the grounds. The beauties of the setting become negligible in the light of that abject gem, a jewel of horror whose rays, as it were, annihilate the rest of the world, and can destroy the heavens themselves. Its fascination (for we are conscious of the element of pleasure even when we are most insistent upon describing our feelings as repulsion) remains almost entirely a secret to us: we can hardly begin to explain it. Anything we can say seems inept and absurd. We have, moreover, a constraining consciousness of our ingratitude, a sense of shame; the grounds are so magnificent, so perfectly laid out. We are ashamed to prefer the canker to the rose. It is difficult to admit that all loveliness goes for nothing as against this appalling eyesore; that ugliness, naked and unashamed, is a far more potent magnet than beauty. But it is so. I have been amused to see how some of the visitors have sought at first to hide the fact that it attracted them so irresistibly, but gradually shed their pretence – one or two with unrestrained terror of the lure that had so inexplicably enslaved them, as if it had revealed some evil predisposition of their souls – as no doubt it had. Others of us never attempted any dissimulation; we were hurried, open-eyed, to this patch like flotsam is to the heart of a whirlpool. It is our Sargossa Sea.

The Scab is unnatural. Any grave is soon covered over; fields champed out of all semblance into obscene messes of mud bestuck with blasted parodies of trees are very soon recaptured by the green grass and the wild flowers. Nature lies just round the corner, ready to seize the first opportunity to recover any territory that is taken from her. But Nature does not lie round the corner here. It is as if Nature recognised that this had never belonged to her and never could, or had been somehow compelled to give it up as forever irreclaimable. There is an invisible barrier beyond which no blade of grass, no runner of a weed, no thread of a root, attempts to pass. Chance of wind may deposit a seed there from time to time, but without result. Nothing grows there. I think that nothing has grown there since Time began, or ever will – that it might be ploughed and reploughed as deep as the centre of the earth and filled with fertiliser, to no end, and that, even were it possible to remove that sterile soil, such of it as was transferred elsewhere, in bulk or in separate particles, would there again produce sterility, in patches or in specks according to proportion, while the place from which it had been taken would remain a ghastly pit which nothing else could fill. I may be wrong: I am of a fanciful disposition, but that is how I feel about it, and others who know it as I do share my feelings despite the most radical differences of temperament.

So far as I can ascertain, it has no particular history. There is no reason why it should be thus infamously differentiated from the rest of the world.

It had a common origin with spots which are now gardens or glades or green fields. In the beginning of things no one could have foretold that it would become so unlike these, or, witnessing the stages of its alienation, if there were any such, could have suggested any reason for its monstrous and unparalleled development. While Nature holds aloof, however, and, so far as human eye can see, attempts no reconciliation, the Scab is stealthily but incessantly encroaching on Nature. Even in my experience it has extended perceptibly, and Nature, while falling back inch by painful fraction of an inch, never attempts to regain the ground she so loses. This is unlike Nature, unlike her infinite patience, her inexhaustible resource. One would expect some sudden sally, some surprising circumvention. But no. Things take their course. Nature knows when she is beaten! – and the Scab apparently has her beaten. All that she can do is to yield only by degrees as infinitesimal as the eternal concentration of her enormous opposition can contrive.

In putting matters thus I am only too conscious, of course, of the inadequacy of language to deal with such a situation. I have called the Scab unnatural, and spoken of it as impervious to Nature. But that is not quite true. It is to green life. But there are forms of life which infest it (apart from the fact that it is a kind of living death itself). Ants, for example! They have succeeded in forming intricate establishments in that sinister and inhospitable soil. They maintain a perpetual traffic on and, to some undetermined extent, within it. Seeing them following their incomprehensible courses (a vicious circle if ever there was one) – which they support upon nothing found within that desolate circle, but upon material they abstract from Nature, to and from which they journey incessantly, without let or hindrance – an extraordinary similarity presents itself to one's eyes between them and this barren soil. They are simply like mobile particles of it, well-nigh indistinguishable from it. Not so is an ant that one may encounter in Nature. The foil of greenery, of infinite variety, sharpens such an ant to our sight, and endows it with lively qualities of enterprise and dexterity and even a tiny burnished beauty these sordid insects entirely lack as they pass and repass (to no other end than the multiplication of their kind) on this wretched surface mechanised to so unendurable a degree that the sight of them going and coming afflicts the conscious but baffled spectator with a sense of meaningless and endless motion alien and repugnant to the human soul. Other insects and tiny reptiles are found here too. The evidences of their existences uncorrected by the diversity of Nature assume a hideous relief: their *formes*, and other commotions or indentations of the earth, are an unsightly testimony to insensate activity.

The whole plot has been mined and honeycombed and corrugated throughout the ages, in countless ecstasies of futile ingenuity: the product of a mindless itch.

And some of those with whom I have discussed the phenomenon believe that the Scab will, slowly perhaps, and perhaps at an incalculably accelerated rate, but surely, spread over the whole earth, and that in the end the blessed light will fall only on an immense panorama of empty 'workings,' established in their time by myriads of ants and other insects and tiny reptiles the last of which are dead.

The Last Great Burns Discovery

So Charlie Crichton has gone to his reward!

Well, he will rank for all time as one of the Great Burnsians, in the direct line of Duncan MacNaught and Thomas Amos and John Muir. Their like will not be seen again. The whole field of Burns lore has been 'redded' with a small-tooth-comb – there is no scope left for the development of such Titans now. Crichton was the last of them. Only minor gleanings, the veriest *minutiae*, remain; these cannot feed the indomitable will of such men. What pigmies in comparison are even the best of our Burnsians today! There is no help for it. It is 'beyond remeid'. Yet even when Crichton first became prominent in World Burns Circles over thirty years ago the same might have been said – it seemed almost equally unlikely that he could find anything sizeable either or be destined to do more than stroke the t's and dot the i's of his distinguished predecessors. Those who thought that reckoned without their host however. The secret perhaps is just that Crichton knew better than anybody else all that had been done already. Heavens, how he applied himself! He had the whole thing at his finger-ends. He wasted no time on false trails. He knew the whereabouts of every scrap of holograph and every relic of Burns himself and his family and his relatives and everybody mentioned in his poems or letters or in any way connected with him, and the birth-places and various dwelling-places and last resting-places of them all. Yet he did not give up hope; he was sustained, I can only suppose, in addition to infinite tenacity of purpose, by some premonition of his high calling, of the momentous discovery which despite all the probabilities, had eluded the myriads of indefatigable searchers who had gone before him and been reserved for his humble self.

I stress the adjective – his *humble* self; since his natural modesty must have had a great deal to do with it – that, and his profound common sense, as the direction in which his researches finally took him, and the very nature of his discovery, show. If he subsequently – and most naturally – became less humble the question is whether he did not remain to the end infinitely more humble than anyone else would have done in like circumstances. I think he did.

All this, of course, is an old story now. It is nearly twenty years since he gave to the world what I feel amply justified (there are certainly no indications to the contrary) in calling the Last Great Burns Discovery. It came at an opportune moment. The Burns Movement had fallen on lean years; and there was a ridiculous attempt in certain would-be-clever quarters to switch it off its traditional lines and concentrate attention on highbrow stuff and nonsense. Crichton put an end to that.

I know what I am writing about because of a fact which I have never disclosed before, simply because, for his own good reasons at the time, he asked me not to. *I was the first man to whom Crichton disclosed his epoch-making discovery.* I divulge this at last with a full sense of the title to immortality Crichton thus – I think deliberately – conferred upon me; and am, of course, in a position to prove it up to the hilt. The time was not ripe then – nor for another couple of years – to make it public. Crichton judged it unerringly; those of us who remember the effect of his disclosure, the worldwide furore, when he decided that the moment had come, can vouch for that. It was a veritable bombshell; the biggest thing in Scottish literary history since the Kilmarnock Edition itself – and probably the last big thing Scottish literary history will register!

Few men could have kept the secret of having been Crichton's first *confidant* as I have done, and I have frequently in these intervening years laughed up my sleeve at nobodies bragging of some petty detail and posing as Great Burnsians without knowing that, like little Jack Horner, I too had had my finger in that pie and had pulled out such a stupendous plum!

I remember that evening as it were yesterday. We had been sitting in Crichton's parlour discussing same teasing, if very trivial, points in current Burnsian controversy – on the musicology side. He worked up to it very gradually; probably afraid of the effect a too-sudden disclosure might have upon me. Finally: 'Now I've got something to show you,' he said, 'something really big. We are going for a walk before the light fails. It isn't very far.'

Off we went; across a field and over a medium-sized hill and through the valley on the far side of it, until we came to the 'larach' of an old cottage, and, beside it, a patch of jungle running down to a little burn. That patch of jungle had been the cottage garden once upon a time. Now, even then I knew my Burns topography as well as most so-called expert Burnsians, and my excitement began to rise. I suspected what Crichton was leading up to; I was right up to a point – Burns *had* lived for a while in the cottage that had stood on those old founds. But Crichton – though I saw him noticing out of the tail of his eye that I had already jumped to that conclusion – had something far greater to show me. He plunged breast-high into the tangled growth of the old garden and I followed him until, close by the burnside, he threw aside a last swathe of rank vegetation, as if it had been a curtain, and said: 'There!'

What I saw was a little ruined old dry closet. There was no door to it; but the roof had been recently repaired, and the seat inside, though rotted away in parts, was wonderfully preserved.

'You don't mean…?' I cried.

He nodded solemnly.

It was an august moment – the most impressive moment of my life – as we stood there in the gathering twilight, and he told me the slow but sure steps, the ten years unremitting study, that had led to his discovery and his final and absolute proof that (though, alas! there was no scrap of writing on the walls, no carved initials on the woodwork even) Burns himself had used that very place, that very seat; the only convenience he had used that was still extant – Burns himself, and Jean Armour.

'Since then;' he said, with a break in his voice, '…You will understand…It has become a sort of temple to me; a Holy of Holies. I am not a rich man, as you know, but I have bought this property…to preserve it for all time.'

What a wonderful thought! That strip of semi-decayed wood bridging the years and bringing one into almost direct physical contact with our national Poet – and on no adventitious grounds but on the immutable basis of common human necessity, of constitutional at-one-ment! Darkness was descending upon us but I felt a glow of supreme exaltation and looked with awe into my friend's eyes.

We stood silent together in unspeakable communion for a little while.

Then swift upon the rapture of revelation came the tragic cry which showed the real genius of the man – his power of thinking of *everything*; literally nothing escaped him – and the way in which the achievement and failure are hopelessly twined together even on such great occasions.

'But the pail,' he cried, 'the old pail wasn't there. If only…'

We left it at that.

Five Bits of Miller

First of all, there is my recollection of a certain fashion he had of blowing his nose: the effect of the sound mainly, and my appreciation of the physiology of the feat. A membraneous trumpeting. Fragments of a congested face, most of which was obliterated by the receptive handkerchief. Like an abortive conjuring trick in which, transiently, certain empurpled and blown-out facial data meaninglessly escaped (as if too soon) from behind the magic cloth which, whipped off immediately after, discovered to the astonished gaze not the expected rabbit or flower pot but only Miller's face as it had been before the so-called trick (the trick of remaining the same behind that snowy curtain when literally anything might have happened) or, rather, Miller's face practically unchanged, for the curious elements that had prematurely broken out of their customary association were to be seen in the act of reconciling themselves again, of disappearing into the physiognomical pool in which they usually moved so indetectibly. – I had invariably present in my mind on such occasions moreover a picture of the internal mechanism, the intricate tubing, as if Miller's clock-face had dropped off disclosing the works. I never really liked the way his wheels went round; the spectacle offended some obscure sense of mechanical propriety in me; I felt that there should have been a great deal of simplification – that there was a stupid complexity, out of all proportion to the effects for which it was designed. I was in opposite case, regarding Miller, to the guest who took for a Cubist portrait of his host a plan of the drains that hung in the hall.

Then the condition in which this weird aggregation was kept revolted me. It was abominably clogged up. What should have been fine transparencies had became soggy and obtuse: bright blood pulsations had degenerated into viscid stagnancies; the tubes were twisted, ballooning or knotted in parts and taut or strangulated in others. Miller could never hoist his eupeptic cheeks with sufficient aplomb to hide this disgraceful chaos from me or dazzle my contemptuous eyes with that lardy effulgence of his brow from which his hair so precipitately retired. 'Yes, yes,' I would say to myself, 'a very fine, and oedematous exterior, but if you were all right behind instead of being so horribly bogged – really lit-up from within, instead of disporting this false-facial animation – man!; if your works could only be completely overhauled and made to function freely and effectively, what a difference it would make!'

Then there was his throat. I hated to hear him clearing it. He was top-heavy as I have just shown. That appalling congestion behind his face consumed practically all his energy. The consequence was that any movement of his throat sounded remote and forlorn, a shuttle of phlegm sliding unaccountably in a derelict loom, the eerie cluck of a forgotten slat, trapping the casual sense that heard it in an oubliette of inconsequent sound. It was always like that; like the door of some little windowless room, into which one had stepped from sheer idle curiosity, implacably locking itself behind one. A fatal and inescapable sound, infinitesmally yet infinitely desolating. How many stray impulses of mine have been thus irrevocably trapped! I feel that a great portion of myself has been really buried alive, caught in subterranean passages of Miller's physical processes as by roof-falls, and skeletonising in the darkness there. Miller clearing his throat was really murdering me bit by bit; blowing bits off me with those subtle and unplaceable detonations of his, of which his over-occupied head behind that absurdly bland face must have been completely unaware –

Thirdly he had a way of twirling his little fingers, almost as if they had been corkscrews, in his ear-holes and withdrawing them with lumps of wax on the nail-ends. Uncorking himself by degrees. But his brain was never really opened: it remained blocked, or rather it had coagulated – his hearing never flowed clear into one. Just an opaque trickle devoid of the substance of his attention. – One felt always that one was receiving a very aloof incomplete audition. The wax itself was inhumanly stodgy and dull – not that bright golden vaseline-like stuff one sometimes sees, silky skeins of it netting the light, flossily glistening, a fine live horripilating honey. But orts of barren comb that had never held honey; dessicated fragments of brawn putty that made one sorry and ashamed.

Even yet I cannot trust myself to do more than suggest in the most elusive way the effect his cutting his fingernails had upon me. He did it so deliberately and his nails were so brittle and crackling. Dead shell. His finger-tips under them were dry and withered. Shaking hands with him was like touching dust and deepening reluctantly but helplessly into the cold clay of his palm. – But meanwhile I am speaking of his nails. They literally exploded. He affected to use scissors like the rest of us: but, watching him closely, I was never deceived. It was not by the scissors that he cut his nails. He blew them off with his eyes. I know that sounds absurd and impossible. But if you could only have seen the way in which he looked at his finger-tips while he was engaged in this operation, and the extraordinary crepitation and popping-off that ensued –

Lastly, there was the way in which he used to squeeze a blackhead out of his chin. He was the sort of person who more or less surreptitiously permits a horde of these cattle to enjoy his cuticle for a certain length of time for the queer sport of killing them, and, at the appointed time, he slew them with amazing precaution and precision. I think this process gave him some strange dual effect of martyrdom and ceremonial purification. I cannot attempt to describe here the rites with which he was wont to sacrifice a black-head of the proper age on the altar of his complexion. For the outsider the ceremony was to a great extent masked by the fact that he only obliquely faced any congregation through the medium of a mirror. In a fragment of it that eluded the blocking back of his head and a thin slice of side-face decorated with a whorl of ear, one saw all that one might, heightened in effect by the liquid light in which such a reflection was steeped. The sqeezing-out process was a delicate and protracted one. Black-heads do not squirt out under pressures like paint from a tube, but emerge by almost imperceptible degrees. A very slim yellow-white column (of the consistency of a ripe banana) that ascends perpendicularly and gradually curves over and finally, suddenly, relapses upon its base again.

Yes! I think that perhaps the most vivid recollection of Miller I still retain is that of some knobly fragment of his chin on which under the convergent pressure of two bloodless, almost leprous, finger-tips the stem of a black-head is waveringly ascending; and then of the collapse – lying there, thready, white, on a surface screwed and squeezed to a painful purple, like a worm on a rasp!

You remember the big toe-nail in one of Gogol's stories? Well, I have only these five somewhat analogous bits of Miller left – mucus, phlegm, wax, horn, and the parasitic worm – five unrelated and essentially unrepresentative bits of the jig-saw puzzle that I used to flatter myself I could put together with blasphemous expertise. All the rest are irretrievably lost. But see what you can make of these five.

Wound-Pie

'Ou, aye. She's aye leevin' – for ocht that onybody kens,' he said.

'Hoo d'ye mean? – for ocht that onybody kens?' I spiered.

'Weel, up to a wheen years syne – mebbe five or sax – she was whiles seen gan aboot. But ane or ither o' them was aye wi' her. Naebody ever got chance of speakin' wi'r by hersel'.'

'That was unco queer, was't no'?'

'Mebbe aye and mebbe no. It's haurdly for me to say. It's only lookin' back yin minds o't. Naebody noticed it at the time – or at first at onyrate.

Gin onybody tried to hae words wi' her whichever o' them happened to be alang wi' her spoke for her and gin the auld body spoke hersel' at a' it was juist to repeat what they had already said. She never said a word that wisna pit into her mooth. There was nae gettin' roon' them; and ye'd to watch hoo ye tried. Ye ken what it is in a place like this whaur everybody's connected through ither.'

'Which o' them does she bide wi'?'

'I canna tell ye that either. There's a fell big family o' them and when she cam' here at the first go-aff she'd bide a wheen weeks wi' Jock in Henry Street, and syne a wheen wi' Dood in Back Mary Street and syne wi' Leeb in the Factory Entry, and whiles she'd gang doon to Mirr'ns at the Tail. And sae on. She was aye on the go. It stude to reason. They were a' keen to hae'r and sin' she couldna' be in hauf-a-dizzen different places at aince she'd to dae the neist best thing.'

He pu'd on his pipe for a meenit or twa as gin he was wunderin' whether to say ony mair or no'; and then he gaed on.

'Of coorse ye ken what a place this is for talk. When she cam' first she'd onies amount o' gear, bonnets an' cloaks an' costumes. Twa three kists pang fu'. An' she stoppit wi' Jock to start wi'. Dood and Leeb and the rest were nane owre weel pleased but Jock was the auldest and what could they dae? And Jock's wife is sic a managin' wumman. Besides he'd the biggest family, and the sma'est pey. Jock was a prood man when he ushered her into his seat at the Kirk the first Sunday, and a'body noticed his wife had a new costume on. There was a lot of talk. Ye see, naebody kent juist hoo the auld body had been left. There were different stories, but, by a' accoonts, she wisna' bare. I forget juist hoo lang she stoppit at Jock's – five or sax weeks onyway; and afore she left Jock's faimly was gey weel riggit oot. Their mither was a skilly craitur wi' the scissors and needle, and the bit bairns lookit' better than they'd dune for mony a lang day when she'd finished makin' doon some o' their granny's things to them. But I will say this for Jock and Jock's wife and some o' the rest o' them – it was a guid while efter that afore there was ony cheenge in the auld body's condition – to a' ootward appearances.'

He took anither sook at his pipe.

'To cut a lang story short, it was noticed that by the time sh'd made her first twa roons and wan back to Jock's, she'd a sicht less luggage wi' her. And the claes she was wearin' at the Kirk werena the claes she'd worn the first Sunday and she wasna quite sae lang at Jock's as she'd been the first or even the seecund time afore she went on to Dood's and she wasna sae lang at Dood's either afore she went on to Leeb's – '

He seemed to hae lost himsel' a'thegither tryin' tae mind a' the oots-and-ins, sae I asked, 'But which o' them was she wi' the last time she was seen?'

'That's juist what naebody can mind,' he said. 'An' it's no' for want o' tryin'. Every noo and again even yet the weemum argie themsel's black in the faces owr't but they never get oot o' the bit. And every noo and then ane o' them plucks up courage and pits a direct question at Leeb or Jock's wife, and I've heard them wormin at the bairns, but the bairns are every bit as fly as thcir mithers. And whiles they've fair provokit me or some o' the ither men to spier at Jock or Dood, but it's nae guid – drunk or sober, there's nae gettin' ony faurer farrit wi' them. Jock'll say she's at Dood's and canna win' oot o' her room, puir body, and the doctor'll no' hae her fashed wi' visitors; Dood'll say she's at Leeb's; Leeb'll say she's doon at Mirr'ns at the Tail – The fact o' the maitter is that she's a'whaur and nae whaur at aince; and like to bide there.'

'An' that's a' that onybody kens?'

He noddit.

'Onything may hae happened?' He noddit again.

'But it's no' the thing – it canna be left at that.'

He lookit as if he'd been aboot to nod a third time but had thocht better o't. And I noticed that he didna' pey me the compliment o' askin' me if I'd onything to suggest that hedna already been tried.

'Yet they're aye talkin' aboot her?' I persisted.

'Ou aye! They'll talk richt eneuch – gin onybody spiers.'

'No' unless?'

'Whiles if they think ye're like to spier.'

'It's a queer business.'

'It's a' that,' he said.

'There's naething ye haena' telt me?'

He was slow in answerin'.

'Weel,' he said, 'there's juist this an' ye can mak' o't what ye like. I canna vouch for the truth o't. But Bob Mackay was courtin' Leeb's man's sister at the time the auld cratur gaed to Jock's for the third time, or mebbe, the fourth. And it cam' frae him. He says that she'd got to sic a state she didna ken whether she got ocht to eat or no'. And – I'm gien ye his vera words – Jock said: "If it's a' the same to her there's nae need to waste the guid mercies."…Sae, accordin' to Bob Mackay it cam' to this that sae lang as she was set doon at the table she'd sit there and gang through a' the motions, and be juist as weel content as though she'd been eatin' like the lave – and never hae a bite.'

'Guid sakes!'

'Mind ye, I canna swear for the truth o't – but there's juist this. The verra last time my wife saw the auld cratur maun hae been as near as we can reckon juist aboot that time. She met Jock's wife an' her a'e efternune and Jock's wife and her talkit back and farrit first about a'e thing and syne aboot anither till my wife said she'd had to rin' a' the way hame to get my tea – I'd been awa' in the country a' day wi' naething but a piece in my pocket and ud be as hungry as a hawk. And wi' that the auld wife opened her mooth and licked her lips and said: "Naething beats a wound-pie." Juist like that.'

And he gied an imitation – like a cuckoo clock.

'My wife says you could hae knocked her doon wi' a feather. She was that taen aback that she fair missed her chance. Jock's wife took an awfu' red face and sterted takin' aboot something else sixteen to the dizzen, as if it had been something unco important she'd near hand forgotten aboot – and she never took the slightest notice o' the auld wife's remark and my wife couldna' get a word in endways tho' she tried sae hard that she's never since been able to mind what Jock's wife *did* talk aboot – and as faur as we can mak' oot the auld wife's never been seen since – And, mind ye, even supposin' far the sake o' argyment that she's aye leevin', there's mebbie a guid and sufficient reason for her never bein' seen oot. Accordin' to the best calculations o' the gear she cam' wi – and' I'm nae coonter mysel' – checkit wi' a' that her dochters and guid-dochters and grandbairns hae been seen wearin' since, it appears that at the time my wife saw her last she canna hae hed a steek left barrin' what she was stannin' up in; an' it's a weel established fact that that particular dress was rinnin' up and doon the braes a month or twa efter that on the backs o' Leeb's brats.'

'And what's wound-pie?' I asked.

'I recollect aince readin' o' cannibalism,' said he, and stumped off doon the close.

The Stranger

'All I can say is that he wasn't born of man and woman any more than the man in the moon,' said old Ben wiping his whiskers and relighting his pipe.

'But how could you possibly know that, even if it were true,' replied young Jake.

'Just the same', said old Ben tartly, 'as most of us can tell that a horse is a horse and a cabbage a cabbage and a man a man.'

'I don't see that,' said young Jake.

'You wouldn't,' said old Ben. 'You've never even been married.'

'But that's not to say,' Peter interposed. 'that he doesn't know the difference between a man and a woman.'

'Or,' added young Jake, nettled, 'that all the rest of us are so blind that if there's an equal or greater difference between him and a mere human being, we can't see it – and you can.'

'What I can't see,' said George, 'no matter what he is – and to my eyes he looks just as human as any of us, which isn't saying much – is why you refused to have a beer with him when he offered it to you.'

'I am not the man to say no, when anyone offers to stand treat,' replied old Ben, 'and the beer would have been just the same paid for by him or anyone here. All I can say is, that I had better not. It's a queer thing – but it goes to prove that I mean what I say. Otherwise I wouldn't have refused the beer. Surely that's plain enough.'

'Well,' said George, 'he's a fine free-handed creature whatever he is and all the rest of us drank with him and aren't suffering any ill effects – as far as I can see.'

'So far as I can see,' repeated old Ben, 'it all comes back to that. But it's a good proverb, that warns us never to judge by appearances.'

'Dammit!' said Philip, 'he belongs to the next village to my own home town, and I know his father and mother.'

'That settles it,' said young Jake.

'Pardon me, but it does nothing of the sort,' said old Ben. 'The world has been quarrelling about a very similar problem for the last two thousand years. I have no doubt all sorts of people knew Jesus Christ's father and mother. A fat lot that mattered!'

'Here! here!' said the landlord. 'None of that now, this argument has gone far enough. I served the man and he paid me in the ordinary way, and as the responsible party in this licensed-house, I say that he was a stranger, but otherwise just an ordinary sober human being, fit to be served in any well-conducted bar. An argument's an argument but when it runs into blasphemy I'll have none of it here.'

'Blasphemy be damned!' said old Ben, 'it's a well-known fact that Jesus Christ wasn't born of man or woman in the ordinary way, and all I am saying is that the same thing applies to the gentleman in question.'

'Well,' said the landlord, 'I don't care a sniff whether that's true or not, but I've warned you. No names, no packdrill. Argue away as you like as long as you don't get too rowdy, but to mention Jesus Christ by name is blasphemy, and if you do it again, out you go.'

'The only thing to do,' said Philip, 'is to ask him point blank if he comes in again.'

'You and he seemed to get on particularly well,' said old Ben, to the landlord.

'I liked him,' said the landlord. 'I could do with a lot more customers like him these days. He seemed to have plenty of money and to be of a very lavish disposition.'

'Yes,' said old Ben, 'I understand all that, but I was thinking of something quite different.'

'You would be,' retorted the landlord. 'What was it?'

'Just that his kind seem to have one thing in common – a curious predilection for the company of publicans and sinners.'

'You're just trying to be blasphemous again in a less direct way, you nasty old man,' said the landlord, 'but I haven't noticed that the gentleman in question was any different in that respect from anyone else here – and you're all human enough, God knows.'

'Who's being blasphemous now?' asked old Ben.

'Here he comes again at any rate,' said George.

'Well, I'll ask him plump and plain,' said Philip, and as the stranger came forward, rose and said, 'We've just been having a friendly argument about you. Do you mind if I ask you a simple, straightforward question?'

'Not in the least,' said the stranger, 'but let's have a drink first. Landlord, drinks round, please, on me.'

They all filled up except old Ben, who refused.

'Why won't you have a drink with me?' asked the stranger.

'Because I don't think it is right,' said old Ben.

'What?' asked the stranger, 'the beer? There's nothing the matter with it. It's damned good beer. The landlord knows his business all right. Besides, he's drinking the same in any case.'

'No,' said old Ben. 'Not the beer. You.'

'What's the matter with me?' asked the stranger.

'It's like this,' said Philip, 'we've just been having a little argument, as I said. The question I want to ask you is this – were you born in the ordinary way of a man or a woman, or were you not?'

'What an extraordinary question,' said the stranger. 'How in the world did it arise?'

'Old Ben says you weren't,' said Philip, 'that's why he won't drink with you.'

'It doesn't say very much for old Ben's experience in the world, to refuse a perfectly good drink, no matter whether he's right about my birth or no,' said the stranger, 'but I am sure the idea did not originate with old Ben himself. Who started this hare?'

'You're right there,' said old Ben. 'It was my missus told me. She saw you across the jug-counter here the last time you were in.

'How did she know?'

'Well, it's hardly for me to say seeing she is my missus,' said old Ben. 'I'm the last man in the world to base much on women's nonsense as a rule. But one of the others will perhaps tell you that what my missus says is a good deal more worth paying attention to in such connections than most folk's talk.'

'Yes,' said George, 'we're bound to admit that his missus is a very remarkable woman. She sees far into the future. Time and again, to the knowledge of all present, she has prophesied rightly.'

'There's no question about that,' said the landlord.

'Does she drink?' asked the stranger.

'Keep your insulting remarks to yourself,' said old Ben.

'I meant no insult,' said the stranger. 'I wasn't inferring that her predictions were the by-products of fuddling. I only asked in a perfectly friendly way. Does she like a drink? The bearing of my question on the argument will be clear as soon as it is answered – in the affirmative, as I am sure it will be.'

'She's very fond of a bottle of stout,' said the landlord. 'Well,' said the stranger, opening his wallet, and laying a ten shilling note an the counter, 'will you kindly supply her with stout to the value of ten shilling with my compliments and best wishes?' He glanced at his wristwatch. 'Good gracious! Is that the time? I must be off. Good night, all.'

'Good night. Good night.'

'Just a moment,' said Philip. 'The point is, was Ben's missus right or wrong?'

The stranger had passed out, his hand on the handle of the swing door.

'Right,' said the stranger, and was gone.

The Dean of the Thistle

The Very Reverend Doctor Thomas MacPhaid, Dean of the Thistle, a courtier, one of the leaders of the Church of Scotland, a brilliant ecclesiastical statesman, and the foremost public orator of his day, stopped suddenly in a wonderful passage of eloquence at the very height of his theme while the crowded congregation – they had even had to have chairs put in all the passage-ways – hung on his words. Many of his hearers had not been competely rapt away, if they had retained the very slightest critical power, it might have occurred to them that this unexpected pause was for the sake of effect. If so, it showed the man's miraculous resource – his supreme self-confidence in the presence of the Divine itself. Any other man would have been carried on inevitably on the tide of his own discourse. Or had he over-reached himself – did the sudden pause indicate that he had come to the verge of the unutterable, 'breathless with adoration'? Would a little downward gesture of those hands which could gesticulate so marvellously confess the limit of their powers and the quiet resumption of his seat say all that needed to be said? In the meantime he kept the congregation poised on the edge of the unspeakable. The silence was intolerable; surely such a tension could not maintain itself a second longer; a terrible cry must arise somewhere – probably no one in the whole church had not a desperate feeling as if his voice or her voice were struggling against the impossible restraint and must instantly burst out in some unthinkable noise. If one had given way they would all have given way and howled together like a pack of dogs. Not to be the first was the prayer in every heart.

Then it was seen that up there in the high pulpit the reverend Doctor was smiling. Ah! Was this to be his way out of it? It was as good as – nay, far better than – a little downward gesture of the hands and a quiet relapse upon his seat. Such a smile was a benediction; it resolved the unutterable into the ineffable, signifying that they had passed into it together, not overcome – but having overcome. What splendid terms it would leave them all on with themselves and with each other! A genial and glorious experience!

The beautiful smile that should have signified all this had suddenly gone too far and gone awry, however. It had spread to his ears and become distorted into an extrordinary grimace. It was difficult to recognise the handsome lineaments of the great preacher in what was now declaring itself as the facial expression of a paroxysm of uncontrollable mirth. A second later he was hanging on to the woodwork of the pulpit and howling with helpless laughter. There could be no mistaking the quality of it either. It was genuine laughter; there was no cruelty in it – it rang through the grey old building with a sheer simple humanity that no one could misunderstand. Surprised and shocked as the audience were, every one was sensible of a sudden access of a feeling of well-being – of, somehow or other, the essential rightness of this laughter at such a moment. They had a sensation of delight, an imitative impulse, a feeling of at-one-ment, in spite of themselves. It was a supreme manifestation of the humour of the Saints. It was redeemed by its utter humility. Gone were all the reverend Doctor's conventional attributes – his learning, his high social and ecclesiastical position, his political acumen and experience, his splendid physical presence, his superb address, his unrivalled rhetorical prowess. He was striving for no effect. He had forgotten the existence of the congregation. He was lost to the considerations of this world altogether. He was just a man laughing helplessly in pure delight in the presence of his God.

And yet, it seemed, not so completely lost after all. Some sense of his position had entered into him again. By a tremendous effort he regained partial control of himself and began speaking. 'I beg your pardon,' he said. 'It was a private joke that carried me away. But I could not share it with you in advance. I did not foresee it myself. You heard my sermon; I was never more sincere in all my life. I was never more moved by what I was saying. I felt inspired as I had never been before. Just before I paused it seemed to me that the very heavens were about to open – that my voice was about to modulate itself into the very accents of God Himself. But there is so very narrow a margin between the sublime and the ridiculous that one sees at such a moment that they are really interchangeable terms – at least, merely aspects of each other. The unutterable absurdity of the whole business struck me with irresistible force. We laugh at the quaint ideas of our forebears – we laugh at old ideas of our own that we have outgrown. I suddenly outgrew all ideas, and broke into a new dimension. If, I said to myself, instead of the priestly convention, if instead of myself in this established guise, the familiar pose, with all my reclamé, and ruffling of phylacteries, and the other tricks of the trade, I was here as I really am, what would the effect on the congregation be? If I were suddenly to become myself they would think I was mad. They could not accept me as God made me, they require that I shall hide myself behind the regulation pulpit robe and the coloured hood. If I tore these vestments off without pausing in my sermon, until as I entered upon my peroration I stood here stark naked, what a sensation there would be! I question if I could keep the thread of my discourse in the hubbub I would set up by trying to do anything of the sort – and certainly I could not, at least my words would not, continue to hold the attention of my audience. And yet that is just what I am. In my mind's eye at least, all these externals dropped away and I saw myself standing declaiming here in the state of nature. My Doctorate of

Divinity, my Royal Chaplaincy, and all the rest of it went by the board –
and here I was, in the year of our Lord nineteen hundred and thirty-five,
set up in these highly artificial surroundings over this great and hopelessly
unreal congregation, just like a monkey up a tree. My friends, I am, of
course, fully aware now of what the practical consequences of this will be
– and fully reconciled to them. But I like to think that as far as you are
concerned it will not be easy for you at any future time to sit at the foot of
any minister, not even the most self-righteous and owlishly humourless of
my brethren, even a creature who cannot see the contemptible farce in
His Majesty, King George V, being offered, and actually accepting, from
the Iron and Steel Institute the Bessemer Medal for scientific metallurgy,
as he did last year, and listen to his sermon without (and here he dropped
his voice to a whisper which nevertheless penetrated with perfect clearness
into every corner of that great building), saying, to yourselves in your heart
of hearts with devastating effect, "a monkey up a tree – just a monkey up
a tree.'"

And he stood there laughing merrily, with great goodwill to all, and
making rapid movements of his hands as though he were furiously
scratching his armpits.

A Sense of Humour

As you say, a sense of humour is a queer thing. The trouble is that it varies
so much, and, here as elsewhere, what is one man's meat is another man's
poison.

A little practical joke that I didn't like probably changed the whole
course of my life. But for it I would almost certainly have married my cousin
Winnie Harrington. We were extremely fond of each other and, child like,
gave all our friends to understand that we would be married as soon as we
grew up, and live happily ever afterwards.

But as things turned out I have never seen her nor any of the family
since I was ten years old, and am exceedingly unlikely ever to see any of
them again. Winnie married into the teens of years ago and is the mother
of a large family. Winnie and some of her brothers and sisters were often
enough in our home, but I had never been to hers and had never met her
father and mother. They lived about sixteen miles away, and her father,
my Uncle Will, was a village blacksmith, and the very image of the one in
the poem. He stood six feet three in his stocking soles and was broad in

proportion and had a beard like a crop of hay. I had long looked forward to going to Lochwood, as you may well imagine, and at last the happy time came. My brother and I were to stay there for a week. I was at once thrilled by and afraid of my gigantic uncle. But the visit came to an end abruptly at breakfast-time the morning after our arrival. It was a glorious sunny morning and we were all at table together. I was sitting next to Winnie and felt as happy as could be, though I was usually very shy and it took me a good while to get on easy terms with people I had not met before. I had a boiled egg, and as I topped it I felt that something was wrong – the top seemed to fly off of its own accord instead of requiring to be cut. There on the top of the egg was a horrible live greeny-black beetle. My stomach heaved inside me, but I saw that all the others were looking at me, and just then my Uncle gave a howl of laughter in which they all joined. This was too much. I caught him fairly between the eyes with the egg which I was glad had not been hard boiled, but was nice and 'runny,' and before anyone could say or do anything I was up and out of the door and on to my bicycle and off towards Waterbeck as fast as I could pedal. They could have caught me easily enough, I suppose, but no doubt they were too disconcerted at first to think of it, and in any case probably thought it better to leave me to myself for a little until I got over it. They can never have imagined that I would take it as seriously as I did and not come back. I went to my Aunt Meg's, just beyond Waterbeck, which was about half way home, and stayed there the night, and then completed my journey the following day. First my Aunt Meg and then my parents did their best to induce me to go back to Lochwood, telling me that Uncle Will had always been 'a great one for a joke', but was really as kind and goodhearted as any man could be, and would be dreadfully upset if I took it so hardly and wouldn't forgive him. And what about Aunt Lizzie, and all my cousins, and, above all, Winnie? But it was no use. I had an idea of all that must have been said as time went on after I dashed away from the breakfast table, and they realised that I wasn't coming back. And I could imagine the attitude my brother adopted – the airs he gave himself as quite the little man of the world of the two of us, and all that he suggested rather than said of my silly sensitiveness and petted and unforgiving disposition. So you see, what with one thing and another it was impossible for me to go back, even if I had wanted to; I had been put in a wrong light altogether. I never thought of my Uncle Will or heard him mentioned for years afterwards without feeling a surge of hatred against him proportionate to the disappointment I had felt in being done in this way out of a holiday I had looked forward to so keenly, and though I came to see that I had been too hasty and that the beetle in the egg had been just an innocent joke on his part – not really intended for me, either, for it was only by accident that I, and not my brother, had got the doctored egg – I could not admit it nor modify my attitude in the least. I swore I would never go to Lochwood again as long as I lived or see my Uncle Will if I could possibly help it. And I never did. He died about fifteen years ago and I would neither go to the funeral nor write a letter of sympathy to my Aunt. I only heard once from Winnie after that affair. A week or two afterwards she sent me a postcard, with a few kind sentences designed to show that she was still as fond of me as ever, and with a lot of multiplication signs for kisses. But I happened to be at the door when the postman came that morning. I put the postcard into my pocket and said nothing about it. I wasn't going to stand any more teasing. Later on I shoved it under the linoleum on the kitchen floor and there it remained until mother found it about a dozen years afterwards, when she was moving to another house and took up the floorcloth.

As I say, a sense of humour can mean so many different things. For example, I suddenly remembered all this about the Lochwood Smithy affair last summer when my brother's oldest boy was staying with me – about the same age as I was at the time in question – and I thought I would try out the same joke on him and see how he reacted. But I varied it a little – not intentionally, but just as it happened. I put the egg in the holder with the end containing the beetle at the bottom instead of on top. And what happened? Nothing. He ate the egg all right and when he came to the last spoonful I got a glint of the beetle and was on the point of saying something, but he was looking at me and not at the contents of his spoon and before I could get a word out he had swallowed it up. He never knew and suffered no ill-effects.

A Scottish Saint

The mind of man, upturned,
Is in all natures a strange spectacle,
In some a hideous one.

When Peter MacIntyre came out of prison he was a changed man.

It was not that he desisted from the criminal practices which provided his means of livelihood – he was then close on forty and would have found it difficult, if not impossible, to make his living in any other way, even if he had wanted to, especially at that time when Glasgow, to an even greater degree than the rest of Scotland (and that was to a considerably greater degree than England) was suffering like all other so-called civilised countries from unparalleled trade depression, unemployment, and widespread hardship and destitution. It was not, so far as I have been able to find out, that he committed crimes more frequently or sought to earn more by means of them than he had previously done. He remained content with a certain modest enough income, and, to secure it, does not appear to have committed more crimes in any subsequent year than he did in the year before his imprisonment, or one or two years before that. It was not that he ceased to drink as much. But what did happen is that he not only got drunk less but ceased to get drunk at all. The essence of the matter, however, is that – except for strictly 'business' purposes – he is not known to have ever again gone outside the Cowgate area of the city, and even that portion of it triangularly bounded by Hogg Street, Bruce Street, and Anne Street. In other words, the very worst section of all the slums of Glasgow. He had lived prior to going to prison close by, but nevertheless in ever so slightly less infernal a section of those 'backlands' which were notorious as the worst slums in Europe, if not in the world; but one of his first actions on being released was to plant himself thus in the very heart of that sore which a contemporary writer well-styled 'the cancer of Empire'. The action was symbolical of that change in him which, effected by his imprisonment, was only realised by any outsider in conjunction with the events it produced three or four years later.

Another thing was that he ceased to associate except with the fixed population of that quarter. Previously he had been ready enough to talk to whoever stood next him in a public-house, for example. That ceased, and I believe he never spoke again to anyone who did not live in that particular densely-populated triangle.

It was only very slowly that an outsider here and there began to notice that something very strange was taking place. There had, for example, been gang feuds, outbreaks of razor-slashing, and the like in the area. These became fewer and fewer and ultimately ceased in the most unaccountable fashion, although there was every reason to believe that the general criminality of the denizens had not diminished. It had simply changed its tactics – but how and why?

Along with this went another phenomenon; the complete withering of Salvation Army and similar activities of all kinds. The so-called 'social workers' in the area were absolutely nonplussed; they became conscious of a frustrating force with which they had no means of coping. It became more and more difficult, and finally impossible, to get into contact with the denizens at all. Any attempt to enter into conversation failed; any proffer of tracts or anything else was simply disregarded as if it had not been made; street-corner meetings ceased to be able to detain any one at all except 'a crawl of bairns', or, occasionally, members of the 'floating population' which used to be as large as the fixed population of the area, but became steadily less – not that the numbers in the area decreased, but that 'coming and going' ceased; the population became as fixed as MacIntyre himself. All these manifestations were exceedingly intangible at first; it was only a year or two after his release that they became appreciable in their full effect to a few keen observers who remained baffled, however, as to exactly what was happening, or, rather, as to what it all meant.

It was in the autumn of 1935 that a friend drew my attention to the matter, and I remember his saying to me that he did not think the people of the area had become any less criminal or less drunken and otherwise vicious in their habits, but that they had somehow or other ceased to do anything that would prevent their deriving the fullest possible enjoyment from, and freedom in, their manner of living and had evolved a pride in being precisely the sort of people they were with which no attempt to change them in any way had any conceivable means of coping.

'It is,' he said, just as if they had come by a full realisation of themselves as a distinct species of humanity. They are as insusceptible of being influenced by other types as dogs or cats are from trying to be fish or birds. Their motto might be Shakespeare's

Simply the thing I am
Shall make me live.

'What other people call crime is their natural mode of life, what other people call law and order is an organised crime against them on the part of their natural enemies. They feel completely justified in their attitude – and it is impossible to deny that despite the hellish houses in which they live, their debauchery, and all the rest of it, they are just as intelligent and physically fit (and a damned sight hardier) as any other section of the community. Not only that, but they are far more intelligent and physically fit now than similar communities elsewhere that have not succeeded in insulating themselves in their inexplicable and extraordinarily complete fashion from Christian and philanthropic agencies and other influences inimical to their chosen (or at least, fully and finally accepted) mode of life, or than they were themselves before the change took place. The result of this insulation, with

No orifice for a point as subtle
As Ariadne's broken woof to enter

has been to make the work of the detectives and police a thousand times more difficult than it was before, and not by any organised or at least obvious defiance – the whole thing is amazing, tacit and undesirable. I am afraid that all the provocation comes nowadays from the police themselves. Nevertheless, the whole population are far warier than they used to be – they do not fall into the hands of the police anything like so easily, and above all they have almost wholly eliminated "aggravating factors" and consequently get off, when they are caught, with lighter sentences. It is an unheard of thing now for any criminal from the Triangle to do physical injury gratuitously when the robbery which is the real object can be accomplished without it. It is an equally unheard of thing for the sleuths to come by the information they are seeking through drunken blabbing. The whole population are on their guard to an unprecedented degree, they keep themselves to themselves and give nothing away. But they have lost both the old furtiveness and desperate defiance. It seems that they have no longer any sense of inferiority, of being at a disadvantage. They are different – that is all, and perfectly understand the margin upon which they operate and are only anxious to have the "necessary intromissions" with the rest of the world. Of what the police are doing by way of retaliation in these circumstances – or rather our suspicions as to the steps they must be taking, when they get the chance – to extract information and secure a reasonable average of prosecutions, the less said the better perhaps, but that can only be intensifying the criminal discipline. The question is, where has that discipline come from – how is it being maintained?

'Although it is operating to criminal ends – ensuring in a far more confident and efficient fashion modes of lives the authorities and all the agencies of religion and public morality deplore – it is unquestionably a moral force, and, having regard to the nature of the human material in which it has manifested itself perhaps the strongest moral force in Scotland today – though that isn't saying much; "moral forces" are few and far between, and generally associated with the free-masonry and practical interests of more favourably situated groups at the expense of their "inferiors". My own idea – though I have nothing to go upon – is that this Cowgate business must all be traceable to some single individual, and a very remarkable individual at that.'

He was right. The individual was Peter MacIntyre. I had occasion (for reasons that need not transpire) to make the matter the subject of intensive study for a long time afterwards, and it was only with the utmost difficulty after months of work that I got on the right lines that led back to this spare, reticent, ruthless middle-aged man. I never spoke to him myself; that was impossible – though I was frequently in the little public-house that now constituted his headquarters and near enough and unsuspected enough to hear him talk to his associates (friends, let alone intimates, would not be the right term) and note his influence upon them and the way in which it radiated out from them to every individual in the area. It was enough to closely observe his face and particularly his eyes for a little to know that here was a man dedicated to an implacable purpose, and wholly without personal ambition other than to serve it disinterestedly. He would do nothing to improve his condition; he wished no more than would suffice to maintain his particular mode of life; he drank readily but I never once saw him affected by liquor, nor do I believe that he ever committed a single crime more than he found necessary to give him the money he required to frequent public-houses and drink with the particular steadiness which had become normal to him and defray his other small expenses, for food and room. Beyond that he had no use for money, he was an alcoholic ascetic, a slum saint. He was less an enemy of society than a defender of the particular type of society in the Triangle. He upheld the Triangle 'culture' and was determined that no outside influence would weaken or subvert it. He derived no personal advantage from his unique power, he was content so far as actual criminal practice was concerned to work his own line and make no attempt to outshine his fellows as a master-criminal. It was simply the spirit, and not the activities, of the area he organised – he was not a gang leader; he got no percentage on the loot of the others. I question if he was ever privy to ninety-nine per cent of their efforts – any more than they were to his; he used no force to discipline them, they were not answerable to him in any direct or practical fashion – his rôle was limited to infusing them with a certain spirit.

It was, of course, a situation that could not last. The end came, not through the police after all, but through the social reformers and the sanitary authorities. There was a wave of civic improvement; a fresh epidemic of jerry-building. The Cowgaters were to be transformed into typical suburban rabbits, like bank-clerks, shop-walkers, commercial travellers, and insurance agents. An order went out in August 1936, for the demolition of the entire Triangle: and a wholesale transplanting of its denizens to new housing schemes. It was then for the first time that MacIntyre showed his hand and his complete ascendancy over the population was demonstrated in an astounding way. The authorities were defied. It was seen at once that the completest arrangements had been made to resist the Order, and that only the most drastic measures would serve to enforce it. The most drastic measures were adapted; the police, galled by years of contempt against which all their methods had proved singularly ineffective, were only too glad to have the chance 'of teaching the scum a lesson at last.'

But MacIntyre knew that the end had come. A baton charge or two, men with showers of stones, bottles, boiling water, and what not, resulted in a number of casualties an both sides, but the Triangle as a whole was securely barricaded in its teeming tenements. Daylight the second morning, however, showed the horrifying spectacle of 'a fine blue flower border' – twenty-seven policemen with their throats cut lying side by side along the pavement in Anne Street. No end of a hullaballoo ensued. Detachments of soldiers and armed police were rushed up; but it was found that the denizens were armed too and amply supplied with ammunition. It was to be a fight to the death, and they were determined to sell their lives dearly. They did. The siege of Sidney Street in London was a mere fleabite to the Battle of the Triangle. Finally, as everyone knows, it ended with the firing of the entire quarter – whether accidentally or of set design by the authorities or by the denizens themselves is not known.

I believe that it was MacIntyre's final order and that it was loyally obeyed with the full consciousness that it would mean the death of every man, woman, and child in these densely-populated warrens. It did. Apart from that, the police and military fatalities numbered over 1,100. So ended the last attempt in Great Britain on the part of any community to remain where it was and preserve its own mode of life in defiance of the over-riding forces which insist that even if, in many ways, the distinctive qualities of such communities compare favourably – as they did in this case, and as the final discipline, heroism, and decision to die together show – with the general tone, they must yield to the so-called march of progress and 'become like other people'.

But even yet I sometimes think I see MacIntyre's eyes contemptuously looking the whole force of civilisation 'through and through', and I have never seen any other Scotsman whose eyes could have made MacIntyre's blink under their scrutiny. Nor, far the matter of that, anyone who wasn't a Scotsman either.

Aince There, Aye There: A Shetland Story

The Parish Council of that great, lonely, scattered parish, which included nearly a score of very sparsely-populated islands – rocky, treeless islands with snaggled coasts divided by belts of water so that they presented an endless collection of silver-points in full daylight; and in the twilights of dawn and dusk, by moonlight, or on days of overclouded skies, of wood-cuts – were astounded.

The islanders led a very bare life, and parochial relief was a matter of mites; the old people lived in their little, low, isolated cottages on next to nothing – 'wind pie' the staple of their lives – and in exceptionally hard cases, bedridden or blind or the like, whether an extra sixpence a week or as much as a shilling might be granted was a matter for weighty consideration. Hours of deliberation – little oases of monosyllabic comment in a desert of doubt and difficulty – would be given to such a problem. It was difficult to tell such infrequent speech from the coughing of sheep outside. And most of it was not devoted to the business in hand, but to fragments of gossip, and to matters of fishing and, above all, of crofting interest.

The recent rains have washed off the 'limy' mildew and new green shaws have sprung up from the centres of the 'castocks'. Is this healthy? No. This recovery means the growth of new shaws from the bulbs must take sap and substance from the turnips....On cutting the centres, nearly all swedes and yellows have a streaky, mottled appearance inside; later this may induce rotting. There is a 'teuchness' about the tapins and want of sap in all turnips... Pigs are in the 'deid thraw' again; retailers are complaining everywhere that pigs bought under the new quota system cannot be sold at a profit, and prices are a little back from those of a fortnight ago. The other side of this is, for years pig breeders and feeders under the chuck-and-chance-it systems were getting far too little for their costs of production. The cure? – further limit the imports of foreign bacon and give home producers a chance....Isn't it evident that rough beef-cattle, fat or stores, are out of fashion?...In the midst of this somehow or other the business of the Board goes forward and decisions are reached. The actual money, of course, was not entrusted to the paupers concerned; they could go a whole year, many of them did, without touching so much as a penny piece; the relief was given in kind – the van from the General Stores allowed the recipients goods to the value which the Parish Council decided upon. Only at the last meeting a month ago the Parish Council had had a particularly difficult case to deal with, and had had – though none of the members could recall afterwards just how they had come to decide in that way – an altogether unusual burst of generosity. It had been a vicious night of wind and sleet, desperately cold, and the members from the different areas having to come considerable distances had no doubt felt they must do something big to justify the ordeal to which they subjected themselves in the public interest. The business in question was an application on behalf of two old sisters living together in a remote spot on the west side for no less than a pair of blankets, and their crave was actually granted, and a pair of nice, thick, winter-weight blankets duly supplied.

It was not pleasant to have the glow of satisfaction – the heroic sense of being ready to defend their action – which suffers members of a Parish Council who make such a gesture replaced almost instantaneously by a realization of the utter unworthiness, the sheer black ingratitude, of the recipients. Yet here they were confronted within thirty days with another application for a pair of blankets from the same parties. The letter of request was handed round like some fearsome curiosity. The members could not believe their eyes. It was incredible.

No mistake had been made. The previous pair – fine, fleecy blankets with a sky-blue line along their borders – had been handed over to the silly old creatures immediately after the last meeting. A joke of any sort was out of the question. It was equally incredible that the renewed application was made in earnest – that they really imagined for a moment that having just been allowanced one pair of blankets they would be given another unless there were wholly exceptional circumstances to warrant such an unprecedented step. Were they too 'dottled' to know they had got them? Had they sold them? Had they accidentally set fire to them? Had they been stolen? Nothing of the sort was specified in the letter. In their slow way the members discussed this grave matter, or rather sat silent about it, for a long time. The more they thought about it the more inexplicable it seemed. Finally it was decided that two of their number who resided nearest the old women should visit them in person, find out all the whys and wherefores, and report to the Council the following month.

In due course, then, Doddy Irvine and Peter Moar came to the dilapidated, ill-lit little cottage on the west side, and found only one of the sisters at home – Molly Shearer, a little, bent old woman with almost the expression of a toad, wrinkled, scaly, yellow skin, and eczema on her left ear.

'Aye,' she said. 'It's the bitter black weather, so it is. A terrible time for old bones without any meat or marrow. There's no keeping a sparkle of heat at all in a poor done body in a winter like this. The cottage is so damp and draughty, one might as well be out on the open hill-side, and, dod, in these long nights the back of a peat-stack would be easier than a bed like mine.'

She told them how she took two cats in beside her and put every scrap of cloth she had in the house on top of her, and yet lay dirling with cold and loneliness as if she'd been standing bare naked on the seashore and the wind from the north.

'That's just what we've come to see about,' said Peter Moar. 'You've applied for blankets from the Parish Council, but the Parish Council is responsible for laying out public money and has far more to do with it than can possibly be done, especially in such uneasy times and seeing that the whole of the money at our disposal is drawn from people scarcely any better off than yourself. So we've got to be careful – very, very careful indeed. It is a very serious matter. Now, about this application for blankets, you got a pair granted to you by us just a month ago. We can't understand why you are applying for a second pair, so soon at any rate. Where are they anyway? You got them all right, didn't you? But I don't see any sign of them on the bed there.'

'Och aye,' Molly replied, 'we got them all right. And a rare heavy pair they were too.'

'Well, they must have made a heap of difference to you. You couldn't be too cold at nights with a couple of comfortable, thick fleeces like that tucked round you, and with two of you in the same bed to keep each other warm.'

'Two old women don't warm each other any; they simply double the misery and cold. It's not like having a man in the bed. I'm not saying that the blankets did not make a lot of difference though. They did that. We were right glad to get them.'

'Well,' said Peter, 'it hardly looks like it. You might have been content for a while at least to be so much better off than you'd been. But instead of that you pop in a second application right away. Do you think the Council's made of blankets? You're keeping something hidden. It's all very mysterious. But where are they? – that's what I want to know – where are the new blankets you got only last month?'

'Eh,' replied Molly, 'I'm just coming to that. You know old Henry Polson lives just through the wall, in the cottage adjoining this – going on for his ninety-third year and nobody to look after him. It's a great age – and Kirsty and I have to do what we can for the poor old atomy. It isn't much – but there are things a man needs a woman's body for. And the poor must help the poor. He's a lot older than us, and far more helpless.'

'Well, well,' said Peter, 'but what's that to do with the present business of Kirsty and you and the two blankets you got from us only a month ago.'

'I'm coming to that – I'm just coming to that,' said Molly. 'Poor old Henry feels the cold terrible. In fact, it seems he gives out cold just as some folk give out heat. It doesn't matter how cold the weather is, he is always ten times colder. And this winter he's been worse than ever – just frozen to death all the time. It's his back that's worst – he scarcely ever says anything else but just how mortal cold his back is – cold water running up and down it all the time. He was awfully bad one night about three weeks ago – cruelled with the pains, and cold, you wouldn't believe a man could be so cold and still alive. So Kirsty – she's eighteen months younger than me, and always a one for her own way. I could never stick out against her even if I wanted to. So Kirsty said we must lend him our new blankets; and before I could get in a word edgeways she pulled them off the bed and took them in and happed him up. But he said he was no warmer and nothing would satisfy him but she'd to get in behind him…'

Molly's voice tailed away as if she was musing profoundly on the mysteries of life and death; there was silence for a while; and then she added: 'So you see – that's why we had to put in a second application for blankets.'

'But,' said Peter…

'Well,' said Molly, 'it's like this. I told you she'd to get in behind him, and you know – well – aince there, aye there!'

Old Eric's Hobby

There is no man in the archipelago who knows more about the history of the islands and the psychology of the people and the secret, subtle, almost indetectible dramas that move beneath the seemingly grey, featureless, and uneventful surfaces of their lives than old Eric Laurenceson – no man with better stories to tell, and, alas, no man less able to tell them. People from the Scottish mainland are apt to think the life of the islanders essentially the same as their own, only much duller and poorer. You have to live a long time on the islands and to shed all the outward signs of being a stranger until the islanders almost forget that you are and accept you as one of themselves, before you begin to realise how utterly different all their little ways and promptings are – how completely different they are in their attitude to the most fundamental things, in the intimate texture of their beings. And once you have got to that stage – and it would be a very exceptional incomer who could ever get any further – you will be in a position to appreciate the great gulf that lies between your insight and the intimate understanding of a man like Laurenceson.

The trouble with Laurenceson, however, is that eagerly gossipy and voluble though he is, his speech is all but wholly incoherent. It is not that he has any actual impediment in his speech, but his manner is an endless outpouring of broken phrases, unfinished sentences, a most disconcerting scrappiness, with lapses into the ancient Island language, insinuations and innuendos, a general taking for granted that you are far more familiar with the background than you can possibly be which makes him obscurely allusive and maddeningly elliptical, and these fragments of speech are eked out with a range of inflections to the significance of which you have no clue, queer little giggles, sly looks, nudgings, and gestures of all sorts. These mannerisms are partly due to his extremely alcoholic past; he has gone all to bits and pieces. He is upwards of seventy now, and though he very seldom goes on a regular 'skite' and indeed cannot afford any longer to spend the pound to thirty shillings a week he used to continue to do regularly until a couple of years ago or thereby on going out in the flit boat to the bi-weekly mail-boat out in the voe (for the mail-boat cannot come in to the little jetty and the flit boat has to convey passengers and cargo out and in), he still pays his visits twice every week without fail to the steward on the steamer and has his sufficient ration of whisky. For there are no licensed houses on the island, and it is impossible to buy any strong drink retail. The only way is to visit the mail-boat; or to buy the stuff by the case or the barrel, which isn't a good plan because one loses the social stimulus, and, drinking by oneself, one drinks more and it becomes at once too expensive and too harmful, besides being a case of a feast and then a famine.

His wife runs the shop now, or, at least, does ninety-nine per cent of the work. Old Eric only diddles back and forward, making faces and mumbling away to himself; but he always carries his gun. He is the sworn enemy of the Shags – the Green Cormorants. These queer bottle-green and black birds are not eaten; he simply pops them off one after the other – he must shoot an incredible number of them every year – and leaves the shattered corpses to float about, bloodying the diamond-like transparency of the waters of the voe.

There are, of course, any amount of them and all that Eric kills has no perceptible effect in reducing their numbers. They are here, there, and everywhere – especially when the shoals of sillocks (the first year saithe) are close to the shore. It is an amazing sight to see these sillocks; in the voe, close up to the jetty, you can see them in the clear water like an enormous army drawn up on parade – the water is simply solid with them, line after line, column after column, thousands upon thousands of them. To catch them is child's play. Throw out a line and twenty of them will leap at the hook at once. You can fill a basket in less than no time. Fine fat little fish they are too, though too oily for some people's taste. The island folk clean them as soon as they are caught and boil them; then leave them to cool and eat them the following day, when they are simply delicious.

The sillocks hang in the waters of the voe like a vast dense swarm of midges. And any day and every day you will see old Eric standing there on the jetty, with a scrubby unshaven chin, a short clay pipe screwed into his toothless mouth, and an overdone look of grim determination, potting away at his detested Shags. The crack of the shots echoes alarmingly over the still waters and along the rocky shores and away over the drab, treeless peat-moors. There is no movement, however, among the interminable lines of the sillocks. Are they deaf? The shattering one after another of these avian periscopes above them and the ruddy staining of the waters has no effect upon them whatever. Crack, crack, crack! On and on and on. He is never tired of smashing the life out of these ludicrous-looking birds, these misshapen ducks, with the ugly oily gleaming plumage.

It may seem wanton brutality. The birds are of no human use; or at least he never attempts to make any use of them, though, of course, their breasts are eatable, if intolerably salty for most people's liking, while in Greenland their jugular pouches are (or used to be) employed as bladders to float the fishing darts of the natives, and in the Far East they are often tamed and trained to fish for their owners, every bird wearing a ring round its neck to prevent it from swallowing its catch. In Britain they used to be trained for the last-mentioned purpose too, but a rather different system was used, the birds being allowed to swallow the fish but being forced to vomit them immediately afterwards. Three hundred years ago a gentleman held the office of 'Master of the Cormorants to King Charles.'

If they are put to no use, at least in the island voe they are doing no harm; and even if they were, the number he kills would make no appreciable difference where they are so limitlessly plentiful. But old Eric justifies himself. He is a man with a mission. It seems that the Shags are hideously greedy and devour the sillocks in incredible numbers. The poor sillocks! Eric's mouth trembles so agitatedly with virtuous indignation that his pipe almost falls out, and there is more than a hint of tears in his bleary old eyes. With the possible exception of the golden eagle there is no other indigenous species of bird which eats so much that it cannot fly. Yet cormorants are often caught when suffering from surfeits which not only prevent them from flying but also – from all appearances – cause them considerable pain. Nor is that the only manner in which they fatally over-reach themselves. Salmon bass have been the undoing of many a cormorant. When a certain cormorant versus bass fight, witnessed some months ago, was ended by the death of both combatants the fish, stuck half-way down the cormorant's throat, was found to weigh four lb. Conger eels, too, have often proved too big a mouthful. A cormorant can certainly eat seven to ten lb. of fish a day. Words fail old Eric to express his hatred of the rapacious shags with their inordinate appetites, and his disreputable old figure struggles queerly to assume a worthy pose as the defender of the innocent defenceless sillocks.

But, of course, nobody likes a good boiling of these delectable little fish better than old Eric himself. He is, in fact, just a human shag, and if you get a close-up of a Green Cormorant and compare it with Eric himself you will see a really startling resemblance. For seen close up the birds have a similar sordidness of aspect, a like tipsy unaccountability of movement, and suggest crude caricatures of their intended forms – birds gone wrong – just as Eric himself does in relation to normal humanity. And if you catch the eye of one of them cruising about with its head held up like a periscope you cannot fail to recall Eric's expression as he takes sight along the barrel of his gun. Finally the sea is almost as much in his blood as in theirs.

In the crude black and white drawings which constitute the aspects of these islands when the sky is overclouded, it is only by an accident as a rule that his figure is distinguishable from its rocky background; but at other times when everything seems to melt into the endless encompassing clarity – when one can scarcely see life's appearances and happenings for the ubiquity of the light in which they immediately pass away – he emerges with his diseased onion of a head in a strange and startling way, like a special creation, incredible as all beginnings are. The effect is strange rather than terrible, but that is due to the ethereal transparency in which he is steeped, for old Eric is no beginning – in this life at any rate. And these shocking arrivals of his out of nothingness fill one with the most curious, subtle, and remote intuitions about the light, since it is its nature, and not his – some weakness of its nature, some nasty and futile propensity – that is illuminated on such occasions, and he moves in a brilliant vacuum in which he assumes a sort of enchantment, just as a single sound shows up an immense surrounding silence. One cannot think much or say much about the islands without using such a metaphysic of light as one finds here and there, but very briefly and sparingly, in the dry periods of the *Enneads* of Plotinus; but one must use it not briefly and sparingly, but in the most lavish and inordinate fashion. We remember that light properly so-called is only a narrowly defined part of a far greater phenomenon, that of radiation in general. It is a pity that light should be suddenly employed in showing us only old Eric again, just when we are most aware of the idea of countless kinds of invisible light and of the existence of innumerable colours we can neither see nor imagine – given as we are but one octave out of some sixty octaves of ether wavelengths already explorable by the methods of physics, a gamut reaching from great radio waves at one end to the inconceivably minute waves of X-ray; and cosmic rays bombarding our planet from outer space, at the other end. Present yourself, old man; come into the light.

'Creation was once, is always. The miracle of creation, the unique event of the calling into being of things describable, never repeats itself but there are always places where it is only just an affair of the past.' It is just here that the scandalous figure of old Eric shuffles into sight, with the slaver of a panting dog at noon – this is what we are brought back to, as if his gunshots – crack, crack, crack! – had riddled the whole illusion of the sun, here where the mind goes out, not in serene reception, but in abstract speculation, disdaining earth.

The Case of Alice Carruthers

Alice Carruthers was not only quite good-looking but a really nice, obliging, and capable girl – so they said, though it was difficult to see how they could possibly know. For there was no getting near her. She never spoke to anyone – until she was first spoken to, and then she only made the reply that remark called for, but never carried the conversation any further. She had no small talk and if not a positive distaste, at least a complete incapacity, for tittle-tattle. It wasn't that she was in any way sulky or vain or queer. On the contrary she was open-faced and clear-eyed, happy-natured if extraordinarily quiet-natured, kindly in disposition, and always willing to help in any way she could. But she never made the slightest advance of any kind. Naturally all her good qualities did not make up for this singular deficiency; in a little town like Whitshiels how on earth could people get on without 'personalities', back-biting, flippancy, easy vulgarity, and endless excitement and volubility about trifles. One might perhaps liken the effect she produced in that milieu to the use of verse in drama. The verse keeps the dialogue at a certain remove from actuality, while stressing the rhythm of speech – not that she ever gave any impression of calculation, of formality; it did not seem a matter of choice at all. She was, in a word, not 'innerly' and innerliness is the most prized quality down there – all over Scotland in fact – and any one who lacks it is a social outcast. But Alice was happier than most of these unfortunates; she was not 'outcast' very markedly or with any vindictiveness; she paddled her own canoe without ever colliding with any other in that press of craft and without any other ever colliding with hers, intentionally or otherwise. No mean feat!

Alice was not disliked as a child when the pressure to make one 'like everybody else' is most insistent and cruel; but she was generally alone – she was no other girl's bosom friend, and seldom to be seen linking along with any school-mates. And as a young woman she was more and more isolated. This did not sour her in the slightest. She was completely self-contained. People knew exactly where they had her all the time. She was always there – she never went out from herself to meet anybody else half-way or quarter-way or at all, but if they came in to her she was hospitable enough, she gave them what she had to give, but never tried to keep them by playing up to them in any way. Take it or leave it; there she was. The consequence was they felt defrauded – felt that she was reserving her real self and only fobbing them off with an anteroom; it did not occur to them that if she gave them no more it was perhaps because she was unaware that she had any more – that if she was not entirely open to them it was because she had not yet explored herself. And she had never had a lover. She was thirty and assumed to be definitely on the shelf. It was a very curious case. She was exactly like the other girls – she gave herself no airs and graces; she did not criticise or dissociate herself from their mode of life; she did not feel superior to them any more than she felt inferior – only she wholly lacked this indispensable faculty of small pretences and insincerities, of conventional hypocrisies, which meant so much more to all the others than their genuine qualities, so much more that the latter could scarcely have been discerned at all by anyone who did not know them intimately. And as to love affairs, so far as external manifestations went, these partook of exactly the same nature as the rest of this social life in which she had no share – plus a little squalid danger. They depended upon a series of silly gambits and gambols – senseless catchwords and clichés, and actions in keeping with them. Love is a pretty poor affair in a place like Whitshiels, and ends very quickly as a rule – in a poorer; a little shallow stream soon lost in the morass of marriage. Did the young men realise that a love affair could not take this easy common course with Alice – that her self-contained character meant that she was capable of a great passion – and were they frightened of that, having no deeps with which to speak to such deeps, no ability to live up to anything of the kind? They probably knew it without knowing they knew it – like Alice herself. They kept clear of her at any rate, and it seemed to make no difference to her – she was conscious of no failure, no strange cravings, no hopeless longings. She did not realise that in the life about her she was like one of these rocks that stuck up greyly out of the river that ran past her door but displays strange colours if the waters rise till they flow over it. The waters of life had never submerged Alice.

But all at once the time came when they did. Ted Crozier had a bad name. He had got several girls into trouble. You never knew who he'd be going with next – or how many different ones in the surrounding parishes he'd be having on a string at the same time. Ted was not to be trusted. He had to go further afield nowadays. No girl in Whitshiels would be seen with him. It was more than her reputation was worth. Was it just this scarcity of 'raw material' that attracted him to Alice – was it because he was tired of easy conquests and wanted to try his skill with the hardest case in the place? Did he suddenly see Alice as a sort of challenge – a final test so far as he was concerned – in Whitshiels at least? He was near the end of his tether; was this to be his crowning triumph – the achievement of the impossible? It must have been the attraction of opposites. Alice and he were soon going together, hot and strong to all appearances. Opinion in the town was sharply divided as to whether it was Alice's inexperience, her lack of previous affairs, her ignorance of his real character through holding herself so aloof, that was responsible for her fall from long-sustained grace – or – or not. The alternative was never defined; some people had a vague suspicion, but they did not formulate it in precise terms – the springs of Alice's nature were too remote and obscure for them. But they were certainly on the right lines. If she had been in any ignorance of Ted's reputation she could not have preserved it long after they were first seen together – plenty of people were at pains to enlighten her (not blurting it out of course – they weren't on terms with her which would allow of anything of the sort – but with innuendoes, double-edged remarks, of all kinds). Alice did not seem to notice or understand any of these hints, and gave none of their makers any encouragement to pursue the matter any further. Alice was certainly no greenhorn; whatever she might have missed in direct personal experience it was impossible for any girl working in one of the Whitshiels tweed mills to remain in any ignorance of the 'facts of life.' Alice's father, mother, and brother were in a different position; they had no hesitation once they realised that it was true, that it was no mere scandal but actual incredible fact that Alice and Ted were walking out together, in giving her their whole minds and vocabularies on the subject. They did their utmost to dissuade her from seeing any more of the fellow – they called her all the hard names they could lay their tongues to – they predicted her inevitable ruin if she failed to accept their advice – they implored her to think of their good name if she had ceased to have any regard for her own. It would be wrong to say that she gave them the feeling that they might as well have spoken to a stone wall. Certainly all they said ran off her like water off a duck's back, without making any impression; they scarcely got a glimmer of her unfamiliar colours, but she listened quietly and reasonably enough to all they had to say, she did not flare up or anything, she did not weep or sulk – but they simply got no further with her, she took in all they said hospitably enough but it produced no result, she just did not discuss the matter with them in any way. That was the maddening thing about Alice; she looked so nice and natural, she was so obviously one of themselves, there were no oddities about her to lay a finger on – and yet she did not react to anything the way everybody else did. It wasn't that you came up against a blank wall – there was no sense of any impediment, any resistance – you simply seemed to come to the world's edge and fall into the void. The ground disappeared beneath your feet. The thread of your discourse vanished into thin air. You could make nothing of her. Or almost nothing. They did elicit, much to their surprise, one definite statement. It was when they were casting up about the other girls he had ruined. 'He won't do that again,' she said.

As if he could help it! And yet for a long time he seemed a reformed character. There was no breath of his having any other on-goings. So he couldn't be having any – or the news would soon have been out. For people were on the *qui vive*. Ted couldn't get away with anything in Whitshiels or near it nowadays. Either he was hiding his tracks extremely well – or he had really turned over a new leaf. As to Alice there was little difference except that she seemed to have ripened – to have changed, mellowed inside herself while presenting an unchanged front, or practically unchanged front, to the world. Then all at once the blow fell. It was a particularly bad business too – Ted's worst yet. Had he had to keep the two extremes going, now that he could no longer have two or more affairs much of a muchness going simultaneously? This would be a criminal case too. The poor little creature would probablty die – in any case it would take a Caesarian operation to deliver her – for he had got a little incomer, a little servant girl from the country, of barely fifteen, in the family way. There was a lot of violent feeling against him in the town. 'He ought to be horse-whipped – he ought to be lynched' were the general sentiments. A few groups of the men were for taking the law into their own hands. Alice's folk could make nothing of her. The sensational news seemed to go into her one ear and out at the other without affecting her in the least. From first to last they never heard her refer to the matter in any way. But they could hardly believe their eyes when they saw her titivating herself that night as usual to go to her tryst with Ted. They tried to stop her but it was no use. It was a devil of a night too – pouring 'auld wives and pipe stapples'. That alone should have kept her in. She'd be drenched to the skin; do water-rats make love?

A gamekeeper found her the following morning at the foot of a tree, under a branch from which Ted was hanging dead.

She said little about it – except that that was their usual trysting place. She had not realised how wild a night it was. Struggling through the pouring rain against a terrific wind she must have been late for her assignation. It was pitch-black, which had added to her difficulties. All at once stumbling along the slippery clay path she bumped into something which swung away and bounded back into her and swung away again and bounded back once more. She knew at once what it was and fell in a faint below the human pendulum.

Alice's mother knew that her new clothes-rope had mysteriously gone missing, however – but she said nothing about it, and just went and bought another, but not at the same shop.

People were surprised that Alice did not find herself *enceinte*. If she did it was with that as with so many other things – she never showed it. But people knew what Ted had been…they were sure…so they just remembered how deep still waters run and remarked knowingly that 'Alice knows the ropes'. Which was true – in one sense if not in the other.

Vouchsafed, A Sign

'Na laddie! Ye mauna say that. Sae mony byordinar things happen that the least a body can dae is to preserve an open and respectfu' mind. It disna dae to jeer at the Unseen, for it aye has the lauch o' us in the hinder-en'. You're young yet, but wait until you've lived as lang as I ha'e and you'll no' be inclined to treat things in sic an off-haun way,' said my Granny.

'Oh, I ken,' I replied, 'There's mair things in Heaven and Earth than my philosophy recks o'. Sae I'm tell't. And nae doot it's true eneuch. But it's real evidences o' that I'm eftir. I may come to scoff, but I'm willin' eneuch to bide to pray – if onything impresses me in that way. Sae faur naething has. I think a' this business aboot spiritualism and second sicht and guid dreams and bad dreams and sae on is juist a lot o' havers. But as you say you've lived faur faur langer than I ha'; and what I'd like to ken is if you can gi'e me ony convincin' first-haund experiences o' your ain o' this kind. Wasn't there something aboot grandfaither's daith?'

'There was that!' said Granny. 'Comin' events aye cast their shadows afore them, if ony yin can read them aricht. Neither your grandfaither, puir man, nor I had ony reason to be lookin' for his sudden daith, but I got as clear a warnin' a wheen nichts afore the fatal accident as ony human being ever had. There was nae mistakin' it. I kent in a meenut, and tell't your grandfaither.'

'But what was this warnin' you got, Granny,' I spiered.

'The Unseen works wi' the vera simplest means,' said Granny, 'Three nichts afore your grandfaither's daith, juist afore he cam' to bed, he lifted up the chamber-pot – and the handle cam' awa' in his hand! I kent then – and shair eneuch he perished in the pit-accident afore the week was oot. Shairly you canna ask for onything plainer or mair convincin' nor that!'

Sticky-Wullie

Galbraith met her in the licht o' the shop window at the fit o' the toon.

'Och aye,' he says, staunin' sae that she couldna win by, 'and ye'll ha'e been for yer wee bit daunder.

'There's waur things,' he says, 'than a braith o' fresh air in the country efter bein' cooped up in a stuffy atmosphere a' day.

'But,' says he, 'Sticky-Wullie tells mony a story oot o' schule.' And he pointit to her legs.

She was wearing a short skirt that haurdly cam' alow her knees and a pair o' what they ca' nylon stockin's: and the tail o' her skirt and the backs o' her stockin's were a' covered wi' the wee green ba's.

She blushed to the roots o' her hair.

'It's a guid job,' says she, 'that everybody's no' a Sherlock Holmes.'

'Aye,' says he, 'for them that ha'e onything to hide.'

'What ill can there be,' she says, 'in a wee daunder on a braw nicht like this?'

'Sticky-Wullie disna grow in the middle o' the road,' says he, 'and there's no' mony hedgbacks here-aboots whaur it's heich eneuch to taigle the knees o' a strappin' young wumman like you. But nae doot ye were a wee thing tired and juist took a bit barley in the syke afore ye turned back. Ye ha'ena been lookin' juist owre weel lately to my way o' thinkin', though ye've a rare colour the nicht.'

'I like a guid sherp walk,' says she, 'it fetches the bluid up.'

'To a' appearances it does,' says he, and on the offshot nae doot, he addit, 'And yin steps oot better when yin's by yinsel'. Ye maun ha'e come back in hauf the time it took ye to gang.'

'What gars ye say that?' says she, wi' a fleggit kind o' look.

'Och, if ye're gaen to ca' a man Sherlock Holmes,' says he, 'for usin' his common-sense, he maun live up to his reputation, and if the cap disna fit ye needna pit it on.'

He said it in a meaningfu' way to gar her wunder no' juist hoo he kent onything aboot it ava but juist hoo muckle he did ken; and as for him he was wunderin' mair and mair juist hoo muckle there was to ken, and at a bit o' a loss what to say neist. It cam' to 'm a' o' a sudden.

'It 'ud set ye better,' says he, 'Mary, if ye kent common-sense when you saw it, and aiblins ye'd no' need to be comin' tearin' back to the toon by yersel' at this oor o' the nicht. It'll be a shock to a' yer freens to see ye hame sae early. It's an oor yet afore the feck o' the courtin' couples'll be turnin' back.'

Wad ye believe it, the cratur sterted greetin'!

'Wheesht, wheesht,' says he. 'This'll never dae at a' – the bonniest lass in the toon staunin' bubblin' and greetin' on the street. He's no' worth greetin' owre. There's as guid fish in the sea as ever cam' oot o't and ye can ha'e your pick at ony time. C'wa and ha'e a bit turn wi' me for a cheenge and it'll mebbe steady your nerves.'

And he yokit an airm in hers and she gaed like a lamb. But when they cam' to the cross-roads he noticed she gar'd him tak' the laich road and he thocht to himsel': 'She's fear'd to meet him again – and mebbe it's juist as weel.'

'I dinna ken what ye maun think,' she says efter a wee.

'Ye needna fash yer heid aboot that,' says he, 'That's juist whaur Sherlock Holmes comes in again. A blush is nae guid but ony fule could tell at the first go aff that you're no' ane o' the hardened kind – and, without bein' that, if there'd been muckle amiss ye'd 'a' been mair particular aboot the incriminatin' evidence. Yet it's something new to see you alane – or at ony rate comin' into the toon – at this time o' the nicht; and it's no' ill to jalouse what's at the bottom o't. But there's juist this; atween you and me, considerin' the kind o' lads you've been knockin' aboot wi' o' late, the wunder is something o' this kind hasna happened lang afore this.'

'You seem to ha'e been keepin' a gleg e'e on my affairs,' says she.

'Aye,' says he, 'I ha'e: and no' afore time – and here's that stuck up guid-for-naething Malcolm o' the Bank. It's no' often you see him by himsel' either at this time o' nicht,' gien her a searchin' look, and syne, when Malcolm cam' alangside, wi' his face a' workin' and his een like to pump oot o' his heid, he said, as easy-osy as ye like, 'Braw night, Malcolm – juist haen your bit daunder?'

'Ye – ,' but Malcolm never got the word oot a' his mooth for Mary was owre to'm and smothered it wi' ane o' her wee hauns; syne, slippin' an airm into Malcolm's, she turns roon to Galbraith.

'Common-sense,' she says, 'is whiles owre common, and the trouble wi' Sticky-Wullie is that it disna aye tell the same tale. Ye mauna judge ither fowk by yersel'. Guid nicht.'

And she whirled Malcolm roond and awa' they sailed and left Galbraith staunin' like a stookie.

Without a Leg to Stand On: A Shetland Sketch

'Talking about the mass production of B.Sc.s – agricultural or engineering – by the Scottish universities nowadays,' he said, 'there's no place in the world perhaps less suitable for the young man in a hurry type than the Shetland Islands.

'A little knowledge is a dangerous thing, and the little knowledge these fellows have is particularly dangerous in such islands where the whole business of life is so largely dependent upon kinds of traditional knowledge that have never been reduced to words on paper at all.

'The natives know what they need to know without knowing how. It's not the sort of thing that can be learned. It's all a question of having knacks like that lucky touch or "green thumb" old gardeners talk about. You see, things must have reached a certain level – which they have not begun to do in the Shetlands – before the application of a little modern science can be useful, and go-ahead B.Sc.s simply can't realise that.

'The nature of their training makes them aggressive, dogmatic, and quite incapable of seeing all round a complicated issue. They think they are being scientific when they are being exactly the opposite – just advocating the application of a few so-called scientific facts to a situation they do not understand in the least and of which they are too constitutionally impatient ever to learn anything worth knowing. That's just it. They fancy they are the last word in up-to-date enlightenment, when the real truth is that they are simply ineducable…

'Well one of these fellows got the headmastership of the school on one of the little north islands of the Shetland group I know. He was a very typical specimen of the breed. He did not wait to learn the lie of the land – but assumed that as Headmaster of Houll School and a B.Sc.(Agriculture) to boot, he ought to be a Force To Be Reckoned With and a Power For Good in the Community.

'So he barged right in. Joined the Badminton Club which played in the Village Hall and was soon at loggerheads with the Hall Committee because they wouldn't give him his own way. Became Secretary of the Model Yacht Club and on the Organising Committee for the Annual Regatta. And he talked to all the fishermen and crofters and thought he was doing fine.

'They were flattered to have him to talk to. So far as book-learning was concerned they were utterly ignorant, and over-valued it accordingly – in others. But let any of their own children waste too much time reading! That was another matter altogether; and of course any idea of keeping their children at school after fourteen was out of the question.

'There was far too much to be done on the beggarly little scratches of crofts, and at the herring fishing in the summer time and the haddock fishing in the winter, so far as the boys were concerned, and as for the girls, they were in immediate demand at the gutting stations during the fishing season, and, at other times, they had not only to help their mothers with the housework and looking after the babies, but they were needed in the harvest field, and in the milking-shed and in the hen-ree and for turning the peats on the hill and later carrying them in the plaited baskets (or "kishies" as they call them) slung on their backs, and for stacking them (a great art in itself) beside the houses, ready for the long black winters.

'And also the second main industry in the Shetlands is the knitting industry, and that is wholly in the hands of the women, who spend every waking moment they have when not busy with some other essential task (and often when doing other things, too – for it is marvellous how many tasks they can fulfil while never ceasing to ply their knitting-needles as well) knitting indefatigably, turning out Fair Isle jumpers, sweaters, stockings and gloves. There is not much time for reading in such a community.

'But the young headmaster I'm telling you about was far too green and too cocksure; he did not realise the shrewdness that lay behind the deference with which he was listened to – he did not realise that these people were shrewd enough to be willing to pick his brains and get him to write their letters for them and get free advice from him in regard to all their little problems without... well, without taking him exactly at his own valuation: and certainly without rushing headlong to act upon the advice he gave them, instead of thinking very cannily about it first and especially when it conflicted in any way with their traditional practices and prejudices.

'And, of course, I have nothing to say about it so long as it stayed at that. It was all right his taking an interest in local affairs and talking to everybody. There isn't much to brighten people's lives up in these islands, and talking to this fellow was a bit of a change – so long as it didn't go beyond talk.

'The young Department of Health doctor on the island hated this new headmaster – Moar, they called him; Peter Moar – like poison. "He thinks it's all plain sailing," he said, "but wait a little. The surface of the water is smooth and sweet enough just now, but life here is just like the Sound between the islands there – it calls for clever navigation, and a great deal of knowledge and experience that is not to be found in any book at all, and, even with that, as the best skippers will tell you, you can never be too careful and patient. The island people will soon see through this fellow. They'll make all the use of him they can in the meantime, but he'll get jammed on hidden and uncharted rocks one of these fine days. Mark my words! He won't last long here....But he may do a great deal of damage in the meantime."'

What the Doctor had in mind was the fact that Moar was going round insisting that something should be done to improve the local cattle. The cows were small, as all indigenous animals are in the Shetlands, but in the course of generations, as the Doctor pointed out, the islands had evolved a type of cow precisely suited alike to the needs of the people – and to the resources of the islands in regard to feeding for cattle.

'Moar wants the Department of Agriculture to send a Bull of a bigger breed next season. He doesn't realise the danger. The type of cattle they have get on all right with the very limited feeding these crofts can afford to give them – and they give a splendid milk yield, which is just what's wanted.

'To introduce bigger cattle will upset the local economy altogether – and these people can't afford to experiment, apart from the fact that to ignore all the lessons of the past, and the way the local animal has been evolved to suit the local conditions and needs, is utterly unscientific. With these very small crofts the people have no margin to come and go on in matters of this sort – one bad calving season would ruin most of them altogether. The idea just appeals to their cupidity at the expense of their commonsense. But Moar thinks he knows it all – on the strength of a little book learning, and no practical experience whatever. Mark my words, there'll be trouble. I don't know very much about the Shetlands myself. I haven't been here long enough, but I was brought up in a farming countryside in the South of Scotland and I remember a thing or two. I know it doesn't do for a farmer from Berwickshire to come down into Dumfriesshire, for example, and forget that times and seasons are different in the two counties. Or like a fool try wheat where oats or rye are the only hope. Or sow potatoes too soon and have them cut down by the late frost. Or with the sheep, try to grow more wool, and forget the need for hardihood, and lose a season of lambs.

'And there are thousands of such-like things to consider in regard to stock or land before you can safely make any departure from established practice. And these aren't the sort of things you can learn in books – none of them – and that's just where a fellow like Moar (and he's a very typical specimen of the whole breed of these B.Sc.s) is so infernally dangerous.'

'But surely the Department will have more sense than send a different kind of bull before they've taken all the necessary factors in the local situation carefully into account,' I said.

'Not they!' hooted the Doctor. 'They all hang together – these Government boards and these mass-produced B.Sc.s and what not. You'll see.'

I did. The Doctor was absolutely right. But that is another story – the story of the Bull; and it cannot be told in other than Rabelaisian terms. The new Bull fiasco was a howler to high heaven in all conscience, yet it was in another connection that Moar finished himself so far as these islanders were concerned, and I'm telling you this story not only because it is a good story in itself, but because it is a perfect example of the way in which these half-baked young know-alls of B.Sc.s fall down when it comes not to theory but to practice, not to airing their book-learning but to giving a hand with the actual job. It's the sort of thing that is happening all over the country with these Government Boards and young graduate teachers – only it's rather an extreme example perhaps.

Well, as you know, all the crofting ground in the islands is portioned off with deep, open ditches, and every now and again a cow falls into one of them and the people come running from all over the place to get it out. Moar by his way of it had established himself as quite a progressive public figure and the accepted authority in every contingency, when one day this happened on old Fred Williamson's croft at Whitefields and they got ropes and had hauled the cow out when they saw that something was seriously wrong with her. It was then they made the mistake. Instead of sending, as they had been accustomed to do for long enough whenever anything was wrong with any of the cattle or pigs or sheep or ponies, to old Peter Barclay at Isbister, they sent to Houll School for Moar. And ere long Moar came tootling along the road in his little Morris car, and hopped out, and came down over the field and across the rigs very brisk and businesslike. He was soon acquainted with the facts and with the opinion that the cow had broken one of its forelegs. He stood and pondered, looking very seriously at the cow. And then he knelt and examined first one foreleg and then the other.

'Nonsense!' he said when he straightened himself again after a fitting interval. 'It hasn't broken its leg at all. Look,' – and he half knelt again, pointing first to the one leg and then to the other – 'they're both the same length. Get it carried up to the byre and give it time to get over the fright it's had. You'll see, it'll be all right in the morning.' And with a confident laugh he strode off up the rigs again, a purposeful little fellow, with, as everybody round the cow agreed, 'his head screwed on all right and his heart in the proper place too.'

When the morning came, however, the byre door couldn't be opened, and finally had to be taken off its hinges. When this was done, it was found that the cow was lying on the floor of the byre and its back had been hard up against the door, making it impossible to open it. Moar, they reflected, would be busy in the school; it would never do to send for him during school hours. So they now sent for old Peter Barclay, and when he came they told him just what had happened and how they'd sent for Mr Moar and he had said that the cow would be all right by morning and hadn't broken its leg since, as he had pointed out, both legs were the same length.

Old Peter laughed in a crafty, sardonic sort of way. 'Aye,' he said, 'he was right enough. Both legs were the same! But the truth of the matter apparently just didn't occur to Mr Moar. The trouble is both forelegs are broken!'

And so indeed it proved, and when the news went round the island that Fred Williamson's cow had had to be shot after all, quite a few ungrateful people muttered that Mr Moar would have been none the worse of a little shooting too.

'Tuts,' laughed the Doctor, 'there's no need for that. Just give him plenty of rope and he'll hang himself soon enough – if he hasn't done it already.'

An Epoch-Making Event

It was while we were living on that little island that my wife came in one day laughing very merrily.

'Great excitement in the village today!' she cried.

It wasn't a village really – only a place where a few houses were built together at the Harbour (all the other houses on the island stood separately on their own little crofts), and where the general store and the post office were located. The bi-weekly steamer comes into the voe there and passengers and goods are taken off or put on by a row boat.

'Phoebe,' continued my wife, 'is thrilled to bits.'

Well, there was nothing very surprising in that. Phoebe is very easily thrilled. If, for example, any new chap comes to the island – a new teacher, or a new doctor, or anything. Until it is ascertained whether he is married or single. If he is single the excitement continues. Phoebe is an old maid, of over fifty. But the appearance of a new bachelor is a sign that she has met her fate at last. She is all over the place discussing him – contriving meetings with him. All the islanders know this little foible and make the most of it. The island lives on little things; it does not take much to interest and divert it. So Phoebe is led on without mercy. The affair is seriously debated in all its bearings. It is reported on all hands that the stranger is undoubtedly in love with her. Has he really said nothing yet? He must be too shy. It is Phoebe's duty to help him out. Let her only look at him carefully and she will see unmistakeable signs of the passion that is consuming him. No wonder. Phoebe is looking younger than ever. So the poor old creature hunts out all her fineries – and togs herself up in the most fetching fashion. One thing is certain; she can blush and giggle like a girl. You never saw such a foolish old creature. And her lover is to be at the Whist Drive on Friday night? Certainly. That is her opportunity. She fusses round him in the most remarkable fashion, prattles away to him with extraordinary animation and fits of merry laughter, feeling that she is making great progress and has him safely in the toils at last – while he wonders what on Earth is wrong with the fantastic old creature, and everybody else in the Hall is fit to die at the ludicrous spectacle. Hope dies hard. Phoebe is not easily put off, and, finally disappointed in one man, comes up again to the conquest of the next with all her colours flying.

Fortunately I was a married man and brought my wife with me when I came to the island. So I was spared Phoebe's attentions of this sort, though I had to stand a great deal of her senseless chatter whenever I went into the shop. So I stopped going; my wife used to go instead. But I had another reason for avoiding Phoebe. I hate all dogs, but Phoebe had one I particularly loathed. This so-called dog was a midget Shetland collie. Our little boy of three called it 'the baby dog' or, in the island dialect, 'the peerie mootie thing'. You never saw such a flea of a dog. You might as well have gone round with a mouse at the end of a lead. But there was never such a dog! It had all the canine virtues. Phoebe thought the world of it. Wherever she went it went. 'Rob Roy' she called it, but she had, it transpired, christened it under a misapprehension, and a month or two later she found it was a lady and had to rename it. Oslo was its new name; and the orgy of adoration of which it was the subject has never been surpassed in all the astonishing history of pet dogs. No wonder Phoebe was an old maid. If she could lavish such a wealth of affection on this horrible little creature, Heaven only knows what she would have done with a man. To see her with Oslo would have kept her a virgin if she had been the only woman in the world.

On this fateful day, my wife had been going round the corner of the shore towards the shop, when she saw Phoebe waving frantically to her from the window of her sitting-roam. My wife waved back but did not want to go in. By the time she got into the shop, however, Phoebe had run in there too through the connecting lobby between her own rooms and the public quarters of the establishment, which, with the assistance of a couple of girls, she managed. Oslo was snuggled – I was going to say *between* her breasts, but in Phoebe's case it is not known that there was any such division. Oslo was, let us say, *on* her breast; and my wife saw at once that something entirely out of the ordinary had happened, that Phoebe was excited to an absolutely unprecedented pitch. And no wonder! My wife naturally had no premonition of the magnitude of the cause; the soul-stirring event that had led to the frantic waving from the window and the wild rush into the shop had cast no shadow before it. Phoebe was dying to communicate the great intelligence. My wife cannot remember whether she asked, or even looked, a question or not, or whether Phoebe just incontinently spilled the beans. Whichever way it was, hugging the little beast in her arms, and dancing about like a hen on a hot girdle, Phoebe cried: 'It's Oslo! It's Oslo!'

My wife is not usually 'slow in the uptake', but there did not seem to be any reason for all this commotion. It wasn't as if Oslo was lost or anything. There she was in Phoebe's arms and nothing seemed the matter with her.

'But there's nothing wrong with Oslo, is there?' she asked.

Phoebe was now a sort of dancing Dervish, emitting looks of tremendous profundity, half-laughing and half-crying and cuddling away at the dog; but in the midst of this whirl of gesture and suggestion my wife at least gathered the central fact...'Oslo, my little darling!...He! He!...You know...I don't quite know how to say it...But you know?...little Oslo's *unwell...*'

My wife was now purposely obtuse. She was determined to make the dithering old creature say it.

'Unwell?' she said. 'She looks all right. What on earth is the matter with her?'

'It – it's – you know. It's her first time. My dear little Oslo – naughty, naughty! – wants a mate – He! He! – Don't you, precious?'; and Phoebe hid her blushes in the little brute as in a muff.

Appendix 1
Hitherto Unpublished or Uncollected Stories, Sketches and Fragments

The Lion of Edinburgh

I know. It is all this talk about the wild new Scottish Nationalist Movement that has got you and now you cannot think of Edinburgh without at once saying to yourself: 'The red lion of Scotland – the Lion Rampant'. But, believe me, you are wrong. I know Edinburgh far better than you do, and the lion of Edinburgh is a very different sort of animal altogether.

Let me tell you a story about it. I have a group of friends who live over in York Place. They are all students together at the Edinburgh College of Art, which is nowadays an enormously wealthy place owing to the magnificent legacies it has received. So my friends, though none of them come of well-to-do families, all have very substantial bursaries and so have a good deal more money between their fingers than the run of Art students in other countries. There is no starving in garrets for them. In other respects, however, they are true to the Art student type. They are wild lads, with broad-brimmed beach hats and irrepressible high spirits and given to heavy drinking. Bohemians, I tell you – as far as Edinburgh will allow it; real Bohemians.

And they all lodge together very comfortably in York Place with a tall black-avised Highland woman, Mrs Riach, for their housekeeper. A very stern proper-backed widow – a woman of granite. Nobody gets any change out of Mrs Riach. She makes my friends an ideal landlady. Nothing they do seems to surprise or shock her; she takes it all for granted – just doesn't seem to see it – as if they were behaving perfectly rationally and properly. I do not think the wildest cantrip imaginable would make that woman blink an eyelid. She is simply marvellous. There is only one thing – she must be paid on the nail. No shilly-shallying about it. And you can bet your boots there have been no end of high jinks in their apartments. Spike MacQueen and his chums are the boys for that – up to all kinds of devilment.

Now one morning at breakfast – which in this ménage was a very movable feast and took place nearer midday than nine o'clock in the morning as a rule – Spike and his pals were sitting round the table in the dining-room, all very unnaturally subdued and much the worse of wear. It was the morning after the night before. They had had a particularly hectic splore. None of them could remember anything whatever about it after a fairly early hour in the evening. But they knew by their condition and by various little signs that there had been, to use their phrase, singularly 'dirty work at the cross-roads' and that it must have been well into the morning before they got back to their lodgings. In short there were six or more hours to account for of which none of them could recall the least thing. They had got home all right – that was perhaps the main thing – for they must certainly all have been extremely drunk and none of them in that condition was apt to be in the least quiet and well-behaved, while they had given the police so much trouble and impudence first and last that they might account themselves lucky not to have been taken up and lodged in jail.

They were far less disposed to be thankful over yet another escape, however, than to be depressed over their present – and prospective – situation. It was no remorse of conscience that was worrying them; you can be sure of that. They were dying of thirst; their throats were like lime-kilns; they longed not for hairs – but the entire pelt – of the dog that bit them. And they had not the wherewithal. Pooling their remaining resources they found themselves in a desperate plight. They would not draw their periodic allowances for another ten days and in the interval they had not enough for the barest necessities – the inescapable incidentals – let alone drinking money. It was a devil of a fix altogether – and at tea-time yesterday they had been unusually flush. That was what had set them off on such a steep binge. They must have had a night of it and no mistake. They could see no way out of their difficulty. No doubt once their heads cleared their natural ingenuity would reassert itself and they would find ways and means of borrowing a shilling or two here and there. But so far as their thirst was concerned that would at best amount to no more than trying to flood the Sahara by discharging a water-pistol. They were in for a spell of horribly short commons. It was a ghastly predicament. They revolved the matter in all its bearings and the situation seemed more and more hopeless with every word that was uttered. Even Spike, their natural leader, could not see the faintest glimmer of light.

A knock came to the door and Mrs Riach put in her head.

'A gentleman to see you, Mr MacQueen,' she said.

'Who is it?' asked Spike cautiously.

'He did not give his name,' said Mrs Riach. 'He merely said to tell you it was the gentleman with the lion.'

'With what?' asked Spike with a note of horror.

'The lion,' said Mrs Riach, as if the delivery of a lion was as commonplace a matter as the delivery of the laundry.

'Er,' said Spike, 'Oh! of course. Has he – has he the lion with him?'

'Yes,' said the imperturbable Mrs Riach.

Spike gave an agonised look round the transfixed faces of his comrades. They were totally unequal to an emergency like this, but Spike was not their leader for nothing.

'Ask him if he'll be good enough to wait in the hall just for a minute or two, Mrs Riach, please,' said Spike, and the landlady withdrew.

'Now what the devil is this?' Spike demanded of his companions in distress as the door closed.

They grunted in various keys.

'I have it,' said Spike, after a moment or two. 'We must have bought the blasted thing last night. Leave him to me. I'll manage him. I'll bring him in here.

Spike went into the hall.

'Good morning,' he said to the grubby unprepossessing fellow he found there. 'Will you please come this way?' And he ushered him into the dining-room.

'Now,' said Spike, 'you've come about the lion, haven't you?'

'Yes,' said the visitor.

'The lion we bought last night?'

'That's right, sir.'

'How much did we pay for it?'

'Thirty shillings.'

Spike looked round the others. Thirty shillings! Ye Gods! What could they not do with thirty shillings now. Suddenly Spike thought he saw a way out.

'Well,' he said quickly, 'the things one does overnight sometimes look a bit different in the morning. My friends and I were just talking about it before you arrived and the fact of the matter is that we have changed our minds.'

'Changed your minds?'

'Yes. You can see how it is. We have no place for a lion here. Besides our housekeeper, whom you saw just now, is a very strict lady. She would not allow a lion in the house. It all seemed easy enough last night. But this morning it is obviously quite impossible.'

'Well, that's got nothing to do with me,' said the man, truculently. 'You bought it and I've brought it as arranged – and a stiff pull-up it's been too, all the way from Leith. And I haven't any time to waste either. I've my business to attend to.'

Spike gave his famous winning smile.

'Well we're extremely sorry to have put you to any unnecessary trouble and loss of time, of course. But you are a man of the world, and you know that we were going through the loops a bit last night. A lion is no earthly use to us. But you're in the line. You sold it to us and you can just as easily sell it again to somebody else. You stand to lose nothing. Of course you have had all the trouble, and danger, of bringing it up here, and we wouldn't have you do that for nothing. What I suggest is that you refund us £1 of the 30/-, keep the other 10/- for your trouble, and keep the lion.'

'I'm afraid I can't do that,' said the man with what struck Spike and his friends as a shockingly short and sinister laugh. 'But I think you'd better come down and see it for yourself.'

'Very well,' said Spike. 'There's no harm in that. But do be a sport. We have our reputation to consider and York Place is a rather select quarter – full of Government offices and lawyers' offices. I'm afraid we'll have done ourselves a lot of harm already by even bringing a lion into it at all. I hope this doesn't get about or we'll be ruined. Too much publicity doesn't do in our profession.' And, slightly changing his tune but not making it too menacing, he added, 'In any case, you must have seen we were not responsible for our actions last night and you would probably get into very serious trouble if you tried to hold us to a transaction made in these circumstances. But I'm sure you'll be reasonable. Let us go and have a dekko at this king of beasts.'

Spike and the animal-dealer proceeded downstairs, and Spike's friends followed hesitantly a few steps behind them.

When the outside door was opened, it revealed standing in the roadway a large hand-cart in which lay an extremely moth-eaten stuffed lion.

All the girls in the Government offices came and they were at the windows surveying the wondrous scene. Spike was equal to the occasion.

'Now you just give me a quid, and take the lion back to Leith and sell it to someone else,' he said, 'and we'll say no more about the matter.'

The man shook his head.

'Well,' said Spike, 'let's go fifty fifty. That's a fair bargain. Fifteen shillings, and you take the lion away and do what you like with it.'

The man shook his head. Spike lost his temper.

'If it wasn't too much bother I'd get a policeman right away. It's pure robbery, that's what it is. But keep your thirty bob and a fat lot of good may it do you. Only – take that lousy object out of this.'

The man shook his head.

'I've no room for it,' he said. 'It takes up too much space that I want for other stock. Besides I've had it for years and years and I'm sick of the sight of it. I'm not taking it back on any account.'

'Very well,' said Spike, 'don't. We've tried you every possible way but you won't be reasonable. You've had thirty bob and you're damned well paid. One good turn deserves another. If you can't take the blasted brute back to your shop, take it and set fire to it in your backyard or dump it into the dock or do anything on earth you like with it – but take it out of this and don't let us see it again.'

The man looked as if he were making the best of a very bad job.

'Very well,' he said, and got in between the shafts of the handcart and off he went.

One of Spike's friends found his voice at last.

'Sold us a lion?' he said. 'Sold us a pup!'

'If,' groaned another, 'we'd only got five bob back out of the blighter… !'

'The worst of it from my point of view,' said Spike, 'is our infernal Mrs Riach. Her face has less expression than a mud-pie. None of us had any idea what we'd been up to last night and, I don't mind admitting, I got the wind up properly when she announced "The man with the lion" in that flat voice of hers. She was having us on. There's more in that old wife than meets the eye. She knew that we'd jump to the conclusion that it was a real live lion – and, mark my words, she'd seen it, she knew exactly what it was.'

Just as the handcart turned out of sight into Leith Walk, Spike said, 'Boys will be boys and you must pay – and pay dearly for your experience. Let that be a lesson to you that all Edinburgh's lions are stuffed lions…I think I am entitled to the balance of the funds for the way in which I have handled the matter.'

But none of the others agreed with him as to that, trifling though the sum in question was.

The Loch Ness Mystery

'I have been an omnivorous reader ever since I was a boy,' he said, 'and I think I may fairly claim to have a very considerable stock of general knowledge of all kinds. I have made a special study, too, of the mysteries, and crimes, and curious stories of Scotland. Now I am neither a detective nor a fiction-writer, but certainly if I read a Crime Club story I am prepared to wager I can see the solution before the author divulges it as quickly as anybody if the author plays fair with his readers in its development, and I can also devise plausible enough hypotheses as to the truth of various unsolved and apparently insoluble mysteries. It is, in fact, a little hobby of mine.

'But there is one incident that has come to my attention for which I can think of no solution whatever – no conceivable motive or explanation. If you can think of any I shall be greatly obliged.

'Of course I do not mean the sort of thing we could all invent – say, for example, that the macabre feature of the matter is to be explained as the sign of some weird secret society, or that it is due to the natural course of a rare disease nobody ever heard of, or to some queer passion which led the objects in question to be treasured by the person responsible just as some people keep the lock of a dead friend's hair.

'As a matter of fact that last explanation is most likely ruled out – if any person had treasured these objects in that way, he or she would not have been at all likely to lose them carelessly, or to fail to reclaim them from the police – unless some crime was involved. I think the second explanation is ruled out too; the objects in question were in no way diseased nor did they appear to have been acquired by torture or violence. Nor could they have been used, so far as I can see, though they could have been acquired, for purposes of revenge; they would not be easily recognisable; they might have belonged to anybody originally. As to the first anything at all might serve as the sign of a secret society, but at any rate there has never been any word of such a Society existing in this country, and no previous or subsequent instance of the recurrence has been recorded.

'Far-fetched scientific ideas do not seem to fit the matter either; the objects in question were not poisoned; nor were they other than just what they seemed to be. They had not previously belonged to a Chinese God, for instance; if they had, or if they had been valuable relics of any famous personage, there was nothing unless they had been acquired or were being used criminally to prevent them being reclaimed. They were very carefully examined by experts; they did not conceal on their surfaces any writing or marks visible or invisible. I have thought a very great deal about the matter and it is improbable that any of you will advance any theory that I have not evolved and been forced to discuss for one reason or another. At any rate do not let us waste time considering any of the obvious shots at a solution that can be made by imaginative persons; I can assure you that I have considered them all.

'Let me tell you the story – not that there is any real story; the one macabre feature is really all that there is to it, and that in itself is what baffles me completely. One Spring afternoon three or four years ago a young gamekeeper found by the side of Loch Ness, in a lonely unfrequented place, a gentleman's leather glove of a very common type (the glove for the right hand) and close to it a little heap of bones. He informed the police and all the ordinary police routine of investigation was gone through, and not only that but some of the best detectives in the country were brought in – not because of the glove or the bones but because of what the glove contained. The glove itself bore the glover's name and so forth; and the bones proved to be the bones of sheep and had no connection with the glove at all. The matter got the usual newspaper publicity but nothing came of it. There is no reason for thinking that any crime had taken place, and yet, as I have said, the contents of the glove removed the matter completely out of the normal and the police and everybody else who had anything to do with the affair were completely at a loss to account for it.

'This in detail was of so extraordinary and gruesome a character that it suggested all manner of weird and horrible possibilities, but there was no means of getting any forrader with any of them. I know that this detail has fixed itself in an amazing way in the minds and imaginations of quite a number of people who heard of it, and certainly it has done so in my own case. It may well be that one or more of you will be affected in the same way. In any case we will see. Now remember disease is definitely ruled out – the things did not drop off inside the glove without the owner being aware of them, or even with his or her being aware of them. They were perfectly healthy, clean, unbroken. If they had shed themselves unobtrusively in the glove in any case it was surely an extreme coincidence that that particular glove should have happened to get lost; and besides if there was any innocent explanation of that sort the person who had lost these objects would have had no reason not to give the authorities that simple explanation. Crime, too, – at least of any ordinary kind – is, I think, ruled out; at least there is no trace of anything having happened with which these objects could have been at all connected and to which they might be a clue. When I say disease and crime are ruled out I do not include insanity or some purely personal crime – of revenge, say, or sadism – which has never come to light and in the nature of the case probably couldn't. Now let me tell you what this single macabre detail was.

'But first of all can any of you guess from what I have already said what the objects in the glove were?

'No, it wasn't fingers.

'No, I did not think that you would. It is not the sort of thing at all one is likely to guess, although one perhaps ought to, seeing that the objects in question are perhaps the only objects apart from fingers, save a ring or rings, generally associated with the inside of a glove.

'The inside of the glove contained three perfectly clean and complete finger nails.'

On Being Sold a Pup

'There's absolutely no limit to the lengths they'll go,' said MacAlister.

We had been discussing women, apropos a certain local affiliation case involving one of our friends.

'You're thinking of a particular case,' said Grieg. 'Let's have the story.'

'Oh, I don't know that it's anything very much,' said MacAlister, 'but it's the most striking example I've come across personally – so far. I wouldn't be surprised if several of you could cap it. It was when I was living in Oban. One of the crowd I used to associate with there – Rory McLeod – had got in tow with a notorious local woman, a regular hard case if ever there was one. At least that was the name she got, but there was nothing the matter with her, except that she was a bit of a prostitute – one of those small-headed Highland women with blue-black hair and exceptional grace of movement. Her eyes were not quite black, though – it was only her eyelashes that were so black, and that's what made her eyes look so dark. She certainly had a far less disgusting way of walking than any other woman I have ever seen. Even then (though I didn't say anything) I understood how pride – Scottish pride – may oust all womanhood, and rejoiced in it, as I rejoice in all the wild and regardless passions of my race. I got to know her a great deal better later on; we became great friends; and all I have to say is that "nous ne connaissons pour notre part quelque chose d'un peu farouche et de si tendre, de sentiment caricatural et de si cordial, et de si *bon*, et d'un jet franc sonore, magistral". It was only a sort of calf-love with McLeod – he was just a shallow romantic, with no real appetite for life. In any case we warned him against her all we could and did our best to break off the association. It may have been our influence finally – I don't know – but one Saturday night he and a couple of other fellows were coming along the street. He had had a lot of drink. Suddenly she appeared on the scene and tried to get him away with her. But he wasn't having any, and all at once he broke away from her, whirled her round, and gave her a hefty kick on the bottom. There was a clean smack as if it had been a football. One of the other chaps, Nobby McQueen, told me that as she stood watching Rory go off she'd the most devilish expression he'd ever seen, or could imagine, on a human face. "All right," she cried after them, "I'll have my revenge." But they paid no attention and went on to the hotel. On the Monday the fat was in the fire. Rory was up against an assault case – but a damned serious one, one that was likely to ruin him. It seemed that she had been pregnant and Rory's kick had caused her to abort that night. The affair created a tremendous sensation in the town and district, where Rory was a very popular fellow – one of the best! Everything seemed black against him. When the denouement came I was having a drink with one or two of the boys in the hotel lounge. Dr Milligan – who didn't come in there often – blew in, looking unusually pleased with himself. Milligan kept himself pretty much to himself and though all of us would have liked a word with him – to hear if there was any new development in Rory's case – none of us dared to approach him. Fergusson of the Bank, however, came in just on Milligan's heels and joined him in a drink. Fergusson was one of Milligan's few intimates and a minute or two later we saw Milligan saying something to him in too low a voice for us to overhear and Fergusson out with an almighty shout, slapping his thigh for all he was worth and then laughing like to burst himself. They had another drink together and Milligan had to go. Just as he was going out, Fergusson shouted to him, "No need to keep that private, is there? Can I tell the boys?" "By all means," cried Milligan, "Share the joke with them. It'll be public property in no time anyhow." So Fergusson came over and sat down along with us. "It's about Rory's case," he said, "You'll be glad to hear that's all cleared up now." Cleared up? We stared at him. Then it all came out, and bears out what I said at the beginning, that there's no limit to the lengths women will go in matters of this sort. What do you think that woman had done? She'd gone home and killed a bitch (you'll all remember it – always about the streets like its mistress – a most unhealthy-looking, yellow-bellied animal, obviously born for just such an end) that was in pup, and took one of the unborn litter and faked it up a bit to pass as the foetus she alleged she'd aborted with. Milligan was completely taken in at first. It wasn't that but something else – something in her attitude or something she said – that made him suspect that all wasn't just open and above board. So he sent the gruesome object off to a pathologist in Edinburgh, and had just received his report back before he came in here.'

[The following concluding part of the paragraph is crossed out in the manuscript. – Eds.]

'It's a good job Milligan and one or two others know the truth,' said one of us, 'Rory would almost let the case go through against him than have this coming out against her.' We did not think that he would have carried his quixotry to that length if he had been in the position to do it, but we all agreed that he'd certainly have thought of it and been inclined that way.

In the Gaelic Islands

'Ah, yes,' he said, enthusiastically, 'I know the Gaelic Islands well. I have travelled all over them, again and again. I am always glad when I can go back to them. You should really pay them a visit. I know they are far out of the beaten track and very difficult of access, but they are worth all the trouble. They are really most interesting. It is like going into another world. There are, of course, several parts of Scotland like that – each very different – each a little world apart. But the Gaelic Islands are at the furthest remove from anything you can find anywhere else. It is a great experience.

'Of course the most interesting places are the most out of the way places. I am not saying anything about the towns where the steamer calls, but they are not just so absolutely foreign, so completely unspoiled. But it is the little lonely villages or the isolated houses that are the main thing to one like myself who has become – if I may say so – a connoisseur of places; of types of life, that seem incapable of co-existing on this little earth with the *normal* existence most people lead. One would not think that the whole world, let alone this small country of Scotland, could accommodate such differences. The distance between Edinburgh or Perth, say, and Tomluachin in Benbecula or Kilreidil in South Uist is far greater than that between the North Pole and the South, and the distance in time is greater than the whole span of history. One goes about in such places with a most delightful sense of the incredible. As a matter of fact, it is true – they have not changed within historical time. The people are just as they were long before Christ. There is no time – no change – in the Gaelic Islands. The people are of an indescribable innocence – absolutely unspoiled.

'It is very difficult, of course, to find one's way about in these outlandish places without some little knowledge of the Gaelic. Fortunately I am a good Gaelic speaker. It is a handy language to have – in Canada, in Patagonia, or even yet on parts of the Scottish mainland. I remember a little Jewish packman who began going the rounds in the wilds of Argyllshire. He made no headway; he was very downhearted; he could not understand it. Until one day a man said to him, "Have you the Gaelic?" He replied that he hadn't.

'"Ah. That's it," said the man. "You will never get on here till you learn to speak the native language."

'The little Jew set to and learned Gaelic in a surprisingly short time and he has gone on like a house afire ever since. He does a roaring trade and is one of the best-known figures all up the West of Scotland. Besides Gaelic's worth learning if only to nonplus the English. They do not mind people speaking French or German or Italian or Spanish – but Gaelic! It is worth learning it just to see their faces. The main difficulty in going about in these remote places is that there are no hotels or boarding houses. That doesn't matter so much in the summer-time. One can always sleep in the open. But in the winter – it is no joke, I can tell you, to tramp all day over a moor without seeing a living soul and come at nightfall to a tiny village or more likely a little cottage standing miles away from its next-door neighbour. But it is no great difficulty really. The people are so hospitable. They will not turn a stranger away if they can possibly help it. They will find a corner somehow. But it is no easy matter. The cottages are so very small; there is no spare accommodation. You could not go to a house on the mainland after dark with a cock-and-bull story of having lost your bearings and be sure of a bed. But in the Gaelic Islands you can. They do not even seem surprised when you suddenly turn up out of nowhere and ask for a night's lodging. They take it all for granted and make you perfectly at home. You are welcome to anything they have – the trouble is they have so little, just next to nothing, and a bed, or, rather, just room to sleep in is the great trouble. But they are not to be stuck if there is a way at all.

'Now you are not to be shocked. They are, as I have said, incredibly innocent people judged by worldly standards. And it often happens that you come to a lonely cottage and... there is no place where you can possibly sleep, unless you share her bed with the daughter of the house. She is not the least little bit embarrassed; if she seems to be shy it is because she is afraid that this will not be good enough for you, that you may scorn to lie with her and feel contemptuous of the artless offer. Probably she is a lovely wild creature of sixteen or seventeen, with purple-black hair she can sit on, and eyes like black diamonds. Apologetically the mother or father explains that this, alas, is all they can offer – but if you stammer any absurdity about the proprieties they will not understand you. You will perplex and grieve their simple hearts to no purpose. And they are proud as Lucifer too in their way.

'The ideas such a suggestion would raise would be – "Is he really too superior by his way of it to care to sleep with Mairi?" And "Does he think we are such fools or that Mairi is so worthless a maiden that he would get the chance if there were the slightest danger?" Of a verity, no. Do not distress yourself, my dear sir, with your evil mind. Nothing is further from their thoughts. It is easily arranged. What happens is just this – Mairi goes off to bed, and her mother goes into the little bedroom with her, and puts both Mairi's feet into a stocking and draws it right up – tight as can be – to Mairi's pretty supple little waist. And there you are. Everything is perfectly all right. You can go to bed beside Mairi with a clear conscience. Mairi has been made inviolable. In the morning it will be seen that everything is as it should be, that the mouth of the stocking still safely encircles that pretty waist.

'A splendid idea, isn't it? So simple and so effective. Occasionally, of course, a man who does not deserve these privileges as we do, happens to come along. But marvellously fresh and innocent as these little Island girls are, they can look after themselves all right. They know their way about though the man who shares their bed overnight may be the first human being they have ever seen outside their own family. I remember just one such case. The good mother had had her suspicions, I think – she had not liked the look of the fellow. But her doubts and fears were set to rest in the morning when she asked Mairi in a whisper first thing if the stranger had tried to interfere with her through the night. He had. The villain! But everything was perfectly all right, for Mairi replied in her simple way: "Oh yes, Mother. He tried hard to get my legs out of the stocking. But I wouldn't let him. He couldn't manage. He only got one of them out."'

The Darkie Baby

'Have you seen the Darkie Baby anywhere about?' asked my wife.

'No,' I said very carefully, 'I have not seen it today at all.'

She gave me a curious look. I wonder if she doubted me. As a matter of fact I had taken it upstairs the night before and locked it in a drawer in my study.

Despite my careful utterance she was probably made curious by my seeming indifference. A week earlier – and before that for a year, two years – I would certainly have dealt very differently with any suggestion that the

Darkie Baby might be lost. And I would not have been careful in my utterance. The Darkie Baby meant far more to me than to anyone else; that was why I had taken it upstairs and put it away in a drawer – not exactly for safety; at any rate, not for its safety, but for mine. The matter had just gone too far. And no sooner had I removed it out of the way than my little daughter, Midge, who hadn't looked at it for months, except perhaps now and then when it was in my hands, and then not desiring it but amused at 'Daddy playing with it,' wanted it.

Let me explain. It was nearly three years ago that my wife made the Darkie Baby out of four bits of firewood and a black woollen stocking. She darned eyes and mouth on to it with light-coloured yarn. It was, I thought, an unattractive object. But, with the perversity of her kind, Midge thought otherwise. Dolls that had cost far more – flaxen-haired dolls with dainty dress and eyes that opened and shut – were no more regarded. The Darkie Baby was her sole concern. She nursed it and played with it and pretended to feed it and to bath it with great fidelity for several months.

And then I began to see that the Darkie Baby was far more alive in a way than either Midge or her mother. They were normal specimens of their kind with the normal limitations. But the Darkie Baby was constantly to be found in the most unexpectable places and postures. No boneless wonder at a fair ever twisted itself into more remarkable shapes. Midge was a little double-jointed and very active; but she could not assume the endless range of unnatural shapes the Darkie Baby took up – shapes with just a crude enough indication of the human and all the rest inhuman and seemingly unlimited in variety.

I think too the colour had a great deal to do with it. If it had been pink or white I would probably never have noticed it. The fact that it was black seemed somehow related to my real but unexpressed ideas on the Colour problem; a problem that had cropped up a good deal in my student days in Edinburgh, where so many of the black students married or associated with white – or Scottish – girls and some of the city restaurants refused black patronage. Negro Art, too, was interesting me a good deal at that time. In one way or another at all events the Darkie Baby began to take up more and more of my attention. It was considerably battered about by this time and that had – not humanised it, but somehow made it more sympathetic, more provocative of a sense of fellow-feeling. The harsh outlines of the eyes and mouth had been softened as the light yarn got dirty. At first I only accidentally came across it. Midge left it lying in my armchair perhaps or I found it cradled in one of my slippers. But soon I – no; did not instantly look for it when I came into the house; not yet – discovered in myself a faculty for immediately knowing where it was; and it got into all kinds of places, I assure you. My eyes turned automatically in that direction. I never managed to carry this a stage further however and foresee where it would be next.

My work was beginning to benefit as a result of having the Darkie Baby about the house. A glance at it seemed to help me to put myself at several removes from merely human feeling. The frisson of the very definitely, yet indefinably abnormal in much of my writing – the attractive awkwardness of many of my rhythms – owed a great deal to the Darkie Baby. And I am afraid this influence extended to my relations with my wife and child. They became too ordinary, too destitute of any element of surprise, and especially of the sort of ugliness of which I was more and more enamoured. The more life I saw in it, the less I saw in them. Now they have been [Four words are illegible here. – Eds.] Darkie Baby was when I saw it first; the Darkie Baby has become all and more than all I could ever have hoped they might be to me as spiritual and intellectual companions.

And now whenever I came into the house about the first thing I did was to get hold of the Darkie Baby and twist it into some new angularity – or sit looking at it until its battered expression took on tragic new significances. I seemed as I held it and gazed at it and played with it to be switched into a different plane of consciousness. Wooden if you like, but so flexible, capable of such incredible attitudes, and of a knack of turning up in such unexpected places that it seemed by far the liveliest thing in the house. You can imagine how this kind of thing grew on a man who lives as I do – on his nerve ends. Finally as I sat writing at nights I would find myself unable to concentrate for thinking on the surprising shapes the Darkie Baby could assume (be given, of course, but assume it seemed, for it had more than its full share of the wilfulness, a malignity of all material things). I would begin trying the effect of new shapes on it – seeing how it looked standing on one leg, or with one leg and the other doubled back to seem amputated at the knee, or with one eye covered up, and so on and on and on. And while I was doing it with one hand I found myself planning out still further shapes and jotting down on paper the linear essences of them – like a lot of Pitman's Shorthand outlines.

No! You are wrong. It was not because I felt this was interfering with my writing – that I was going mad, a little mad, perhaps – that I took it upstairs. On the contrary! I was afraid it got lost. Midge might take it out and fail to bring it back one day. Or it might even get lost somewhere in the house – or I mightn't be able to find it as quickly as I wanted to. I might come in lusting with some notion of a new shape for it, and not be able to lay my hands on it. You see I wanted to get equivalents in rhythm for all the shapes it could possibly take – I wanted to work these out systematically, without anybody else butting in on my experiments – and as long as it was not in my own study Midge or even her mother might take it up and do things to it. I did not want other people to do things to it that might possibly conflict with mine – especially now that I was exhausting the possibilities in definite sequences, and getting notations for all kinds of primitive and marionette and toy and wooden Pegasus and like effects.

The wool? No. That's curious. The black woollen stocking that covers the bits of firewood has never seemed to matter in itself, for the quality of its material, that is to say. I will certainly think about it. Many thanks for the idea.

Anyway the Darkie Baby is in the drawer in my study, in the position in which I left it last night and so far as shapes are concerned – texture will be another matter – I can rely on being able to start right away at the point I left off at last in the particular series I am now writing out and go right ahead.

Enemy's Daughter

I was, of course, infinitely cleverer than Sally, though I was only idling about at home, not earning a penny, dreaming of writing poetry and of the stupendous literary fame I would have one day, while she was the typist in one of the local tweed mills, very exact and efficient and proud of her work, and earning an excellent salary.

She was an exceedingly pretty girl but made no friends in the town. She kept herself to herself, extraordinarily self-contained, but never in the least bit morbid, and though proud, not conceited. She had indeed a certain blitheness, a bright bird-like quality, but as difficult to get on terms with as an old boot. She was far too fine for the vulgar mill-workers to get near at all. She made them, not intentionally, feel far more clumsy and inferior than they really were, which was bad enough, but yet they were just, they knew she was not unfriendly or stuck up or giving herself airs or siding with the bosses against the workers or anything like that. She wasn't one of themselves, could not possibly join in their coarse fun, but she was among them like sunlight all the time. She was so pretty and her eyes were so bright and her ways so delicate and dainty.

She lodged with my mother, and the Devil still finds plenty to do for idle hands. We were thrown closely together. I appreciated her beauty to the full and her perfect integrity and gallant way with the rough and largely incomprehensible world about her. I was sufficiently sensitive and well-educated to handle the matter, I did not frighten her off or repel her with any vulgarities. I was something new in her experience, the witty intellectual; and I could talk so interestingly about all sorts of things. I led her on ever so gently, the thing elaborated itself into a play. It was understood that it was only an elaborate comedy, not to be taken seriously. We had our respective roles, just vaguely adumbrated and apprehended at first but soon splendidly developed. We became letter-perfect and exceedingly dexterous, introducing subtle new [words missing. – Eds.] and gay gags. It was a private world the two of us built up, just for ourselves. My mother and others of course could see, and to some extent share, the merry teasing that was going on, but they were external to it all – they missed all the finer points.

Sally and I pretended to be in love, not in any silly obvious way, of course, but in a highly polished fashion, a matter of elaborate jokes which nobody could possibly see but ourselves, inflections, moues, lifts-up of the eyebrows, wrinklings of the nose which conveyed their meaning to ourselves alone. We became more and more expert and daring. It was so perfectly understood that it was just a game, the point being to make it seem, to treat it ourselves, as if it was a very real affair while never forgetting that it was only make-belief. I would kiss her so passionately, and so cynically. The note was: 'Heavens, what perfect lovers we would have been, if I had not so completely and irrevocably outgrown women.' I trusted I was treating her fairly. I pretended to hesitate at times, to feel a real compunction for the poor little thing. No doubt she was trying to play the game and would hide her real feelings as cleverly as one could possibly expect, but what if, under it all, her feelings were really engaged! It was a case of a bird and the serpent. She had acquired the patter wonderfully, I would concede, and often gave the illusion that our wits were equally matched, but that was merely superficial; she lacked my complicated intellectuality, my powers of word-play.

Now and again, just for a flash, I was not so sure of myself. Might she not outwit me in the long run, succeed by imperceptible degrees in turning the makebelief into reality? Was she not, in fact, playing with this very possibility, invisibly intriguing to that end?

I insinuated as much, making it clear that she needn't trouble, I was up to all the conceivable tricks. You are really very naïve, Sally; you needn't imagine for a moment that you can ever deceive me. What I am not sure about is that you are not deceiving yourself? I gave her my condolences in advance on such a terrible *faux pas*; I showed her how anxious I was that she should not humiliate herself; I infuriated her by my assumption that, after all, she could not be blamed, it was inevitable that she should fall in love with me. And so on and on and on, all in a spirit of banter, never degenerating into more than mock seriousness, mock sentiment.

Time passed lightly, gaily, in such an atmosphere. There were substantial gains on both sides as a matter of fact. We gave each other a great deal, of fun, of companionship, of practical help in little things. She had been very lonely inside herself; I gave her the illusion of finding an ideal companion, of being something she could play up to and almost become in order to fit herself for such a connection. As for myself, well, I was doing nothing else. My capacity for genial persiflage, glittering many-edged utterance, and the lightest and most intricate of equivocal relationships would have been hard put to it to find anything like so good an outlet. I could have amused myself as elaborately as I liked at the expense of the other inhabitants, but they could not have taken part in the comedy, save on a far lower plane. This was better than playing solo. And I genuinely delighted in her beauty which all this by-play brought out and permitted me to enjoy to the full.

She was really by far the loveliest girl in the district and I had her all to myself. I loved to take down her splendid chestnut hair, rippling five feet down her back to below her hips. I amusingly exaggerated the way in which, unavoidably, we were thrown together in my mother's little house. I embarrassed her by pretending that we were far more intimate than we really were. I scandalised her by giving that impression to one or two of my mother's friends who came about the place. My mother did not know how to handle the situation. She knew, of course, though even she may have had an occasional doubt, that Sally and I were not really misbehaving ourselves. She may have thought – I think, finally, she hoped, for she had got very fond of Sally – that 'things would turn out all right'. She tried to speak to me once or twice, but I made fun of her fears, her hopes. Why did Sally permit me these liberties, sit on my knee, let me take down her tresses, let me kiss her? I went as far as I could, of course, but I thought as time went on that she was disappointed, hoping against hope, unable to understand how I could go so far and no further. She was careful never to give me the impression that she would have let me; careful, too, never to give me the impression that she wouldn't, that she had a sticking-point. She cunningly left the matter in doubt. While inside me a small still voice [word missing. – Eds.] 'No quarter! No quarter!' but I paid no attention to it.

She would have made an excellent wife. There is no question about that. But I had other fish to fry. I decided to end the game. She happened to develop a couple of small warts just under the tip of her nose; the first physical blemish I had ever seen on her. I plagued her cruelly about them. I exaggerated the extent to which they got in my way when I wanted to kiss her. I made far-reaching and disquieting remarks on what warts were really a sign of, what they betrayed of the inner secrets of one's constitution. I was ruthless, macabre about them. She was frequently on the verge of tears. Something was happening to me, too; my usual mercurial disposition was often queerly and heavily overclouded. I had spasms of sheer black temper, brutal and ugly moods, unlike my customary debonair bearing altogether. I was showing her the worst in myself; she thought I was doing so deliberately, as a new development of the game. But the warts did not grow and become more disfiguring; they disappeared almost as suddenly as they had come. I had made up my mind now to end the little farce once and for all. I changed the tone of my banter.

I now made it appear that she had been too clever for me after all, that I had succumbed, yet that it was impossible. I cursed my luck. I made what I said about her endearing qualities sound genuine enough, as it was. I left her in doubt as to whether I had only got hold of some mad, unshakeable conviction, or whether the very depth of my being, the essence of the phylogenetic instinct in me, was not really, and legitimately, involved. Or had I really just been playing with her all the time? – in that [words missing. – Eds.] to care at all.

In any case I made it clear to her that all would have been well – but for one insuperable barrier. I could never marry an English girl. All my desperate frontier blood surged up against such a monstrous betrayal of my race, of the great function of my ancestors, there were oceans of spilt blood between us. The countless dead would cry out against such an anomaly; I would never know a moment's peace. True, she only belonged to just over the Border, only a matter of ten miles from my own birthplace, but the little it was, and yet how much. If our birthplaces had only been an inch apart and yet that fatal imaginary line – the division between England and Scotland – had run between them it would have been all the same. I ought to have realised it sooner. But I did not think I had done her any irreparable injury, no more than she had done me by letting me go so far before she was sure of me. And so on and on and on. She thought I was only joking cruelly again, more cruelly than ever.

But an unmistakeable note crept into my voice. I said more and more caddish and wounding things, things that would have been instantly intolerable but for the peculiar relationship that had subsisted so long between us. She tried hard, desperately hard, to persuade herself that this was just a fresh variation, a more intense and difficult stage, of the old game, that that terrible note was not really in my voice but only in her apprehensive imagination. She felt like a good player who is inexplicably off form, not up to my moves today, but without a doubt that they were all in the game, if she could only see it. I was simply playing better than ever, but her mind wouldn't work. But I knew that some of the caddish and wounding things I had just said, which had not been instantly intolerable for the reason stated, would only take a certain time to act – once she was by herself, and could think out the matter properly.

I was right. I went away on my cycle very early the following morning and did not come back till late. Sally had gone to bed; but my mother was sitting up for me.

'What have you done to Sally?' were her first words.

'Sally,' I said, feeling sure that Sally would not be sleeping and knowing that in that case she could hear, 'Oh, that little English lodger of yours, you mean?'

Mother and I had a terrible row. Sally, it seemed, had told her that she must change her lodgings and had, in fact, at once gone and secured new ones. And she went the following day. I saw her very seldom after that, and never to speak to. I have not been back in the old town for quarter of a century now. Sally is still the chief typist in the mill. No, she never married. She never took up with any other man. And yet I hesitate to say: 'Poor Sally!'

Of course I was young then; my blood had not really begun to assert itself; I did not hate the English as I do now – or it might have been 'Poor Sally' all right.

The best joke would have been to have heard Mother 'explaining' the rupture to some of her cronies.

She missed Sally greatly.

'You'll be sorry for this,' she said. 'You'll go a long way before you find another as good.'

She was right there – as to the second [words missing. – Eds.] – but this is another story.

The Jackknife

Dick had asked Santa Claus for an air-gun, and Tommy had asked for a jackknife with all sorts of fitments, but when morning came, and the wild rush was made to the fireplace, what was the surprise to find that Dick had got both the airgun and the jackknife. They had both all sorts of other things, of course – packed pillowcases, in fact – but Tommy was inconsolable.

'I expect the old man is getting a bit dottled and mixed up his orders,' said Dick, laughing. 'Of course,' he added, 'I would give you the jackknife, only that might spoil my luck. It doesn't do to give away things that Santa Claus gives one.'

Now what was puzzling the boy's mother and father, of course, was how the jackknife came to be in Dick's pillowcase – or, at least, how both the airgun and the jackknife came to be in the same pillowcase, for they were certain that they had put the airgun in one and the jackknife in the other. They might have made a mistake and put the wrong one in Dick's, and consequently the wrong one in Tommy's too – but assuredly they had not been so careless as to put both these presents in the one pillowcase. But of course they could not say anything about that to the boys, without giving away the whole Santa Claus illusion.

The father, indeed, was tempted to do that – for, if the mother did not, he at least suspected that Dick had already seen through the illusion, and was only now pretending to be still believing in it for reasons of his own.

Dick was so plausible in all the discussion that went on. He was not to be caught out in any way, and it was also evident that he meant to keep the jackknife. He was maddeningly confident that he could not be found out – so confident that the father could not be sure whether this was because he really still believed in the Santa Claus fiction after all, or because he knew his parents well enough to be sure that they would not make any suggestion which would tend to reveal that they, and not Santa Claus, filled the pillowcases, or just because he felt sufficiently ingenious to get out of the matter in any event.

He must certainly have had it all very carefully planned, and been ready with explanations in case he was caught. If he wasn't caught in the very act of transferring the jackknife to his own pillowcase but only in going to or back from the fireplace, it would of course suffice to say that he had wanted to see Santa Claus actually coming down the chimney, whereas, if he were caught in the very act, he would pretend to be walking in his sleep and not responsible for his actions. But he had not been caught, so his parents could not prove that he had been near the fireplace at all. They might think what they liked, but they could not prove it. And what the father hated most was this sense of Dick mocking at them in the fix in which they were caught between the kindly old fiction and the actual facts; that, and his absolute callous unconcern for his brother's grief and disappointment.

The father could, of course, have ordered Dick to give Tommy the jackknife, though there would not only have been at once a scene which would have spoiled this Christmas morning far more than it had already been spoiled, but the matter would have kept cropping up for long enough afterwards – he could hear how Dick would jeer at Tommy, assert that the jackknife was really his, tell the other boys they played with all about it, and generally give Tommy a very miserable time. So he simply said: 'Well, I do not understand it – we must just make the best of a bad job.' After breakfast he went to the shop, taking Tommy with him, and bought him a jackknife – but a far better one, costing twice as much in fact. Tommy was pleased as Punch.

The father did not know what to do really. The headmaster of the school had said to him one day not long before when discussing the two boys: 'Tommy is a fine little fellow, but he's the plodding type, steady but sure. Dick is no problem. He's much the cleverer – in fact, probably the cleverest boy that has ever been through my hands, but, as these very clever ones so often are, sadly lacking in moral ballast. I'm not suggesting that he has criminal tendencies. The way it works out just now is, taking his lessons for example, instead of careful preparation and proper attention and application in class, he just trusts his own wits to solve any difficulties on the spur of the moment as they arise. That's what accounts for his surprising ups and downs in class. When he really works he can be top every time, but when he trusts himself to improvise a solution to a mathematical problem at a moment's notice, or invent out of his own head the right answer to some quirk in French or Latin, well – he naturally comes a cropper.'

Dick knew after that fateful Christmas, of course, that he was being carefully watched at home, and his parents knew that he knew. They also knew that he did not care a bit about that; his sole concern was just not to be caught – exposed. And he never was. I have heard him attribute a good deal of his subsequent success to this early training in following a crooked course without ever putting himself in such a position that it could be brought home to him effectively.

That early training has certainly stood him in good stead. No wonder that from such a beginning he has become a Cabinet Minister of Great

Britain. His success, of course, delighted his father, and his brother, too, who if he ever suspected the truth had long ago forgiven and forgotten all about what happened that Christmas morning; but, though the old man was very proud, too, of his elder boy's career, he was cast in a different mould. Success did not make up for everything to him, and you may remember that there was a good deal of newspaper comment and speculation on the fact that when he died he left everything to his son Tommy (who had got on in the world too and was by then Provost of his native town) and nothing to Dick, except the receipt, which he had made the shopkeeper give him that Christmas morning, for the more expensive jackknife he had had to buy for the disappointed Tommy.

A curious legacy for a Cabinet Minister to get! Doubtless the old man in his simplicity had never reckoned on the fact that his son's eminence would ensure that such a bequest would be given world-wide publicity, and raise all sorts of questions. Or he may have muttered to himself: 'Let them say what they like – Dick will be able to explain the matter satisfactorily enough and in a way that redounds to his own credit.'

But all that Dick said when he was pressed by the journalists was: 'Oh! My father knew I needed nothing else.'

Nor did the worthy Provost, on being approached, throw any further light on the matter.

A Land of Fruits

Just use the phrase, 'a land of fruits', and you all think of Spain or the South of France or Italy or the Orient or the South Sea Islands. Bah! What do you know of Scotland? Let me tell you I am thinking of no tropical country and I deliberately use the phrase, 'land of fruits'. That is what sticks out above all – I might have said flowers or fish or birds; it would be equally true; but it is fruits I think of first and foremost when I think of the place where I was born, and bred, in Scotland here, just like the Riviera or in Samaria. Imagine to yourselves just over a great field full of meadowsweet and marsh marigolds and wild orchids a little wood on the side of a hill and the sunshine playing through it – or is it the golden hair of a certain girl I am chasing in and out between the boughs – and then a light wind springs up and sets all the branches of the copse swaying. And what do you hear? Everywhere the soft wooden knocking of nuts – bunches of them like the knuckles of a man's closed fist hanging on every twig – and tapping gently in the wind on the sunny air, or, if the breeze becomes just a little stronger, clicking like castanets. Greeny-brown scrog nuts with splendid white kernels. That is one of the things I am thinking of, and there they are – free to all – a great harvest of them every year to the end of time. Does that sound like Scotland to you?

And crab apples. There are various places in the neighbourhood of my birthplace I used to go for them. But I preferred a place away out lonely, hilly Wauchope Road, five or six miles out. I used to cycle there, taking a pillowcase with me. It was fine to come coasting back in the evening – free-wheeling most of the way especially down the very steep hill that falls so abruptly, with a dangerous corner at the bottom, into the town, with the packed pillowcase (do you know the word) 'dunting' on my carrier. Plenty of crab apples for whoever cares to go for them – and knows where to go. But what does anybody know about Scotland? People have such stupid ideas about it – cold, gray, wet, miserable. A land of fruits, I tell you.

If you have plenty of patience and love a long day on the tops of the hills, the things to go after are the blae berries. There are any amount of them on each of the three hills that overhang my native town and on all the hills that rank, top after top, behind each of these. You must not be afraid of getting your knees wet as you kneel to pick them. It takes a long time to get a decent basketful – a making of jam – but it is worth it. You get to know where the big beauties are to be found too – fine fat fellows, purple under their light coating of grey bloom. Blaeberry jam is one of the things I always think about when I think about Scotland – as characteristic delicacies of the country, blaeberry jam and heather-honey. And no doubt near you wherever you are picking the blaeberries there will be a row of bee-hives. You will come upon other berries too – the speckled crane-berries, which make delightful jelly; and the tiny hard black cranberries which, unlike the others, you can pick a dozen at a time by letting the wiry stems run between two of your fingers, thus stripping them and making the little jet balls drop off into your cupped palm.

Most important of all in the life of the community I am thinking of were the great stretches of wild raspberries to be found in the woods on all sides of the town. It is vast fun picking the rasps on a fine summer's day. I remember as if they were related to each other – part and parcel of one lovely phenomenon – the bright eyes of the girls, the glitter of dewdrops on the little jagged leaves, and the deep cordial sparkle at spirtling raspberry juice. Dewdrops, I said; for the wise gatherers get to the best places first thing in the morning – carrying all kinds of cans and baskets as receptacles for the fruit; but most of them, the older ones at any rate, used to carry what we called store-baskets, brown woven baskets with a handle across the middle of the top and lids, flaps, opening at both sides of it, though the baskets were not compartmented inside, but roomy – they held a lot of rasps. Yet, in a good year – and if you knew where to go, and got there early – you were not long in filling them. Occasionally too you came across a cane or two bearing white raspberries instead of the usual red ones. All these rasps were for anyone to go and pick who cared to. In one or two of the great woods – though the public were never debarred – there were little rules and regulations that had to be observed, however, but that was because some of the more thoughtless had incidentally done some little damage to young trees or by frightening the game.

There were of course brambles, (what the English call blackberries) and – though they were far less important – wild strawberries (and here too one occasionally came upon white berries instead of the usual red ones). But have I not said enough, to show that here indeed is a land of fruits, when you have nuts and apples and blaeberries and raspberries in plenty and free to all for the picking?

But where is this particular district of which I am speaking?

It is down in the Borders, in Dumfriesshire to be exact.

How long is it since I was there? Let me think – it must be – yes, it is over a quarter of a century ago now.

But I must have been young at the time of which I am speaking. Yes, I was just entering my teens. I have never been back there since then. But I think of it now and then, and, above all, when I do, as a land of fruits. They say that stolen fruit is sweetest, but I am not at all sure that that is true; in any case I see that I have omitted to say anything about the apples, and pears and plums we boys were in the habit of stealing from the orchards of the Duke, the mill owners, and other wealthy people of the town. I had my fair share of these, too, I can assure you, but though there was a spice of danger in these raids it is not stolen fruits, but the abundance of wild fruit, free to all, that leaps first to my memory.

Here's How: A Glasgow Story

The man in the pub said: 'A joke's a joke, but… '

He spat with disgust, and took another swallow of beer. Then he went on:

'Well, you may say we did a certain amount of work and got the agreed payment, and that's that. What have we to complain about? And besides we ought to count ourselves jolly lucky to have had it at all. As long as we get the work what need we care what the job is and who it's for? Most of us had a long spell of unemployment before that – and most of us were certain to have it again. It was a Godsend, and it doesn't do to look a gift-horse in the mouth, eh? Well, that's one way of looking at it, but it doesn't take us very far – though it all comes to the same thing in the long run, perhaps. The Royal Family must have the wind up pretty badly these days. Anyway, they're trying to bolster up their position by all the publicity possible – and that's plenty in all conscience. Biographies serialised in the papers and magazines, not only of the grown-up members, but of the very youngest. The life-story of a five-year-old Princess has to be all set out in print nowadays. With photographs galore. Talk about making bricks without straw. They'll be telling their pre-natal histories next. They miss no chance. You can't pick up a paper but there's a splash of some kind about them. They stick at nothing in the self-advertisement business. There's bound to be a reaction. People aren't going to fall for that sort of ballyhoo indefinitely. But I think this Cunarder business was the bloody limit. I'm only a rivetter, and I was desperately needing the work – but I am black ashamed to have had anything to do with it. It wasn't so bad while the work was going on (though calling it by a number gave a sort of convict or Army effect to the whole thing) – but once the job was nearly through and the Royalty boosters got busy… My God! all the infernal fuss about naming it. Columns and columns of twaddling speculation and suggestion in all the papers. Then the announcement that the Queen was to name it in person, and that what it was to be called was to be the Queen's own secret till she pronounced the sacred word. What do you call that classical woman who had a face to launch a thousand ships? Well, the Queen's face isn't like that – unless by frightening them into the water! My own dutch would be no great shakes in a beauty competition, but I'd back her against the Queen any day of the week. It isn't the face to launch ships the Queen has – it's only the neck. And then all the snobs collected – all the hangers-on who never did a hand's turn in their lives and didn't know one end of a ship from the other. And the Queen got up on the platform – the whole world hanging on her lips, breathlessly waiting for the momentous declaration. And it came! You bet your life. The biggest anti-climax in history. Mary, says she, as bold as brass and as proud as Punch. People don't seem to react in a decent human way at all nowadays. I can't understand why the whole crowd didn't burst out laughing. Talk about a sell! But no, they all took it seriously and the whole world swallowed it like a butter-ball and said how splendid it was – what a divine inspiration! the perfect name! trust the Queen's taste, her inimitable tact. Mary!'

He spat again.

'People who'll stand for that sort of guff'll stand anything. You just can't insult them. You can do anything you like with them – and they'll lick your... boots. Yet we pride ourselves on our commonsense – hard-headed intelligent people! Oh yeah! Sez you! A hell of a lot of expert knowledge and skill goes into a job of that kind and we Clyde workers are the finest craftsmen the world has ever seen, or probably ever will. We had all been unemployed for ages – starved and insulted in every possible way. Demoralised by hanging about the street-corners, they told us. But we hadn't lost our skill. We made a masterpiece of it. It was a great sight as it took to the water – a miracle – a floating Cathedral! It doesn't matter a damn about us, of course. We can be out of work, hopeless, demoralised, starving – as long as we like – though they'll expect us to toe the line like nine-year-olds and have all the skill in the world if and when the time comes to build another. But with the launched ship we have nothing to do. It doesn't give much of a thrill to us who've been working in it to see the finished article – just like getting the last word to complete a crossword puzzle there's no prize for. Nay; those who get it right are penalised instead. A mug's game. The finished article is us finished too and we might as well take to the water too in a different way. We have nothing to do with the launched ship. Its splendid appointments are not for us; it may win the blue riband of the Atlantic – we'll read about it in the newspapers or hear it over the radio, we won't be there to see, we won't be on board. It is not for us – luxury cruises to foreign countries we'll never see. These are only for the toffs – *we* can rot in the slums... I tell you I wouldn't have had a second's hesitation when I saw all that mob becking and bowing, and thinking what a stroke of genius it was to christen the contraption Mary, in turning a battery of machine guns on them and blowing them to hell out of the way. I don't grudge the old ship the bottle of champagne smashed over her snout; what I do grudge are the bottles of champagne or anything else but vitriol smashed over theirs. If I'd my way of it there'd be no sham pain about the smashing I'd give them – and nine-tenths of the men on the Clyde felt the same way. I'd give them a souvenir of the launch all right, and launch them into hell with it.'

I had had his glass replenished.

'Well,' said he, lifting it, 'Here's *how!*'

It was a toast I had no difficulty in accepting. I know *how* all right: I only wish I also knew *when*. But it can't be long now. There's a limit to all things. 'Mary! By jees... !'

The Man with the Hole in His Sock

Then there was this man, and he had a hole, and it was in his sock. That is, in his left sock. It was a very small but very open hole, showing white like a bright white eye looking out over the heel of his shoe, wherever he went. And this man, he hated it.

Until it had been pointed out to him – until some fool, some idiot, had made the extreme blunder of drawing his attention to it – the hole had lain quite still, bothering no-one. Quietly, with no complaint, it had rested there, coming out to wink at the world through which he walked. Now it cried out loud to all who passed by, made itself bold, called loud and clearly: 'Look at me. I'm a hole in a left sock. Down here, down near the pavement.'

Until that moment when some imbecile had made him aware of it, the man had spent an easy, calm, unhurried, unflurried sort of day, bright with the odd joke, the restrained laugh, the raised eyebrow, the courteous smile. Lunch had gone by easily, conversation flowing from him, around him. The warmth of a graceful manner had surrounded him; people had shown their amusement at his wit, his pleasant and unaffected style. He had crossed his legs, nonchalantly.

Supposing someone had noticed it then, when he had so nonchalantly, so elegantly crossed one leg over the other? Supposing Forster had noticed it – Forster of the prim and proper, over-dressed mind? Or Wallace, with all his talk of the wife and her tidiness, her neatness, her never a hair out of place? No doubt, as he had stood up to move easily, smoothly (even triumphantly) away, Forster had leaned over the table to Wallace with a whispered 'I say, old man... but did you see... the hole... in his left sock?'

The man tried, bravely, to screw his left foot down into his shoe, to order it to stay there and not come rising out as he put his weight on the left toe. He felt the hole staring out again and screaming 'Look at me. I'm a hole. I'm growing *bigger.*'

If he put his left hand into his trouser pocket, then perhaps he could force the left leg of the trousers to hang lower, and he would not then need to limp in this extravagant manner, for the hole would come up to look at nothing but a stretch of dark cloth.

To put his hand into his pocket meant unbuttoning his overcoat. He transferred the two books and the newspaper from under his right arm to under the other, and with his right hand unbuttoned the overcoat. He transferred books and newspaper back again and then plunged his left hand under his jacket, into his trouser pocket and down, down, dragging the left leg down. Ha! that had it fooled! That stifled its crying! Still with a slight limp, trying to keep the pressure on the left heel rather than the toe, one hand in his trouser pocket, one trouser leg hanging lower than the other, his coat open, he stood at the bus stop and waited.

He would have to go downstairs on the bus. To go upstairs – even though he longed for a cigarette – meant taking the hand out of the pocket, allowing the trouser leg to ride up. People behind him would see it and think – *well!*

It had been – until that fatal moment when some absolute moron opened his big mouth – a perfect day, quite one of his best, with everything going perfectly.

It was one of those days which felt as if they had been planned in advance, and was going off smoothly, entrances and exits coming up bang on time, all your little remarks going home exactly as you placed them. Even the sun had made an early appearance. Now it was cloudy. There was a slight chill in the air. He could feel it on his heel.

His shoes were not old, nor new, but perfect, showing just the right degree of care. His suit was obviously not his best but was far removed from being anyone's worst, and the crease in his trousers, though not sharpened, was very definitely there, and led like a signwriter's arrow down, down to the well-brushed heel of his shoe and the hole behind it. He was quite formally informal, as one should be when going to a small party to meet with a few friends.

Except, of course, for the one huge mistake, he was just right.

It could not have been there that morning: of this he was certain. With such a perfect day almost planned from the start, one just did not make mistakes like that; besides, he was never the one to make *any* mistake. One was extra-careful for one never knew whom one might meet. One made a special effort to ensure that things went right, that one was quite charmingly proper, that one was quite obviously effortlessly correct.

It could not possibly have been there that morning. When had he put the sock on? First – or almost last? He had put it on carefully, of that he was sure. Even a hint of a hole, a mere suggestion that the material was wearing thin, and he would have discarded this pair and taken the blue ones. It was not as if he was down and out, not as if he had no others.

He climbed on to the bus platform, pulling his shoe up into his trouser leg as he did so. He chose the first vacant seat from the entrance.

The conductress asked for his fare. She smiled at him as he fumbled.

He had to take his hand out of his pocket, transfer the books and the newspaper, dive into his back pocket for change: no change. He had to transfer the books and the newspaper back again, and reach with the other hand into his wallet pocket. He had only a note.

The conductress smiled at him again, almost as if she KNEW.

He mumbled his apologies and thanks as he took the change, and dropped a sixpence onto the floor. He reached down to look for it. The hole was staring at him, and he jerked his foot back, deep into his shoe, and let the sixpence lie wherever it had fallen. Now he was hot, even though it had become remarkably cool for August.

The real problem, of course, would not arise until he got to Miriam's. There he would have to be careful. He must keep up the right appearance. His manner had to be fairly suave, to be neat and easy; the conversation had to flow, the wit to be ready. The hole had to be dismissed. He could feel the possible awkwardness, everyone standing there with a glass and looking at him and being carefully polite to him, and all of them KNOWING.

Of course, he might stand with his back to, say, the sideboard – but not all the evening; he could not move crabwise round the room, sliding from one piece of furniture to a wall, to another piece of furniture, to another wall. Nor could he stand all evening with his legs crossed, one foot delicately poised behind the other, hiding the naked heel. Perhaps if he could keep his hand in his pocket… but that would look odd.

He had learned something, though. Wherever he might be in the future, whatever the room, whatever the occasion, as soon as he SAW a man standing for any length of time with his back to the sideboard, or with one hand plunged down deep in a trouser pocket, or balanced precariously, one toe behind one heel, he would KNOW the man had a hole in his sock, and he would go up to him, and laugh, and make a joke about it, and put the fellow at his ease.

For after all, what is a hole in a man's sock? Even in a man's left sock? Such a small and insignificant thing, it was all part of the untidy business of living, and no matter how careful you were, it had to happen to you some time.

But supposing, just supposing, his feet were dirty!

The horror in this thought made him hotter still. He began to sweat, small, fresh spots appearing on his brow. As a small boy his mother had made him change his underwear every two or three days in case he had an accident and was taken to hospital and there they found he was wearing a dirty vest. He suddenly knew just how horrible a thing this might be; the same sort of horror was on him now.

It was not a thing one could laugh off nonchalantly, dirty feet. Or foot. A hole in one's sock – well, what was that? He might even have shrugged it off, carried it away by a brilliant remark; might, even, have used it, for a slight unconformity is invaluable in the right place. It could have made him a character among the others, all so stereotyped.

His charm could surely overcome his awkwardness? But not if his feet were dirty! Fancy making some bright remark, some jest about making a hole in one, or about having to get someone to darn his socks, and exhibiting the hole – and then finding his feet were dirty and the dirt showed! He shuddered.

All the way from the bus stop to the door he walked with a slight limp, one hand firmly in his pocket, his coat open, books and newspaper under his right arm. The conductress had smiled at him as he left the bus, and he was sure that she knew, which did not help him at all.

He had bathed his feet only two days ago, but the city was full of dirt and dust, and he had big feet which were bound to have collected some of it, and if it showed – well!

He stood at the foot of the steps leading up to the front door of the house, and looked at the curtained front-room window, from behind which came warm laughter and the ring of glasses. He could just see them laughing as he made the joke about finding someone to darn his socks, or as he asked Miriam for a needle and thread and told her why. Then he felt the warm air freezing, the laughter ceasing, turning to awkwardness as he bared his grinning heel...

Suddenly determined, he turned away from the door and walked two streets to the nearest public telephone. He rang Miriam and told her how sorry he was but he had a cold and could she ever forgive him? She could, and would, and did, but she was terribly disappointed, for they had all looked forward so much. And it was quite obvious that she did not believe a word, and that was the last he would be hearing from her for some time.

Still limping, he made his slow way back to the bus route, and went home. There he had a bath – which was quite unnecessary, for the skin on his heel was a milky white. He laid his clothes out for the following day, folding his blue socks on top, and went to bed.

Nothing Like Flannel

I had the mumps. It was before they were notifiable or there was any question of the schools being closed or even the affected children being allowed to stay away. My glands were swollen up to a great size right up to my ears which felt as if they were going to crack any moment under the strain.

Now my mother was the best mother in the world but there was never any question of my playing truant with her winking at it or staying at home any day on some trumped up excuse of my mother needing me, as so many of the children did. Wet or shine I went to school as regular as the clock and never missed a single attendance if it could possibly be helped. Nor did I ever want to play truant or to stay away on some pretext. Going like this with my face all blown out with the mumps was a different matter, however.

My brother whose face was as badly swollen as mine had gone off all right with his face in a framework of red flannel, but then he was so utterly insensitive, not like me at all. And it was no use my mother saying that half the children in my class would be in the same predicament. I was determined not to go. There were special reasons. I was very fond of my teacher that year – Miss Graham; but what mattered most, of course, was that I was madly in love with one of the girls in the class, a lovely golden-haired little creature called Nelly Brodie.

So I wouldn't go. I would not go. My mother swathed my face in a red flannel bandage and fastened it on the crown of my head with a safety-pin. Even if I was going at all – which I wasn't – I couldn't possibly go in a red flannel bandage of all things. So she got out a big white flowered silk handkerchief of my father's and put that on me instead.

But I can't go now. It wouldn't have been so bad if I'd gone off along with my brother at the usual hour, but now I was late and I would be the target of all eyes. Besides the register would be marked, so I'd lose an attendance anyhow. I simply could not bear it. My mother knew how terribly sensitive I was, but, late though I was, she was determined that I should go. So she put on her coat and hat and went with me – right to the school gate, and saw me safely inside it.

I crept up the stairs and along the corridor, suffering agonies of shame, and half-minded – since there was no sign of the janitor – even yet to run downstairs again and go away up the hillside till dinner time.

I had got to the door of my class by this time and I suppose Miss Graham had heard someone moving about there, for she suddenly opened the door. 'Oh, it's you, is it? You're very late. I thought you weren't coming. So you've got the mumps too, like the rest of us. Are they very painful?'

I looked up and – would you believe it? – Miss Graham's own face was swathed in a roll of red flannel.

I felt better when I saw that; and better still when I allowed myself to be drawn into the room and found not only that half the class simply could not laugh at me if they wanted to for the same reason, but that my darling Nelly had her pretty face all rolled up in red flannel too.

I did not feel the least bit self-conscious or ashamed of myself as I went and sat at my place, which was next to hers, in the back row of desks. But I am afraid we made a very poor attempt to smile at each other; I knew my own ears went crack-crack-crack, just like a zig-zag firework.

Wells

My mother was one of the most profoundly Scottish women I have known. You still meet them occasionally – I myself know several others hardly a whit behind her who are still living – but she was even forty years ago a 'quaint survival', born at the very tail-end of her true period and living most of her life through an era of increasingly rapid change in which she was more and more out of place.

People who are used to having their emotions about nature dragged up and inflated instead of preferring to have them left quiet and even cryptic could have made nothing of her or would have completely misunderstood and undervalued her. Her sort – their quiet selves need to be known as fully as people know each other who listen to music together. One heartening fact is true of them all; their lives suffice them. These lives are spent most fully in that human relationship in which pretence and pose are alike impossible, in which each person, stripped by familiarity to single-heartedness, is known wholly and accepted and still loved. They pass their days in ordinariness without personal ambition or worse emotion, and know contentment.

People like myself cannot avail ourselves of their qualities – their endless services – without a feeling of shame, since we know only too well what inhibition and atrophy of their potentialities, and what secret suppressions and frustrations underlie that glow of patient and acceptant serenity which characterises them, very like the effect of castration on tom-cats. Yet it should be impossible not to recognise the rare quality of a mind like hers both instantaneously responsive and stable; of a spirit which, without losing lived or lighter elements, is acquainted with the deepest sources of happiness and grief, and in one respect at least – its humility – is among the greatest of the great. Just as there are thousands of women teachers only a tiny percentage of whom really love their work and have a true vocation for it, so there are tens and hundreds and thousands of women who are wives and mothers but only a tiny (and dwindling) percentage who have a true vocation for wifehood and motherhood. My mother had both, and the latter most abundantly.

Her everlasting theology was, of course, a bore to me, and though I know now that though perhaps it was just that enabled her to go to one's heart. Thinking of all the church activities in which my parents were always involved – and the incessant theological argumentation in our home, however, even yet I cannot for the life of me understand how my mother living so marvellously all the time at the level of mere life (an occasional enforced descent to which is well-nigh insupportable to most men) could tolerate all those ministers (odd how many square heads, Byzantine noses, and circumflex eyebrows I remember among them), among most of them the parsonic voice and style distressingly conspicuous, and almost all of them leaving an impression of vague substance, professional repetition, and remoteness from the life of the time. All that seemed out of keeping with mother altogether; on the contrary, it was – whatever the solution of the riddle may be – very much part of her, and in fact the guise in which her personality appreciated in stillness, generally, most disconcertingly, revealed itself in public (for churchgoing was about the only form of public life in which she ever participated).

In the Middle of the Field

It's a queer business, she said, mortal queer. There's naething the maitter wi' him to look at (except a lost look in his een whiles – as if he was puzzlin' aboot it himsel') – a muckle upstan'in' man in the prime o' life. I canna understand it ava'. There's been naething o' the kind in the faimly afore as faur back as we can trace its ins and oots – which is no yesterday; and I've never heard o' anither case o' the kind or come across onybody else that has. He never kens when ane o' the turns is comin' owre him. He hasna as muckle as a meenut's notice – no eneuch time to sit doon in even. He'll gang oot as fit as a fiddle, whether in the mornin' or in the efternune, and it's no' till he doesna come in till it's lang efter his usual time that we jalouse what's happened and gang oot to look for him. We never ken the meenut or the day. Sometimes months gang by withoot a break; sometimes he'll ha'e as mony as half-a-dozen fits o't in a single week, and when that happens he'll no' ca' off work and bide in the hoose till the bad spell passes. No' him! He's as thrawn as they mak' them – a gey handfu' to deal wi', I'm tellin' you. But whether they come close thegither or faur apairt, yin's aye on the tenterhooks, kennin' that suner or later it's bound to happen again. It's that – and the infernal mystery o' the haill thing, and no' kennin' what the end o'ts to be – that's the constant plague. It's no as if there was ocht to gang by – disna gang off his meat nor his sleep when ane o' the attacks is due. There's nae warnin' ava'. He'll gang oot just as he does at ony ither time – fu' o' energy and lookin' the very picter o' health – and syne be fund like Nebuchadnezzar in the middle o' a field. And whiles the field tak's some findin'. He has a big swatch o' grund to cover and we never ken what airt he's in at ony particular time. We're on the hop whenever he's mair than an 'oor late in comin' in for a diet – but whiles it tak's us 'oors to find him, and him in that fearfu' plight a' the time. It's queer hoo often, workin' roond the haill countryside, it's in the vera last field we reach that we find him. It's a God's blessin' it only comes owre him in fields. We'd hae the deil's ain job if he was liable to't in the wuds as weel. But it maun aye be in an open space. Of coorse a'body else in the district kens a' aboot it – that's to say as muckle as we dae oorsel's, which is hanged little when a's dune – and keep an eye on him whenever they can, withoot lettin' him ken't, of course, for he's mortal touchy. It's that that keeps him frae tellin' us whenever he gangs oot exactly what pairt o' the estate he's ga'en to. That 'ud save time and trouble, but he'll no' dae't. It's nae use speakin' to him. He'll aye hae his ain way whatever happens. But he s'ud think o' ither folk. He'll scarcely discuss the maitter at a'. Efter ane o' his bouts there's nae gettin' a word oot o'm on ony subject, let alane that, for days on end. A' that I ken aboot it is juist odds and ends I've pieced thegither owre the years since it first sterted and the little I've seen mysel' or heard tell o' frae ithers that ha'e. It's no' muckle to gang on. He never had them, as faur as onybody kens, afore he was thirty. It's only in the past hauf-dizzen years that he's been liable to them – and a queer thing is that they never seem to get ony waur or ony mair or less frequent. I ha'ena worked oot the year's average, of coorse. What I mean is that for the six years they've whiles come close thegither and whiles he's only had an odd bout for months at a time, but there's nae sign o' ony real development o' the trouble. What happens as faur as I can mak' oot is juist that a' at aince as he's crossin' a field he has to get down on his haun's and knees, and he can try to rise again or claw at the grass and try to crawl or dae onything else he likes, but he canna win oot o' the bit. It's a pitifu' sicht. The yett may be starin' him in the face but he canna get an inch nearer't. He has an idea that if by hook or crook he could get oot o' the field he'd be perfectly a' richt again. Mebbe aye and mebbe no'. The fact remains that get oot o' the field to pit the maitter to the test is the vera thing he canna dae. I've asked him why, since he kens he canna win off the bit, he disna juist sit 'quiet till the fit gangs off, instead o' tearin' at the grund and workin' himsel' into sic a terrible state. But it seems he canna help it. The need to struggle for a' he's worth is pairt o' the trouble. No' that he gangs gyte or bites his tongue or onything like that – he tak's it canny eneuch in a way. What happens is juist that he needs to pit oot a' his strength – and a' his cunning tae. He disna lose his heid. Fegs no! I've seen him whiles lookin' roond and roond for ony possible way oot in as sensible a way as ony man could – weighin' up the chances, as it were – lookin' at this break in the hedge or that. But no' gi'en owre tearin' at the grund or movin' his body roond and roond like a teetotum, though his knees never move a hairsbreadth off the a'e spot. It's queer to compare that wi' the deliberate look in his een – as if he was tryin' to get oot o' his predicament in twa different ways at aince. The look in his een seems a different method a' thegither frae the clawin' and whirlin' o' his body. Yet when we find him and get him oot o' the field where the thing seized him, he's back to normal again in twa or three meenuts. Thank Guidness it's never happened through the nicht. We micht never find him. Imagine it on a wild winter's nicht o' rain or snaw. He'd dee o' exposure. His ain idea and oor fear tae is that whether by nicht or day a time'll come when we'll no' find him sune eneuch. He's never been exhausted to oor knowledge – there seems to be nae end to his energy – but if 'oor efter 'oor ga'ed by and nae help cam' he couldna keep up that desperate fecht and there's nae sayin' what 'ud happen then. He micht only wear himsel' oot and fa' asleep withoot ony mair harm till we fund him, or if we didna find him and he woke up syne I whiles wonder if the fit 'ud ha'e passed and he could rise and walk oot o' the field withoot ony mair adae, or whether the fecht 'ud ha'e to stert a' owre again. But I dinna think he'd wear himsel' oot and fa' asleep nae maitter hoo lang we were. As time passed I think he'd get mair and mair desperate and burst the muscles o' his hert or gang mad a'thegither. It's impossible to tell. We'll juist ha'e to wait and see. But it's a terrible anxiety; and it's nae use sayin' he s'ud bide mair in and aboot. He's a gamekeeper born and bred, like his faither afore him, and fit for nocht else; and even if he could get a job where he'd be mair under ither folks' een he'd hate it like hell and that micht pit him in a waur state still. It's no easy to ken what to suggest for the best; to me and ither folk his trouble is juist like what the middle o' a field is to himsel'. The haill thing… *Wheesht! There's his fit. No' a word!'*

It was twenty past nine. My uncle walked in, gave me a smile, made a few remarks about the weather, and putting away his gun and game-bag, sat down in his armchair and began undoing his boots. I thought I saw or heard him wince... or was it just my imagination? I couldn't see his hands which in his bending posture were drowned in his shadow.

The Affair at Hawick

My dear Jim, I was sorry to hear of your death the other day and ever since I have found myself thinking, scarcely at all of any of the other elements of our friendship, but almost entirely of your line of argument with regard to the Blackburn case five years ago. It is strange it is only now, on hearing casually of your death, after being completely out of touch with you since a few months after Blackburn's trial, that I should realise how profound an influence your conversations then have had upon me.

We were in the Buck bar together the night of Blackburn's arrest. It was the sole topic of conversation. Young as I was, I was a little disgusted at the general excitement, the fatuous comments, the lack of sympathy with those concerned. I did not know Blackburn or any of his family except by sight nor had I been long enough in the town to know many of the men who were discussing the matter in the bar. Besides, Scottish border psychology was largely antipathetic to me. I did not understand it and up to then had not wanted to. Suddenly its most intimate aspects were thrown open to me – flaunted before my eyes, as it were – and the more I understood (or thought I understood) it the more I hated it (or thought I did). You were in very different case. You were a native of Hawick. You knew it inside out. Besides you had been away from it and had returned to it after a much higher education and far wider travel and more diverse contact with men and women of different races and stations in life than any other of its fourteen thousand people or, indeed, all of them put together. For the most part you met your fellow-citizens on their own level, and kept your real self to yourself. Despite a difference in your speech – which was one of the things, together with the fact that you were a doctor and a relatively rich man, that gave you the standing you had, the general respect in the community – you were regarded as essentially 'one of themselves', whereas an incomer like me is kept in his place and woe betide him in all sorts of matters if he fails to know what is permissible nay, proper to a native but forbidden to him. I was handicapped by not quite knowing some of these niceties, and, of course, in the excitements of the argument, when you were allowed to say things no one else could have got a moment's hearing for, my silence, my occasional obvious acquiescence perhaps, and still more my occasional failure to agree' with or even to understand you, while not, of course, agreeing with any of the others, made me disproportionately unpopular and enabled them to transfer to me the resentment and intolerance with which they would fain have treated you. I did not know you well enough either to understand why you felt moved in this particular connection to take the strong line you did. You could quite well, I thought, have met them on their own level in this respect as in all others, and kept your real opinions to yourself. What did it matter? It was so obvious that you could not convert any of them to your view, no matter how clearly and incontrovertibly you stated it. I wondered if it was something you had come up against in your profession that accounted for the urgency of your interest and the energy with which you expressed it. I wondered if it was some abnormality in your own sexual life, or if you had had some closer connection that I knew of with one or more of the Blackburn girls yourself. It was so unlike you to make 'much ado about nothing' – for the essence of your position was simply that the whole case was about nothing; that there should never have been a case. I rule out now of course all three of the possible explanations I thought of – indeed, they were each dismissed almost as soon as I entertained them. The third would inevitably have been verified at once in that town where everybody knew everybody else and all about them and a great deal more. In the heat of the debate somebody would quickly have let that cat out of the bag. Nor do I think you could long have concealed the second; in fact, at the crest of the discussion, you would have been quick to admit it yourself – and I have sometimes wondered that you did not put more fat in the fire by making a bogus confession. As to the first, it ran counter to the course your arguments developed. So I am still puzzled as to why you threw yourself so ardently into the unprofitable fray.

I remember perfectly how it began. You and I were talking of something else – some new books, for that was our principal point of contact; everybody else in the bar was avidly canvassing the pros-and-cons of the Blackburn sensation and advancing the most ribald fatuous or mean-spirited speculations. In the course of our own conversation we could not help overhearing all the rest of the talk. All at once you intervened. Someone – I think it was little Phillips, the tailor – had said that Blackburn should be lynched, and somebody else thought that Blackburn would get his deserts all right but that Mrs Blackburn should be lynched and that if there was any proper public spirit in Hawick the thing to do was 'to burn out the whole bloody nest of them.'

'Look here,' you said quietly but in a way that silenced everybody else, 'Tom Blackburn has been a thoroughly well-known citizen of Hawick for forty years – and, though he wasn't born in the burgh himself, came of an old Hawick family, and married a Hawick woman. And all his children were born here and most of them are married here to Hawick men and have Hawick children of their own, and the unmarried ones have all Hawick sweethearts.'

'Except Jean,' said a little dark-faced man whose name I didn't know, in a very significant way, though the significance of it completely eluded me at the time – naturally, as no details of the affair were available yet.

'Except Jean,' you agreed, 'Jean has never had a sweetheart so far as I know. But what I was going to say was simply this – that there isn't a responsible person in the town who would have believed a word to the discredit of any of the Blackburns yesterday, let alone what you (and almost everybody else) regards as the perfectly monstrous situation that has now been disclosed. That throws a curious light on what we know of each other. If a man like Tom Blackburn can go in and out amongst us all these years unsuspected of such atrocious practices, repeated and repeated over a long period, how can we know that there aren't lots of others of us in like case – and if Tom Blackburn could get off with it so long, why can't others get off with it altogether? Not one of us would have suspected Blackburn – any more than we would suspect ourselves.'

'I notice,' said the little dark-faced man, 'that you do not question Blackburn's guilt. You might have pointed out that the charge has not been proven yet – that none of us know for certain what it is. But you have not done so and it seems therefore that you take for granted something that puts him in a very different category compared with all those who may be guilty of similar practices, but against whom, so far, there is certainly no breath of suspicion.'

'I am not concerned to argue that just at the moment,' you continued, 'My next point is that all that earned for Blackburn the general esteem of the community cannot have been changed by this discovery. Either that esteem over all these years was well-founded or not. For our own credit let us assume it was. If it wasn't, it shows we can so misplace our confidence and friendship over the best part of a lifetime that we ought to be very chary now of trusting our powers of censure and repudiation. The sudden swing-over so many of you have executed shows the hollowness of your pretensions. If your likes are so fickle and shallow your dislikes are probably just as worthless.'

'You are not trying to defend the crime of which we understand Blackburn is accused, are you?' asked the little dark-faced man.

'Not at the moment,' you replied, 'I am charging most of you with a different offence. But there is this to be said, following immediately on what I have already said – Blackburn was not the less useful and intelligent a citizen, none the less diligent and capable a business man, and – one of the things that concerns me more as a doctor – none the less admirable a physical type, as the consequence of his practices. In the last-named respect he could give points, as you know, to most of the men in the town and certainly to almost all the men of his own age. So far as I know he never had a day's illness in his life. Not one of you can deny that he was a first-class mill manager – or that he was a thoroughly intelligent man – or that he was a responsible citizen and took an active and useful part in the affairs of the burgh. But there is much more to it than that. Most of us know Mrs Blackburn by sight. She is a personable woman and does not show any signs of having been ill done by. Nor do any of the nine daughters. They all look physically fit and temperamentally happy enough. They all got a decent education and were brought up in a comfortable home, and the six married ones all seem perfectly normal efficient wives. Neither they nor their husbands have given any signs of having a grisly skeleton in the cupboard; those of them who have families have healthy children – and the grandchildren and their mothers and fathers have always seemed to be on happy family terms with the old folks. None of you can deny any of these things.'

'But where is the argument leading?' inquired the dark-faced man.

'I will tell you in a minute,' you said, calling for drinks for me and you and having thrown yours back, went on: 'I am not discussing the alleged crime at the moment. What I am discussing is the advantage or disadvantage of its having been discovered. Most of you have the good name of Hawick at heart, haven't you? Is the stink that will be in all the papers tomorrow going to redound to the Glory of Hawick? A horde of sensational journalists are rushing into the town. Where the carrion is there will the vultures gather. Hawick is going to be written up as a modern Sodom or Gomorrah. Do you relish that? If not, why set the ball rolling? You are only forestalling the yellow press – and, some of you, being a little yellower. Then most of you have wives and children of your own. Do you want them to be discussing this sort of thing? Do you – all radgie enough at any time – relish seeing it act as a sort of aphrodisiac on your wives or sweethearts, and yourselves? Oughtn't some of you to be thankful that such things happen occasionally to give you an excuse for talking about the things you think about so much but can so seldom and only surreptitiously talk about, and give you a much needed stimulus in other ways, no doubt. I bet a lot of Hawick children will be getting their bottoms well warmed the next few days – and not knowing what for. Convention doesn't allow us to talk about such things except in a hole-and-corner way – except when an occasional Tom Blackburn becomes a public benefactor. Hypocrites! And then there is the glorious indifference to other people's feelings – the revel in their humiliation and shame. Take the six married ones. Leaving them and their unfortunate husbands out of account, isn't it nice for all their in-laws (most of whom are friends of ours and constitute no inconsiderable part of this community which is revelling in the fouling of its nest) – and won't it be a pleasant thing for their bairns to have thrown at them in the years to come? No, no, don't let us think of any of them; let us enjoy our virtuous indignation. Above all do not let any of us inquire whether his own sexual practices have not had far less defensible results – no matter how 'normal' these practices may have been – than Blackburn's malpractices. It is no concern of ours if this damnable disclosure breaks up the hitherto happy homes of some of the daughters – it is difficult (if our general belief that this sort of thing is monstrous and intolerable is justified) to see how it can do otherwise. For the husbands to remain with these daughters now would be a kind of condonation of the father's offence – besides, the new knowledge (if it is new – and if it isn't that, of course, makes the matter infinitely worse) would import into their subsequent relations infernal shades of sensuality surely! The onus is on the husbands to show that they were not deceived when they married. That involves delicate considerations. There is no end to the enticing ramifications spreading out for our delectation in all directions. We are in for a thoroughly enjoyable time. God grant that we have sufficient malice and conscious carnality to take full advantage of it. My mind plays with the picture of Mrs Robson discussing with Dick his first relations with Jessie Blackburn – poor Dick casting his mind back to the marriage night, or earlier. And then there is the holy horror of the Reverend Mr Smith and his changed attitude to his daughter-in-law, the whilom Katie Blackburn. Such spectacles multiply in my imagination. There are such excruciating embarrassments to conjure up – such subtle difficulties, and lovely tit-bits. I know the people of Hawick so well that I can picture perfectly the receptions that Dick Robson and Tom Smith and Harry Melville and Fred Gray and Kenneth Thompson and Willie Fergus will have at their respective places of business tomorrow, and how they will feel themselves when they venture forth as usual (if they do) and encounter the changed reactions of all sorts of people I can visualise to a nicety, and how their wives will feel in the shops. I wonder if Nelly Blackburn will be at the cash-box in the co-op as usual; it will take some nerve, won't it? Nice girl, Nelly. Probably Bob Anderson has thrown her over already – or has suspended his love for her until she is certified still virgo intacta. And all these are only the frills, the trimmings, of the case. The real core of the matter hasn't been touched yet.'

'You're right,' said the little dark-faced man, 'I was wondering when you were coming to it.'

'Oh, were you?' you retorted pleasantly, 'What is it, then?'

'Surely that is obvious – the charge itself.'

'No,' you replied, 'I don't think so. What intrigues me far more is how the charge became public and, above all, how it arose. I know it is practically impossible to keep a secret in Hawick, but after all Blackburn did it for umpteen years (and so apparently, did most, if not all, of his family, and the authorities ought not to have been less reticent at this juncture. Besides, they are supposed to be public servants, and it is not public service to have the reputation of Hawick – not to mention Scotland, and mankind at large – besmirched in this way, and all the tongues in the place canvassing lewd speculations, when the case could properly have been heard *in camera*, and any wrong this sensational disclosure may do to innocent parties restricted to an irreducible minimum. But that is assuming an official leakage? Surely the premature blazoning-forth of the business could not have been done by any of the Blackburn family or their in-laws. I shall be very interested to know exactly how it got out and about and how the final shape of the business corresponds if at all, to the ideas concerning its nature current among us now. But I shall be infinitely more interested to know how the charge came to be brought at all. I don't suppose any of you wiseacres can throw a light on that.'

'Lots of people saw Tom Blackburn being taken to the gaol,' said Phillips.

'But he might have been guilty of any of a thousand and one other offences far less juicy than this – or it might just have been a mistake. Nobody but some of his own people, and the officials concerned, can have known the charge against him. Even the evening papers simply phrase it "unnatural crimes". Whence comes all the information that purports to define the precise nature of these? In any case that wasn't what I was asking about. I was asking how the charge came to be made against him. Very deep problems are presented here, assuming the idea of the nature and extent of the charge that is going the rounds is substantially true. (Turning to the little dark-faced man) You think Jean has been the nigger in the woodpile?'

'Probably' said the little dark-faced man, 'She is the oldest of the family, and has never married.'

'You mean that she was the first to fall a victim to her father, but if so why – assuming her hatred of him – has she been so long in divulging the secret? Why should she let all her sisters share her fate in turn? And why should each of them – not to speak of the mother, if she was in their confidence – have kept the secret?'

'She probably hated all her sisters as well as her father and did not see why they should not suffer the same fate as herself.'

'If you have not some definite reason to know that that is so you are making a very large assumption there. I think it is much more probable that they all loved the father. That would account better for the keeping of the secret, wouldn't it – besides fitting in better with the air of well-being and family happiness they have all shown. On the data in our possession (which may or may not be correct) all eight fell to the father, only the youngest escaping. That's what we're told. Presumably the trouble arose through Nelly's refusal to comply, or through her sweetheart, Bob Anderson, if he had any inkling of her difficulties, or through one of the other husbands if, belatedly, he learned what was what, or through Jean if, having most to do with the father, she was jealous of Nelly, or through the mother if she suddenly learned what she's been in ignorance of all these years or if she suddenly developed a determination to save Nelly – or through any of a hundred and one other causes. The whole thing is extremely puzzling – and unfortunate. None of the family will be a whit better off with the possible exception of Nelly, so far as I can see, and nobody else was a whit the worse of Blackburn's malpractices, except perhaps the daughters' men, and they seem to have disguised any loss of which they were aware remarkably well. I shouldn't be surprised if Blackburn hasn't some sort of feeling that he has done well by them all and that each and all of them might have come by sexual experience less desirably than through his agency. After all he was responsible for their very lives. He was, I imagine, not the man to be deluded by the usual bunk about love, which is the disguise under which lust gives the world so many mental defectives and inferior physical types. And I imagine most of the girls, if not all of them, would agree with him. There can be no question that if he and they do think so he and they are right on almost every conceivable ground. They have come to no harm – certainly no harm comparable for a moment to that which society will now inflict upon him and upon them, for his refusal to respect the prejudices of this particular country, prejudices which have not been universally shared, have not demonstrably led to better results than obtained under other conditions, and the sanctions of which have not been at all adequately considered – least of all by those who are most vocal now in their abhorrence of Blackburn's alleged crime. They have had little or no previous experience of this sort of thing; they are not in a position to present any facts or figures showing its evil effects. So far as I know no authoritative treatise on the matter is available anywhere; it is simply taken for granted, and in my experience things which are taken for granted in this way by most people generally

[Here the typescript ends. – Eds.]

A Friend of the Family

It isn't any use trying to make honest, old-fashioned love to any of these cuties nowadays, complained Abe Jack. I know, because I've tried it. It's my nature to be sentimental. I'm old enough to belong to a time when that was regarded as the only right and natural disposition of any fellow worth the name of being a man. But look at young Bella Laird. Going on nineteen. I'll hit any man on the point of the chin who denies that she's the bonniest lass of her age hereabouts that isn't yet married and settled down. So one day I walked up to the cottage and found her in alone as I knew she would be. I took the arm-chair by the fireside – but could I get her to come within arm's reach? Devil a bit of it. And her standing just beyond it just as bonny and as damned irritating as anything I ever saw in my born days. So at last, fair worn out, I says to her: 'Bella, my dear, you're not just a lassie now, so let us talk plump and plain as a man to a woman. As you are well aware I am no stranger to this cottage. I've slept here both with your mother and your mother's mother. God rest them both. But you and I are left, and what I'm wondering is whether you're a true daughter or granddaughter of either of them. You know what I mean?' Surely that was fair enough and I spoke just as nicely as I possibly could to make it easy for the creature – just as, in days gone by, with good results, I had spoken first to her grandmother and then to her mother. But times are sorely changed. What do you think she did? She threw back her head and laughed a good one, and then she said, 'Aye, Abe, you're an auld freend o' the faimly sure

eneuch, and I'll no' let you doon. I've a present for you.' She went out of
the room and I thought that she was mebbe a bit shy and had gone to
undress in one of the bedrooms, but again I wondered, for she seemed to
be taking a longish time and I began to doubt that she was making a fool
o' me and had cleared oot o' the cottage a'thegither and thought I'd ha'e
to go and see, when in she came, carrying the faimly cat in her airms, and
threw it on to my lap, crying 'There you are Abe – just as I promised you
– a present for an auld freend o' the faimly.'

And she threw back her head and laughed again till you might have
heard her in the next village or the next again and was out of the door and
up the stairs and locked her bedroom door against me before I had time
to utter a single word. Now what do you think of that?

Poor Pussy

I get on well enough with most people. On the surface, that is. So long as
I don't get to know them too well. But I don't like to see deeply into them.
I avoid that instinctively. Now and again, however, I can't help somebody
saying something that opens things up. I hate it like Hell. But there you
are. And just the other day a woman said something that has haunted me
ever since. It wasn't the sort of thing one could possibly see coming at all.
Otherwise I'd have dodged it.

It was in a little job-printer's place in Glasgow. A cat had come in off
the street a week or two ago. It was the most miserable scraggy terrified
little specimen I ever saw. It had an extraordinarily thin neck and looked,
though much thinner, very like a hen does when most of its feathers have
been pulled off, though in this cat's case there was no raw flesh showing.
Only it looked as if there should be. – It was no thicker than a pipe-stem,
and its head waggled on it as if it would fall off any minute.

The printer said it looked a hundred per cent better than it had when
it first came in. It was cleaner for one thing; for another it was getting
something to eat fairly often. And there was nothing chasing it now. But
he agreed it must have had a terribly bad time before that, and it would
still take a long time before it got back anywhere near to normal. While he
was saying this, the cat sat looking at me out of eyes that were the very
essence of misery.

It was then the woman spoke.

'I've seen that kind of look often enough before', she said, 'You sometimes see it in a restaurant for example. A girl at a table near you will look just like that. Apart from her eyes the girl looks quite all right – pretty even, and well enough dressed. The sort of girl I'm thinking of is nearly always very pretty. And you wonder what on earth makes her eyes look like Hell, and you can't solve the problem until she rises to go out – and then you notice that she has a club foot. There's something radically wrong with that cat. It may fatten up and get to look all right – except for its eyes. But they'll never lose that look. It isn't just a Hunger-Gesicht but far worse, though just what I don't know. The trouble is we don't know enough about cats to have any real idea what's wrong. It's nothing on the surface. Being starving and dirty and ill-used before has nothing to do with it at all, I *know*.'

That was all she said, but the clumping of a club-foot has gone through my mind every since. And probably always will. I know I couldn't help looking down at her feet before she finished speaking. They seemed all right.

Putting the Lid On It

By this time I had got up into the far corner by the bar, beside the little middle-aged man whom nobody knew, who had not spoken all the evening and had not even seemed to be conscious of what was going on at all. I had had my eye on him quite a lot, a little curious about his power of isolating himself, holding himself quite intact and unaffected in such a Babel. But I had seen no interest, amusement, or indignation in his eyes at all; his face had never broken into a laugh or coloured up, nor had he scowled or manifested any impatience or disgust. It was good to get out on to the edge of the Niagara of dirty cracks and cachinnation and horse play again; the beer tasted better here, much cooler and more exhilarating.

After a little he began talking to me. He had a very still small voice. I don't think anyone else in the bar could have heard a word he said to me, or, looking in our direction, even known he was talking to me. 'I don't believe in this brave new world,' he said, 'Malthusian belts and all the rest of it. It's mostly just talk. Too many people know about all these things and are constantly talking about them, but, under all the talk, the amount of ignorance is really incredible. They know the names of all these things, just as children at school can reel off the names of all the rivers in India and the principal towns of China and all the rest of it. But that's all! The extraordinary thing about modern life is that the more superficially

informed most people are the more essentially ignorant they are –
especially about the very things that come closest to them and which they
think – and everybody else takes for granted – they know best. The fact is
they know nothing at all – nothing at all; I never hear anyone speaking who
seems to know a tremendous lot without suspecting that he, or she, really
knows far less (especially about the things they talk most about – and above
all about sex) than those who talk least. It's all a sort of epinasty... you
know, curvature of an organ, caused by a more active growth on its upper
side. That's it, funny like hell on the surface, but all hollow below, just
empty, not a thing in it. Reminds me of a doctor friend of mine who said
to me once: "Educated! Good Lord! Do you realise that in Great Britain
ninety-nine per cent of the married women, mothers of families, go
through life without ever once experiencing an orgasm." In other words,
most people don't know how to copulate even. That's what the general
ignorance amounts to, the utter ineducability... The art of copulation is
still in its very infancy.'

I nodded, but what I was really thinking about was another fellow who
had recently said to me on the same subject at the same zinc counter: 'Let
her experience an orgasm? No bloody fear! What do you take me for?'

'This general ignorance,' he went on, 'is *literally* incredible, you know.
So nobody can believe it. Everyone takes it for granted that they – that
most people – know a hell of a lot. The gentle art of seeming to know it
when you don't is far and away the most flourishing of the arts today – in
fact, the only art that *is* flourishing at all and drawing everything else into
itself. The same doctor once said to me: "Physicians learned in the action
of remedies have never studied the effects of a dose of castor oil on a
constipated girl. It is the pitiful truth that such a study of constipation has
never been made, though whole libraries of books on the subject have been
published. No one has gone out in search of a guiding principal, and
therefore the 'essential symptoms' which might lead to a recognition of the
true cause of the trouble have never been identified. Thus, the victims of
this common affliction try hundreds of remedies and visit as a rule, large
numbers of doctors. Sometimes they obtain benefit, sometimes not.
Elaborate examinations are carried out by the latest methods of 'science',
elaborate and irksome diets are imposed; operations are performed. But
nobody knows the answer for the simple question, 'Why is it that, of two
persons who live much the same lives and eat much the same foods, one
is always constipated and the other never suffers from the trouble?' Until
that question has been answered the treatment of the affliction will remain
in its present unsatisfactory state." And that's only one example of the

monumental ignorance which prevails about the action of most drugs and remedies.'

'"I resolved to test the action of heart drugs," my doctor friend told me on another occasion. "Strychnine had a great vogue, its effects being insisted on by physicians and surgeons – the latter, indeed, often refusing to operate on a patient under an anaesthetic unless the patient had a preliminary dose of strychnine, while anaesthetists had often beside them a hypodermic syringe ready charged, lest the heart should fail. To my surprise, I could get no result with strychnine whatever. In medical doses, by the mouth or hypodermic injection, no effect could be traced on the healthy heart, nor on people in a state of collapse. I read up the literature, and, beyond assertions as to its value, there was not on record a single instance where there was proven any evidence to justify the belief in its properties!" So there you are!' said the little man, 'Such examples of abysmal ignorance in regard to the things that come closest to us, and are really vital to our very existence, could be multiplied indefinitely. So you see why I take all these bright young people with a dose of salt! They've got a lot of patter off. But that's all. They know nothing really. They can jabber through the whole Marie Stopes, Aldous Huxley litany – natter away, as they've been nattering here all evening, about lesbianism and homosexuality and contraceptives and all the rest of it – yet they don't *know* any more than dolls about anything.'

I just nodded again and called for more beer, and then the little man went on: 'But I'll tell you a story – a case in point. You'd think the shop assistants in some of these big Oxford Street stores couldn't afford to not know a lot, couldn't avoid learning all that there is to know, wouldn't you? They think so themselves – think they know the whole business from A to Z. A girl has got to be careful, you know! So there are no flies on them. What? But especially in one of these big hostels – like that one in the next street, where there are between seven hundred and eight hundred girls in residence. How the blazes can any girl stay in a place like that without learning the whole bag of tricks? They're all high steppers too. The firm insists on good lookers and good dressers, pays them well, dredges the whole country for well-educated girls from good families and do they have a time? You bet! Just go along that street any evening and watch the procession of cars to the door of that hostel. And all the bright young things coming out and going off with their beaux! Dressed up to the nines, and carrying a wonderful soignée – every mother's daughter of them. It's like a Mohammedan's dream of paradise. Well, think of the inside of that hostel, all the bedrooms, and the baths and the gymnasium and the lounges and all the rest of it, and all these hundreds of young women up to the eyes in their love affairs, and how the Hell can any girl go there – and not just have everything taped off to the last degree in a few days? What else *can* they think about, talk about, and do? It stands to reason. – And yet I don't believe a word of it. I believe ninety per cent of the girls are, and will always be, as green as cabbages – invincibly innocent, ignorant, and pathetically anxious to do their best. They haven't the least idea of the how and why of things at all – don't know how babies are born, whether they come out of their ears or mouths or navels or where. It beggars belief. It's hopelessly fantastic. And here's the story which illustrates that. And mind you I don't think it's exceptional. I think the approach of ninety-nine girls out of every hundred to the so-called "facts of life" is just like this at best! People like you and I thinking about a whale of a great harem like that, and all the talk, the hectic confidences, that must keep such a beehive buzzing, naturally get hot under the collar – but don't you believe it! You might as well be at a village Sewing Bee, a damned Dorcas Society! Here! I have a letter about it – from one of the girls in that very hostel. That proves it's genuine – that I'm not making it up.'

He took a long pull of beer, wiped his mustache, and plunged his hand into his inside pocket and pulled out a batch of papers, from which he selected one and, putting the rest back, opened it out, and held it in front of me, so that I could follow the words on the actual paper as he read: –

'You remember my telling you Elsa's getting married next month. She has been slogging at the "bottom drawer" all the winter; sitting in the lounge night after night, embroidering this and gathering that. (I ask you is it worth it? Men don't notice things like that, do they? You should know.) But she has made six really beautiful nighties, exquisitely embroidered – just like those you see in Madame Anne's for five guineas. On Thursday night about a dozen of us were sitting round the fire in the lounge, smoking, talking, and what not, when Elsa looked up and asked if someone would lend her a half-crown. She wanted to cut a circle. Madge handed her one, and naturally we gave her our attention and watched with admiration the deft way she manipulated the half-crown and the scissors. The whole six exquisite nighties were treated in the same way. I vaguely thought something was wrong, but I was too lazy to comment and none of the others seemed to notice anything amiss. She then sat down and started to embroider the circles she had cut out, turning one into a rose, another into a shamrock, and so on, and sewed the pieces on again. At last she finished and heaved a sigh of contentment and started folding them up. She must have forgotten herself – forgotten she wasn't in her own bedroom but in the lounge and had an audience. She held one of the nighties up over herself – admiring it – when suddenly Rena (she's the one I told you about, Polish, supposed to be a Countess or something blobby like that) startled us all: with "Oh!" and a swift indrawing of the breath. "Elsa", she said, "Why have you made a hole in the middle of your nighties and put a lid on it? It looks so funny somehow".

'By this time we were all gaping at the nightie, which Elsa still had held up in front of herself, and slowly the truth was dawning on us, the little grey cells were beginning to throb.

'Elsa looked wildly around, recovered, started to fold up the garment somewhat perkily, turned to Rena and said, quite seriously, "Well my dear, I rather loathe the idea of – of turning it up! This will simplify matters, don't you think?

'Don't ask what happened then. We just sat like graven images, eyes goggling, lips compressed. One by one we left the lounge, how I don't know. I do remember falling over Madge just outside the door. She'd collapsed – convulsions or something. Then something snapped in me too. God blast the girl!'

At Sixes and Sevens

'Oh! – It's a new one,' she cried.

Just like that – right off the reel.

Well, there *was* a new one, but how did she know which?

It was, of course, obvious that by new she meant new to us as compared with the others; newly arrived, so far as we were concerned, not newly made. For the matter of that, it might have been the oldest of the lot. There was no knowing. They were practically of a size. There was no visible indication of relative age whatever, but, in any case, new would have been a most inaccurate adjective. Her loose use of the word jarred upon me. Thinking back, I realise that I profoundly mistrusted her from that moment. Not that I let the effects upon me get out of proportion to the cause, however!

How did she distinguish the new-comer? There was absolutely nothing to go by. They were as like each other as split peas – a phrase frequently used to express absolute identity in appearance, though I must admit I have never actually studied two such peas, or parts of peas, to see if I could not differentiate between them. So like each other in fact that we had never been able to give the others names – to tell one from another. Yet here she was, christening this one with complete confidence at the very outset as 'The New One'. How did she know? I confess my first impulse was to deny that it was the new one – to declare that one of the others, it did not matter which, was responsible for the obvious increase from six to seven. But somehow I couldn't. Her eyes shone far too certainly upon me. They can be enchantingly candid at times. It would have been obvious that I was lying, and it would have been singularly mean and futile to lie obviously and in a manner that gave her no compensatory pleasure in the face of that radiant certitude – like pretending to a rose that it was a weed, like trying to see it as such.

She knew I was debating with myself along these lines. Her eyes narrowed a little, half-challengingly, half-apprehensible. Easy to pick upon one, any one, it doesn't matter which, I thought, and swear that it is the new one. Was that just what she had done? Why hadn't I thought more of the increase from six to seven before she came in and made her incontinent remark? I had noticed the increase – just noticed it; that was all. I had incredibly enough thought nothing of it. No doubt I could have done so later. But the fact remains. What would she have said if I had greeted her when she came in – before she had had time to notice it herself – with the news? What would she have done if I had had the forethought to have kept the number six – put away one of the old ones and kept the other five and the new one? (But I couldn't have done that; I didn't know which was the new one until she told me.) Would she have known it then? I have this element of caddishness in me – of baffled caddishness really, for I almost invariably think of all manner of adroit expedients after the event and wish I had thought of them timeously. I can't get rid of it. She knows it as well as I do. Her eyes can never quite clear me of such tricks; and they spoil things between us – in some ways.

But I said nothing, only nodded and laughed as usual; and her eager brightness heightened into pride and love. This was more than I deserved. My nod must have been a shade too reassuring; my laughter rather too spontaneous seeming. I was surprised at myself. I am seldom so accommodating; but almost immediately I realised that I had done this not so much because she was right as because I knew she was right. I had never been able to distinguish between the others any more than she had, but I knew at least as well as she did that she was right about the new one and that there would be no sense in pretending that she wasn't. To pretend that the new one was not the one she indicated would have led to a mere argument and she would have known that I was deliberately sacrificing the subtler issues inherent in the situation. I am not the man to do that. Besides my confidence was not in her rightness yet, not quite that, but in something inside me that corroborated and confirmed it; and to lie in that way would have been even more a stupid injustice to myself than to her. And it wasn't that I didn't [Line missing. – Eds.] rightness with her – altogether – without testing her own knowledge of it, although I was quite alive to the fact that my knowing she was right neither proved that she really knew it herself nor explained how she knew it – still less how the rightness was hers and only mine through her. I capitulated, then, so far as these initial issues went, to something unusually pretty and persuasive in her eyes; and also because I wished to concentrate on more important elements of the matter.

For, of course, I couldn't tell how I knew any more than I could tell how she knew. There was absolutely nothing to go by. It gave me a queer thrill to feel so perfectly positive. It is a feeling that most of us, who are worth anything, experience very seldom, if ever, nowadays, or, at least, can retain for more than a moment or two, if there is any intelligent discussion; and it was an extraordinary and – I felt at first – regrettable thing that such an unusual and exceptionally exhilarating sensation should be concerned, and in my case indirectly at that, with such a trifling issue. If only I could have acquired it in relation to something really big and vital! And, if indirectly, through some more flattering medium than my wife – through [page missing here. – Eds.] in our places? Apart from that it was not fair to the others – the other six – to regard as trifling any matter that concerned them, however remotely. But did this concern them? They did not seem affected in any way except numerically. There was absolutely no difference between any of them that the eye could see, or the microscope discern. On the tray there, by the window that looked down upon the busy street, urgent with such very other concerns, in the oblique grey light, they huddled enigmatically, identical in the infinitesimal crookedness of their mouths and the devilish intentness of their eyes, concentrated to pin-points of a menacing blackness. Deadly – literally deadly. If the former had been magnified to a certain degree they would have afflicted the universe with an appalling, an impossible, appearance of deformity; if the latter had dilated even a little they would have reduced the cosmos to a cinderheap. And, when they moved, it was with the same certain-uncertain elfin clank-clank, their innumerable wispy legs twirling fantastically and their noses cocked at the prescribed angle. Nor was there the slightest variation in pace. Either they were huddled enigmatically there – or moving at the same slow unchangeable rate round and round, in circles. For they could not go straight...

I wondered how I could contrive to become nettled, with an effect of justification, over her delighted cry that it was a new one. Wasn't there an element of disloyalty in her excitement? (as if I had not already been disloyal myself in thinking of them, however momentarily, as too insignificant a *point-de-departure* for such a discovery!) Had her interest in them, I found myself asking, been only pretence, had she been tiring of the old ones that she should hail so joyfully this addition to their number – this novelty of being able to tell one from the others? I had no sympathy with this craze for novelty. It was over-emphasising a mere numerical difference, and arithmetic, for its own sake, merited no such tribute. Other people (albeit in other connections) made no such fuss over their power to recognise the difference between six and seven...

The original six showed no sense of the fact that they were now seven. Nor did the new-comer act otherwise than as if they had been everlastingly together. They were all constitutionally incapable of surprise, curiosity, delight, or even recognition of anything – beyond jealousy, interest or interaction of any kind. [The following part of the paragraph has been crossed out. – Eds.: They lived in a world insusceptible of change – since change is a matter of perception, and whatever their perceptions might be (for in attempting to think of them one was hopelessly handicapped by the human fallacy) they were obviously incapable of conceiving of change.] Their autocentricity was perfect.

Seven was the same to them as six. One would have been the same; none would have been the same. They were no mathematicians. They simply could not know. Her excitement over a mere addition to their number, then, was most irritatingly misplaced in the circumstances. But even as I argued this I knew that I was being deliberately unfair to her (and even as I recognised my unfairness I was conscious of subtle and far more serious accusations I could not formulate yet but must later – conscious that all these were but very tentative and sketchy reactions to this momentous happening and poorly indicative of the amazing intricacy and importance of the speculations it must yet arouse in me). Her excitement was due not to the fact that where there had been only six there were now seven – not to any absurd speculations as to the consequences the change might entail for the original six, when, as she knew as well as I did it could not entail any, for there were no means whereby they could even become aware of it – but to the fact that for the first time it had been possible to distinguish one from the others, the fact that she had succeeded, inexplicably but none the less surely, in doing this.

It was her own feelings, her own reactions, she was concerned with. I endeavoured to whip myself into an acute displeasure with this unrestrained display of egocentricism. What difference could it possibly make to her, or to anybody or anything else, that she should be thus unaccountably endowed with the ability to recognise one of them and distinguish it infallibly from the others? That would not bring her, us, anybody into closer touch with them; since the one recognised had no means of knowing that it was recognised, of recognising in return, of responding in any way, (even if it had wanted to, which would have been by no means sure – it might very well, probably would, have resented the intrusion, deemed her outrageously perceptive) – but, even if it had – if it had been able, and willing, to reciprocate – would that have been fair to the other six? Why should this new-comer be accorded recognition at the very outset when all these years the others had gone undifferentiated, indistinguishable. It was grossly inequitable. There was something disloyal in this incontinent recognition. She had been too precipitate – exclaiming so egregiously. A wiser woman would have meditated long and carefully over such a discovery before she disclosed it. She would have considered it fully in all its bearings – so far as she possibly could. And then she would have justly, considerately, hinted at her feeling that she had acquired this extraordinary faculty of discrimination and debated the matter in detail with her husband before committing herself and him in this irrevocable fashion. She might even have put it to him in the first instance as a hypothetical matter and seen how he took it before going any further (although, of course, there would have been an element of disingenuousness in such a method). But in any case – even if behind her indulgence in her impulses there is a faith that I will be equal, for both of us, to any emergency that arises – it was to some extent unwifely and certainly rash to blurt it out like that...

Unfair to her again. For of course (apart from the immediate impulse to share her knowledge with me – even if only to surprise me into some new appreciation of her) the reason for her eagerness, her excitement, had been that she instantly thought that if she could recognise one she might yet learn to recognise the others. A typical non-sequitur certainly. Or she had thought that since she could recognise this new-comer there must be reciprocity, it must know that it was recognised, and through it, in course of time, she – we – might get into touch with the others which had hitherto baffled us so completely. All this was very ingenious, very womanly – what they call intuition. Still it re-established her loyalty to them in a way. Her welcome to the newcomer had not been just pride because she could recognise it – not relief at being able to recognise one of them at last instead of having the prolongation of a mutual incomprehensibility that was beginning to be too tiresome for her, with her inevitable womanly flair for intimacy, but a joyful irrepressible sense of having unexpectedly, unaccountably, but unmistakeably found a means to an end. She did not care for the newcomer in itself, just because it was new, or because she could establish relations with it of which the others had proved insusceptible (lowering her standards – the line of least resistance) but because through it she could the better, the more consciously and fully, maintain her loyalty to the others. And, so far as I was concerned, had not her first thought been that if she could tell this one from the others, so of course must I – her cry 'Oh! – It's a new one' had been really interrogatory; she had scarcely been able to believe her own eyes and had turned naturally, and as in duty bound, to me for confirmation. The dear creature!

But why that strange way of expressing herself? – 'Oh! – It's a new one.' Surely the natural thing to have said, the really spontaneous womanly thing, would have been: 'Good gracious – there's *seven* of them!'

Oh, it was all very well arguing in this way, – but was it loyal to take advantage of the difference, decadent probably, whatever it was, of this newcomer as a means towards achieving an intimacy which the older six had so far unanimously refused to entertain? Was it right? Was it playing the game? I felt that I had a great many questions to ask her, a great many aspects to discuss. How far did her recognition go, for example? On what was it based?

'At least we'll be able to recognise the other six now,' she said, and, as I regarded her blankly, added, 'in contradistinction to this one.'

Of course, of course! The little fool! But what had we gained really so far as the other six were concerned? Hadn't we always been able to recognise the other six by the fact that they were six, and severally indistinguishable and, accordingly, treated them all alike?... The woman *would* rattle on so, jumping to conclusions like that. Heaven only knew what she'd say next! It all wanted careful thinking out. One could not be too cautious in a matter of this kind. She seemed to have no sense of finesse at all – rushing in like that where even I was not sure that I could move 'highly and disposedly' enough. But I made up my mind that I was not going to be stampeded. She was so radiantly, so irritatingly *épris*. It was impossible to think in such unsubdued conditions. If she would only go away and give me a chance! Surely she could trust me to do justice to the matter – or couldn't she? She did not want justice done perhaps. Wasn't her precipitancy disloyal to me, too: jealous, selfish, wanton? Not that I wanted deference exactly, and I could not have tolerated to have had her either indifferent or dependent. Still, in a matter of this sort…

Another smile springs flickeringly upon me and in an agony of apprehension I realise that she is going to speak again. God only knows where this will lead. The creature must be *mad*. There is no stopping her. She won't give one a moment's chance. I can't get a word in edgeways. That's the worst of these over-bred, highly-educated women. Jingling their ear-rings and rustling their silks and insinuating an endless succession of glances and smiles till one's brain is simply a chaos of contending lights, scintillant sensations, like – like a damned chandelier!

The Frontier

(A Border story that is also on – but doesn't cross – the border line of politics.)

It was a remarkable situation for one of the leaders of the Scottish Nationalist Movement to find himself in, and Blacklaw smiled a little as he thought of what the newspapers would make of it if they got hold of it – as, of course, they wouldn't.

He had sufficient knowledge of the powers which had carried him to leadership to be certain of that, though these same powers were apparently quite incapable of extricating him from his immediate pass. But the man's quality transpired less in his determination, and confidence in his resource, to avoid that ribald publicity, than in his recognition that this contretemps ought not to have occurred at all and that he had only himself to blame, and in his resolve to profit by the experience if only – as he put it to himself – by 'deepening his consciousness of Scotland'. But *was* it Scotland? That was just the trouble. 'Very well then,' he amended his resolve – fully conscious of the national quality of his hairsplitting habits of thought – 'By deepening my consciousness of Scotland in the light of this experience.' English was far too vague and confused a language to think in; the absurdity of that metaphor in relation to the facts irritated him. It was a pitch-black night, and yet to 'throw light' on his predicament was precisely what his mind was trying to do. He was trying to make bricks without straw in the complete darkness of a howling void. He had ceased to be concerned with the fact that he was lost on a trackless moor; what was of far more consequence was how he stood intellectually and spiritually. Would this force him to alter his established positions? Scarcely; but it might make them more superficial – more arbitrary and artificial – and so sap a force of conviction which had hitherto seemed to derive from unplumbed but adequate depths. His nationalism had never been a shallow thing, relatively to that of most of his associates, yet he had increasingly felt that it might be in comparison with certain manifestations of nationalism in other countries. It was not based, perhaps, on equally profound intuitions of reality, nor even on a corresponding knowledge of Scotland itself, historically, culturally, or physically. He was compelled to take stock again of his equipment in this way. Juggling with little political schemes was one thing but the nature and destiny of a country quite another. Part of his strength had come from the fact that unlike many of his associates he was conscious of many of the disabling gaps in his knowledge, but, somehow or other, this had never forced him to repair them. It would have been extremely difficult; in many directions the data were hard to come by; concentration on the deeper issues would certainly have left him little or no time for dealing with current affairs. Scotland might have gained a poet or philosopher, but it would have lost an active politician who, at least, in the absence of the forms, recognised one of the deficiencies of the Movement and was able to some extent in comparison with his colleagues to make a little imaginative compensation for it, if only in the negative way of deprecating facile generalisations, resisting premature formulations of policy, and, generally, giving a greater impression of profundity. He knew how poor a substitute all this was for exact and detailed knowledge, sweep of historical comprehension, and proleptic faculty. But these would never be his, and, in their absence, at least he had a good Scottish precedent for his alternative tactics, for had not Kant blamed David Hume for declaring certain questions to lie beyond the horizon of human knowledge without determining where that horizon fell, whereas the real difficulty of discussing Hume's philosophy lay, not in his having omitted to do that, but in his having drawn that line in different places at different times.

It was encouraging to feel this resemblance to Hume in circumstances that offered no other encouragement. It was becoming intensely cold, and he had to pick his way too cautiously for fear of 'cricking' his ankles or plunging into a moss-boil to be able to keep warm. He had no idea what direction he was going in, but the core of his cerebration was the question of whether he was – in what was well-called this 'debateable land' – in Scotland or in England. He felt that he ought to know, instinctively. But he didn't and so it was necessary to fortify his spirit of nationalism on other grounds. The phrase 'on other grounds' amused him. 'Carrying the war into the enemy's camp – what?' And certainly this question of where the frontier lay was not necessarily a fixed one; it might also be drawn 'in different places at different times'. That was the solution. No wonder he did not instinctively recognise a line of demarcation that was purely arbitrary and might be shifted by treaty or military action or – for all practical purposes – by a regrouping of economic interests any day. Perhaps this was the hidden meaning of the experience he was undergoing – to disabuse him of his fixed idea that the frontier ran hereabouts instead of further north or south. And he extracted a second encouragement from the very heart of his plight when he remembered that in an inspired moment in one of his speeches he had referred to the North of England – down to the Humber-Mersey line – as Scotia Irredenta, and contended that 'the economy of these islands had been completely distorted by the cancerous parasitism of London, since the real centre, the heart of all the great industries, corresponded to the old Brythonic Kingdom, between Glasgow on the North and Liverpool on the South'. No wonder his pulses were normal; he was not in England after all, no matter if he had overstepped the so-called Border by a mile or two.

Apart from moving slowly and picking his footsteps very warily, he was pleased to find that he had no sensation of fear in circumstances of solitude and darkness he had not encountered before. Perhaps his blood was responding to some ancestral familiarity in this – perhaps it had some knowledge of imminent requirements, though the second notion was (he recognised in an instant) derived from the past too. Conditions of warfare had changed, and in the unlikely event of actual hostilities between Scotland and England little was likely to depend nowadays on individuals' night-knowledge of lonely moorland tracks. Guerilla warfare on the Border hills would hardly be an essential part of the proceedings. Still – one never knew! He was more impressed, however, by the sudden sense of experiencing the countryside as the overwhelming proportion of Scotland actually was for about half the time (not to mention that other 'darkness' of depopulation and unfrequentation) and as only the tiniest percentage of the population ever experienced it. Most of the people were herded in the cities and knew little or nothing of the land as a whole – least of all under conditions which presented it in a guise so utterly unfamiliar and yet at least as valid, as essential to a synoptic view, as any day-time appearance. What Scotland most of them had was a mere figment of the light. Night was older than light and still as frequent, and they could not ignore that aspect of Scotland if they were to base their nationalism deeply enough. 'What can they know of Scotland who only street lamps know?' He was in touch with the traditional, the immemorial, Scotland – before it was warped away from its real nature by modern industrialism. He was in touch with Scotland in the guise in which it had been familiar enough to the fathers of the race but ever in decreasing measure to their degenerate sons. He must carry back some of this blackness and wildness and loveliness into their National Movement which was far too congested with little urgencies, too like a stream of street traffic and not corresponding

[Here the manuscript ends. – Eds.]

Standing by the Pool

Like all others of her species Mrs D had passed through many transitions in her time. From a baby erroneously described as a little Venus by her mother and a skinned rabbit by her father, she had turned into a plain but not ugly child with a heavy mind that accepted unquestioningly a strange and unknown world. Beauty never came to her but the transition to young womanhood imparted to her plainness a momentary quality of youth that made her physically desirable to men of limited choice and the fact that she found herself desirable to anybody lifted her heavy mind into a temporary wonder. Sunlight lay upon the dull land, bathing it with surprising warmth. For a short spell to look into her eyes was to look into happiness. For an unbelievable week it was to look into sheer joy. Then the brightness of the eyes grew dull, the expectation died out of them, and she entered the long and dreary phase from which there seemed no escape, saving in rare moments of daring imagination. Reality held nothing, acceptance returned, but now it was not acceptance of a strange and unknown world but of familiar specific burdens. Patience itself became a routine mood. This, she thought, was the final change and would go on for ever. But into this patience entered a new Mrs D. She did not enter nor take complete possession. She slipped in and out slyly, or burst in with volcanic violence, to leave the evacuated body clammy and limp when she departed. 'That wasn't me' came the desperate thought, 'Oh, no! Not me!' But it was. And the red intruder increased her visits, becoming more and more violent each time, until at last she had her way. And then, born of the violence and its consequences, Mrs D changed again, and became a person beyond her own comprehension. It was a person without any feeling whatever, a person completely numb. What was done could not be undone, and since there was no effacing it, it had to be accepted; like all the other phases of her unenviable existence. Only this time one accepted it without any sensations. One watched oneself do this or that, but it was like watching someone else, not really watching oneself at all. It was not a day-to-day affair. It was minute-to-minute. Every minute was interminably long and it merely led to another that was just the same. Of course, things happened. One watched them happening, going on doing things and saying things, gaining a little comfort from familiar operations that had never before held any pleasure in them. Yes, she was conscious of doing things but they all seemed flat and meaningless. They made no impression, responding to instincts for movement, and for movement away from people. But she had no plan, neither short-term, such as breakfast, nor long term, such as escape. The future did not exist for her any longer. They were all separate, disconnected spots joined by no central design or purpose. She stood for a long time by the pool. She was quite prepared to watch herself entering it. Eventually she turned away with vague surprise. And the long moments continued to lead endlessly and meaninglessly from one to another.

The First Clock in Barra

When I was a young man, my elder brother, Calum, left home and sailed for Canada. He was about seventeen years old at the time and I was five.

After he had gone, I used to sit for hours on the west cliffs of Barra looking out over the vast stretches of the Atlantic and I used to say to myself: 'Somewhere out there is Calum and some day, no doubt, when I am grown up, I'll go out there too.'

However, the days and the weeks and the months passed and life went on as usual on the island, until one day, just before Christmas, the postman came down from Castlebay with a parcel, addressed to my mother, and it was tied with a piece of tape with 'A Present from Montreal – A Present from Montreal – A Present from Montreal' written all round it.

My father was in the house at the time and he looked at the address and the tape and said *'Oh A'Mhairi's ann bho Calum 'tha so'* – 'Oh Mary, it's from Calum this is' and proceeded to open the knot on the tape. He eventually succeeded in undoing what must have been about the most difficult of knots to loosen, and started unwrapping the parcel. Well, he took off about half-a-dozen sheets of brown paper and uncovered a beautiful cardboard box. He carefully lifted the lid and removed a few handfuls of shavings, and there, wrapped in tissue paper was – a clock!

Now nobody in Barra had seen a clock before, but my father knew immediately what it was and he also knew that a clock should make some kind of noise; so he put his ear to the clock – without removing it from the box – and said in Gaelic, 'Oh, it's a clock, but it's stopped – there's something wrong with it. Now no-one must touch this.'

He carefully put the packing back round the clock, put the lid on the box and wrapped it up in the half dozen sheets of paper and tied it up with the tape and put it through to the *culaist* (the bedroom).

Well, it turned out to be a boisterous night; the rain was pattering against the window panes and the wind was howling around the house, but as soon as the tea was over my father put on his oilskins, his sou-wester and his sea-boots; tucked the parcel under his oilskin and away he went to the priest's house.

It was about three miles away and when he knocked at the door the priest came and answered it, saying *'Oh Thighearna, A Micheal, gu de tha ga d'thoirt a mach Leithid an oidhche tha so?'* 'Oh goodness, Michael, what takes you out on such a night as this? Is there something wrong? Is somebody ill?'

'Och no,' said my father, 'there's nobody ill at all, but we've just had a parcel from Calum from Montreal; it's a clock, but it's broken – it won't go.'

'Oh, thig a stigh, a dhuine.' – 'Oh come in, man; come in and let me have a look at the thing.'

So my father went in and handed the parcel over to the priest, who cut the tape with a knife and unwrapped the box, somewhat unceremoniously, opened the box and took out the clock. He looked at it for a second and turned a handle at the back of it and the clock went all right.

'Och, Michael,' he said, 'there's nothing wrong with the clock, it just needs winding, that's all.' And he said to my father, 'Now, every night, before you go to bed, you must turn this handle like this, eight or nine times – until it won't turn any more – and you'll find the clock will go all right.'

My father thanked the priest for the information and, without even waiting for a cup of tea, came straight home.

He arrived back about nine o'clock and my mother and I were eagerly awaiting him, to hear what the priest had to say.

'Och, there was nothing at all wrong with the clock, except that it was needing winding,' he said, with an inflexion of authority in his voice. 'And now,' he said when he had taken the clock out again, 'I'm putting this up here on the mantelpiece and nobody is to touch it but myself.'

And there was the clock, sitting on the mantelpiece, going 'Tchik-tchok, Tchik-tchok, Tchik-tchok' without a moment's pause. And we all three sat down and gazed in wonder and amazement at the hands that moved ever so slowly, without ever uttering a sound, until my father, about eleven o'clock asked my mother if they were to have any supper at all that night.

The news soon got around the island and people came from every part to see this wonderful thing that told the time – every night the house was full of people sitting round the fire, gazing in silence at the clock. It was as if the clock had the power to strike everyone dumb as soon as they looked at it. Men who used to come in for a *ceilidh*; to sing songs and tell stories, now came and sat transfixed before this most wonderful engine.

My father was soon the most revered man on the island. The children and the young ones used to keep out of his way when they saw him coming along the road. '*Seo Bodach A Chloc*' they used to say. 'Here's the man with the Clock'; and my father was soon the most famous man in Barra, with the magnificent title of '*Bodach a' Chloc*'.

As I said, I was only five and as time passed, I became ever more eager to get my hands on this clock, just to see how heavy it was, or just to feel it maybe.

However, spring had come and my father and mother were out all day on the croft and I was out with them, of course. Well, one Saturday, while we were out, my mother said to me about eleven o'clock: 'Run away home, Donald and poke the fire up a bit and put the kettle on, it'll be a help for me if it's boiling when we come home,' so away I went (the croft was about a mile from the house on the other side of a little bay). I put on the kettle and looked up at the clock. There it was going Tchik-tchok, Tchik-tchok, Tchik-tchok on the mantelpiece, so I said to myself, 'Now, Donald here's your chance.' So I dragged a chair up to the fire, got up on to it and reached down the clock.

I looked at the back of it and started turning this handle and that handle and the next handle – oh, I was having a grand time when I looked out of the window and saw my father and mother leaving the croft, so I jumped up on the chair and put the clock back on to the mantelpiece. I looked out again and could see my parents coming down about a hundred yards from the house, when, all of a sudden – Tr-r-r-r-r-r-r-r-r-r-r-r went the clock. Oh clearly I didn't know what on earth to do. I jumped up on to the chair, shook the clock, tucked it under my jersey – did everything with it, but it wouldn't stop. So I ran through the '*culaist*' and tucked it under the bedclothes; but still it went on, much more quietly Tr-r-r-r-r-r-r. And just as I came back my father and mother came in.

My mother, for some reason, went straight through to the bedroom and came running out immediately shouting, *'Oh A Micheal, tha an Diobhal anns a leabaidh'* – 'Oh Michael, the devil's in the bed.'

My father went through and threw the clothes off and there was the clock, as it seemed, in its last gasp, Tr-r-r-r-r-r – r.

My father picked up the clock and listened to it, and sure enough it was still going Tchik-tchok, Tchik-tchok, Tchik-tchok and he put it back on the mantelpiece.

I'll never forget the thrashing I got for that. *BUT – I was the first man on Barra to discover an alarm on a clock.*

Note
Ceilidh = a sing-song or impromptu concert, one of the great features of Hebridean life.

The Murder

Mitchell did not intend to commit murder. Nothing was further from his mind, and he, and anyone who knew him, would have regarded it as inconceivable that he should ever do anything of the sort. He was not of a fighting disposition. Very much the opposite. The set-to was forced upon him, suddenly, and without the slightest provocation on his part. It was a purely wanton assault, and the two blows which his assailant rained on the head before he struck out in self-defence were barely enough to be really dangerous. Looking back he always remembered that his first feeling was one of surprise that he had not collapsed under them, but they had had instead the unexpected effect of 'clearing his head'. His opponent was bigger and stronger than he was and knew 'how to use his fists – a knowledge of which he lacked the very rudiments. In self-defence he might have appeared to strike out blindly and register a mere fluke, but actually he had had a soaring suggestion of mastery. He felt as if instincts and abilities quite equal to the occasion but hitherto unsuspected in him had instantaneously mobilised themselves. How surprised his opponent and the onlookers must be! He was as cool as a cucumber, and about to teach this hulking bully the sharpest lesson of his life. The impact of his clenched fist on his assailant's nose – the spurtle of blood – had awakened in him incalculable powers. Brutes like this should not be allowed to exist.

Exultant in his consciousness of power to avenge the brutal and uncalled for attack, strong in his virtuous indignation, he recalled how he had realised that he could make the punishment that he liked. There was nothing to prevent him killing this vicious pest, temporarily blinded with the blood which he – Mitchell – at the first blow had sent spraying into his goggling eyes. In a sudden telescoping of thought and feeling he was conscious of his second blow and his third – the cracking of the skull beneath his knuckles – a few ludicrous spasmodic movements and then the collapse of his enemy – his own impassivity as the little ring of spectators closed in on him and the motionless shape at his feet – the realisation that the man was dead – his own sense not only of perfect justification, of the impossibility of any conscience pricking – but of being able to 'get away with it' in any court of law – his enjoyment of the tremendous sensation in the town and further afield – the effect of it all on his subsequent port and mien among his fellows.

It was queer that it required such a wanton assault by a callous inferior to bring out the unsuspected qualities of brain and brawn in a man. Perhaps this was one of the justifications of evil, that it was a touchstone of good.

All these ideas and the fullest sensations of exemplifying them went through him like a flash of lightning at that first impact of his hand on his opponent's face, and, later, he was always able to re-experience that peak moment of his life with the same vividness – the same comprehensive realisation of everything that was involved, and the same soaring sense of perfect coordination and mutual adequacy of mind and muscle.

And as quickly upon it ensued an utter darkness. It was not till an hour later that he had recovered consciousness and slowly and painfully realised what had happened. His opponent's third blow had felled him as if he had been a bullock in a slaughterhouse.

Ballet: Barley Break (The Scarecrow)

Harvest-field. Haystack centre rear of stage. Harvesters, all fine young folk, dancing – except Old Man, Lame Girl, and Local Idiot. Idiot, avid to dance, seizes upon Lame Girl who makes pitiful efforts to comply to the callous amusement of the others. Farmer's Daughter comes disdainfully by. Idiot discards Lame Girl and seizes upon her, whirling her into wild dance. She makes desperate efforts to free herself but they avail nothing against his imbecile frenzy. The Old Man has given the Lame Girl a Scarecrow to console her and she is vainly conjuring the Muse of Dancing with it in steps of her own impotent devising. The other harvesters, who hate the Farmer's Daughter, are all dancing in a fashion to emphasise the antitheses between the demoniacal dance of the Idiot and the ineffectual efforts of the Lame Girl. Farmer's Wife comes on the scene, mightily indignant, and tries to free her Daughter. Old Man, suddenly galvanised into incredible activity, won't let her and whirls her up into dance. Farmer's Daughter escapes from Idiot and runs round behind haystack. Idiot follows. Farmer's Wife follows. Old Man follows. All the crowd follow. Last of all Lame Girl & Scarecrow. Reappear, Farmer's Daughter with Idiot who has partially taken on the guise of Skeleton Death; Farmer's Wife and Old Man who has discarded his breeks to display the legs of his true character, the Devil; and the harvesters. All except the Devil and the Idiot afflicted with lameness and dancing in fashion reminiscent of first efforts of Lame Girl. Reappear Lame Girl no longer lame and Scarecrow changed into Handsome Youth but with elements of dress to connect him still with Scarecrow. Farmer's Daughter recognises him and ludicrously tries to reclaim him. Enter Farmer, uproariously drunk, with Gipsy Baggage. Infuriated Wife tries in vain to shake off the Devil and reclaim him. Farmer's Daughter and Death; Farmer's Wife and Devil; Lame Girl and Handsome Youth; and Gipsy Girl and Farmer do Eightsome Reel. Death claims the Farmer's Daughter and they disappear beind the haystack. The Devil claims the Farmer's Wife and they disappear behind the haystack. The remainder begin to enjoy themselves in earnest. At the height of dance they break off and, the men chasing the girls, disappear behind the haystack. Only the Lame Girl – after a little – reappears, dancing forlornly with the Scarecrow.

Lechois: A Play in One Act

Dramatis Personae
Mother
Old Woman (who might almost be her double, except for her old-fashioned attire)
Jean, the daughter
Alick, the son
Common, a business man in a good way of doing

Enter Jean, to find her mother in conversation with a lady like an old-fashioned and cruder version of herself.

Jean: (1) Mother – Oh!

Mother: This is an ancestress of ours – a century or two ago.

Jean: But she's bound to be dead.

Mother: (2) She is, so far as that goes, but it doesn't go so far as most people imagine as long as they are still alive. [Just as children think you are dreadfully old at twenty.] You're too young to understand [perhaps but by the time you are my age you'll come to see that the difference between life and death as they are called is no more than tweedledum and tweedledee]. Most folk are either dead, so to speak, or not born yet; we're in the minority that are temporarily neither.

[Page missing. – Eds.]

Mother: All women are sisters. I think it is because of something I lack and she has – something extremely necessary just now – that she has come today. We might change places. I would do it in a moment if I thought her kind of power could be brought to bear today – But I don't. Life's got beyond human control. Machines have made such a difference. The dead are just as helpless as the living.

Old Woman: The dead are the living – in so far as they are anything.

Mother: They played their part in their own day. If we could do the same in ours, and all the generations still to come did just as well – it would be all right. But, for the first time in history, mankind is impotent and I can see no way in which it can regain the power it has lost.

Old Woman: There must be a way.

Mother: There isn't.

Jean: I'm sorry, but I'll have to go. I have an appointment. – *(To the Old Woman)* I'll be seeing you again.

Mother: Jean!

Jean: Now, mother –

Mother: You're not going – after all our talk this morning.

Jean: I must. It's no use talking. I'd simply lose my job if I didn't, and where would we be then? Common would see that I didn't get another – that Alick lost his – that we lost this house. And after all what's love and marriage but camouflage for the same old business. As well do it comfortably as not. (Exit)

Old Woman: Common?

Mother: (3) Her employer. Employers are common. So are employees.

He'll marry her, of course. She'll be very well off. There isn't a girl in the place wouldn't jump at the chance.

Old Woman: Common! I killed him once.

Mother (soothingly): I know. But can you do it again. He was one man then. He is legion now. And his victims are one with him. Jean says his real name is Everyman.

Old Woman: No. I can't do it again. One man was the problem as I met it and overcame it in my own day and generation. Long ago. It is always for the living to meet and overcome it in its changing guises in their own age.

Mother: Would to God I could act as you did! My whole life has become a futile quest for the power to do so. – But it is hopeless. It is beyond me.

Old Woman: Perhaps it is only because you lack hope that you lack power.

Mother: Perhaps – but how can I manufacture hope?

(Enter Alick)

Mother: This is Alick.

Alick (without paying any attention to the introduction): Where's Jean.

(Mother bows her head. Alick clenches his fists and moves towards the door as if his mind were made up to settle the matter by violence – then he suddenly subsides into a chair, with a gesture of impotence.)

Mother: How's the strike?

Alick: It's broken down. The men are going back.

Mother (4) *(to Old Woman):* Alick is one of the men's leaders. [Everywhere] the employers are attacking the standard of living [of the working classes]. They say they must work longer hours for less money. [Some sections of the workers have struck. A great deal depended upon Alick's section, but] the strike's breaking down. The more cowardly and short-sighted of the workers are streaming back. – The road is being made. [Common is dead: Long live Common. And his methods are as ever those of the slave-driver. The only difference is that today the slavery's been so subtilised that the slaves do not recognise themselves for what they are. Or, rather, they are so well educated that they know they are not fit for anything else. And they aren't; they aren't. All they want is to have everybody else in the same position.] They say: it is the only way of getting the road made. They are as anxious to see the road made as the employer is.

Old Woman: They can't all be. There must be rebels amongst them. You spoke of strikers? They haven't all gone back.

Mother: (5) But they are not rebels in the right way or for the right ends.

All they want is a mean little bribe of one kind or another – some petty concession. But practically all of them want the road to go on. At best they want to get rid of Common and elect somebody else who'd do practically the same as he does. All Common has to do nowadays as a rule is to stop work for a week or two. That brings most of them to their senses. 'For God's sake, good Mr Comyn [*sic*], please restart the road, and we'll work under any conditions you care to impose.' That's what's called common sense – public spirit – good citizenship.

Old Woman: And the women work with them?

Mother: (6) The women work with them. One never hears of a woman living in a slum saying: 'Life here is so foul that I won't bring babies into it, whatever happens.' They breed like rabbits. One never hears men say – as hundreds of thousands should – life is not worth living on these terms. Or, if they do say it, they don't act up to it. No. They carry on to the most abominable and futile lives and make women and children share them. And an employer has only to say – wages must come down – and most of the workers no matter how wretched their circumstances agree with him and submit to worse and thereby force the few who might resist to submit too. And if they show the slightest tendency not to their wives and children make them. All families would rather subsist on the breadwinner's dehumanisation than starve.

Old Woman: And are the employers any better off, themselves?

Mother: No, except materially, which doesn't matter. Their lives are just as dull and stupid and essentially meaningless. Though they can buy enough sensation of one kind or another or deceive themselves. They are just calloused in a different way; it comes to the same in the long run. They don't live any longer. Being wealthy doesn't usually mean being any happier or freer really, or any surer of the things that make life worth having and for which life was intended. It can't buy love, for example, or wisdom. Rich men's daughters sell themselves even more deliberately than poor men's. – I tell you there's no ground that the road's not being driven over. Honour, love, and the like are no longer obstacles: the levies now at work make short shift of them all.

Alick: What's all this talk about the road?

Mother: I'm sorry. I forgot you didn't know. – This is an ancestress of yours.

Alick: Indeed? She looks like it – I'm pleased to meet you. You've a great deal to answer for.

Old Woman: I was burned as a witch in the long-run.

Alick: (7) That wouldn't have mattered, would it, if you'd really been one.

Old Woman: No doubt there's some folk would like to burn you too.

Bolshevism is the latest name for witchcraft, I'm told.

Alick: But I'm not a Bolshevik either. So far as I can learn about what's happened in Russia the very same business is being carried on there as in this country, under, if anything, even worse conditions, and a different name.

Old Woman: Then you're an Anarchist.

Alick: If I must have a label I suppose that will do as well as any. But before we go any further, if you don't mind, what about this road?

Old Woman: (8) It was the road from Kilmavonaig to Badenoch – not that our place-names matter. [The same thing has happened in almost every district of the world: but this happened to be mine.] The Lord of Badenoch at that time was Walter Comyn. [Cruel, bloodthirsty and vindictive he was hated by all his people.] He had the right of 'pit and gallows' and made the most of it. [For the most trifling offence, and, indeed, for none, he strung up his vassals on the gallows tree which, all the year round, never wanted its quota of ghastly fruit.] There was none but would have gladly ended his existence, [but dread of any such attempt proving unsuccessful stayed their hands.]

Alick: They never thought of the other way out – ending their own. [Let us call that the Condition under which most men live – subject to futile existences, loathsome diseases, and death. But most of us are resigned to it. –]

Old Woman (ignoring the interruption): [He never moved without his armed escort.] There was nothing he wanted that he did not obtain. [If opposition was offered blood was unstintedly poured out to gain his ends. When] he determined to make a road from his castle of Ruthven through to Kilmavonaig [he had no human opposition to encounter – it was the formidable difficulties Nature interposed that had to be overcome.] The country was such that the task was stupendous, herculean, well-nigh impossible. Yet he swore to make it though it cost him a thousand lives and a thousand crowns to do it. Blood and money were no object.

Alick: Blood and money never are, and nature has long since ceased to offer any effective opposition. – [What did he want the road for?

Old Woman: Merely to get regular supplies of Kilmavonaig ale which he deemed the best in the land.

Alick: We have plenty of diplomats today who would find cause enough for world warfare in things no bigger than that.]

Old Woman: Hundreds of men were put to work. All the vassals of his domains, from childhood to old age, were called upon: and to them he added hundreds of serfs, bought and sold like cattle. [Fifteen shillings was a common price for a husband and wife and all their issue.] Despite the numbers engaged the work prógressed but slowly. Every day Comyn came and urged them on with curse and lash to greater and still greater efforts. Harvest came on, but men could not be spared to secure the crop – [although the continuance of the work depended upon it.] Orders were given that it should be reaped by the women.

Alick (bitterly): Great man! The first of the land army. But our WAACS were a big advance on his idea.

Old Woman: One September afternoon returning from visiting his workers [in even a worse mood than usual] Comyn suddenly came in view of a glade in the forest. There two young girls were busy reaping a little patch of oats. The day being hot they had taken off part of their clothing and ashamed [at being caught in such a state by their lord and his attendants] they tried to hide themselves in the shelter of the trees. Comyn saw them. 'What do they mean by running away?' he cried. 'Every minute is valuable [and must be spent in work. To fritter away time cannot be allowed. An example must be made.] Seize them and take them to the castle. Let them be brought before me tomorrow.' [Two of his followers carried out his orders and] the girls were duly brought up for judgement. They were charged with idleness and neglect of work. [But they were graciously permitted to make any statement they could on their own behalf.] They explained the cause of their flight. 'A pretty excuse!' said Comyn. 'It is high time you learned that your bodies and clothes are alike my property, to do with as I deem fit. – Three days from now you shall reap in the same place clad as Mother Eve was in the Garden of Eden and all the other reapers shall be summoned to see you do so. Take them away.' And the girls were removed. One of them was my grand-daughter. I was a serf – the property of the Lord of Badenoch [as my ancestors had been and as my descendants were. All our family tree was entered in the stud-book of Ruthven Castle. But] at that time I was very old and decrepit. [It was many years since I had ceased to be a toiler and Walter Comyn had forgotten my very existence. Though physically weak] I had acquired power in another direction. I was regarded as the most terrible witch in Badenoch. I made up my mind to exercise all my power to prevent this outrage. [And the mother of the other maiden – a much younger woman than I was – was of like mind and came to my hut to contrive a means. 'This must be stopped,' she said. 'It shall,' I said, 'It's a hard task – but the girls must be saved from this shame at all cost. Great power will be needed but between us we can obtain it. Before this time tomorrow the Black Comyn must dree his weird' –] And, to cut a long story short, he did!

Alick: Excuse me interrupting again but there's just one thing I want to know – before you go any further. Do you still think it was worth it? Were the subsequent careers of these girls any better really than they would have been if they had been exposed in the way Comyn intended.

Mother: Oh Alick!

Alick: Didn't it all come to the same thing in the long run? Didn't it? Isn't life just such an exposure?

Old Woman: You must answer that question for yourself. No one can answer it for you.

(Silence for a little.)

Alick: All right! I suppose you mean what I am and other people are or can be is the result of this or that happening instead of something else. [You mean that the long run isn't over and that the final upshot still depends to some extent upon us. –] Well, fire ahead! What did you do? What happened?

Old Woman: We made our plans. My helper insisted that Comyn should get one chance – that his life should be spared if he cancelled his sentence. I agreed – because I knew that he would not take it. If I had had any doubts I would not have agreed. – On the fateful morning Comyn arose in the worst of tempers and was early on the scene of the road-making. Where his road narrowed to a single file, overhung with boulders, covered with dense undergrowth, I suddenly appeared. His horse shied violently and if Comyn had not been an expert horseman he would have met his end there and then. Well for him if he had! He saw me as soon as he regained control of the beast and burst into a storm of abuse. But without heeding what he said I delivered my warning. 'You dare to threaten me,' he shouted, 'Vile carrion! You should have disappeared with your usefulness many years ago but your belated hour has come now. Seize here and string her up to the nearest tree.' 'Then dree your weird,' I cried. Two or three of his mess dismounted and plunged into the undergrowth. – But of course I had disappeared. Comyn's temper did not improve as he waited or when they returned from their fruitless quest. When he reached his workers he gave full vent to the fury of his passion. With curse and lash he urged them on to doubled and redoubled effort. Finally taking some of the foremen along with him he rode on a distance ahead of the workers and said: 'If you do not reach this point a week hence you will pay the penalty with your lives'. As they came back a hill hid the workers from their view for a little but when they came to the top of it an extraordinary spectacle presented itself. Soon after Comyn's arrival two eagles had appeared in the air – so high as to be mere specks. Gradually – after Comyn and his party went on ahead – they descended in long sweeping circles and as they neared the workers began giving vent to loud piercing screams. Latterly the attitude of the great birds became so threatening that all stopped work and tried to scare them off. Resistance seemed to infuriate them. With angry screams they swooped for the attack. With beak, wing, and talon they struck and tore at man and beast. The men fled in all directions. Horses and bullocks stampeded in terror, taking with them the frail contrivances that served for carts. Just headed straight for certain precipices over which they fell headlong and were dashed to pieces on the rocks below. – This was the indescribable scene that met Comyn's eye as he topped the hill. Thunderstruck he gazed for a moment, then with an oath exclaiming, 'Why didn't the fools strike down the birds?' he galloped forward to destroy them. But the eagles did not wait for his assault. No sooner did he appear on the scene than both birds, despising meaner victims, made for him with trebled fury and wilder screams. The rush of their wings as they cleft the air sounded in his ears like ocean surf and their cries pierced his very soul. He had all to do to keep his seat. Realising that his only chance lay in flight he headed his horse for Ruthven Castle. Apparently divining his intention one of the eagles met the steed with a mighty blow of its wing. The animal wheeled and bolted. Confused and terrified, Comyn dashed his spurs into the horse's flanks, his one idea being to get away from the fateful place, no matter in what direction. Again and again he applied his spur and was carried he knew not whither. For a time his fleet steed left the pursuing eagles behind. Crossing a ridge of the Grampians he galloped at fearful speed towards Craignaheilar. There the birds overtook him, and buried beak and talons in his quivering flesh. Bit by bit the clothing was torn from his back. Steaming flesh and broken bone scattered over the heather marked the course of his long last wild career. But the noble horse could not endure for ever, and when, unscathed by the eagles, it dropped dead on the banks of the Tarff, all that remained of the Lord of Badenoch was one leg dangling from a stirrup. – Thus were the maidens saved from shame. Thus was the road-making ended.

(Enter Common and Jean)

[*Common:* I am sorry to spoil the story.

[*Old Woman:* Comyn!

[*Common:* (9) The same – at your service. Why don't you people face all the facts? Call me the Lord of Badenoch or Commons Ltd or whatever you like – times change but the two contending forces in human life remain the same at bottom. Activity verses inertia. Brain – and less brain. Anything you like. You may kill me in one form – in so far as anything ever is killed – but what does your victory amount to. The struggle goes on forever. It's two essential elements in humanity at war with each other. And as long as humanity continues to exist the struggle between them will continue. Don't talk nonsense about stopping the road making! If the Kilmavonaig project was held up – were the men any better off? Hadn't they to tackle road making or something similar elsewhere as long as they lived. Under a slightly less tyrannical master, perhaps – but did that make any – fundamental difference. Both sides learn as they go along. No British employer nowadays would use the same methods as were used in Badenoch then, if he could – he knows how to get more out of his men. And the men have learned – there wasn't any talk about independence and 'a man being a man for a' that' in Badenoch. But what does it all amount to? Is the mass of the workers any better off fundamentally? Are they fit for anything else than manual labour – soulless routine – and if they were given more wages than just sufficient to keep them working wouldn't they stop working – and would they be any better off then? – The spot where my horse dropped may still be called Lechois or One Foot and the road I planned may never have been completed. But circumstances have changed. There is no need for it. Kilmavonaig ale – or a better – can be obtained everywhere – if you know how. There are roads in all directions. Cruelty? Yes. But the cruelty is inherent in life itself – in the fact that the great masses of the people are unfit to be anything more than 'hewers of wood and drawers of water' – and don't really want to be. Perhaps a time's coming when we'll be able to do all the routine work of the world by machines – will the great masses of the people be any happier then even if they get a good minimum wage for doing nothing but bringing more and more into the world to do nothing in turn too. Not a bit of it! –

Jean (to Old Woman): (10) And you say that saved the maidens from shame? It depends what you call shame. What was their subsequent history? Weren't the very conditions of life shameful and intolerable?

Alick: I don't agree with you – or with you either. I consider your doctrines opposed to the intentions of the Creator. Life can be made worth living for everybody – work can be directed to noble ends, each striving for the good of all –

Comyn: Old chap, I admire your ideals and I wish you could make them practicable. Only I don't see that you can. But if you think so – fire ahead, and good luck to you. Talk less and do more. In the meantime we must carry on with what we've got – *(puts an arm through Alick's and draws him towards the door, passing the Old Woman, to whom he gives his other arm) – (to Old Woman)* And Death hasn't changed your point of view, I see? The trouble is it hasn't changed mine either. *(To Alick)* When folks are alive they're too apt to regard Death as a solution instead of a mere continuance of their problems. *(Turning to Old Woman again)* (11) Well, I don't bear you any grudge now, you know – I understand and respect your motives although I cannot agree that they are practical – and I will say this… that the story of how you bested me in Badenoch… makes a rattling good story. You tell it so dramatically, too… But they laugh best who laugh least [sic – Eds.]? –

(Exit Comyn, Alick & Old Lady).

Mother (starting as from sleep): …Oh.

Jean (running over to her): What's the matter, mother.

Mother: Oh, Jean, I had such a terrible dream.

Jean: What about.

Mother: About you and Common, and about Alick too, all mixed up with a dreadful old Highland story about a witch who might have been my double… It's given me quite a shake.

Jean: Don't think about it… Besides dreams always go by contraries.

Mother: You're not just marrying Common because he's in a good way of business, Jean.

Jean: What a question!

Mother: I mean… you really do love him – for himself.

Jean (kissing her): Of course, I do. You silly old mother.

Appendix 2
Provenance and Publishing Data

ANNALS OF THE FIVE SENSES (Montrose: C.M. Grieve, 1923; Edinburgh: Porpoise Press, 1930; Edinburgh: Polygon Books, 1983, with an introduction by Alan Bold)

PUBLISHED STORIES AND SKETCHES

The Black Monkey (*The Broughton Magazine*, Christmas 1909)

All Night in an British Opium 'Joint' (*The People's Journal*, 15 March 1912)
Below the story is a photograph of the young Chris Grieve curled up on a settee, eyes closed, long-stemmed pipe in mouth, and the materials on a tray before him. On the left is the paragraph: 'The Confessions of a Scotch opium smoker. He had some whiffs of the so-called magical drug, but instead of producing sweet dreams, it made him want a breath of good fresh air.' On the right, there is this: 'Our opium-smoker says he could get as much exaltation out of a smile from a *People's Journal* prize beauty as from all the poppy juice in creation.'

Casualties (*The Broughton Magazine*, Summer 1919)

Nisbet, an Interlude in Post War Glasgow (*The Scottish Chapbook*, vol.1, nos.1 and 2, August and September 1922)

Following Rebecca West in Edinburgh (*The Scottish Chapbook*, vol.2, no.3, October 1922)

Some Day (*The Scottish Nation*, 30 October 1923)

In the Fulness of Time (first published under the title 'In the Fulness of Time' in *The Scottish Nation*, no.33, 18 December 1923; reprinted as 'The Dead Harlot' in John Gawsworth, ed., *New Tales of Horror*, 1934)

The Purple Patch (*The Northern Review*, May 1924)

Old Miss Beattie (*The Gallovidian Annual*, 1927)

The Common Riding (*The Glasgow Herald*, 12 March 1927)

Wound-Pie (first published under the title 'A Dish o' Whummle' in the *Scots Observer*, 19 March 1927; reprinted with the title 'Wound-Pie' and with the phrase 'wound-pie' [or 'wund-pie' meaning a pie made of wind, or air] replacing 'a dish o' whummle' in the text, in John Gawsworth, ed., *New Tales of Horror*, 1934. Also published as 'Wind Pie' in Aberdeen Students' Charities Magazine *Eureka*, 1961. In the original text, the ending was as follows:

'"And what's a dish o' whummle?" I asked.

'"Wund-pie," said he, and stumped off doon the close.')

Murtholm Hill (*The Scots Magazine*, April 1927)

The Waterside (*The Glasgow Herald*, 16 April 1927)

A'body's Lassie (*Scots Observer*, 14 May 1927; reprinted in John Gawsworth, ed., *New Tales of Horror*, 1934)

The Moon Through Glass (*The Glasgow Herald*, 16 July 1927; reprinted in J. Rowland, ed., *Path and Pavement*, 1937)

Maria (*The Glasgow Herald*, 27 August 1927; reprinted as 'Tam Mackie's Trial' in Peter Haining, ed., *The Clans of Darkness: Scottish stories of fantasy and horror*, London: Gollancz, 1971. In this collection, the story ends in the third-from-last paragraph, with an exclamation mark instead of a long dash after the words 'Maria was deed'.)

The Visitor (*Scots Observer*, 1 October 1927)

Andy (*The Glasgow Herald*, 22 October 1927)

Holie for Nags (*Scots Observer*, 22 September 1928)

The Scab (*The Glasgow Herald*, 15 August 1932)

The Last Great Burns Discovery (*At the Sign of the Thistle*, London: Stanley Nott, 1934)

Five Bits of Miller (privately published by MacDiarmid in an edition of forty numbered copies, 1934)

The Stranger (John Gawsworth, ed., *New Tales of Horror*, 1934)

The Dean of the Thistle (*New Scotland*, 9 November 1935)

A Sense of Humour (*New Scotland*, 23 November 1935)

A Scottish Saint (*New Scotland*, 25 January 1936)

Aince There, Aye There: A Shetland Story (*Outlook*, June 1936)

Old Eric's Hobby (*The West Fife Annual*, 1938)

The Case of Alice Carruthers (John Lehmann, ed., *New Writing*, 1939)

Vouchsafed, A Sign (John Singer, ed., *New Short Stories 1945–46*, 1946)

Sticky-Wullie (*Scottish Journal*, September 1952)

Without a Leg to Stand On: A Shetland Sketch (*Saltire Review*, Spring 1960)

An Epoch-Making Event (undated mansucript in Edinburgh University Library, signed by Richard Bell, c/o Wood Hazel, 14 Viewforth Gardens, Edinburgh. The typescript is signed by Hugh MacDiarmid. Posthumously published in Alan Bold, ed., *The Thistle Rises: An Anthology of Poetry and Prose by Hugh MacDiarmid*, London: Hamish Hamilton, 1984)

APPENDIX 1: HITHERTO UNPUBLISHED OR UNCOLLECTED STORIES
AND SKETCHES

In the National Library of Scotland, Edinburgh, the C.M. Grieve collection contains two separate lists of titles (MS.27082, ff.68, 82–3) of stories and sketches for proposals MacDiarmid must have made or intended to make towards a collection of his work in the genre of prose fiction. Some titles indicate texts we have gathered in the present collection; some titles are suggestive or reminiscent of others collected here but not identical (for example, the title 'Girl with the Club-foot' is probably the story we have collected as 'Poor Pussy'); some have remained elusive.

The first list is headed with what was, presumably, MacDiarmid's proposed title for the collection: 'On Making Beasts of Ourselves' and a subtitle, 'Short Stories and Essays' is crossed out and replaced with 'A Scottish Miscellany'.

1 The Common-Riding
2 The Waterside
3 Tam Mackie's Trial
4 Sticky-Wullie
5 The Case of Alice Carruthers
6 The Dour Drinkers of Glasgow
7 On Making Beasts of Ourselves
8 The Epoch-Making Event
9 The Five Bits of Miller
10 The Last Great Burns Discovery
11 In the Middle of the Field
12 The Moon Through Glass
13 Vouchsafed A Sign
14 Jenny A' Thing
15 ['Marble Story' crossed out. – Eds.] Holie For Nags
16 ['Wound' crossed out. – Eds.] Wind Pie
17 Christ in pub story [Presumably 'The Stranger' – Eds.]

2 plays	Woman who put out dry clothes on
Wiseman	line at dawn
2 Profiles	The cow broke its two fore-legs
1/ Wiseman	
2/ Muir	The stuffed lion

Bill Cumming's Story
The Plant That Wasn't Told
Girl with Club-foot

The second list is headed 'Contents':

The Lion of Edinburgh
The Loch Ness Monster Mystery
The Waterside
On Being Sold A Pup
In The Gaelic Islands
An Epoch-Making Event
Nellie Fairlie's Downcome
A'abody's Lassie
The Dean of the Thistle
The Punishment
Old Eric's Hobby
The Darkie Baby
Enemy's Daughter
The Jack-Knife
Aince There, Aye There
A Sense of Humour
My First Rabbit
The Fuschia That Wasn't Told
A Land of Fruits
The Case of Alice Carruthers
Castle of Balbate
Here's How
An Awkward Meeting
The Miser
The Stone of Destiny
Make-Weights: –
    1/ Achilles' Heel
    2/ A Merry Christmas
    3/ Nothing Like Flannel
    4/ White Heather
    5/ Scottish Women
    6/ Ultima Thule
    7/ Clothes
    8/ The Worm In The Heel

9/ Otter Hunt
10/ The Pleasures of Angling
11/ The Art of Guddling
John James Milroy
Mrs Woodhead's Servant
The Middle of the Field
The Affair at Hawick

The Lion of Edinburgh (Text supplied by John Manson from NLS MS27093 ff.13v 14–22, 23r. *c*.1934.)

The Loch Ness Mystery (Text supplied by John Manson from NLS MS27093 ff.23v 24–27 28r. *c*.1934.)

On Being Sold a Pup (Prepared from the manuscript in the NLS. The author is named as Hugh MacDiarmid.)

In the Gaelic Islands (Text supplied by John Manson from NLS MS27093 ff.8–12, 13r *c*.1934.)

The Darkie Baby (Text supplied by John Manson from NLS MS 27093 ff.28v, 29–33.)

Enemy's Daughter (Text supplied by John Manson from NLS MS27093 ff.34–35, 36r, 37v, 38–42.)

The Jackknife (Prepared from the manuscript in the NLS.)

A Land of Fruits (Text supplied by John Manson from NLS MS27093 ff.2–5, 6r. Published in *Markings* no.7 [Kirkcudbright, 1998].)

Here's How: A Glasgow Story (This item exists in typescript in the James Barke/James Leslie Mitchell correspondence in the Mitchell Library, Glasgow. It was made available to the editors by John Manson and Richard Price. It refers to the launch of the Queen Mary in 1934 and is clearly related to the poem 'Die Grenzsituation' ('Was *this* the face that launched a thousand ships?') published in the '1946' section of the 'Hitherto Uncollected Poems' in volume 2 of MacDiarmid's *Complete Poems*, edited by Grieve and Aitken.)

The Man with the Hole in His Sock (Prepared from the typescript in the NLS MS 27066, ff.43–9, dated 'Feb 9 1959'. A crossed-out note on the title-sheet, not in MacDiarmid's hand, reads: 'Submitted to *London Magazine* April 36'.)

Nothing Like Flannel (Prepared from the manuscript in the NLS. The story is marked 'III' under the general heading 'Make-Weights'.)

Wells (Text supplied by John Manson from NLS MS27095 15v, 16, 19. 1935–9. Published in *Southfields* 5.1 [Glasgow, 1998].)

In the Middle of the Field (Prepared from the typescript in the NLS

MS 27066, ff.83–8. A note suggests this was published in the *West Fife Annual*, 1937. The author is named in the typescript as Hugh MacDiarmid, but this is crossed out and in MacDiarmid's hand, given as James MacLaren. Also in MacDiarmid's hand, on the last sheet, are the words: 'From James MacLaren, c/o MacCaig, 7 Leamington Terrace, Edinburgh. This was Norman MacCaig, MacDiarmid's closest friend after they met in the 1940s.)

The Affair at Hawick (Prepared from the typescript in the NLS MS 27066, ff.148–61. Preceding the typescript are two manuscripts. The first reads as follows:

The Hawick Horror
Why should we upset everything. All the rest of us went through it. Nobody knew. Father well respected: ditto Mother. Does she know? What reaction would be – quality of comment etc – are these people any better. Who knows? Nobody knew about it either. Affair would be relished – savagely relished – by some. What is the scientific fact?

The second reads as follows:

The Affair at Hawick
Part I
I must write this in English unfortunately, but even if it were possible for me to write it, not only in Scots, which would be little better than English, but to reproduce the Hawick dialect it would be impracticable for various reasons. The best I can do is to remind readers that in order to get the proper hang of my story they should pronounce it in their minds *more boreali* all the way through (not that I actually think in that fashion myself but that I am continually conscious of the actual sounds of the life I am thinking about and writing about in this alien tongue – and give a few examples of veritable [An illegible word in quotation marks here. – Eds.] utterance so that they can appreciate what a poor appriximation even in Scots is and how terribly translated any account (and not only linguistically as I shall show – since if I attempted to write all I remember, in its full circumstantiality I would require at least a chapter in place of every sentence I pen and even then only be able to seize upon a moiety of the details infesting my memory; anything approaching a full understanding is utterly impossible and at every point it is as necessary for me to depend upon my readers' sense of the difference in complexity, in kaleidoscopic changes of mood – to mention only two respects – between any living

person and any written or writeable account of him [or] her as upon their ability to think the people of whom I am writing into something much more like their proper linguistic setting and so fill out my account with some appreciation of the tempo and colouring and feel of the particular streams of consciousness with which I am concerned). There is, for instance, the old gag of my schooldays – the Hawick spelling of Egypt. Not ee, gee,

[Two pages missing. – Eds.]

cratur.' It is pronounced 'peh-weh-ow'. The lean, wry, active people hate 'peh-weh-ows' – anaemic, feeble, ineffectual folk of any kind – and as I hope to show their outstanding characteristic is their thrawness, their spleen, their indefatigable cussedness. They know no let or hindrance. Knocking their heads against stone walls is their favourite pastime. The great majority of the Borderers today – even in Hawick, 'The Queen o' a' the Borders' – are, of course, sadly decadent – mere shadows of what they ought to be. The genuine article, the real thoroughbred, is few and far between. But when you get him, or her! For sheer recalcitrance, devilment, they have no equals. But with a very large proportion still at least something of the old quality survives under the surface and asserts itself quickly enough in times of stress or excitement – or (this is the important point) when they are amongst their own kind, when they allow themselves to be really themselves and let themselves go, and feel no need to be on their guard – and, above all, in their love affairs and intimate family relations. Their vitality is magnificent. In no other part of Scotland is life lived with such intensity, such gusto – and such a preference over the sweet fruits of life of those whose sourness pulls the lips together and twists and screws them. In no other district is excess in sensuality and hard living so generally a function of strength. Their scale of values is illustrated by the story of the farmer who went into his stockyard one morning and found his young son – a lad in his early teens – having sexual intercourse with a servant-girl. He looked on for a few minutes and then shook his head, muttering 'Ech, but ye're an awfu' lad, Jock. Ye'll be smokin' next.' They must be seen in their sensual life, in the avidity they bring to it, in the conscious joy they feel in it, in the endurance they show. And it is difficult to feel that – through the medium [of English.]

[Four pages are missing here. – Eds.]

Strathearn Ewart did not belong to Hawick though he came in his early teens from somewhere in Perthshire but whether his parents had moved to Hawick or whether he had other relatives in Hawick to whom he came for some reason or whether he simply got a job and came on his own I have no idea. Perhaps it is only the name 'Strathearn' which is misleading me with some false association. But, at all events, whether his parents belonged to Hawick or nearby, matters little. He had not a real Hawick tongue in his head although he had assimilated a great deal of the local twang and could use it almost indistinguishably at times. He did not use it habitually; that's what gave him away. Not that it matters; he undoubtedly came of stock that belonged to the Borders originally – and no matter how his parents and perhaps their parents had diverged and established themselves

The manuscript ends at that point. The title of the typescript as reproduced here, 'The Affair at Hawick', is written in MacDiarmid's hand over the typed title and byline: 'The Blackburn Case by C.M. Grieve'.)

A Friend of the Family (Prepared from the untitled manuscript in the NLS. The present title has been supplied by the editors.)

Poor Pussy (Prepared from the manuscript in the NLS.)

Putting the Lid On It (Prepared from the manuscript in the NLS. The author is named as Hugh MacDiarmid.)

At Sixes and Sevens (Prepared from the manuscript in the NLS MS 27066, ff.164–82.)

The Frontier (Prepared from the manuscript in the NLS. The author is named as Hugh MacDiarmid.)

Standing by the Pool (Prepared from the untitled manuscript in the NLS. The present title has been supplied by the editors.)

The First Clock in Barra (Prepared from the typescript in the NLS MS 27058, ff.58–63. The title is crossed out, so the story may have been given another title.)

The Murder (This item is printed from the manuscript and typescript in the possession of the University of Delaware Library, Hugh MacDiarmid Papers, Box 2, Folder 38, with the permission of the University of Delaware. The manuscript is dated 7/3/32 and signed C.M. Grieve.)

Ballet: Barley Break (The Scarecrow) (Prepared from the manuscript in the NLS. Under the heading 'Ballet' the title 'The Scarecrow' has been crossed out and replaced with 'Barley-Break'.)

Lechois: A Play in One Act (Prepared from the manuscript in the National Library of Scotland, Edinburgh The author is named as C.M. Grieve. The numbers in round brackets seem to have been added to the manuscript in another hand, possibly indicating structural design for performance. The passages in square brackets (except for those inserted by the editors) are marked as such in the manuscript, perhaps suggesting cuts to be made for performance; the final opening square brackets after the Old Woman's description of Comyn's demise seem unclosed, so perhaps MacDiarmid considered ending the play before the entrance of Common and Jean, with the Old Woman's words 'Thus was the road-making ended.' The play may have been written for radio, rather than the theatre. Alick's allusion to WAACS is a reference to the Women's Army Auxiliary Corps, founded in 1917.)